WOMEN, IMAGINATION
AND THE SEARCH FOR TRUTH IN
EARLY MODERN FRANCE

Women and Gender in the Early Modern World

Series Editors: Allyson Poska and Abby Zanger

In the past decade, the study of women and gender has offered some of the most vital and innovative challenges to scholarship on the early modern period. Ashgate's new series of interdisciplinary and comparative studies, 'Women and Gender in the Early Modern World', takes up this challenge, reaching beyond geographical limitations to explore the experiences of early modern women and the nature of gender in Europe, the Americas, Asia, and Africa. Submissions of single-author studies and edited collections will be considered.

Titles in this series include:

Edinburgh University Library

Books may be recalled for return earlier than due date;
if so you will be contacted by e-mail or letter.

Due Date	Due Date	Due Date

Women, Imagination and the Search for Truth in Early Modern France

REBECCA M. WILKIN
Pacific Lutheran University, Tacoma, USA

ASHGATE

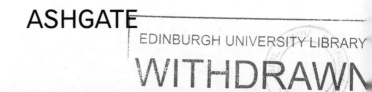

Published by
Ashgate Publishing Limited
Gower House
Croft Road
Aldershot
Hampshire GU11 3HR
England

Ashgate Publishing Company
Suite 420
101 Cherry Street
Burlington, VT 05401-4405
USA

Ashgate website: http://www.ashgate.com

British Library Cataloguing in Publication Data
Wilkin, Rebecca May
Women, imagination and the search for truth in early modern France. – (Women and gender in the early modern world)
   1. Women in science – France 2. Learning and scholarship – France
   I. Title
   305.4'2'0944'0903

Library of Congress Cataloging-in-Publication Data
Wilkin, Rebecca May.
  Women, imagination and the search for truth in early modern France / by Rebecca M. Wilkin.
     p. cm. — (Women and gender in the early modern world)
  Includes bibliographical references and index.
  ISBN 978-0-7546-6138-2 (alk. paper)
     1. Women in science—France. 2. Learning and scholarship—France. I. Title.

  HQ1397.W55 2008
  305.43'5094409031—dc22

2008002367

ISBN: 978-0-7546-6138-2

Printed and bound in Great Britain by MPG Books Ltd, Bodmin, Cornwall.

Contents

Note on Translations

For the sake of space, I have included only English translations in the text and kept the notes in the original language. When too much meaning or beauty would be lost in translation—for instance, in the case of poetry—I include both the original French along with an English translation in the text. I have sometimes included words or expressions that cannot adequately be translated from the original in brackets alongside my best English approximation. Translations are mine unless otherwise signaled. For majors works I have used standard translations where they exist and are satisfactory.

List of Figures

Acknowledgements

The search for truth joins together "the lives and labors of many," according to Descartes. It is with gratitude that I recognize the labors of those who have joined with me to produce *Women, Imagination, and the Search for Truth in Early Modern France*. Domna Stanton's exhortations to move "upward and onward" account for the scant resemblance this book bears to the dissertation I wrote under her direction at the University of Michigan. I would not have had the courage to write on Montaigne had I not studied with Floyd Gray and worked alongside Eric MacPhail. Eric and Guillaume Ansart read multiple drafts of all five chapters; their insights and encouragement improved the book immeasurably. Domenico Bertoloni Meli, Jérôme Brillaud, Karin Eckholm, Constance Furey, Kevin Grau, Joel Klein, Ellen MacKay, Evan Ragland, Jonathan Sheehan, and Allen Shotwell commented usefully on various drafts of Chapter One, for the purposes of which Stuart Clark kindly sent me his just-published *Vanities of the Eye*. Virginia Krause kept up an enriching correspondence with me about Bodin and Montaigne; she moreover sent me a word-searchable file of *De la démonomanie des sorciers* as a palliative to her and Christian Martin's forthcoming critical edition of that work. Virginia, Jérôme Brillaud, Shannon Gayk, Patricia Ingham, Oscar Kenshur, Chris Semk, and Rob Schneider offered valuable suggestions for improving the second chapter. Mark Greengrass graciously met with me to speak about the *politiques* and neo-stoicism during an auspiciously-timed visit to Bloomington; Ann Carmichael, Kyla Dennedy, and Karin Ekholm commented helpfully on the resulting third chapter. Erec Koch served as a sounding board for parts of my argument in the fifth chapter on Descartes.

Practical matters can be daunting when the writing process expands to fill all time available. A pre-tenure leave combined with a grant and semester's teaching release administered by the former Office of the Vice President of Research at Indiana University allowed me to get this book underway. Chris Semk located most of the images for the book, hunted down missing page numbers for citations, and compiled the initial draft of the bibliography. Guillaume Ansart, Cynthia Bannon, Jérome Brillaud, Katherine Ibbett, Rosemary Lloyd, and Michael Lundell emended various drafts of my prospectus. Erika Gaffney at Ashgate responded immediately to my proposal with a plan for how to proceed. She guided me through the publishing process with patience and humanity. Allyson Poska and Abby Zanger welcomed my book to their series. The anonymous Reader evaluated the manuscript in a timely and thorough fashion, and Meredith Coeyman through her care brought order to an unwieldy text. *Women, Imagination, and the Search for Truth*, like too many scholarly monographs these days, was written under intense pressure. For a while it appeared that although I would publish, I might perish anyway. For their steadfast support in hard times, I thank Guillaume Ansart, Nico Bertoloni Meli, Margot Gray, Kevin Hunt, Eileen Julien, Oscar Kenshur, Erec Koch, Virginia Krause, Eric MacPhail, Michael Moriarty, Todd Reeser, Tim Reiss, Rob Schneider, Lewis Seifert,

Domna Stanton, Barbara Vance, and Kathleen Wine. They have all been "d'une parfaite générosité."

My family has lived with *Women, Imagination, and the Search for Truth* for several years now. It has been a blessing to be able to share the writing process with my parents, David and Betty Wilkin, both former teachers of French. As always, my father had a hand in simplifying my prose. My mother lent a hand with childcare at critical junctures (as did Dorothy Ansart, Jamie Kirkley, Barbara Vance, and the wonderful teachers at BDLC). I am fortunate to be married to someone who knows the value of hard work and appreciates a job well done. Cédric Picard never once suggested I cut corners for the sake of expediency. He did the lion's share of housework and spent Sundays with our daughter to allow me more time to write. Marian went from toddler to kindergartener as I wrote. When children grow and change so fast and books take shape so slowly, it is hard to justify all the time spent on the latter. Marian's salutary unconcern for the state of my book reminded me that my value as a person was not contingent upon its completion.

No parts of this book have been previously published.

For Cédric Picard and Marian Aurélie Picard

Introduction

"Even women," René Descartes wrote in 1638, would be able to read his *Discours de la méthode* (1637); he had written it in French for that very reason. Yet he would go on to write the *Meditationes de prima philosophia* (1641) in Latin for fear that the skeptical reasoning his meditations required might prove dangerous for women and other "esprits foibles" (weak minds). More than revealing a personally ambivalent attitude towards women's access to knowledge, Descartes's cautious overture to women reflected a consistent feature of early modern thought: To define an epistemological program was also to define an intellectual community, and women were the truth-seekers through whose inclusion or exclusion intellectuals (mostly men) sought to articulate the limits of the search for truth. In *Women, Imagination, and the Search for Truth in Early Modern France*, I argue that in the late sixteenth and early seventeenth centuries, the effort to define woman and the nature of gender difference was a response to intellectual upheaval and a crucial ingredient in the epistemological experimentation that culminated in the "new science"— the reform of *scientia* (knowledge) to which we now trace the origins of modern science. Building on three decades of feminist scholarship, my purpose, like that of the historians, literary scholars, and philosophers who have preceded me, is to demonstrate the importance of women and gender notions to this pivotal chapter in intellectual history. However, my conclusions differ from those of my predecessors. Past analyses have stressed the sexist ideology behind the emergence of a monolithic and masculine enterprise. The contradictory representations of women and the diverse commitments to notions of gender difference that I bring to light in the five chapters of my book speak instead to the fragility of human confidence in its claims to knowledge.

By the 1560s, it was clear that the authority of the ancient *auctores* was fading, and with it, the standard that had served to ascertain the truth about the natural world. The discovery of peoples unacknowledged in sacred history, the humanist recovery of competing philosophical traditions, and the restless impatience with ecclesiastical abuses that led to the Protestant Reformation—all disseminated through the recently invented printing press—had irreparably undermined the careful amalgam of Christian theology and Aristotelian natural philosophy composed by the medieval Schoolmen. Some Renaissance intellectuals strove to replace or buttress claims of truth derived from authority with positive (that is, rational or empirical) criteria. These authors emphasized women's illiteracy with respect to the book of nature, just as scholastic natural philosophers had underscored women's ignorance of Latin. In effect, even though epistemological experimentation led to widely divergent and sometimes contradictory representations of women, the idea of woman served a consistent function.[1] Through the exclusion of women, they articulated the limits of the search for truth and sought to ensure their privileged place within it.[2] Others, however, magnified the void left by the dissolving scholastic system. Skepticism, a school of thought whose driving hypothesis was that nothing could be known for sure, flourished amid the intellectual upheaval of the late Renaissance.[3] Skeptics underscored the presumption of human claims to knowledge. The subversion of gender hierarchies and/or notions of sex difference abound in their writing. What indeed could moderate man's presumption more than to argue that women were just as worthy as men? And what could demonstrate the elusive nature of truth better than to reveal the speciousness of the supposedly obvious fact of sex difference?[4]

Descartes thus inherited two opposing conceptions of the search for truth, each characterized by a divergent attitude towards women: a positive endeavor culminating in the attainment of truth, from which women were excluded; and a skeptical search in the pursuit of an indefinitely deferred destination that challenged all that could be taken for granted, including gender notions. Descartes's original contribution to intellectual history was not his wholesale rejection of Aristotelian natural philosophy, to which he merely delivered the coup de grâce, but rather his confrontation of positive and skeptical modes of seeking. Indeed, what was truly novel about his approach to an old dilemma was his claim to overcome the doubt that had undermined previous attempts to establish firm bases for knowledge. Descartes sought to out-doubt even the Skeptics to found a rational epistemology that would surpass skepticism once and for all. His claim that "even women" could read and profit from his method was not just the result of his hostility to scholasticism; it was part of his appropriation of skeptical arguments. Albeit conventional and

---

1   Because I focus on the epistemological function served by representations of women, my analysis differs significantly from Ian MacLean's descriptive study, *The Renaissance Notion of Woman: A Study in the Fortunes of Scholasticism and Medical Science in European Intellectual Life* (Cambridge: Cambridge University Press, 1980).

2   As William Eamon observes in *Science and the Secrets of Nature: Books of Secrets in Medieval and Early Modern Culture* (Princeton: Princeton University Press, 1994), "[t]he problem of what qualifies as knowledge is intimately connected with the problem of who owns it" (351).

3   Richard Popkin, *The History of Scepticism from Savonarola to Bayle* (Oxford and New York: Oxford University Press, 2003). This is the latest expansion of *The History of Scepticism from Erasmus to Descartes* (Assen: Van Gorcum, 1960).

4   Scholars have only begun to address the important link between the skeptical search for truth and gender-bending arguments. See Kathleen Perry Long, "Jacques Duval on Hermaphrodites," in *High Anxiety: Masculinity in Crisis in Early Modern France*, ed. Kathleen P. Long (Kirksville: Truman State University Press, 2002), 107–36. She points out that the manual for all early modern French skeptics, Sextus Empiricus' *Outlines of Pyrrhonism*, is rife with examples of contrary customs regarding sex. Richard Regosin underscores the theme of gender reversibility that runs throughout Montaigne's *Essays* in *Montaigne's Unruly Brood: Textual Engendering and the Challenge to Paternal Authority* (Berkeley, Los Angeles, London: University of California Press, 1996). Constance Jordan does not connect pro-woman arguments to skepticism in *Renaissance Feminism: Literary Texts and Political Models* (Ithaca and London: Cornell University Press, 1990), despite the fact that several key champions of women were inclined towards skepticism.

ambivalent, Descartes's opening of the search for truth "even" to women broke new ground. The Skeptics accepted established institutions (laws, religion, and customary, social practices), because they rejected novelty as the manifestation of vain, human pretensions. Descartes, however, insisted on the possibility of scientific progress, and his provisional deference to custom in the *Discours de la méthode* could not prevent later Cartesians from questioning institutions and practices founded on prejudice. Pro(to)feminist Cartesians argued that "the mind has no sex;" that women's intellectual inferiority resulted from nurture rather than nature; and that this situation should be corrected, not just for the sake of justice, but also for the betterment of society as a whole.[5]

In sum, Descartes transferred an inclusive attitude towards women from a *skepsis* (search) with no term to a rational quest that promised continual progress. Sapping skepticism of one of its most successful rhetorical strategies, Descartes incorporated women into an endeavor that would carry subversive gender play well beyond the realm of rhetoric. The effects of this appropriation, however inadvertent, cannot be underestimated. Open "even" to women, a collective endeavor whose purpose was to ameliorate the human condition would inevitably be shaped by them. To be sure, women's initiatives to ensure their participation in the pursuit of knowledge would be contradicted, thwarted, and denied. But the rationale behind them could not be undone.

Women, Imagination, and the Search for Truth in Early Modern France revisits two narratives that have become standard in feminist scholarship. First, it nuances the thesis that the Scientific Revolution—that roughly contemporaneous cluster of scientific discoveries and methodological innovations associated with the beginnings of modern science—was a masculine enterprise that triumphed at the expense of women. In her pioneering study, *The Death of Nature* (1980), Carolyn Merchant strove to show how the proponents of the new science proclaimed the domination of a masculine, knowing subject over a feminized object of knowledge, nature.[6] Yet the story of how masculine science subdued "disorderly, active nature" couched historical change in terms of an eternal war of the sexes, reinforcing gender stereotypes rather than breaking them down.[7] Merchant mourned a prescientific golden age when nature was understood to be both alive and female, paradoxically validating an essentialist view of nature that, as Merchant showed, lent itself so well to construing science as a masculine enterprise. Historians of science have since challenged the revolution model of intellectual history that underpins the death of nature narrative.[8] The new

---

5   Siep Stuurman, *François Poullain de la Barre and the Invention of Modern Equality* (Cambridge and London: Harvard University Press, 2004).

6   Carolyn Merchant, *The Death of Nature: Women, Ecology and the Scientific Revolution* (San Francisco: Harper, 1980). Others who rehearse this narrative include Evelyn Fox Keller, *Reflections on Gender and Science* (New Haven and London: Yale University Press, 1985); Susan Bordo, *The Flight to Objectivity: Essays on Cartesianism and Culture* (Albany: State University of New York Press, 1987); and Londa Schiebinger, *Nature's Body: Gender in the Making of Modern Science* (Boston: Beacon Press, 1993).

7   Merchant, 164.

8   For instance, Steven Shapin, *The Scientific Revolution* (Chicago: The University of Chicago Press, 1996) and Daniel Garber, "Descartes, the Aristotelians, and the Revolution

emphasis on continuity invites a nuanced analysis of the exceedingly complex time that spanned the late sixteenth and early seventeenth centuries. Moreover, the emergence of queer theory, masculinity studies, and attention to transgender issues point to a more dynamic response to the question of how gender notions contributed to the emergence of modern science.[9]

Mindful of the unacknowledged debts that the proponents of the new science incurred toward their Renaissance predecessors and inspired by recent work in the field of gender studies, I argue for a more gradual, less triumphal, and ultimately more positive view of this exciting, yet eminently untidy chapter in early modern intellectual history. Considering women as potential rivals or partners in the search for truth, rather than as mere objects of science, allows me to underscore their increasing importance within that quest. Indeed, I show that whereas in the late Renaissance, intellectuals elaborated particular ideas of women in order to define and legitimate various constructions of knowledge, the new science, at least in its French—that is, Cartesian—incarnation, sought to secure the participation and support of real women. Furthermore, far from revealing a hegemonic and monolithic gender ideology, my analyses reveal great variation in representations of women, as well as varying investments in the notion of gender difference.

Second, my book challenges the dominant feminist interpretation of Cartesian philosophy, according to which Cartesian rationalism and corresponding dualism merely reconfigured the exclusion of women from the search for truth insofar as the unsexed, truth-seeking mind was invariably—and invisibly—gendered male. Articulated by Genevieve Lloyd, this thesis continues to frame most feminist discussions of Descartes, including Erica Harth's excellent and timely study of women's "versions and subversions" of Cartesian philosophy in the seventeenth and eighteenth centuries.[10] Nevertheless, recent developments in Descartes studies

---

that Did Not Happen in 1637," *Monist: An International Quarterly Journal of General Philosophy Inquiry*, vol. 71 (1988), 471–86. These studies take aim at structuralist narratives of rupture with the past: the "paradigm shifts" of Thomas Kuhn in *The Structure of Scientific Revolutions* (Chicago: University of Chicago Press, 1962), and above all, the "epistemic breaks" alleged by Michel Foucault in *Les Mots et les choses: Une archéologie des sciences humaines* (Paris: Gallimard, 1966).

9   Scholars of the early modern period have made important contributions to unseating facile oppositions by historicizing scientific definitions of sex difference, reconstructing the experience of gendered embodiment from earlier times, and by demonstrating the centrality of "gender trouble" to major literary works. Influential representatives of these trends include: Thomas Laqueur, *Making Sex: Body and Gender from the Greeks to Freud* (Cambridge and London: Harvard University Press, 1990); Barbara Duden, *The Woman Beneath the Skin: A Doctor's Patients in Eighteenth-Century Germany*, trans. Thomas Dunlap (Cambridge and London: Harvard University Press, 1991); and Jonathan Goldberg, *Sodometries: Renaissance Texts, Modern Sexualities* (Stanford: Stanford University Press, 1992).

10   Genevieve Lloyd, *The Man of Reason: "Male" and "Female" in Western Philosophy* (Minneapolis: University of Minnesota Press, 1984). Erica Harth, *Cartesian Women: Versions and Subversions of Rational Discourse in the Old Regime* (Ithaca and London: Cornell University Press, 1992). See also Londa Schiebinger, *The Mind Has No Sex? Women in the Origins of Modern Science* (Cambridge: Harvard U.P., 1989) and Joan Scott, *Only Paradoxes to Offer: French Feminists and the Rights of Man* (Cambridge: Harvard U.P., 1996).

suggest that feminist wariness with respect to Cartesian dualism may result more from the philosophical tradition that has been handed down to us than from a thorough reading of Descartes. In the past decade, interest in the ethical aspect of Descartes's search for truth has attenuated an almost exclusive emphasis on epistemological questions, while new work on his physics (that is, natural philosophy) has gone some way toward balancing the traditional focus on metaphysics. Both trends situate Descartes's projects with respect to historical context; both challenge the caricature of the Cartesian subject as disembodied mind.[11] The incorporation of these perspectives leads to a more congenial picture of the possibilities of Cartesian philosophy for feminism than would otherwise have been possible.

Five chapters comprise *Women, Imagination, and the Search for Truth in Early Modern France.* Each chapter takes one or two authors as its focus. Some are major figures: Jean Bodin, Michel de Montaigne, and Descartes. Others deserve to be better known: Johann Weyer, Guillaume du Vair, André du Laurens, Marie de Gournay, Elizabeth of Bohemia. With the exception of Weyer, with whom I begin and whose influence in France I reveal in each subsequent chapter, and of Elizabeth, Princess Palatine, all were French. All except Weyer and Elizabeth were (nominally) Catholic and responded in some measure to the confessional controversy that bled France. Most were professionals (jurists and medical doctors); their training and corporate loyalties shaped their attitudes towards knowledge to varying degrees. I chose these authors because of the originality of their intellectual contributions and the impact that they had, but also because each one can be seen as contributing to the definition of a broad intellectual trend.

The book as a whole shows an evolution in the early modern search for truth from ad hoc, opportunistic, and often inconsistent responses to epistemological instability to an increasingly self-conscious and systematic reflection on the need for epistemological reform. The chapters move from hermeneutics, to ethics, to epistemology proper in roughly chronological order. In Chapters One and Two, I show how disagreement regarding Biblical interpretation inflected conflicting readings of witchcraft, a subject of intense interest to nearly all Renaissance intellectuals.[12] Was the witch mad or did she know something illicit? It depended on how one interpreted her testimony—literally (Weyer) or allegorically (Bodin). Neo-Stoics and skeptics pushed hermeneutical differences under the proverbial rug as sectarian strife reached its apex. In Chapters Three and Four, I show that the search for truth became the quest for peace: neo-Stoics recommended quelling feminizing passions to achieve tranquility, while skeptics (Montaigne and Marie

---

11   See Timothy Reiss, *Mirages of the Selfe: Patterns of Personhood in Ancient and Early Modern Europe* (Stanford: Stanford U.P., 2003); Erec R. Koch, "Cartesian Corporeality and (Aesth)Ethics," *PMLA* 121 (2006), 405–20; and Catherine Wilson, "Descartes and the Corporeal Mind: Some Implications of the Regius Affair," *Descartes' Natural Philosophy*, eds. Stephen Gaukroger, John Schuster, and John Sutton (London and New York: Routledge, 2000), 659–77. Michael Moriarty challenges the very idea of a Cartesian "subject" in *Early Modern Thought: The Age of Suspicion* (Oxford and New York: Oxford University Press, 2003).

12   Stuart Clark, *Thinking with Demons: The Idea of Witchcraft in Early Modern Europe* (Oxford: Oxford U.P., 1997).

de Gournay) cultivated the suspension of judgment through bemused reflection on the reversibility of gender categories. This ethical turn in the search for truth was effective in proscribing conflict and establishing a stable political regime. However, it exacerbated the unresolved question of how to make knowledge and ascertain the truth of what one knew. The last chapter deals with the newly self-conscious efforts of Descartes and his contemporaries, notably Elizabeth of Bohemia, to define the epistemological foundations of continual scientific (and social) progress and their consequences for women.

Chapter One

Common Sense:
Johann Weyer and the
Psychology of Witchcraft

My investigation into the deployment of gender distinctions by early modern intellectuals in order to define truth and to legitimate particular means of attaining truth begins in the mid-sixteenth century with the polemics surrounding the witch trials. The witch trials, long the purview of social historians, may at first seem remote from the philosophical inquiry that we associate with Descartes. This distance collapses, however, once we recognize that the late Renaissance obsession with demonology, a subject of intense interest to political theorists and physicians as well as theologians both Catholic and Protestant, mediated questions of philosophical as well as theological import. Stuart Clark has shown that to gauge the power of illusion wielded by demons was also to call into question the validity of human perception. Throughout the sixteenth century, vision was considered the most noble of the senses, but also the most vulnerable to demonically induced error. When Descartes in his *Meditationes de prima philosophia* (1641) established the foundations for future knowledge despite the possible distortions caused by a melancholic imagination or an evil demon, he was evoking a problem that had arisen in the demonological literature of the late Renaissance: how can we be sure that what we see is, indeed, outside of us? The attention that Descartes paid to optics in his mechanistic physics, and particularly his rejection of the Aristotelian doctrine of *species*, further reveals how important it had become by the early seventeenth century to ascertain finally the reliability of visual perception. The skeptical crisis of the late Renaissance, heralded by Charles Etienne's 1562 translation of Sextus Empiricus' *Outlines of pyrrhonism* from Greek into Latin, was fueled by a pervasive loss of faith in the veracity of visual perception.[1]

While the signs of the unreliability of vision were everywhere, one book brought the question of visual perception to a head: a treatise authored in 1563 by a Lutheran physician from Flanders in the employ of Duke Wilhelm of Jülich, Cleves, and Berg—the small but politically important duchy in the lower Rhine valley, not so far from where Descartes would later spend his most productive years. In *De praestigiis daemonum*, Johann Weyer (1515–88) condemned the witch trials as the unjust persecution of mentally unstable women. In the process, he modeled a hermeneutical

---

1   Stuart Clark, *Vanities of the Eye: Vision in Early Modern European Culture* (Oxford: Oxford University Press, 2007), especially chapters 4, "Glamours: Demons and Virtual Worlds" (123–60), and 10, "Signs: Vision and the New Philosophy" (329–64).

stance designed to enhance the prestige of the physician. Combining the literalism redolent in Luther's approach to the Bible with a traditional understanding of the practice of medicine as the discernment of the body's ailments through the reading of signs on the exterior of the body, Weyer defined the search for truth as a hermeneutics of surfaces, wherein "common sense"—the inner faculty thought to synthesize sense impressions before passing them along to the understanding for analysis—served as the arbiter of truth. Thanks to an epistemology in which sense perception played the decisive role, the physician, whose expertise was usually circumscribed to natural phenomena, claimed a stake in the investigation of supernatural occurrences. However, in his eagerness to establish the physician's authority in demonological matters, Weyer overlooked a contradiction in his argument: his emphasis on the Devil's power to distort and deceive human perception undermined the authority he granted to the senses. *De praestigiis daemonum* advanced an untenable paradox: through sensual perception one could ascertain truth, but the Devil was a master of sensual deception.

Claiming that Weyer was the first to identify those women persecuted in early modern Europe for being witches as misunderstood hysterics, a disease label that had no currency until the nineteenth century, Gregory Zilboorg called Weyer "the father of modern psychiatry."[2] Less anachronistic, certainly, would be to call *De praestigiis*

---

2   Gregory Zilboorg, *The Medical Man and the Witch during the Renaissance* (Baltimore: Johns Hopkins Press, 1935), 205. The disease label "hysteria," as Helen King has demonstrated, was only invented in the nineteenth century. "Nineteenth-century hysteria, a parasite in search of a history, grafts itself by name and lineage onto the centuries-old tradition of suffocation of the womb" (64). In search of an ennobling ancestor, late nineteenth-century researchers of hysteria hailed Johann Weyer as a man ahead of his time. Désiré Bourneville, a disciple of Jean Martin Charcot (1825–93), the hysteria expert at La Salpêtrière, published the 1579 French translation of Weyer's book in 1885 as part of a collection called the *Bibliothèque diabolique*, which featured mainly sixteenth- and seventeenth-century works on possessed nuns. Charcot's circle pronounced a retrospective diagnosis on all early modern women accused of witchcraft and nuns claiming possession: they were hysterics, and the rational, humanitarian Weyer had been the first to recognize this fact. Another of Charcot's students, Sigmund Freud (1856–1939), named *De praestigiis daemonum* one of ten "most significant books." Cited in George Mora, "Introduction," *Witches, Devils, and Doctors in the Renaissance: Johann Weyer, De praestigiis daemonum*, eds. George Mora and Benjamin Kohl, trans. John Shea (Binghamton: Medieval & Renaissance Texts & Studies, 1991), lxxiii. The anachronism persists. Ilza Veith, whose 1965 study, *Hysteria: The History of a Disease* (Chicago: U. Chicago P., 1965), informs very recent Anglo-American scholarship, states that in the Middle Ages and Renaissance, "Hysteria ceased to be a disease—it became the visible token of bewitchment and thus fell within the domain of the Church, the Inquisition.... With the exception of the few who were fortunate enough to come into medical hands, hysterics became victims of the witch craze" (56). Relying on Veith, Laurinda Dixon affirms that "Weyer ... vociferously denied the existence of witches and blamed the symptoms of *furor uterinus* on natural causes" in *Perilous Chastity: Women and Illness in Pre-enlightenment Art and Medicine* (Ithaca: Cornell U.P., 1995), 47. In "A Strange Pathology: Hysteria in the Early Modern World, 1500–1800," *Hysteria Beyond Freud*, ed. Sander Gilman (Berkeley: U of California Press, 1993), G.S. Rousseau heralds Weyer as "a type of Renaissance Philippe Pinel or J.-E.-D. Esquirol." "Already by the sixteenth century," he claims, "Johannes Weyer

daemonum a foundational text for early modern "psychology", a term first employed in the 1580s by Catholic demonologists like Noël Taillepied, the Canon of Pontoise and author of *Psichologie, ou Traité de l'apparition des esprits* (1588). "Psychology" for Taillepied is the science of distinguishing perception from illusion with the aim of affirming the existence of demons, souls separated from bodies, ghosts, prodigies, and other "spirits."[3] In his *Quatre livres des spectres* (1586), probably the most important work in the subgenre of demonology that was "psychology" (as Taillepied defines it), Pierre Le Loyer (1550–1634) refutes four kinds of doubt expressed with respect to specters. One of these is doubt in the trustworthiness of the senses.[4] We recognize Weyer's argument here, pushed to its logical extreme: the Devil's power of illusion is so great that we can never be sure of what we really see, hear, feel, or sense in any other way. *De praestigiis daemonum* left its readers with an urgent problem. If Luther's "repeated insistence on the reality and presence of the Devil and his assault on humans, and his detailed and frequent testimonies of the Devil's physical and spiritual assaults on himself" made the Devil the intimate moral foe of each and every Christian, Weyer in *De praestigiis daemonum* can take credit for making the Devil an epistemological enemy of unavoidable proportions.[5]

De praestigiis daemonum was symptomatic not only of the epistemological trouble of the late Renaissance, but also of the gender strategies through which enterprising intellectuals like Weyer sought to capitalize on such instability.[6] The words and bodies of the women whom Weyer claims are falsely accused of witchcraft serve as "texts" through whose "reading" the physician demonstrates the pertinence of his literalist, sense-based hermeneutics. Anyone can see that these so-called witches are simply deranged, the physician insists; to go prying beyond what is easily apparent is perverse and cruel. We might imagine that knowledge gleaned through common sense, unlike book learning, would be within reach of everyone, just as we might suppose that the Devil's illusions would be universally misleading.

... pronounced that hysteria ... must be semiologically construed.... He exonerated hysterics from the charge of diabolism and pronounced them innocent of witchcraft" (114–16). Rousseau evokes "melancholy" and "hysteria" almost indiscriminately (114–16, 128–9, 122–3, 137). Misled by Rousseau, Cristina Mazzoni states in *Saint Hysteria: Neurosis, Mysticism, and Gender in European Culture* (Ithaca: Cornell University Press, 1996) that Weyer "declared" that women accused of witchcraft "were nothing but hysterics," even though she recognizes that "the identification of witches with hysterics" is a "historical commonplace" and one that she does not seem particularly eager to accredit (9).

3   In his *Introduction aux Sciences Humaines: Essai critique sur leurs origines et leur développement* (Paris: Editions Ophrys, 1974), Georges Gusdorf locates the first use of the Latinized noun *psichologia* in Germany in the late 1590s (11).

4   On Le Loyer see Terence Cave, *Pré-histoires: Textes troublés au seuil de la modernité* (Genève: Droz, 1999), 70–73, and Clark, *Vanities of the Eye*, 214–15.

5   Alan Charles Kors and Edward Peters, *Witchcraft in Europe, 400–1700: A Documentary History* (Philadelphia: University of Pennsylvania Press, 2001), 261.

6   I borrow the notion of "trouble" from Cave: "Le dépistage d'un 'trouble' permet de localiser une région problématique de la perception, de retrouver une sorte de fêlure dont l'auteur et ses contemporains ne sont peut-être pas pleinement conscients, mais qu'ils ressentent comme un malaise, une tache floue à l'horizon de la pensée" (15).

Weyer, however, claims that certain people are naturally more vulnerable to demonic deception than others. The essentially melancholic imagination of women, he argues, makes them incapable of the sense perception to which he assigns pride of place in the search for truth. The madness with which Weyer diagnosed witches thus masked the contradiction that vitiated his plea. Identifying the susceptibility to demonic illusion as a feminine trait was to compartmentalize it, to limit implicitly the damage that the Devil could inflict elsewhere—for instance, on the perception of learned physicians. Those who refuted *De praestigiis daemonum* rejected the hermeneutical advantage that Weyer claimed for himself. To the gender strategy by which he claimed this advantage, however, they did not object. Weyer's vociferous adversary, Jean Bodin, decried the physician's medical diagnosis of witches; nevertheless, he called upon woman to embody his opposing hermeneutics. The phenomenon that Clark has felicitously termed "thinking with demons" was thus, I argue, inseparable from another thought process: "thinking with women."[7]

Making Sense of Misogyny

Weyer's defense of women accused of witchcraft rested on a diagnosis: they were melancholic. Although the diagnosis was conventional, what is striking in *De praestigiis daemonum* is the way in which Weyer generalizes that diagnosis to all women. Extrapolating from medieval concerns regarding the discernment of true mystical experience from delusion, Italian jurists and physicians of the early sixteenth century emphasized the difficulty of distinguishing witchcraft from possession facilitated by melancholy.[8] Melancholy was known as the Devil's bath (*balneum diaboli*), a dark humor that facilitates the Devil's infiltration of minds and souls. That is why, according to the Italian naturalist Pietro Pomponazzi (1462–1525), "the first exorcists, whom they call *praecantatores* or enchanters, before the conjuring, would purge the possessed victims' bodies of black bile."[9] Legally, the problem was that under the influence of melancholy, one who was possessed might sincerely believe that she was a witch. She might, therefore, be punished as the Devil's

---

7   I refer to the phrase coined by Stuart Clark in *Thinking with Demons: The Idea of Witchcraft in Early Modern Europe* (Oxford: Oxford U.P., 1997).

8   The scholastic Guillaume d'Auvergne (d. 1249) disparages the visions alleged by female mystics as the product of melancholy, arguing that women were particularly susceptible to the melancholic delusions wrought by demons. "Many of these visions and fantastic apparitions are produced ... by the illness of melancholia. This is especially true with women, just as is the case with true visions and revelations. And the reason is, in addition to what doctors say, the nature of female souls—namely, from the fact that they are far easier of impression than male souls." Guillaume's "extensive treatment of the spiritual ramifications of physiology" made him, in Dyan Elliott's words, a "mainstay for future theologians with a diagnostic bent," Dyan Elliott, *Proving Woman: Female Spirituality and Inquisitional Culture in the Later Middle Ages* (Princeton and Oxford: Princeton University Press, 2004), 206.

9   Pietro Pomponazzi, *De naturalium effectuum admirandorum causis, sive de incantationibus* (1556), cited by Johann Weyer, *Witches, Devils, and Doctors in the Renaissance: Johann Weyer, De praestigiis daemonum*, eds. George Mora and Benjamin Kohl, trans. John Shea (Binghamton: Medieval & Renaissance Texts & Studies, 1991), 447.

accomplice when in fact she was only his victim. The physician, mathematician, and magus, Girolamo Cardano (1501–76) emphasizes the resemblance between melancholic witches and the possessed in *De rerum varietate* (1557). Weyer cites him at length: "[Witches] are misshapen, pale, and somewhat gloomy-looking; one can see that they have an excess of black bile in them just by looking at them. They are taciturn and mentally infirm, and they differ little from those who are thought to be possessed by a demon."[10] Melancholy blurred the line between illness and evil, victimization and accountability; as a result, the jurist Andrea Alciati (1492–1550) simply recommended hellebore, a purgative prescribed for melancholy, for women supposed to be witches.[11]

Weyer claims, like Alciati, that witches are women who suffer the delusions of black bile and whose "eyes are blinded." He invites his reader to consider "the thoughts, words, visions, and actions of melancholics" to "understand how in these persons all the senses are often distorted when the melancholic humor seizes control of the brain and alters the mind."[12] He compares the illusions wreaked by Satan to those resulting from black bile. Witches are women whose imaginations are corrupted by Satan "just as we see it happen that the mind is wounded, troubled, and filled with various fantasies and apparitions in those whose brains are fogged up with melancholy or by its vapors."[13] Mixing melancholy with devilish hallucinations, the Devil cloaks himself, Weyer explains, in the inky shadows of melancholic smoke to facilitate his illusions: "From black and melancholic vapor something horrible appears—a demon-image, as it were; accordingly, the Devil loves to insinuate himself into this vapor, as being a material most suited for his mocking illusions."[14] As for his female victims, they may be melancholic or just melancholic-like, but the important thing is their susceptibility to persuasion. Thus the sly Devil may win over women who are (among other things) melancholic: "[T]hat crafty schemer the Devil thus influences the female sex, that sex which by reason of temperament is inconstant, credulous, wicked, uncontrolled in spirit, and (because of its feelings and affections, which it governs only with difficulty) melancholic."[15] Or the evil one has as easy a time persuading women as he does persuading melancholics: "[T]he sort of person most likely to be attacked is one who ... is so moved by external or internal causes ... that as a result of specious inducements he will readily present himself as a suitable instrument of the demon's will. Melancholics are of this sort." So, too,

---

10 Girolamo Cardano, cited by Weyer, 510. Cardano stopped in Cleves on his way to England in 1552; perhaps he met Weyer there?

11 Weyer, 537. Alciati spent a few years teaching law in Bourges just prior to Weyer's medical studies in the nearby town of Orléans.

12 Weyer, 183.

13 Johann Weyer, *Cinq Livres de l'Imposture et Tromperie des Diables: des enchantements et sorcelleries ... faits François par Jacques Grévin de Clermont en Beauvoisis, médecin à Paris* (Paris: Jacques Dupuys, 1567), "Préface," (n.p.). This edition was reissued in 1569; I cite from it occasionally if Grévin's French translation presents interesting differences from the 1991 English translation by John Shea. The translations from Grévin's French to English are mine. I distinguish between these texts by their date of publication, that is, 1569 or 1991.

14 Weyer, 1991, 188.

15 Weyer, 1991, 181.

are "old women not in possession of their faculties, and similarly foolish women of noted malice or slippery and wavering faith."[16]

As a medical diagnosis, Weyer's assessment is inconsistent. His hesitation between either diagnosing women as melancholics or comparing them to melancholics betrays his awareness that melancholy was a condition associated with (male) genius. Weyer apprenticed for three years with the occasional physician, occult philosopher, and alchemical dabbler, Heinrich Cornelius Agrippa von Nettesheim (1486–1535), who in *De occulta philosophia* (1531–33), relates the thesis of Aristotle's famous Problem 30: "[B]y melancholy ... some men are made as it were divine, foretelling things to come, and some men are made poets ... all men that were excellent in any science, were for the most part melancholy." Agrippa furthermore claims that the melancholic temperament predisposes "men's bodies" to receiving "celestial spirits"—a claim that would lead many of his critics to suspect him of trafficking with the Devil.[17] I return in Chapter Two to the controversy engendered by Weyer's attempt to associate melancholy with women. Here it is enough to note that his diagnosis served the purpose of the legal defense he crafted. H.C. Erik Midelfort has shown that Weyer's defense of women accused of witchcraft comprised one of the most influential developments of the Roman insanity defense in early modern Europe. Considering the witch's pact, signed and sealed with Satan's cold semen, in terms of Roman contract law rather than as a feudal oath of homage, Weyer questioned its validity in addition to underscoring its implausibility. *Even if* women did abjure God and commit the crimes to which they confessed, Weyer argued that they could not be held responsible on the grounds that contracts involving fraud or a power disparity, such as that between an adult and a child, were illegal by Roman standards.[18] Emphasizing the Devil's power of persuasion and women's inability to resist it, Weyer dismissed as null and void the pact contracted between them, consistently opposing the Devil's "fineness, subtlety, and long experience" to "the grossness of [his female victims'] nature and the incapacity of their spirit."[19]

The legal implications of the melancholy diagnosis were well understood by Weyer's readers; so much is evident in Thomas Erastus's (1524–83) summary of Weyer's plea. Erastus was a Calvinist physician based in Basel; his point by point rebuttals of Weyer's argument were included in the 1579 French edition of *De praestigiis daemonum*. Since Erastus organized his rebuttals in dialogue form, they help to understand how Weyer's arguments were received. Summarizing Weyer's central argument, Erastus sharpens the contract issue: "Those who have

---

16   Ibid., 180–81.

17   Heinrich Cornelius Agrippa von Nettesheim, *Three Books of Occult Philosophy*, trans. James Freake, ed. Donald Tyson (St. Paul: Llewellyn Publications, 1993), 188. On Agrippa and melancholy, see Winfried Schleiner, *Melancholy, Genius, and Utopia in the Renaissance* (Wiesbaden: Otto Harrassowitz, 1991), 27.

18   H.C. Erik Midelfort, *A History of Madness in Sixteenth-Century Germany* (Stanford: Stanford University Press, 1999), 213–14. Midelfort furthermore argues that Roman law provided relief from the late medieval emphasis on witchcraft as heresy, as a willed abandonment of God, insofar as the pragmatic Romans distinguished actual acts from thought, wishes, and intentions that were not inherently criminal.

19   Weyer, 1991, 263.

no communion cannot make a contract. Item, those who are of a contrary opinion do not contract. Finally, there is no consent where fraud, violence, cruelty, error and ignorance intervene." Hence the gallant verdict, delivered sarcastically by Erastus: "[O]ne should pardon the more fragile sex." [20] Sarcasm aside, Erastus in no way misrepresents Weyer's argument. Although Weyer often qualifies those accused of witchcraft as old women, it is without a doubt the female sex in its entirety whose susceptibility to satanic illusions he purports to prove. Weyer approves Euripides' opinion that it is "a thing of reproach, to kill women" and Virgil's claim that "no lasting renown comes from punishing a woman." [21]

Weyer's characterization of women replicated the views of the *Malleus Maleficarum* (1487), or "witches' hammer," one of the first and certainly the most influential manual for identifying and prosecuting witches. Authored primarily by Dominican Inquisitor Heinrich Kramer, the *Malleus* "elevated witchcraft to a pivotal position in the struggle between man and the Devil" and gave new responsibility to witchcraft "for the world's ever increasing ills." [22] The *Malleus* was a repository of the tropes of medieval misogyny, among them that of female malleability: "women are naturally more impressionable," claims the Dominican, and thus "more ready [than men] to receive the influence of a disembodied spirit." Kramer invents roots for the Latin *femina*: "Femina comes from *fe* and *minus*, since she is ever weaker to hold and preserve the faith." He concludes that "woman is by her nature quicker to waver in her faith and consequently quicker to abjure the faith, which is the root of witchcraft." [23] Weyer draws from the same sources as Kramer to argue that women cannot be held accountable for the crimes for which they stand accused and to which

---

20   Thomas Erastus, *Deux dialogues de Thomas Erastus, Docteur en medecine à Heidelberg, touchant le pouvoir des Sorcieres: & de la punition qu'elles meritent*, trans. Simon Goulart de Senlis, in Johann Weyer, *Histoires, disputes et discours, des Illusions et impostures des diables* ... (Geneva: Jacques Chovet, 1579), 779 (see also 857–8), 781. Of the two dialogues published by Chovet, the first figured in Erastus's *Disputationum de medicina nova*; the second was his *Repititio disputationis de lamiis seu strigibus*, published independently in 1578. In the dialogues, Erastus designates Weyer as "Furnius." Furnius was one of Cicero's correspondents; there are two letters to him in the *Epistulae ad familiares* (*Letters to friends*), written during the Civil War period. The relation between Cicero and Furnius, who evidently served as a go-between and confidant, is one of trust and respect. The only hint of disagreement is about the choice between "giving up Narbonese Gaul and fighting a risky battle"; Cicero finds the first option "alarming." Could Erastus have seen Furnius's defeatism comparable to Weyer's emphasis on the risks of battling witchcraft? I am not convinced. Marcus Tullius Cicero, *Letters to Friends*, ed. D. R. Shackleton Bailey, vol. 3 (Cambridge and London: Harvard U.P., 2001), 383.

21   Weyer, 1991, 540.

22   Hans Peter Broedel, *The Malleus Maleficarum and the Construction of Witchcraft: Theology and Popular Belief* (Manchester and New York: Manchester University Press, 2003), 19. The other name that figures on the *Malleus* was that of the more learned and less contentious Dominican, Jacob Sprenger; Broedel explains that Sprenger lent his prestige to the work, authoring the "Apologia auctoris" that prefaces it, but surmises that his authorship of the text was at most minimal (18).

23   Heinrich Kramer and James Sprenger, *The Malleus Maleficarum*, trans. Montague Summers (New York: Dover Publications, 1971), 44, 47.

they often confess. He quotes Chrysostom's homilies on Matthew: "The female sex is heedless and pliant … because it is easily bent from evil to good or from good to evil." He rehearses the inevitable story of how easily the first woman succumbed to temptation: "it was not Adam but Eve that he approached, as being an instrument more suitable for his persuasion; it was she that he overcame in argument with only a light skirmish." Vying with the author of the *Malleus*, Weyer inscribes in etymology the correspondence between the soft female body and her persuadable mind: "the word 'woman' [*mulier*] seems to be derived, rather appropriately, from 'softness' [*mollities*], with one letter changed and one removed, as though the word should have been *mollier*."[24] Weyer's portrayal of women diverges from that of Kramer only in his assessment of the witch's responsibility. Whereas the Dominican Inquisitor emphasizes the witch's willful abjuration, Weyer's women fall prey to the illusions of the dexterous Devil; they are the wily one's gullible victims. The reasons for their vulnerability are, nevertheless, the same as those alleged by Kramer. Weyer reasons that since those whom we take to be witches are "[because of their sex] inconstant, dubious in the faith, not sufficiently stable in their minds as a result of their age," they are also "much more subject to the Devil's trickery."[25] Alas, while defending women from a gruesome death, the physician revived many of the misogynistic commonplaces typical of the medieval witch hunting manuals he was ostensibly combating.

Clark points to Weyer's negative portrayal of women as evidence of the unremarkable character of the misogynistic sentiment that pervades the *Malleus*: so widespread were claims regarding women's susceptibility to devilish persuasion that even a physician who defended women from torture and death did not hesitate to invoke them.[26] This observation invites a salutary rethinking of the causal relation that has been too readily drawn between misogyny and the witch hunts, as if the pursuit of witches were merely an elaborate pretext to eliminate certain kinds of women (midwives, wealthy widows, and so forth). If Weyer's negative characterization of women did not lead him to argue for the culpability of witches, why should we view misogyny as the principal motive of those authors who did advocate the killing of witches? Early modern people put witches to death because they feared witches, Clark emphasizes, not because they hated women.[27] We would, nonetheless, be wrong to assume that misogynistic statements were simply a reflex to which learned men were prone. To view misogynistic expressions as part of the background décor to the drama of the breakdown of intellectual certitude in late sixteenth-century Europe would be to miss half the action taking place on stage. While the learned men who pondered witchcraft and demons were no more determined to eradicate the female sex than the mother fearful for the health of her infant, gender was a crucial component of the intellectual preoccupations mediated by demonological inquiry.

---

24 Weyer, 1991, 181–2. The French translation is less awkward: "Ce n'est donc pas sans raison que les Latins ont nommé la femme Mulier quasi venant du mot Mollier …, qui signifie mollesse." Weyer, 1569, 221.

25 Weyer, 1569, "Préface," [n.p.].

26 Clark, *Thinking with Demons*, 118.

27 Ibid., 110.

That expressions of misogyny were more than part of the mental *"outillage"* of the time becomes clear if we consider that misogynistic motifs, albeit commonplace, could be avoided and even condemned, and thus that their invocation was not culturally determined but was a conscious choice on the part of an individual author. It is significant to the interpretation of Weyer's dismal representation of women that the two figures to whom he incurred the greatest debt—Desiderius Erasmus and Agrippa—eschewed misogynistic commonplaces. Midelfort has shown that Weyer's defense of women accused of witchcraft was modeled on the plea for clemency in the treatment of heretics made by Desiderius Erasmus (1466–1536).[28] Johann III, who ruled the Duchy of Cleves, Jülich, and Berg from 1511 to 1539 had granted an annual pension to Erasmus in 1533, and during the 1560s, even after his death, the latter's benevolent spirit of tolerance, in retreat in nearly every other corner of Europe, was still very much alive in the duchy.[29] During the Spanish occupation of the Low Countries, Weyer's employer, the duke Wilhelm of Jülich-Cleves, welcomed a number of Protestant refugees, including Charles Utenhove, a humanist and protégé of Erasmus whose son by the same name was to marry Weyer's sister Elizabeth.[30] In Erasmus's *Apology* of 1520, which Weyer reproduces in its entirety in the sixth book, "On the punishment of witches," that he added to the 1568 edition of *De praestigiis daemonum*, Erasmus defines heresy as a mental crime that does not hurt anyone but the heretic himself.[31] Erasmus is clearly addressing the question that preoccupied the Catholic elite in Luther's day: What to do about Protestants. But since the witch ostensibly abjured her faith, witchcraft, too, had been classified as heresy since the founding of the Inquisition in the late thirteenth century. Weyer applies Erasmus's dovish logic to the crime of witchcraft. Witches are the victims of their own deluded imaginations, Weyer argues, and as a result, punishment is superfluous and cruel. Worshipping the idols of the imagination is its own punishment; like any false prophet, it leads at best to disappointment: "Relying too willingly [*Ajoustans ...trop de foy*] upon this 'teacher' in many instances, they are wretchedly deceived and wholly ruined."[32]

Erasmus positioned himself against medieval scholasticism, which in his view vitiated basic Christian faith with philosophical hubris. Opposition to arid scholasticism and the fideist critique of reason led him in turn to adopt a

---

28 Midelfort, 204.

29 Mora, xxvii.

30 Willem Janssen, *Charles Utenhove: Sa vie et son oeuvre (1536–1600)* (Maastricht: Gebrs. van Aelst, 1939), 12–13.

31 In the *Apologia Erasmi qua respondet duabus invectivis Eduardi Leei* (1520), Erasmus asks, "How is it ... that in times past, when no schools of theology had been established, people fought successfully against heretics by using the Word of God alone, whereas now, when the whole world is filled with famous academies of learning, the struggle is carried on by means of legal articles and bundles of firewood?" Cited in Weyer 1991, 532. For the complete letter, see the *Erasmi opuscula: A Supplement to the Opera omnia*, ed. Wallace K. Ferguson (The Hague: M. Nijhoff, 1933), 225–303. For Erasmus's views on heresy and the appropriate response to it, see Jacques Chomarat, *Grammaire et rhétorique chez Erasme* (Paris: Belles lettres, 1981), 1129–39.

32 Weyer, 1991, 263 and 1569, 332.

pro(to)feminist stance. In keeping with his general disregard for scholastic pedantry, Erasmus eschewed the misogynist commonplaces of medieval scholasticism and instead turned the usual gender polarity topsy-turvy to underscore what was wrong with the Church. A learned woman upbraids an ineffectual abbot in the *Colloquium Abbatis et Eruditae* (1524), of which Clément Marot (1496–1544) published a versified French translation in 1526. After failing to elicit the abbot's interest in anything but eating, drinking, and hunting, and after defending her study of Latin from his benighted objections, the learned woman issues a warning to her limited interlocutor:

> C'est à vous à y prendre garde:
> Car, si tenez tousjours ces voyes,
> A prescher se mettront les oyes
> Plutost qu'elles vous souffrent estre
> Pasteurs, sans voz brebis repaistre.[33]

> [It is up to you to watch out:
> For if you keep on in this manner,
> The geese will begin to preach
> Rather than suffer you as
> Shepherds, who do not lead your sheep to pasture.]

It was probably not Erasmus's intention to suggest that women should become priests; the point is that the situation must be really bad if a "goose" would make a better priest than a gander. Along the same lines, Erasmus disagreed with those who opposed translating scripture into vulgar tongue lest they "be read by the uneducated" and expressed his wish "that even the lowliest women [could] read the Gospels and the Pauline Epistles."[34]

The same pattern aligning Christian charity, antischolasticism, and pro(to)feminism, obtains in the work of Weyer's exuberant mentor. Agrippa risked his life in 1519 to defend a young peasant woman accused of witchcraft from the "bloodthirsty" inquisitor of the then German town of Metz. The inquisitor, Nicolas Savin, had argued that the young woman was assuredly a witch because her mother had been one. In his letter to the judge appointed to oversee the trial, Agrippa disparaged the Dominicans as a wayward "sect" and mocked Savin for the certitudes he drew "from the depths of the *Malleus Maleficarum* and the principles of peripatetic Theology."[35] Agrippa argues that as a result of his overzealous, unthinking faith in dubious authorities, Savin had forgotten one of the most basic components of Christian doctrine. How could witchcraft pass from mother to daughter when the

---

33   Clément Marot, "Colloque de l'abbé & de la femme sçavante," *Oeuvres*, vol. 2 (Geneva: Slatkine Reprints, 1969), 213–14.

34   That Erasmus makes these remarks in the preface to his Greek edition and Latin translation of the New Testament, the *Paraclesis* (1516), significantly diminishes their radicalism.

35   Cited in Donald Tyson, "The Life of Agrippa" in Heinrich Cornelius Agrippa of Nettesheim, *The Three Books of Occult Philosophy*, trans. James Freake (Saint Paul: Llewellyn Publications, 1993), xxv.

very good point.

↑ *purpose*

purpose of baptism was precisely to cleanse the soul of the hereditary tares devolving to each and every one of God's creatures as a result of original sin?[36] For Agrippa as for Erasmus, challenging the assumption of female intellectual inferiority was part and parcel of an antischolastic stance. In his *Declamation on the Nobility and Preeminence of the Female Sex*, delivered (in Latin) at the University of Dôle in Burgundy in 1509 (presumably to an all-male audience), Agrippa refutes various prejudices against women.[37] Nothing could better illustrate the skeptical gambit that "all sciences are nothing but decisions and opinions of men" than the demonstration of the superiority of women over men.[38] Indeed, I show in Chapter Four that Renaissance pro(to)feminism was often symptomatic of a skeptical attitude towards the possibility of human knowledge.

Inspired by Erasmus's decriminalization of heresy and emboldened to speak out by his mentor Agrippa against the petty logic of inquisitors, Weyer set out to discredit the *Malleus Maleficarum* that had by his time assumed the status of an authoritative juridical reference manual all over Europe. Mocking the Dominicans' credulity and decrying their inhumanity, he refuted point by point the narrative of the satanic pact, arguing that it was nothing but the bastard brainchild of perverse inquisitors and the demented women whom they tortured. Significantly, however, the rehabilitation of women was not part of Weyer's contestation of late medieval demonology. Whereas Erasmus and Agrippa had challenged misogynist *topoi* along with the "peripatetic Theology" that circulated them, Weyer reproduced those commonplaces. Why?

In an influential thesis, Foucault argues that interventions of physicians against witch trials and possession cases constituted a bid for control in a discursive power struggle.

---

36 "Are we not all from the nature of our humanity born one mass of sin, malediction, and eternal of his perdition, children of the Devil, children of Divine wrath, and heirs of damnation, until by the grace of baptism Satan is cast out, and we are made new creatures in Jesus Christ....?" Cited in Tyson xxv.

37 Albert Rabil, "Agrippa and the Feminist Tradition," in Henricus Cornelius Agrippa, *Declamation on the Nobility and Preeminence of the Female Sex,* trans. and ed. Albert Rabil Jr. (Chicago and London: The University of Chicago Press, 1996), 11–12. Louis Vivant's French translation of the *Declamatio* was published in 1530 by Galliot du Pré as *Déclamation de la noblesse et préexcellence du sexe feminin.* Galliot du Pré also produced a new edition of Martin Le Franc's *Le Champion des Dames* that year. Rabil notes this publishing coincidence, 27, n. 48.

38 Heinrich Cornelius Agrippa, *Of the Vanitie and Uncertaintie of the Artes and Sciences*, ed. Catherine Dunn (Northridge: California State University, 1974), 17–18. How do we reconcile Agrippa's pursuit of natural magic in *De occulta philosophia* with his skeptical tract, *De incertitudine et vanitate scientiarum and artium* (1530)? Charles Nauert argues that the contradiction between Agrippa's occultism and skepticism is only apparent, insofar as "distrust in the powers of the human mind to attain truth was the basic presupposition of occultism rather than the product of disillusionment with it." Charles G. Nauert, Jr., *Agrippa and the Crisis of Renaissance Thought* (Urbana: University of Illinois Press, 1965), 201. This interpretation is supported by the fact that just before composing *De vanitate*, Agrippa had written another work, *Dehortatio gentilis theologiae* (*Against Pagan Philosophy*), in which he argues for the primacy of faith over reason. See also Michael H. Keefer, "Agrippa's Dilemma: Hermetic 'Rebirth' and the Ambivalences of *De vanitate* and *De occulta philosophia*," *Renaissance Quarterly* 41 (1988): 614–53.

Redefining the criminal witch-heretic as a patient, he claims, served to remove her from the jurisdiction of the law and the Church and to place her within the realm of medicine: "The characters of sorcerers or *possédés*, who were entirely integrated into the very rituals that excluded and condemned them, became the objects for a medical practice which gave them a different status and excluded them in a different way."[39] Adopting Foucault's thesis, Jean-Michel Sallman describes the witch's new status as an object of medicine: "The witch slips quietly from the domain of heresy to that of illness. She who had once concluded a pact with Satan, becomes a victim of her imagination.... When she was a witch, the gallows or the stake manifested in all their cruelty her complete penal responsibility. As a victim of her imagination or corporeally mad, she becomes a legally diminished being, of limited personal responsibility."[40]

Foucault is right to observe that sixteenth-century physicians strove to raise the standing of medicine relative to the other liberal arts, although they did this mostly by emphasizing their humanist training, and only exceptionally by intervening in witch trials and possession cases. However, in characterizing women as pawns between vying "discourses," Foucault grants too much coherence to the positions of the players and ignores their investment in the witch as a rival in the pursuit of knowledge. Medicine was not a monolithic entity with a clearly defined mission and appointed apologists. Although Weyer's book was representative of a larger effort on the part of physicians to ennoble their profession, the hermeneutics he essayed in *De praestigiis daemonum* were idiosyncratic, experimental, and logically flawed. Furthermore, Foucault's thesis attributes far too much importance to the witch-as-potential-patient. Although many of the women accused of witchcraft were probably unhealthy, they were not likely to make for enriching patients. The women pursued as witches were mostly marginal figures, living in poverty. If a physician such as Weyer struggled to assert the relevance of his training to discerning witchcraft, it was not because he eyed "witches" as an untapped share of the medical market. Rather, Weyer's negative characterization of women reflected, in reverse, the physician's privileged access to knowledge. The clear-sighted physician asserted his privileged access to truth over and against the melancholic imaginations of women, just as the learned (male) humanist called upon the illicitly savvy (female) witch to confirm the exclusivity of his bookish knowledge.

Orthodox Hermeneutics and the Witch

As the least prestigious of the liberal professions throughout the sixteenth and seventeenth centuries, medicine was also one of those disciplines in which

---

39   Michel Foucault, "Médecins, juges, et sorciers au XVIIe siècle," *Dits et écrits: 1954-1988*, vol. 1 (Paris: Gallimard, 1994), 753–56, 754. Note the masculine: "sorcerers and *possédés*." Midelfort offers a lucid critique of Foucault's "radical nihilism," 7–8.

40   Jean-Michel Sallman, "Sorcière," *XVIe-XVIIe siècles*, eds. Natalie Zemon Davis and Arlette Farge, *Histoire des femmes en occident*, eds. Georges Duby and Michelle Perrot, vol. 3 (Paris: Plon, 1991), 467.

"the professional *mentalité* of the Renaissance" asserted itself most emphatically.[41] Physicians had cultivated their scholarly training from the very beginning of the humanist ferment, when, according to Douglas Biow, doctors "wished to be viewed as humanists to help elevate the status of their profession—to make the profession of medicine appear, as they had for so long tried to make it appear, less a mechanical and far more an intellectual art."[42] The first complete editions of Hippocrates and Galen in Venice in 1525 and 1526 signaled the doctor's new calling as philologist. the University of Paris, one of the most illustrious faculties of medicine of the time in Europe, made its international reputation as the center of translating and editing Greek medicine, including Hippocrates and especially Galen.[43]

From the middle of the century, competition from an array of alternative medicines created a consumer's market for medical services, and trained medical practitioners sought to protect their markets from unqualified healers by tightening existing statutes or by incorporating into *collèges*, to which the crown granted a monopoly in exchange for protecting the public through the policing of local medical services. Virtually stagnant from 1450 to 1550, incorporation flourished in France in the second half of the sixteenth century.[44] Since most doctors practiced in towns too small to sustain corporations (and, therefore, could not prevent untrained individuals from practicing), publicity campaigns were even more crucial than restrictive legal measures. No individual aroused more impassioned fulmination among the medical elite than the Swiss-born, self-taught alchemist, Philippus Aureolus Theophrastus Bombastus von Hohenheim (1493–1541), better known as Paracelsus.[45] Though hardly a Lutheran himself, Paracelsus was known to his detractors as the "Luther of medicine," a comparison he seems to have encouraged. In a gesture of defiance not without its resemblances to Luther's incineration of the canon law and bull of

---

41 In France, medical students brought up the rear in university processions, had less voice than future lawyers and priests-in-training in university assemblies, and once gainfully employed, aspired to put their sons or grandsons in the position to join the more upwardly mobile ranks of the robe. Laurence Brockliss and Colin Jones, *The Medical World of Early Modern France* (Oxford: Clarendon Press, 1997), 86. On the "professional *mentalité* of the Renaissance," see George McClure, "The *Artes* and the *Ars moriendi* in late Renaissance Venice: The Professions in Fabio Glissenti's *Discorsi morali contra il dispiacer del morire, detto Athanatophilia* (1596)," *Renaissance Quarterly* 51(1998): 95.

42 Douglas Biow, *Doctors, Ambassadors, Secretaries: Humanism and Professions in Renaissance Italy* (Chicago: University of Chicago Press, 2002), 17.

43 On "The Gospel according to Galen," see Brockliss and Jones, 107–19. On Hippocrates at the University of Paris, see Iain M. Lonie, "The Paris Hippocratics: Teaching and Research in Paris in the Second Half of the Sixteenth Century," *The Medical Renaissance of the Sixteenth Century*, eds. A. Wear, R.K. French, I.M. Lonie (Cambridge: Cambridge U.P., 1985), 155–74.

44 Self-governed and often flanked by tightly knit confraternities, guilds had once been viewed as seedbeds of sedition. That perception changed dramatically when Huguenots and the Catholic League succeeded in alienating entire municipalities from royal control; guilds became a means for the crown to obtain and control loyalty. Brockliss and Jones, 178, 175, 180.

45 For a more developed comparison of Paracelsus to Luther, see Andrew Weeks, *Paracelsus: Speculative Theory and the Crisis of the Early Reformation* (Albany: State University of New York Press, 1997), 1–19.

excommunication, Paracelsus burned a medieval compendium of medical theory (Avicenna's *Canon*) in front of a crowd of students at the University of Basel. Capitalizing on a strand of Luther's eschatology that Luther himself eventually abandoned, Paracelsus proclaimed the legibility of God's word in nature and claimed to decipher its eschatological subtext through divine inspiration.[46]

Weyer famously excoriated untrained medical practitioners. Where surgeons butcher their patients, Weyer warns, Paracelsians practice an "uncertain and dangerous sort of experimentation [*empeiria*]." The followers of Paracelsus rely on the credulity of their patients to excuse their failures; they "cover up their own ignorance in matters pertaining to the hallowed art of medicine" by blaming their shortcomings on witchcraft, just as "that unlearned crowd of surgeons ... immediately attribute gangrene, necrosis, eating ulcers, or other malignant or hard-to-heal sores to the saints." "There are many of this ilk," complains Weyer,

> recently "elated" by the fumes of the fire of chemistry, who boast that they have arisen from the school of Theophrastus Paracelsus. They are the special slaves of arrogance, self-love, and vainglory, who can accomplish all things whatsoever by Stentorian cries, and by promises and sesquipedalian words, in perfect imitation of their master. Thus they have committed to memory the foul sayings of that insane man, and with them they rail at the ancient and sacrosanct art of medicine, and slander and reject it, and bend their efforts to trample it underfoot, fabricating new principles and new expressions, which even they do not understand or defend by rational argument, content as they are with the confused heap of useless words with which Paracelsus filled his writings.[47]

Contrasting "the ancient and sacrosanct art of medicine" to the "new principles and ... expressions" of Paracelsus, Weyer describes Paracelsianism as a textless and illegitimate science. Weyer mocks the ex nihilo source of the Paracelsian "school": Paracelsus was "insane;" his writing, nothing but a monstrous mound of verbiage. Paracelsus's disciples transmit his utterances through a kind of oral history, notoriously subject to human distortion. They engage in shameless self-promotion ("arrogance, self-love, and vainglory") with empty and impotent rhetoric ("stentorian cries, promises, and sesquipedalian words").

Weyer's anti-Paracelsian invective set the tone for the attitudes of French physicians toward alchemy until the reign of Henri IV. Jacques Grévin (1538–70),

---

46   Luther portrayed Nature as being saturated with God's word. "By God's grace," he claimed in the *Tischreden*, we "are beginning to see his glorious work and wonder even in the flower.... We see the power of his word in the creatures." Cited in James Bono, *The Word of God and the Languages of Man: Interpreting Nature in Early Modern Science and Medicine* (Madison: University of Wisconsin Press, 1995), 71. Luther manifested no interest in resolving nature's mysteries, preferring wonder to knowledge. He remarked on one occasion that the creation of the human fetus "is God's alone, something which we cannot perceive." Cited in R. Po-Chia Hsia, "A Time for Monsters: Monstrous Births, Propaganda, and the German Reformation," in *Monstrous Bodies/Political Monstrosities in Early Modern Europe*, eds. Laura Lunger Knoppers and Joan B. Landes (Ithaca, London: Cornell University Press, 2004), 77. Paracelsus, on the other hand, purported to divulge in *De vita longa* (1526) the secrets of how to live as long as the patriarchs of the Old Testament.

47   Weyer, 1991, 154.

a Calvinist physician and a minor star in the constellation of poets orbiting around Charles IX, who would publish the first French translation of *De praestigiis daemonum* in 1567, cites Weyer's scathing indictment of Paracelsians as bookless, raving madmen in his *Discours ... sur les vertus & facultez de l'Antimoine* (1566), a tract against antimony that he wrote in the context of the first French debate on the Paracelsian laxative.[48] The medical faculty of the University of Paris quickly rallied to Grévin's side in the antimony debate, banning the substance for medical use.[49] Grévin's translation of Weyer's book a year later coincided with Jacques Gohory's translation of *La grande, vraye et parfaicte chirurgie* (1567), the first compendium of Paracelsian writings to become available in French. Whatever their attitudes toward witchcraft, those physicians who read *De praestigiis daemonum* could only have felt buoyed by Weyer's outspoken vituperations against this new breed of competitor. Humanists beyond the medical profession lauded Weyer for his anti-Paracelsianism. Weyer's nephew, Charles Utenhove the Younger, devoted one of the encomiastic poems of the *Xenia, seu illustrium quorundam nominum allusions* (1568) that he published in collaboration with the Pleiade poet Joachim Du Bellay, to his uncle.[50] In his invented etymology, Utenhove puns on Weyer's name and on the title of Paracelsus's *Labyrinthus Medicorum Errantium*. From "Weyer," which the French spelled "Wier" (the "W" being pronounced as a "V"), Utenhove spins out "via" a road or path. He congratulates Weyer on the high course he charts in contrast to the errant Paracelsians. Jacques Chovet included Utenhove's poem as an epigram in his 1579 French edition of *De praestigiis daemonum*.[51] In a 1583 letter to his uncle, Utenhove hints at a somewhat more disillusioned appreciation of his uncle's superior path. Complaining of Weyer's failure to respond to three of his previous letters, he ruefully wonders if the physician scorns all those who are not as learned as he is.

---

48   Grévin wrote his *Discours ... sur les vertus & facultez de l'Antimoine* (1566) in response to the La Rochelle physician Loys De Launay's *De la Faculté & vertue admirable de l'Antimoine* (1564). De Launay had learned about antimony in a 1561 French translation of Pietro Andrea Mattioli's *Commentaries* on Dioscorides, where Mattioli credits Paracelsus with having been the first to prescribe antimony for laxative purposes. In a rare instance in which an early modern doctor plays the patient, Grévin claimed that he had tried antimony and that it had left him good for dead for a whole week. Allen G. Debus, *The French Paracelsians: The Chemical Challenge to Medical and Scientific Tradition in Early Modern France* (Cambridge: Cambridge U.P., 1991), 21–30.

49   Debus, 6–7.

50   Janssen 27–31, 50, 65, 74, 129. Utenhove became quite friendly with Weyer's son, Galen (also a physician), once settled in Dusseldorf. Utenhove's missives to Galen Weyer include dinner invitations, thank you notes for loans, as well as requests for medication for himself and his wife. Utenhove knew Grévin as a result of having served as preceptor to the children of Erasmus's Parisian friend, Jean de Morel (1511–81).

51   "Ille VIA tota totóque ERRARE videtur / ERRO vagus coelo, docte WIERE mihi, / Qui Paracelsiste latitans sub nomine sectae, / Nomen ab ERRANDO credibit esse tibi. / Ni quod ABERRANTES recto de tramite, rectam / (Ceu Paracelsistas) cogis inire viam." I am grateful to Eric MacPhail for identifying Utenhove for me and to David Wilkin, Matthew McGowan, and Vivian Holliday for helping me to decipher the poem.

Empirics of all stripes claimed literacy in the book of nature in the wake of Paracelsus's alchemical therapies. Moreover, his "artisanal epistemology" validated those medical practitioners—apothecaries, surgeons, and midwives—whose subordinate status resulted from their hands-on engagement with the human body.[52] Female medical practitioners, few of whom had access to formal medical instruction, were a favorite target for learned physicians in works dedicated to educating the public as to what constituted legitimate medical practice. In his best selling *Erreurs populaires* (1578), Laurent Joubert juxtaposes women's illiteracy to the learning of the (male) physician. Although women are the constituency to whom Joubert addresses his book (and services, presumably), they are also the popular err-ers whom he most emphatically denounces. Joubert chides women who take their health into their own hands, resorting to nefarious douching in cases of reticent fertility, or who, in tending to their family members, ignore the physician's prescriptions, feeding them too much, refreshing them too little, and unwittingly bringing about their untimely death.[53] As for women whose profession is to tend to the health of other women, Joubert does not deny their greater experience in matters dealing with childbirth. Instead, he questions the validity of experience. Midwives, he says, "go about [their work] blindly like empirics, without knowing what they are doing."[54] Though they have little experience, "men have more knowledge" than practiced midwives, and are thus more qualified.[55] Surgeons sounded the same notes of derision, even though their training was, like that of the midwife, practical rather than theoretical in orientation. The autodidact Ambroise Paré (1509–90), surgeon to four Valois kings, insists on the "imprudence of matrons" in his *Deux livres de chirurgie* (1573), while his student and aide-de-camp, Jacques Guillemeau (1550–1613), in *De l'heureux accouchement des femmes* (1609), claims that midwives are all too often hampered by "the limit of their experience."[56]

The well-known story of the male medical establishment's gradual takeover of childbirth in early modern Europe led some feminist historians of the 1970s to hold

---

52   On Paracelsus's "artisanal epistemology," see Pamela Smith, *The Body of the Artisan: Art and Experience in the Scientific Revolution* (Chicago: University of Chicago Press, 2004), 82–93. Smith argues that Paracelsus's application of the metaphor of alchemy to all of nature's workings and even to God's creation thereof validated medicine as a craft, as a vocation concerned not only with the created but also with the process of creation itself.

53   According to Joubert, women who fail to conceive "use all the recipes in the world, rational and empirical, one after another without ever stopping" and he warns women "once and for all to believe and to obey physicians, not less in the quantity of food than in the quality." Laurent Joubert, *Popular errors*, trans. Gregory David de Rocher, 2 vols (Tuscaloosa: University of Alabama Press, 1989–95), 1: 123, 84.

54   Joubert, 1: 173.

55   Ibid.: 208–9.

56   Jacques Guillemeau, *De l'heureux accouchement des femmes*, Cited in Wendy Perkins, *Midwifery and Medicine in Early Modern France: Louise Bourgeois* (Exeter: University of Exeter Press, 1996), 99–100. For the story of the development of obstetrics and the decline of midwifery, consult Jacques Gélis, *La Sage-femme ou le médecin: une nouvelle conception de la vie* (Paris: Fayard, 1988) and Jean Donnison, *Midwives and Medical Men: A History of Inter-Professional Rivalries and Women's Rights* (New York: Schocken Books, 1977).

physicians responsible for the witch hunts. Barbara Ehrenreich and Deirdre English claim that "the rise of the [medical] experts ... began with a bitter conflict which set women against men, class against class." They go on to assert that the early modern medical man claimed a monopoly on the practice of medicine and handily sent the female healer qua midwife up in smoke by decrying her as a witch.[57] It is true that at least until the early seventeenth century the midwife was particularly vulnerable to accusations of witchcraft as a result of the anxiety-provoking processes with which she dealt: pregnancy and childbirth. Kramer devotes a chapter to explaining "How Witch Midwives commit most Horrid Crimes when they either Kill Children or Offer them to Devils in most Accursed Wise" in the *Malleus*.[58] Yet those who accused midwives of witchcraft were clients more often than competitors, women rather than men.[59] Joubert never once suggests that the midwife has anything to do with witchcraft, despite his jealous attitude towards her practice. Nor does Paré make any statements to this effect, despite the fact that he did not hesitate to invoke demonological causes for monstrous births alongside natural ones in *Des monstres et prodiges* (1573).

The relation between the midwife and the witch was a matter of conceptual proximity, not practical identity. Like the Paracelsian or the midwife, the witch was a rival whose knowledge came from an illicit source. Erastus, who is best known for his four-volume work against Paracelsus,[60] explains the etymology for one of the Latin words for witch: "*Sagae* seem to have taken their name from the word *sagire*, as Cicero says: because they want to know lots of things. They purport to know and be able to do things that no one can do ... naturally."[61] As a result, he insists, "witches are even more execrable [than magicians] in that they learn from Satan himself what magicians learn in books."[62] Through his explanation of the origin of the word *saga*, Erastus emphasizes that the witch transgressed orthodox ways of

---

57   Barbara Ehrenreich and Deirdre English, *For Her Own Good: 150 Years of the Experts' Advice to Women* (Garden City: Doubleday, 1978), 33, 39. Diane Purkiss provides a contextual analysis of early feminist interpretations of witch trials in *The Witch in History: Early Modern and Twentieth-Century Representations* (London: Routledge, 1996).

58   Broedel, 27.

59   Lyndal Roper, *Oedipus and the Devil*, 201.

60   The first book—*Disputationum de medicina nova de Philippi Paracelsi pars prima* (Basel: Peter Perna, 1571)—included a brief disputation on witchcraft directed against *De praestigiis daemonum*. Insofar as Erastus targets the heresies implicit in Paracelsus's natural philosophy and emphasizes the heretical nature of witchcraft in his refutation of *De praestigiis daemonum*, it seems plausible that he was eager to assert his religious orthodoxy following his fall from favor. Erastus became involved in church politics after being elected rector of the University of Heidelberg where he was also on the medical faculty. When the party that he supported lost out in a controversy regarding church discipline in 1568, his prestige flagged, and he even had to rebuff accusations of Antitrinitarianism. Charles D. Gunnoe Jr., "Erastus and Paracelsianism: Theological Motifs in Thomas Erastus' Rejection of Paracelsian Natural Philosophy," *Reading the Book of Nature: The Other Side of the Scientific Revolution,* eds. Allen G. Debus and Michael T. Walton, *Sixteenth Century Essays and Studies* 41 (1998), 45–66. See 49–50 for Erastus's biography.

61   Erastus, 813.

62   Ibid., 773. See also 841.

knowing as well as the moral order. The elimination of the witch thus served not just to protect Christendom, but also to defend a construction of knowledge in which books reigned supreme. It is no coincidence that witch-hunting and prosecuting manuals by Dominican inquisitors—Johann Nider's *Formicarius* (1437) and the *Malleus Maleficarum*—were among the earliest printed books, or that early centers of printing such as Mainz and Bamberg in Germany witnessed extensive witch hunts.[63] The gender of the witch—Jean Bodin claimed that there were fifty witches for every sorcerer—underscored her epistemological deviance.[64] Observing that the witch "knew her secrets not from reading books, but strictly from following Satan's direct instruction," Gerhild Scholz Williams argues that

> Knowing without reading, which was thought to be characteristic of witches, was tantamount to knowing beyond orthodox hermeneutics. The struggle over access to knowledge—the prohibition of texts designated as unsuitable to an uninitiated reading public—was always a struggle for control over women and part of her persecution as a witch.[65]

Williams nicely elucidates the relation between the gender and the knowledge of the early modern witch: The learned woman was already an oxymoron; that her knowledge came from Satan added moral perversity to the inversion of intellectual/ sexual order. In addition to enacting the triumph of good over evil, the eradication of the witch proclaimed the ascendancy of proper over illicit ways of knowing; it reaffirmed the authority of the book and the exclusions operated by it.

Weyer boasted the finest medical pedigree, and his diatribe in *De praestigiis daemonum* against the Paracelsians earned him the approval of the learned medical and humanist elite. Yet if "orthodox hermeneutics" and belief in the illicit knowledge of witches went hand-in-hand, what are we to make of Weyer's denial that the women accused of witchcraft had the knowledge they claimed or that others attributed to them? Erastus perceived that Weyer flouted the conventional portrayal of the witch as illicitly learned. Sardonically paraphrasing Weyer, Erastus writes, "it appears that the witches of our time are old *radotees*, who know nothing, have no books, and cannot read; in short that they are pure beasts." And again, "But witches have no science, nor [have they] ever left the house to learn it, they have no books and for the most part do not know how to read."[66] Comparing Weyer's characterization of the witch to his critique of Paracelsus helps understand the role she played in his promotion of the physician. The Paracelsian and the witch support, by inversion, complementary facets of Weyer's medical authority. The ignorant Paracelsian represents the converse of the learned physician, substituting the imagination's

---

63   Christina Larner, "Crimen Exceptum? Witchcraft in Europe," *Crime and the Law: The Social History of Crime in Western Europe since 1500*, ed. V.A.C. Gatrell, Bruce Lenman, and Geoffrey Parker (London: Europa Publications, 1980), 67.

64   Jean Bodin, *De la Démonomanie des sorciers* (Paris: Jacques DuPuys, 1582), 224.

65   Gerhild Scholz Williams, *Defining Dominion: The Discourses of Magic and Witchcraft in Early Modern France and Germany* (Ann Arbor: The University of Michigan Press, 1997), 69.

66   Erastus, 786, 773.

facile chimeras for the solid doctrines painstakingly acquired through long study. Furthermore, his failings justify the privileges enjoyed by the trained physician. The melancholic imagination of the debunked "witch," on the other hand, ensures the exclusivity of the physician's claim to common sense. Witches interpret fantastical forms fabricated by the Devil as the "truly substantial figures" of sense experience, with the result that their thought processes are hopelessly corrupted. Based on a curious blend of medical empiricism and Lutheran literalism, Weyer's surprisingly medieval representation of women enhances the physician's authority.

To Cut or Not to Cut? Women and Their Secrets

When Weyer derides *empeiria* in his anti-Paracelsian tirade, he is not condemning an epistemology founded on sense experience—what we would call "empiricism." To the contrary, Weyer was one of a growing number of physicians within the Holy Roman Empire who looked to observation as a crucial source of knowledge.[67] Twenty years before publishing *De praestigiis daemonum*, Oporinus had produced the work that signaled the renascence of anatomy, Andreas Vesalius's (1514–64) *De humani corporis fabrica* (1543). In *De humani corporis fabrica*, Vesalius's aspired to restore anatomy to the perfection it had attained in ancient Rome; he wrote in Ciceronian Latin and adapted the bodies of the executed criminals he dissected to the proportions and poses of classical sculpture in magnificent woodcut plates.[68] At the same time, as he followed Galen's prescription to observe nature directly, he found himself obliged to contradict the master. "Even [professors of dissection], drawn by their love of truth, are ... placing more faith in their own not ineffective eyes and reason than in Galen's writings."[69] Testimony to the credibility of visual experience, the images in *De humani corporis fabrica* promote autopsy (seeing for oneself) as a crucial complement and sometimes corrective to knowledge gleaned from books. In an age when manual labor—especially the kind that involved contact with diseased or dead bodies— remained the mark of the *roturier* if not of the reviled gravedigger, Vesalius gestures powerfully toward the value of sense experience when he portrays himself manipulating the cadavers he anatomized.

Flemish, as was Vesalius (né Andries van Wesel), Weyer matriculated the year after the future anatomist at the University of Paris, where he studied, as Vesalius had, with the great medical humanists Jacques DuBois (Sylvius) and Jean Fernel (1497–1558).[70] Jacques Grévin, who was the first to translate *De praestigiis*

---

67 According to Midelfort, "early modern German publishers of medical books led a general European drive for increased attention to empirical detail" (165).

68 Glenn Harcourt, "Andreas Vesalius and the Anatomy of Antique Sculpture," *Representations* 17 (1987), 2–61.

69 Andreas Vesalius, *On the Fabric of the Human Body*, trans. William Frank Richardson and John Burd Carman, vol. 1 (San Francisco: Norman Publishing, 1998), liv.

70 Mora points out that Weyer manifested the "same attitude in regard to the study of the mind that Vesalius was then pioneering in his scientific approach to the study of the human body" (lxi).

daemonum into French, also translated Vesalius's work.[71] Although Weyer's formal study of anatomy was probably not very extensive, he knew the work of Alessandro Benedetti, Gabriele Fallopio, and Vesalius, and presented himself as a competent anatomist. Throughout *De praestigiis daemonum*, Weyer challenges testimonies involving corporeal transformations by emphasizing the body's irreducible volume and immutable structure. To the confession of a Schiedam woman who claimed to have "plunged into the sea in a mussel shell," after having slipped out of her house "through a hole in the windowpane" in order to drive away herring from fishing nets, Weyer objects with a verbal dissection of the human body. "We are not speaking of an airy creature made only of spirit, or one fashioned from a substance that can be drawn out fine or melted," he insists, "but of a human being compounded of solid bones, gripping cartilage, firm tendons, ligaments, nerves, and membranes, as well as muscular flesh." [72] Moreover, "we must apply the norm of reason" to ask why the woman needed to plow through the water in a mussel shell when she had already managed to fly through a tiny hole in a windowpane. Could she not just swim through the water just as she had squeezed through the hole? In the case of a girl who claimed to have a knife lodged in her side as the result of evil-doing, Weyer challenges his credulous reader to "tell me how and by what passageways [the knife] was injected." He reviews the one possible path (the digestive tract) only to exclude it. "Even if I should grant that the knife was conveyed by way of mouth, it still could not have been carried to that area of her side unless the stomach and the peritoneum had first been cut laterally, with greatest danger for life itself." The knife would have encountered resistance at every turn in its trajectory. Weyer assures his reader that there was no place for the knife to hide within her body: "Where, pray tell, could that long knife have lain hidden, or where could it have lodged securely for a whole year? If in the muscles on the left side, this would have been apparent, as I say, to the touch and to the eye." [73]

Interestingly, Weyer included an image of the rusty knife in the 1586 edition of *De praestigiis daemonum*. In addition to testifying to the author's impartiality—"here you see the length and shape of the knife"—Weyer's presentation of the evidence reminds the reader of his experience wielding such an object in dissections and thus of his superior knowledge of the human body.

Although Weyer vaunts his knowledge of anatomy, the traditional role of the physician as a discerner of external signs, so emphasized by the medical faculty at the

---

71   Grévin reproduced for Henry VIII of England the woodcut engravings accompanying *De Humani corporis fabrica* in *taille-douce* along with a French translation of Vesalius's explanations thereof in *Les Portraicts anatomiques de toutes les parties du corps humain, gravez en taille-douce, par le commandement de feu Henry huictiesme, Roy d'Angleterre. Ensemble l'Abbregé d'André Vesal, et l'explication d'iceux, accompagnee d'une declaration Anatomique* (Paris: André Wechel, 1569).

72   Weyer, 1991, 508. Weyer does not say how he learned of the case; in similar instances occurring within the Holy Roman Empire, he requested records of confessions from judicial registers. This is perhaps the kind of document that he paraphrases in the case of the Dutch woman.

73   Weyer, 1991, 316.

Fig. 1.1   Knife. Johann Weyer, *De praestigiis daemonum* (1583).

University of Paris, is far more important to his argument.[74] In the 1568 edition of *De praestigiis daemonom*, Weyer added a sixth book, "On the punishment of notorious magicians, witches, and poisoners," that Jacques Chovet included in his edition of a new French translation published in Geneva in 1579.[75] The addition of the sixth book transformed a treatise framed by rather predictable Protestant polemics into an indictment of inquisitional procedure and a manifesto on the prerogatives of the university-trained physician in adjudicating demonological questions. Despite the anticipated objections of "legal experts" and "peevish theologians," Weyer justified his entry into the "labyrinth" of demonology by underscoring that what is really at stake is the exclusive property of no profession.[76] "Anyone may investigate the truth that lies hidden in the depths," Weyer declares; "[T]he authority of antiquity should not outweigh that truth." Nevertheless, he claims, certain truth-seekers have a distinct advantage: "Why then will it not be granted to the physician—by profession an investigator of hidden things, who has long devoted himself to this discipline (with what success it is for others to judge)—to come forth in public and advance his own opinion[?]"[77] Since the physician is "by profession an investigator of hidden things," Weyer reasons, he is particularly adept at unveiling "truth that lies hidden in the depths." Weyer is alluding to the traditional division of medical labor, instituted by the Hippocratic Oath: the physician leaves it to the surgeon to break the surface of the body, and acts himself as "an interpreter of signs," relying on "the outside of the body to know its inside."[78] "Hidden things" refers in the Hippocratic context to things hidden within the body—what we might call "internal medicine." Weyer encompasses within that denomination the truth that has been veiled by the illusions of demons. The physician is a specialist in the discernment of hidden things; demons and witchcraft are hidden things; thus the physician's training is pertinent to demonology.

Weyer's evocation of the Hippocratic Oath contradicts his flashy verbal dissections; both, however, serve his critique of the witch trials. Whereas Weyer uses

---

74   I thank Allen Shotwell for pointing out to me that this division of labor and its accompanying hierarchy was a salient feature of the training Weyer received at University of Paris. About the complex relation between Paris medical faculty and surgeons, see Pearl Kibre, "The Faculty of Medicine at Paris, Charlatanism, and Unlicensed Medical Practices in the Later Middle Ages," *Bulletin of the History of Medicine*, 27 (1953): 1–20, and C.D. O'Malley, "The Inception of Anatomical Studies in the University of Paris," *Bulletin of the History of Medicine,* 23 (1959): 436–45.

75   Johann Weyer, *Histoires, disputes et discours des illusions et impostures des diables, des magiciens infâmes, sorcières et empoisonneurs: des ensorcelés et des démoniaques, et de la guérison d'iceux: item de la punition que méritent les magiciens, les empoisonneurs et les sorcières. Le tout comprins en Six Livres (augmentez de moitié en ceste dernière édition).* (Genève: Jacques Chovet, 1579). This edition consisted in a revision of Grévin's translation along with a translation of the sixth book that Weyer had added into the Latin edition of 1568. It also includes a translation of Erastus's *Repititio disputationis de lamiis seu strigibus* (Basel: Pieter Perna, 1578), his rebuttal of Weyer's plea for clemency.

76   Weyer, 1991, 480, 581.

77   Ibid., 479.

78   Page DuBois, *Torture and Truth* (London and New York: Routledge, 1991), 89.

his anatomical knowledge in a naturalistic vein to discredit the evil deeds attributed to witches or claimed by them, his traditional characterization of the physician as a decipherer of signs structures his protestations against torture. Weyer insists that truth is readily available to the senses; one need only look at and listen to these women to know that they are mad. To resort to torture to obtain the truth is gratuitous and cruel. Far from removing obstacles standing in the way of truth, he argues, torture creates confusion, analogous to the illusions crafted by the Devil. Weyer's contradictory portrayal of the physician's role—an investigator of the body's interior and a reader of exterior signs—might be reconciled if we consider them as diverse means to a single end: that of sparing wrongly accused "witches." Weyer "proves" the fantastical experiences claimed by witches to be impossible through anatomical facts, just as he rejects the confessions they make under torture. Both actions work to deny witchcraft and thus to establish the innocence of the accused. But both also result in a devaluation of the woman's testimony. Weyer grants full authority to the perception of the physician, while denying the legitimacy of the symptoms reported—whether voluntarily or through coercion—by the woman.[79]

Katharine Park traces a similar displacement of authority from the female patient to the physician through her study of the meaning of the expression "secrets of women" in *Secrets of Women: Gender, Generation, and the Origins of Human Dissection*. In the thirteenth century, "secrets of women" referred to knowledge known to women (but not to men) about the ailments and therapies pertaining to the female body.[80] By the fifteenth century, vernacular, medical writers were using the term "secrets of women" to talk about women's sexual and reproductive organs, about which physicians, they claimed, had more knowledge than women.[81] Vesalius, too, would capitalize on the secrecy theme, portraying himself in the transgressive guise of Nero, the sadistic Roman emperor who according to an apocryphal legend reported in Jean de Meun's *Roman de la rose* (ca. 1275) and other medieval narratives, ended his mother's life through vivisection. Vesalius's title page is a deliberate allusion to late medieval visual representations of Nero's matricide.[82] More symbolic than anecdotal,

---

79   This section owes much to Kevin Grau, who encouraged me to think about the difference between medical signs and symptoms as they pertain to Weyer's indictment of torture.

80   See especially Pseudo-Albertus Magnus, *Women's Secrets: A Translation of Pseudo-Albertus Magnus's De Secretis Mulierum with Commentaries*, trans. Helen Rodnite LeMay (Albany: State University of New York Press, 1992). On the development of this genre of medical writing, consult Monica Green, "From 'Diseases of Women' to 'Secrets of Women': The Transformation of Gynecological Literature in the Later Middle Ages," *Journal of Medieval and Early Modern Studies* 30 (2000): 5–39.

81   Katharine Park, *Secrets of Women: Gender, Generation, and the Origins of Human Dissection* (New York: Zone Books, 2006), 77–120. William Eamon, in *Science and the Secrets of Nature: Books of Secrets in Medieval and Early Modern Culture* (Princeton: Princeton University Press, 1994) explains that "the metaphor of the 'secrets of nature' has been one of the most prominent and most powerful metaphors in the history of science" because it serves to define a restricted ownership of knowledge (351).

82   Katharine Park, "Dissecting the Female Body: From Women's Secrets to the Secrets of Nature," *Crossing Boundaries: Attending to Early Modern Women*, eds. Jane Donawerth

Fig. 1.2   Title page. Andreas Vesalius, *De humani corporis fabrica* (1543).

and Adele Seeff (Newark: University of Delaware Press and London: Associated University Presses, 2000), 39.

the open female cadaver in the title page to Vesalius's *De Humani corporis fabrica* celebrated the autoptic authority of the anatomist, who through his art purported to lay bare the most mysterious of bodily functions: generation and gestation. "What is depicted," writes Jonathan Sawday, "is no less than a demonstration of the structural coherence of the universe itself, whose central component—the principle of life concealed within the womb—Vesalius is about to open to our gaze."[83]

For Vesalius, however, the opening of the woman's cadaver is the punch line to a big joke. The anatomist dramatizes his exclusive role as a discoverer of women's secrets, but he builds up a rhetoric of transgression only to deflate it, for it turns out that there is nothing to be known about the open female body in the title page of *De Humani corporis fabrica*. Evidently to avoid punishment or perhaps torture, the female criminal had falsely claimed to be pregnant (French law prohibited administering *la question* to those whose lives would be endangered by it, including pregnant women). "By placing an empty uterus at the center of his title page," Park explains, "Vesalius suggested that its mysteries were illusory, just as he rejected *Women's Secrets* as an 'ignorant book' in his chapter on that same organ. The principal secret of women was that the uterus held no secrets at all."[84] Vesalius takes full advantage of the paradoxical status of the secret that Julius Caesar Scaliger (1484–1558) would bring to light in his 1557 response to Girolamo Cardano's *De subtilitate* (1551). Cardano, a spokesman for the esotericism of Renaissance magic of which Weyer's mentor Agrippa was perhaps the most important representative, claimed that "If secrets are divulged and made common, they lose their beauty and dignity ... a secret is not a secret because it is hidden; it is a secret because it is worthy of hiding."[85] Scaliger, in contrast, denied that there was any intrinsic essence or value to things that Cardano might designate as secrets. Scaliger questioned the ontology of the secret, pointing out that once discovered and divulged, a secret is no longer a secret; it becomes something else.[86] We can see that Vesalius is playing with this paradox, too; he derives his power and authority not from his exclusive

---

83 Jonathan Sawday, *The Body Emblazoned: Dissection and the Human Body in Renaissance Culture* (London and New York: Routledge, 1995), 70. Evocative of a microcosm, the perfectly spherical womb, exposed but as yet uncut, graces many an early modern anatomy book. See, for instance, the title page of Helkiah Crooke's *Mikrokosmographia,* a collection and English translation of works by late Renaissance anatomists like Caspar Bauhin and André du Laurens. The title page of Crooke's compendium becomes progressively more elaborate in the many seventeenth-century editions, but the willowy woman remains, standing in a graceful S-curve, despite her missing abdominal muscles. Compare, for instance, the title page of the 1615 edition, published by William Lagard, to the 1655 edition published by "R.C.," both in London. The former features the woman against a blank, white background; she was probably lifted from one of Crooke's sources. The 1605 Frankfurt edition of Caspar Bauhin's *Theatrum Anatomicum* features a similar, but not identical figure with an exposed spherical womb. In the 1655 edition of the *Mikrokosmographia,* the same figure, somewhat reduced in size, stands as a supporting statue in an elaborate architectural structure around the text of the title page.

84 Park, 39.

85 Girolamo Cardano, *De secretis*, cited in Eamon 280.

86 Eamon, 280.

possession of a secret, but from being the one who lifts the veil, as it were, and who, thereby, initiates the ontological transformation of the secret into something else.

Weyer performs a similar gesture of demystification, except the veil is not located in nature at all but results from the illusions imposed by the Devil or created by torture. His focus is, therefore, on the futility and injustice of cutting when there is no secret to be known. Although Weyer was clearly familiar with ancient, legal arguments against torture, his objections to torture were, nonetheless, unusual.[87] Because early modern jurisprudence, deriving from Roman and Canon law, privileged confession as the proof of choice, torture became an unavoidable means of establishing the guilt of the accused. Both the *Constitutio Criminalis Carolina* (1532) in the Holy Roman Empire and the ordinance of Villers-Cotteret (1539) in France delineate the proper administration of torture.[88] According to John Langbein, "The law of torture survived into the eighteenth century, not because its defects had been concealed, but rather in spite of their having been long revealed. European criminal procedure had no alternative: the law of proof was absolutely dependent upon coerced confessions."[89] And as Edward Peters puts it, "Confession, the queen of proofs, required torture, the queen of torments."[90]

In reference to Vesalius's self-unraveling *écorchés*, Sawday has argued that it was above all the cadavers of executed male criminals that provided opportunities for penal spectacle beyond the grave.[91] Yet the female body was that which best figured the epistemological logic of confession and torture. Vesalius's title page portrays the body of a female criminal who, condemned to death, had claimed to be pregnant to avoid execution. Consistent with the gendering of nature's secrets, the confessions required for the establishment of the crime of witchcraft revolved around women's (sexual) secrets. Central to any conviction for witchcraft was the establishment of the witch's pact with the Devil, a pact sealed through sexual intercourse. Inspired by *De Secretis mulierum*, Sprenger and Kramer emphasized women's sexual desire as

---

87   Although torture, as an element of judicial procedure, would not meet with sustained criticism until the Enlightenment, opposition to torture as a means of finding truth can be traced back to ancient Rome, where the torture of slaves was the central mechanism for elucidating litigation. Those in whose interest it was to deny a confession argued that pain could elicit lies as well as the truth, and that torture served only to verify a particular individual's threshold for pain. Quintilian (ca. AD 35–95) explains the usual debate accompanying torture in his twelve-volume textbook on rhetoric, the *Institutio oratoria*: "[O]ne party will style torture an infallible method of discovering the truth, while the other will allege that it also often results in false confessions, since with some their capacity of endurance makes lying an easy thing, while with others weakness makes it a necessity." Cited in Edward Peters, *Torture* (Philadelphia: U. of Pennsylvania P., 1996), 21. Similarly, Isidore de Seville (560–636), author of the *Etymologiae*, western civilization's first encyclopedia, purports to link *tormentum* (torture) to *torquens mentum* (the twisting of the mind), pointing out that "by the suffering of the body, the mind is also twisted" (Peters, 55).

88   For a comparison of these documents on the question of torture, see John H. Langbein, *Prosecuting Crime in the Renaissance* (Cambridge: Harvard U.P., 1974), 239–41.

89   John H. Langbein, *Torture and the Law of Proof: Europe and England in the Ancien Régime* (Chicago: U. of Chicago P., 1977), 9.

90   Peters, 69.

91   Sawday, 54.

the principal symptom of their weakness and copulation with the Devil as the motive of their abjuration. "All witchcraft comes from carnal lust," write the authors of the *Malleus*, "which is in women insatiable." [92] Sex reified responsibility; it bridged vacillating weakness and obdurate will, contrary characterizations of woman that were equally crucial in the narrative of her initial seduction and ensuing evil deeds. A witch's forced confession of sex with demons doubly satisfied the ideal of laying truth bare. The female body contained and concealed mysterious truths, and the witch's memory was a repository of sordid secrets concerning that body. Women's secrets and torture thus formed a mutually reinforcing pair. The inquisitor's instruments, like the anatomist's scalpel, provided access to woman's secrets, and the presence of a secret—preferably a secret involving sex—justified, in turn, the coercion central to inquisitorial procedure.

Weyer refutes the characterization of the female body as a repository of secrets in his critique of torture. He consistently skirts the issue of women's supposed lust in his discussion of witchcraft; he is careful in his establishment of the insanity defense to avoid a diagnosis that would foreground women's secrets. Like any Renaissance doctor, Weyer knew that the retention of seed in a woman could result in a serious affliction called "suffocation of the mother" or *furor uterinus*, a disease best cured through sexual intercourse. He was probably also familiar with the theory that the noxious vapors resulting from rotting, unreleased "seed" could induce the illusion of demonic "ecstasy," a phenomenon mentioned by an anonymous commentator on *De Secretis mulierum*.[93] Yet Weyer, in his defense of suspected witches, steers clear of an etiology that emphasizes sexual desire, because he recognized that the insatiable *paillardise* of women was the prosecution's centerpiece: "[I]f I can carry my point that there is no truth to this sexual union, then the whole structure of demonically induced phantasms will collapse."[94] It was, therefore, to melancholy, rather than to a uterine malfunction evocative of women's secrets, that he turned to make his case

---

92   Kramer and Sprenger, 47. Helen Rodnite Lemay speculates on Kramer's debt to *De Secretis mulierum* in "Introduction," *Women's Secrets: A Translation of Pseudo-Albertus Magnus's "De Secretis Mulierum" with Commentaries*, trans. Helen Rodnite Lemay (Albany: State University of New York Press, 1992), 50.

93   The commentator discounted old women's reports of divinely and demonically induced ecstasy, claiming that these mental peregrinations were simply the result of uterine vapors: "They think that they have been snatched out of their bodies because vapors rise to the brain. If these vapors are very thick and cloudy, it appears to them that they are in hell and they see black demons; if the vapors are light, it seems to them that they are in heaven and that they see God and his angels shining brightly." Commentator B, Albertus Magnus, *Women's Secrets*, 134. Weyer speaks of ecstasy but does not connect it to suffocation of the womb (1991, 194). Although Weyer does not allege uterine malfunction as a cause of the illusions experienced by witches, he mentions suffocation of the womb as one among many possible causes for strange symptoms often attributed to witchcraft: "Rare and severe symptoms often arise in diseases that stem from natural causes but are immediately attributed to witchcraft by men of no scientific experience and little faith. This often happens in the case of various convulsions, melancholia, epilepsy, suffocation of the uterus, decaying seed, and the many and varied effects of poisons" (1991, 447).

94   Weyer, 1991, 260.

in defense of witches. Weyer claims that there is an easy way to verify that witches do not engage in demonic sex:

> The vanity and falsity of this sexual congress will by shown by clear "eye-witness" testimony and irrefutable proof, if the maiden who is disturbed by this bewitching of her depraved imagination and who is suffering these illusions ... be examined visually and manually by a skilled midwife or by some other trained woman. She will be found to be still protected by this "girdle of virginity," namely, the hymen, provided that she has not lain with a man on some other occasion.[95]

Consistent with Weyer's emphasis on the physician's role as a reader of signs, the evidence of a woman's sexual history is not to be found inside of her, but rather on the surface of her body, available through visual and manual inspection.

When all there is to be known is evident at the surface of things, the imputation of secrets to women's bodies or minds can only lead to "sinister interpretations."[96] Weyer insists that rather than clearing away the obstacles standing in the way of truth, torture buries truth under layers of pain-induced hallucinations. The women tried for witchcraft are "twice wretched," misled by the illusions of Satan and then prodded into voluble delirium by pain.[97] The Devil insinuates and mixes into the imaginations of these women

> fantastical forms and apparitions, stirring up humans and vital spirits to accomplish his subtleties, with such dexterity and skill, that they know not what to confess except that they did these things, accomplished in truth by the Devil, following the permission and will of God: and that they are the cause of calamities befalling men or animals, of premeditated evil, or of afflictions arising in accordance with natural order.[98]

First, the Devil's manipulation of humors and animal spirits blurs perception and imagination to the extent that a woman comes to believe that she is responsible for human calamities, livestock mortality, and natural disasters, when in actuality it is he who has orchestrated them. Second, coercion requires them to articulate something, anything—why not their visions and dreams, for they do not know what else to confess? "[I]t is not to be denied that these poor silly women [*miserables femmelettes*] 'know' these things just as if they were true, because they have been so maddened by the demon through forms impressed upon their powers of imagination. Therefore when they are subjected to questioning and brought near to the flames, they openly acknowledge as their own crimes [those] which are known to them only by dreams and images."[99] Brought to ebullition by adjacent fire, chimeras instilled

---

95   Weyer, 1991, 233–4.
96   Ibid., 523.
97   Ibid., 195.
98   Weyer, 1569, "Préface," [n.p.].
99   Weyer, 1991, 176 and 1569, 213. Weyer recounts how, apprised of an imminent execution in the neighboring duchy of Berg, he hastened "eagerly" to the scene, interviewed an eighty-year-old woman accused of witchcraft, and through the "stronger power of reason," persuaded the duke of Berg to free her on the grounds that the accusations were based solely

by Satan spill over willy-nilly and are solemnly collected, recorded, and collated as truth.

Whereas Vesalius's title page can be read in terms of justice being rendered—the woman who flouts truth with her lies is not spared—in Weyer's narrative, women's tortured bodies are transparent signs that Truth has been violated. He cites a chilling case in which a woman accused of witchcraft was left to hang from the *estrapade*, while her interrogators went off for a bite to eat, with the expectation that the accused would be mollified upon their return.[100] Strung up in this excruciating posture, the woman expired before her interrogators returned. They announced the death of their victim as a suicide, knowing that the public would take suicide as confirmation of guilt.[101] Weyer makes a gruesome point: masked as suicide, death by torture ends up legitimating torture, for a suspect would only kill herself if she were guilty. Thus, do lies perpetuate lies, and injustice, injustice. Weyer's consistent use of the word "torture" to describe the travails that the Devil inflicts on the women that he possesses reinforces the idea that inquisitors are unwittingly carrying out a process initiated and sponsored by the Devil.[102] Yet Weyer warns that the slayer of the innocent is certain to lose in the game writ large.

> But when He finally appears Whom nothing escapes—the searcher of hearts . . .Who knows and judges the most hidden truth—your deeds will be made public, you stubborn tyrants and bloodthirsty judges stripped of humanity and far removed from all mercy because of your blindness. I challenge you to appear at the most just tribunal of the Supreme Judge Himself, Who will decide between you and me when the truth that has been buried and trampled underfoot will rise again and oppose you to your face, exacting vengeance for your villainy.[103]

Here the witch becomes an allegory for mistreated truth itself. Not just "hidden," but deliberately "buried and trampled underfoot," Truth will, like innocent woman suspended from the *estrapade*, demand that justice be rendered by the "Supreme Judge Himself."

To cut or not to cut? Whether in the secrets-of-nature vein that inspired the witch-hunting manuals of Dominican inquisitors and that was appropriated and mocked by Vesalius, or in the science of surfaces championed by Weyer, the answer depended on how truth was construed. Kramer associated the attainment of truth with the prying out of the secrets of women. Vesalius, in turn, posed as a violator of nature's secrets only to show that penetrating nature to her very core revealed nothing in particular. Weyer argued that cutting was gratuitous because the signs of truth were

---

on uninformed hearsay. As for her previous confession, he dismisses it: "[B]oiling oil was poured on her legs so that a false confession might be wrung from her" (1991, 524).

100 In both inquisitional and parliamentary tribunals, the *estrapade* was the most widely sanctioned form of torture; it involved hanging the suspect by her wrists, bound and pulled behind her back, so that the full force of the body pulled on the shoulder sockets. Often, weights were attached to the body to exacerbate the painful effects of gravity.

101 Weyer, 1991, 490.

102 Weyer calls the Devil a "Tormentor" because of whose cruelty a girl's "whole body was racked with truly frightful torture" (1991, 291).

103 Weyer,1991, 490.

readily accessible to the senses. These opposing models share a common feature of course. As a container of secrets or as a transparent record of cruelty, woman's body is a text that calls for a certain kind of reading and in so doing valorizes and legitimizes that reading.

"Imagining Things"

Weyer flaunted his anatomical knowledge in verbal dissections of the human body, all the while invoking the Hippocratic Oath to promote the physician's traditional authority as an expert discerner of signs revelatory of truths "hidden in the depths." How did Weyer's confessional allegiance factor into his appeal for the relevance of the physician's expertise to demonology? Martin Luther (1483–1546), whose critique of indulgences culminated in a full-fledged rejection of pontifical authority in 1520, had located Truth in Scripture. Only what his conscience compelled him to believe upon reading Scripture would he accept as truth. *Sola scriptura*: anything else remained opinion, no matter how many popes and councils sanctioned it. Luther also promoted a particular way of reading Scripture. Whereas the medieval Church recognized four levels of interpretation, in which ascertaining literal meaning was only a necessary first step towards grasping allegory, Luther warned against allegorical interpretation; the literal sense of Scripture was always to be preferred.[104]

Several scholars have linked the new anatomical emphasis on seeing for oneself to the Protestant imperative of reading for oneself. Commenting on a dispute between Vesalius and his former professor DuBois, a prominent Galenist, Andrea Carlino remarks:

> It may not have been accidental that the epistemological break achieved by Vesalius and the forms of the debate over ancient authority coincided temporally with the theological conflicts between Catholics and Protestants. Du Bois posed the problem of the acceptance of the Galenic anatomical paradigm in terms of faith, belief, and orthodoxy, as was the case for sacred texts during those same years. Religious controversy and the climate that it generated may be the source of the language employed by Du Bois on the one hand, and Vesalian empiricism and its challenge to ancient authorities on the other.[105]

Andrew Cunningham goes a step further, positing not just a parallel but a convergence: Vesalius, he argues, was a Protestant.[106] Beyond the implausibility of this assertion (Vesalius's patron was Charles V, the Holy Roman Emperor), the claim that Vesalius's anatomical stance resulted from a confessional allegiance suggests a one-to-one correspondence that ignores the versatility of religious hermeneutics in general as well as the diversity of their application. Interestingly, we shall see

---

104 Peter Harrison, *The Bible, Protestantism, and the Rise of Natural Science* (Cambridge: Cambridge U.P., 1998), 108–11.

105 Andrea Carlino, *Books of the Body: Anatomical Ritual and Renaissance Learning*, trans. John Tedeschi and Anne C. Tedeschi (Chicago and London: The University of Chicago Press, 1999), 212.

106 Andrew Cunningham, *The Anatomical Renaissance: The Resurrection of the Anatomical Projects of the Ancients* (Aldershot: Scolar Press, 1997), 235.

that in *De praestigiis daemonum* the literal interpretation espoused by Luther serves Weyer's argument *against* cutting open the human body, where that cutting consists in torture. To read literally, for Weyer, is to read the signs available at the surface of the body, whereas to cut open the body is already to impose a specious interpretation on it.

It was above all the fifth and (until 1568) final book of *De praestigiis daemonum*, which Weyer devoted to debunking cases of possession, that identified him as a Protestant. According to Catholics, possession provided palpable confirmation of a vast hierarchy of evil, whose discovery legitimated the Church as the arbiter of truth, yet whose lessons were available to all.[107] Exorcism dramatized points of Catholic doctrine, an ensemble of truths rooted in tradition and sanctioned by authority. The possessed writhed in response to the exorcist's talismanic tools—the Eucharist, holy water, the sign of the cross, relics; her skin bore the bloody traces of the holy names he invoked to cast out her demonic squatters; sometimes even demons spoke on behalf of Truth, explicitly castigating Huguenot heretics via a kind of vehicular ventriloquy. Protestants concurred with Catholics regarding the didactic value of possession. Philip Melanchton (1497–1560) viewed the possession epidemic afflicting Roman maidens as the just desserts of the sins of the papacy, while the Calvinist Pierre Viret (1511–71), in *Le monde à l'empire et le monde demoniacle* (1561), cast possession as emblematic of the condition of mankind on the eve of the apocalypse.[108] Exorcism, on the other hand, was an exercise in idolatry in Protestant eyes. Adopting Luther's rejection of human intermediaries, Weyer compares the formulae deployed by exorcists to magical incantation. "[E]xorcists should be fittingly classed with enchanters," he opines.[109] He relates titillating anecdotes peopled by fraudulent demoniacs and oversexed clerics, both stock characters "in the humanist, and especially Protestant, literature directed against monasticism and the monastic way of life in the sixteenth century."[110] One story tells of a young woman from Werl

---

107 Pierre de Bérulle calls exorcism "the Devil's school," a last chance for doubting Thomas to see the light before experiencing "the presence of God and the rigor of his judgments" at the hands of Satan's everlasting torture. Through the spectacle of exorcism, God stoops to meet the didactic needs of the most obtuse: "[F]or here the atheist ... is convinced by his senses, the sole witnesses to withstand the reproach of his incredulity, that there is a divine essence!" *Traicté des Energumènes, suivy d'un discours sur la possession de Marthe Brossier: Contre les calomnies d'un Medecin de Paris* (Troyes, 1599), 25.

108 On Protestant eschatology and possession see Stuart Clark, *Thinking with Demons*, 419–22. Melanchton's views are reported by Weyer, 1991, 470.

109 Weyer calls a magician "anyone who willingly takes instruction from a demon or from other magicians or from books, who employs a formula of known or unknown exotic words ... , or who employs any kind of magical signs, or exorcisms and dreadful execrations, or ceremonies and solemn rites, or many other practices in an illicit attempt of his own volition to summon forth a demon for some deluding, deceiving, or otherwise mocking task, so that the demon will reveal himself in some visible assumed form, or make himself known in some other way, and respond to questions by voice or whisper or by pictures or marks or in any other manner" (1991, 431).

110 Michael Heyd, *Be Sober and Reasonable: The Critique of Enthusiasm in the Seventeenth and Early Eighteenth Centuries* (Leiden, New York, and Köln: E.J. Brill, 1995),

who was traveling to Düsseldorf to be exorcized; she came equipped not just with a letter attesting to her possession, but also with a monk, whose presence, she claimed, lessened the effects of the demonic attacks she suffered. As it turned out, the monk was above all indispensable for the nocturnal services that he provided to her.[111]

Published in Basel, the center of Protestant humanism, *De praestigiis daemonum* was received in France as the work of a Protestant. The publication of *De praestigiis daemonum* in 1563 coincided with the conclusion of the second, decisive session of the Council of Trent and the peace of Amboise. The French crown, then managed by Henri II's widow, Catherine de Médicis, showed unprecedented latitude to the *parti Protestant*; Catholics who had not previously viewed Protestantism as a threat now did. In such circumstances, the fact that Grévin translated Weyer's book into French a year after the spectacular exorcism of Nicole Aubry is highly significant. Various demons had borrowed Aubry's teenage vocal chords to lambast Huguenots for their heresy, and Catholic chroniclers loudly publicized her delivery from Beelzebub and his associates as "the miracle of Laon," because it caused so many Huguenots to convert to Catholicism, or so they claimed.[112] Grévin surely perceived that Weyer's saucy anecdotes regarding fraudulent possession and exorcism offered a powerful antidote to the toxic unctuousness of ultramontane persuasion deployed in the miracle of Laon.[113]

Despite joining the Holy See's *Index* of books prohibited on pain of excommunication in 1570, *De praestigiis daemonum* served as a source for anticlerical jabs in France during the convent-wide possession scandals of the seventeenth century.[114] On the verge of deriding the unladylike postures of the

---

60. Heyd identifies the Italian humanist Polydore Vergil's *De Prodigiis* (1531) as the first work in the genre.

111 Weyer, 1991, 350.

112 Jean Boulaese, professor of Hebrew at the Collège de Montaigu in Paris, authored pamphlets in five languages heralding the "miracle," and even delivered the Spanish version personally to Philip II of Spain. Later, he collected and published eyewitness accounts of the exorcisms from the notables in attendance. D.P. Walker analyzes the "miracle of Laon" as anti-Protestant propaganda in *Unclean Spirits: Possession and Exorcism in France and England in the Late Sixteenth and Early Seventeent Centuries* (Philadelphia: University of Pennsylvania Press, 1981), pointing to the deployment of the host as a distinguishing feature of Aubry's possession: "Indeed these pious Catholics, bent on demonstrating the Real Presence, came near to using the host as a medicine" (24). On Eucharistic devotion and the display of the consecrated host in processions against heresy, see Barbara Diefendorf, *Beneath the Cross: Catholics and Huguenots in Sixteenth-Century Paris* (New York and Oxford: Oxford U.P., 1991), 32–3; 45–7.

113 Grévin condemns the "superstitions to which simple people lend their faith" in the introduction to his French translation of a series of poems on poison by the ancient Greek grammarian and didactic poet Nicander of Colophon (fl. 130 B.C.). Jacques Grévin, *Deux livres des Venins, ausquels il est amplement discouru des bestes venimeuses, thériaques, poisons, et contrepoisons* (Anvers: Christophe Plantin, 1568), 31. These two books include the translation of Nicander of Colophon's poems as well as a treatise by Grévin on poisons.

114 Ludwig Lavater takes up Weyer's account of "the exorcism of the spirit of Orléans" almost verbatim in *De Spectris, lemuribus et magnis atque insolitis fragoribus* (1570). This was the story of some Franciscan monks, who irked by the mayor's stinginess upon his

communing nuns of the Hospitaler Convent of Louviers in 1643, Pierre Yvelin, a physician in the service of Anne d'Autriche (1601–66), claims to "suspend judgment, when I reflect on what Weyer reports in his third book of *De Lamiiae*, on a girl from Werl."[115] With his oblique allusion to the "girl from Werl," Yvelin is clearly counting on the reader's familiarity with Weyer's book to supply the judgment that he finds it expedient to finesse: namely, that the nuns of Louviers are in the grip not of Leviathan or Beelzebub but of a pent-up libido.[116] Yvelin's allusion to Weyer—his only allusion in fact to a medical authority—shows how prominent *De praestigiis daemonum* had become as a reference in medical antipossessionist polemics. Riposting to Yvelin's irreverent *Examen de la possession des religieuses de Louviers,* an uncle and nephew medical team from Rouen, Lemperière and Magnart, inquired with more than a hint of suspicion, "Of what religion are you?"[117] Yvelin was no Protestant, but the imputation of religious unorthodoxy indicates that the medical critique of possession continued to be associated in the seventeenth century with Protestant polemics.

The condemnation of exorcism was recognizably if not exclusively a Protestant phenomenon by the 1560s. In contrast, Weyer's dismissal of the powers of witches, his denial of the culpability of women accused of witchcraft, and his condemnation of their torture and execution were no more common to Protestants than to Catholics. In his rebuttal to Weyer, the Calvinist Erastus justifies the use of torture, explaining that it was to be used only in cases with a strong suspicion of witchcraft. "Criminals are not subjected to *la question* for all kinds of suspicion, or by light conjecture, but when the fact can be proven fully by clues and arguments." Erastus speaks for the mainstream here: torture was to be used sparingly, with discretion, only in cases where other methods of ascertaining truth failed. Although Erastus allows that "there are some who under the pressure of torture, admit to crimes they never committed," he insists that "despite that, there is no wise man who would say that we should not

---

wife's burial in their church in 1534, staged nocturnal interviews with an unquiet spirit (in actuality, a young novice stationed above the vault of the church) to show that the woman was damned as a Lutheran heretic and that her body must be exhumed. The farce was detected and Weyer, who finished up his medical studies in Orléans, notes that "this incident later passed into a proverb, and, when some fiction is told, people say '*C'est l'esprit d'Orléans,*' that is 'It's the spirit of Orléans.'" Weyer, 439; Ludwig Lavater, *Trois livres des apparitions des esprits, fantosmes, prodiges, & accidens merveilleux* (Zurich: Guillaume des Marescz, 1581), 33. The story had everything to recommend it to French Huguenots starved for royal affection: lying anti-Lutheran clerics forced by the king to submit to justice and confess the truth. Other examples of Weyer's Lutheranism abound. He devotes a chapter to debunking "a false story concerning the 'demonic' origin of Martin Luther," and among the melancholics he enumerates, he claims to "know of" an "Italian who believed that he was the monarch and emperor of the whole world," a likely swipe at the Pope (243–4; 183).

115 Pierre Yvelin, *Examen de la possession des religieuses de Louviers* (Paris, 1643), 15.

116 From an error in his citation of the Dusseldorf anecdote, it is evident that Yvelin cites the story of the girl from Werl from memory. It is not in the third book of *De praestigiis daemonum* ("On witches"), as Yvelin says, but in the fourth, "Of those who are thought to be afflicted by the witchcraft of *Lamiae.*"

117 Lempérière and Magnart, *Response à l'Examen de la possession des Religieuses de Louviers, à monsieur Levilin* (Evreux: Jean de la Vigne, 1643), 6.

elicit truth through torture."[118] In contradistinction to Weyer's critique of exorcism, no clear ideological connections can be drawn between the physician's protestations against the witch trials and the Lutheran faith he professed.

There is, nevertheless, an important parallel to be drawn between Lutheran hermeneutics and Weyer's discernment of the body's state through external signs. Weyer's rejection of the "secrets of women" in favor of self-evident signs recalls the literalism characteristic of Luther's approach to Scripture. Luther construed Scripture as something that interprets itself (*sui ipsius interpres*); consequently, for Luther, the rod of faith was the only reading aid necessary for deciphering Scripture.[119] Analogously, Weyer denies that there is anything to be known about a woman's body besides what can be plainly "read." Indeed, Weyer's condemnation of interrogation by means of torture bears a striking resemblance to Grévin's comparison of Protestant to Catholic hermeneutics in one of the sixty-odd sonnets that comprise the two books of his "Gélodacrye":

> L'un ne veut rien couper, et l'autre tout allonge;
> L'un s'arrête au certain, l'autre sur le songe.

> [The one is loath to cut anything; the other elaborates on everything.
> The one stops at what is certain; the other is distracted by visions.][120]

The physician respects the integrity of the body, just as the Protestant respects the integrity of Scripture. The physician works with immediately available evidence; the Protestant likewise deals with the words that are present. In contrast, inquisitors torture witches to make them avow "symptoms" that are purely imaginary, just as Catholics read into Scripture, substituting exegetical visions for the true Word of God.

For neither the Protestant nor the physician were matters as straightforward as they might at first appear, however. If the meaning of God's grammar was sometimes difficult to access, Luther taught, this was not because of the opacity of the words on the page, but because of the pride or other moral failing that stood in the way of the illumination of the Christian reader. Analogously, although Weyer characterized the exterior of the body as an accessible witness to the state of its interior, he reveals that vision cannot be taken for granted when the Devil insinuates melancholy or other obstacles between the object of perception and the perceiving subject. *De Secretis mulierum* and the demonological literature that it inspired located the obstacles to

---

118 Erastus, 858.

119 Scripture is a rock in the desert, and the reader is Moses who must strike at Scripture with the rod of faith until its meaning gushes forth. Heiko A. Oberman, *Luther: Life between God and the Devil*, trans. Eileen Walliser-Schwartzbart (New Haven and London: Yale U.P., 1989), 223–4.

120 Jacques Grévin, *Théâtre complet et poésies choisies*, ed. Lucien Pinvert (Paris: Garnier frères, 1922), 336. The neologism "gélodacrye," which Pinvert attributes to Ronsard, is an oxymoronic mix of tears and (bitter) laughter. Grévin addressed the poem to Marc Antoine Muret (1526–85), a surprising choice since Muret, later in life, would write a panegyric of Charles IX lauding the Saint Bartholomew's day massacre.

truth within the object of analysis (nature, woman). For Bodin, as we shall see in the next chapter, it was the essence of truth to be hidden. For the Lutheran physician, in contrast, the concealment of truth results from its *having been* hidden. At every turn, Weyer portrays Satan as an artisan of *trompe l'œil*, expert of special effects, and master of persuasion. Weyer rejects the logic of secrecy and the tropes of interiority that accompanied it. But rather than disappearing, the obstacles standing in the way of truth have migrated from the object of knowledge to the perception of she who apprehends it.

Weyer relates many stories illustrating the Devil's distortion of perception. In one, a woman named Magdalena was accused of "lying with a demon" because she gave birth to "strange and unnatural objects." Weyer argues that Magdalena was framed, so to speak, by the Devil; this "mass of strange, incomprehensible, lifeless objects [was] displayed by the arch-schemer as the offspring of that coition, so that the imaginary sexual congress might be judged real." Weyer claims that a simple inspection of Magdalena's hymen would have sufficed to prove her innocence against this planted evidence, evidence that consisted in objects that were "large, hard, uneven, rough, and sharp" and that would surely have not left her maidenhood intact on their way out.[121] Similarly, in the story accompanied by the engraving of the knife, Weyer evokes the charades of early modern performance artists to suggest that the Devil could have quite easily rigged up the illusion of a knife exiting the purulent wound at the hands of a surgeon. "And the illusion should not surprise us, since we see such things done daily by mountebanks and vagabond beggars when they pass daggers and writing styles through their jaws or their arms without any bloodshed ... and so they present to view a thousand other marvelous things, but there is nothing to them but subterfuge and artifice."[122]

The service that Weyer claims to perform for the reader is thus to disperse the shadows that have obstructed the perception of a truth that is self-evident. He presents himself as an ophthalmologist who corrects vitiated vision. He relates anecdotes and analyzes them so that others

> may look upon such tricks with a clearer mental vision and not allow themselves so rashly to be deceived by this illusion, this clouding of their eyes, [so that they] may not remain like blind moles in the filth thrust upon them by the demon, but that they may rather allow the cloudy spots or the film to be cleared from their pupils by a physician who offers this salve free of charge to all who wish their eyes to be clear and free of the spirit that dims them.[123]

Weyer's filth-flushing, cloud-clearing activity places the sense of sight at the center of the search for truth. The vitiation of visual perception leads us astray, and conversely, the recovery of our sense of sight allows us to grasp the extent of our error. If only people would allow the physician to apply the salve of his superior vision to their clouded eyes, many lives could be saved.

---

121 Weyer, 1991, 233–4.
122 Ibid., 318.
123 Ibid., 511.

Paradoxically, through a rhetoric of demystification, Weyer emphasized that what should be obvious to everyone is not in fact evident to many people. Weyer rejected secrecy as a metaphor for knowledge only to replace it with a new formula for limiting access to knowledge. The association of knowledge and secrecy confirms scientific inquiry as that which goes "beyond the obvious or the 'naively' empirical ... to discover a deeper reality than that revealed to the senses."[124] When the Devil gets involved, however, there is no such thing as an "obvious" reality revealed by the senses, not even for the clear-sighted physician. The problem in Weyer's argument is that no standard exists for determining where demonic illusion stops and perception begins and, hence, no way to know who sees clearly. How could the physician be so sure that, in the case of Magdalena, the Devil had not created the illusion of an intact hymen rather than the illusion of the bizarre objects to which she claims to have given birth? Moreover, if "clear eye-witness testimony" is the standard that Weyer applies in *De praestigiis daemonum*, then in the young woman who claimed to have a knife lodged in her side, the truth would presumably reside with the people who observed the surgeon's extraction of the knife. But Weyer dismisses their collective observation, claiming that the Devil pulled the wool over the eyes of the entire assembly, a fcat no more economical than lodging a knife in one person's body. If Weyer's intent in his comparison of the Devil to street performers is to downplay the marvel of the illusion he credits to the Devil, the same comparison of demonic illusion to the subterfuge of early modern performance artists taken up a half-century later by Henri IV's physician has the opposite effect. In *De mirabili strumas sanandi* (1609), a book on the healing of scrofula through royal touch, André Du Laurens magnifies the marvel of the Devil's trickery. "If charlatans and acrobats [*basteleurs*] can fool the eyes of the people and make it so that by their artifice, people think that they see things that are not and cannot be: how much more quickly and easily will the Devil be able to do so, seeing that he is sly and dexterous in covering his fraud and trickery: Great then and quasi incredible is the power of the Devil ... to fool and abuse the senses by [*prestiges*] and illusions."[125]

Weyer's argument founders on a contradiction. On the one hand, the physician's harangue against the witch trials may be read as an apology for the authority of sense experience. On the other hand, Weyer so emphasizes the Devil's powers of illusion in his defense of women accused of witchcraft that he completely undermines the validity of sense perception, including his own. Weyer's confidence in "common sense" appears untenable in the face of the power of illusion that he attributes to the Devil. His contemporaries attacked his claim to be able to distinguish reality from illusion, a discernment that (he claimed) demarcated him from nearly everybody else. Erastus, Weyer's first critic, objected to the arbitrary nature of the privilege that the physician claimed in the search for truth. The problem, Erastus points out, is that the Devil's illusions cannot be proved. To Weyer's "they are dreaming" mantra,

---

124 Eamon, 351.

125 André Du Laurens, *Discours des Escrouelles*, In *Les Œuvres de M. André du Laurens, Sieur de la Ferrieres, Conseiller & premier Medecin du Tres-Chrestien Roy de France & de Navarre, Henry le Grand, & son Chancelier en l'Université de Montpelier*, trans. Théophile Gelée (Paris : Michel Soly, 1646), 222.

Erastus replies, "but how will you prove it?"[126] Erastus meets Weyer on his own ground, insisting, "The senses of those who with their eyes saw the shadows of the evil spirits are sound."[127] Taking Erastus's point regarding the arbitrariness of Weyer's exclusive claim to sound sight one step further, others turned the physician's argument against him: it was not witches who were imagining things, they insisted, but the physician. Taillepied levels the charge of illuminism against Weyer and his fellow witchcraft skeptics in "everything they say about the appearance of spirits comes from their own fantasy, cauterized with new opinions."[128]

Strangely, Weyer himself appears to have been blind to the totalizing implications of his argument. This was perhaps because the arbitrary quality of the distinction that he claimed for the physician was masked by a gender opposition. At the same time as he proclaimed the superior vision of the physician, Weyer undermined the authority of the witch/patient by denying her testimony/symptoms, burdening the female mind with layers of illusion that disguise truth. Rather than engaging witches through material acts such as eating, singing, wanton dancing, sexual intercourse, flying about on brooms, or smothering newborn babies, Satan, Weyer claims, tricks his victims through "strange apparitions" that are "conceived in the imagination and generally shared with the visual spirits and humors through the medium of the optic nerve."[129] Weyer insists on the extent to which the Devil's illusions have the consistency and appearance of true perception. The women fail to discriminate between real objects and satanic simulacra because his figures truly look, sound, smell, taste, and feel as if they had originated from outside the body. He corrupts "their mind with empty images, lulling or stirring to this task the bodily humors and spirits, so that in this way he introduces certain specious appearances into the appropriate organs, just as if they were occurring truly and externally." Satan's power of suggestion joined to his victims' superstitious faith in their imaginations lead them to interpret demonic *trompe l'œil* at face value: "They think everything that he suggests is true [ils se laissent aller à ce qu'il persuade], and they are devoutly confident that all the forms imposed by him upon their powers of imagination and fantasy exist truly and 'substantially'."[130] Preferring the chimeras concocted by the ape of God to faithful reproductions of God's creation, witches "revere and cherish

---

126 Erastus, 863.

127 Ibid.,780.

128 Noël Taillepied, *Psichologie, ou Traité de l'apparition des esprits sçavoir des âmes séparées, fantosmes, prodiges, et accidents merveilleux qui precedent quelquefois la mort des grands personages ou signifient changemens de la chose publique* (Paris: G. Bichon, 1588), "Epistre" (n.p.). Taillepied sets out to refute Weyer as well as "Lavater, Cardan, Bodin, Agrippa," all "persons of quality and of eminent literature." This goes to show the extent to which Bodin, although he refuted Weyer, would be quickly lumped together with him. Taillepied's other major publication, *Histoire des vies, meurs, actes, doctrines, et mort des trois principales hérétiques de nostre temps* (1616), confirms his interest in defending orthodoxy.

129 Weyer, 1991, 186.

130 Weyer, 1991, 181 and 1569, 219.

one teacher only, their imagination [reverent & adorent seulement leur fantasie, comme leur seul docteur]."[131]

In *De praestigiis daemonum*, the Devil is not the witch's tutor, as in the demonological literature that characterizes witches as illicitly knowledgeable women. Instead, Weyer insists, women glean their "knowledge" from their imagination. Given that Weyer conducts his "search for the truth that is hidden in the depths" through an almost stubborn refusal to go beyond surfaces; given that his claim to truth is that of seeing things more clearly, it is highly significant that he defines the imagination that is in women so susceptible to distortion in opposition to "common sense." "Persons who stray from common sense are sometimes popularly said to be 'imagining things', and their distortion of understanding or reasoning or thought is termed their 'imagination'."[132] In scholastic parlance, "common sense" denoted the inner faculty whose job it was to collect and assemble perceptions from all five senses before passing a unitary picture on to the understanding. It was, in other words, the faculty upon which Weyer relies for his observations that is entirely corrupted in the women whom he defends. Weyer replaced an opposition between licit and illicit learning—knowledge from books and knowledge from the Devil—with an opposition between he who perceives things as they are and she who imagines them as they are not.

"Keen-Witted Theseus" versus the Amazon

In arguing for the pertinence of the physician's expertise in matters demonological, Weyer identifies Theseus as the ideal seeker of hidden truths. "This business of demons is involved in such inextricable labyrinths that one can scarcely get out himself, even with the keen-witted Theseus for his guide."[133] Weyer's allusion to the Attic hero is obviously self-referential. Theseus famously annulled Athens' annual debt of seven boys and seven girls to the tyrannical Minos when he volunteered to enter the labyrinth himself. There he killed the Minotaur, found his way out of the labyrinth, thanks to the thread provided by Minos' amorous daughter, Ariadne, and freed the tyrant's hostages. Similarly, in purporting to deliver women unjustly accused of witchcraft from the "dark and villainous cells" from which there is no egress but death, Weyer offers to lead the reader from the "labyrinth" of late medieval

---

131 Weyer, 1991, 263 and 1569, 332.

132 Weyer, 1991, 213.

133 Weyer, 1991, 479. Weyer mentions Theseus in a similar passage in the third book: "If, like stubborn men, they harden their hearts toward my words, I predict that they will stumble into a Devil's labyrinth so inextricable that no 'thread of Theseus' can lead them out, but only the Son of the One and Merciful God" (1991, 222). Theseus' exploits were common knowledge, to judge by Louise Bourgeois' use of the myth at the outset of her *Observations diverses sur la sterilité, perte de fruict, foecondité, accouchements, et maladies des femmes et enfants nouveaux naiz amplement traittées heureusement practiquées* (Paris: A. Saugrain, 1617). Here vainglorious language is the labyrinth: "[cet enfant de mon esprit] n'a point le fil d'une Ariadne pour te conduire avec un plaisir doucement trompeur, parmy les contours d'un labyrinthe de paroles" ("Au Lecteur," n.p.).

yet they are barbarians.

demonology. But an additional component of the Theseus legend brings out another facet of Weyer's self-fashioning. In one of his more dubious claims to fame, reported by Plutarch (ca. 46–145) in his *Life of Theseus*, the Attic ruler battled the Amazons, that nation of virile warrior-women to whom Agrippa, along with all subsequent prowoman interlocutors in the *Querelle des femmes*, pointed as examples of women's potential to succeed in the eminently masculine art of warfare. So adept were these horse-straddling women on the battlefield that, provoked by Theseus' ravishment of their queen, Hippolyta, the Amazons besieged Athens and, so the story goes, came very close to conquering it. Plutarch comments, "such were the grounds for the war of the Amazons, which seems to have been no trivial nor womanish enterprise for Theseus. For they would not have pitched their camp within the city, nor fought hand to hand battles in the neighbourhood of the Pynx and the Museum, had they not mastered the surrounding country and approached the city with impunity."[134] Given the importance of Athens, it is not surprising that in antiquity, the Amazons were represented in the guise of barbarians threatening civilization.[135]

Throughout the sixteenth and seventeenth centuries, the epithet "Amazon" designated a woman on horseback and was usually offered as a compliment. Agrippa states that Joan of Arc (1412–31) "took up arms like an Amazon in 1428;" François Malherbe (1555–1628) decries the unhappy end of the "Belle Amazone" in a six-line poem "Sur la Pucelle d'Orléans brûlée par les Anglais"; and Jean Chapelain (1595–1674), in the preface to his ill-fated epic *La Pucelle* (1656), cites "the republic of Amazons" as irrefutable proof of women's military might.[136] In the final painting of the cycle representing key moments of Marie de Medici's life, Pieter Paul Rubens (1577–1640) portrays the dowager queen in the guise of Minerva Victrix, her left breast bared (albeit not amputated) in an allusion to the Amazon's athleticism. Marie de Médicis's had waged open battle against her son, Louis XIII, and the armor and especially the gaping canon behind her indicate that her rebellious streak has not been quelled; the Amazon is still ready to take up arms against the rightful heir to the throne of France.[137]

The figure of the warrior-woman was ambiguous, and the topos of the Amazons' barbarism remained commonplace. Citing the infanticide by means of which they achieved their single-sexed nation, one of the interlocutors in Jacques Tahureau's *Dialogues* (1565) decries "the cruel and abominable government of the Amazons."[138] In his *Singularitez de la France antarctique; autrement nommée Amérique* (1558), the explorer and cosmographer André Thévet (1503–92) reports

---

134 Plutarch, *Plutarch's Lives: Theseus and Romulus*, trans. Bernadotte Perrin (Cambridge: Harvard University Press, 1998), 61.

135 Page DuBois, *Centaurs and Amazons: Women and the Pre-History of the Great Chain of Being* (Ann Arbor: The University of Michigan Press, 1982), 32–48.

136 Agrippa,88. François Malherbe, *Poésies*, ed. Antoine Adam (Paris: Gallimard, 1982), 178. Jean Chapelain, *La Pucelle ou la France délivrée*, vol. 1 (Paris: Librairie Marpon & Flammarion, n.d.), xlix.

137 Ronald Forsyth Millen and Robert Erich Wolf, *Heroic Deeds and Mystic Figures: A New Reading of Rubens' Life of Maria de' Medici* (Princeton: Princeton U.P., 1989), 224–7.

138 Jacques Tahureau, *Les Dialogues non moins profitables que facetieux*, ed. Max Gauna (Genève: Droz, 1981), 25.

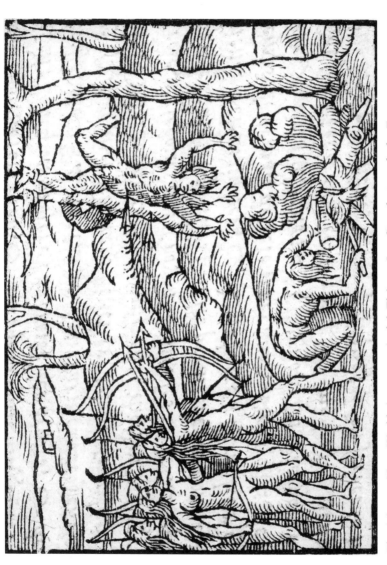

Fig. 1.3   New World Amazons. André Thévet, *Les Singulariez de la France antarctique, autrement nommée Amérique, & de plusieurs Terres & Isles descouvertes de notre temps* (1558).

that the Spanish discovered a nation of women who "live just as the Amazons of Asia lived"—that is, they kill baby boys and treat their prisoners of war "quite inhumanely [*inhumainement*]." "To make [a prisoner] die," he explains, "they hang him by one leg from the high branch of a tree: after leaving him for some time like that, when they come back, if by chance he is not yet dead, they shoot him with ten thousand arrows: [and] do not eat him like the other savages would, but burn him until he is nothing but ashes."[139]

Burning rather than eating one's prisoners—an unusual practice among savages,Thévet points out—is akin to the barbarity against which Weyer inveighs. The hang-and-wait technique prefigures Weyer's story about the woman who died while suspended from her wrists while waiting for her barbarous tormentors to return from lunch. Savages, as Montaigne would famously point out, were not only to be found in the New World. The nuptials for Henri de Navarre's marriage to Marguerite de Valois on 31 August 1572, featured a tilting-match between Catholic and Protestant gentlemen. The latter were attired as turban-bearing Turks, an allusion Frances Yates suggests, to their "unbelieving status."[140] The Catholic gentlemen were, on the other hand, disguised as Amazons. This may have been an allusion to Henri III's recent performance as an Amazon in a ballet; it may also have been an ominous allusion to the upcoming bloodbath of what turned out to be the Saint Bartholomew's day massacre.[141] Towards the end of the seventeenth century, Racine will recall the Amazon's savagery in *Phèdre* (1678) through his characterization of Hippolyte—the son of Theseus and the Amazon he vanquished.[142]

The Amazonian episode of the Theseus legend is pertinent to Weyer's self-representation as the "keen-witted Theseus" insofar as the Amazon who laid siege to Athens, "August Queen of Greece and of the Sciences," was a close, conceptual cousin to the witch who besieged Christendom.[143] The witch's gender underscored the transgression represented by the illicit knowledge and powers she gained without reading.

---

139 André Thévet, *Les Singularitez de la France antarctique, autrement nommée Amérique, & de plusieurs Terres & Isles descouvertes de notre temps* (Anvers: Christophe Plantin, 1558), 121, 123.

140 Frances A. Yates, *The French Academies of the Sixteenth Century* (London: Jarrold and Sons, 1947), 255.

141 The savage warrior-woman continued to shadow the heroic horse-straddling heroine throughout the seventeenth century. In his *Galerie des femmes fortes* (1647), authored during the regency of Anne d'Autriche (1643–61), Pierre Le Moyne uses the epithet to praise a woman who exhorted the inhabitants of Cambrai to resist the Spanish in 1595. Sylvie Steinberg, "Le Mythe des Amazones et son utilisation politique de la Renaissance à la Fronde, *Royaume de Fémynie: Pouvoirs, contraintes, espaces de liberté des femmes de la Renaissance à la Fronde*, eds. Kathleen Wilson-Chevalier and Eliane Viennot (Paris: Champion, 1999), 266–7.

142 Provoking Phèdre's monstrous confession, Oenone designates Hippolyte as "Ce fier ennemi de vous, de votre sang, / Ce fils qu'une Amazone a porté dans son flanc" (I, 3, v. 203–4). And Hippolyte in his declaration to Aricie elaborates on the link between his pride and his savage origins: "Avec quelques couleurs qu'on ait peint ma fierté, / Croit-on que dans ses flancs un monstre m'ait porté? / Quelles sauvages moeurs, quelle haine endurcie / Pourrait, en vous voyant, n'être point adoucie?" (II, 2, v. 519–22).

143 De Gournay, 969.

Analogously, the gender of the Amazon articulated the threat that her military prowess posed to civilization. At least one demonologist drew an explicit parallel between the witch and the Amazon. Bernhard Albrecht, a German demonologist, refers in his *Magia; das ist, Christlicher Bericht von der Zauberey und Hexerey* (1628) to an etymology suggested by the Bavarian historian and philologist, Johannes Aventinus (1477–1534). This correspondent of Melanchthon and Luther drew a link between *hexen*, the German word for witch, and Heza, "the Amazon who was a manipulator of men [Heerführerin] and who must have been a great witch full of spite and thirst for blood whom witches still follow."[144] Whereas belief in witchcraft was universal in early modern Europe, there was no consensus as to the historical existence of the Amazons. Thévet cites the New World Amazons, unaccounted for by "the Historiographers," as evidence that the Amazons of old were no mere legend, while Girolamo Mercuriale (1530–1606), an antiquarian physician, opined that the story of the Amazons, "which many people believe to be fictitious," must be true, because Hippocrates, "the most truthful of all ancient authors," speaks of them.[145] Madeleine de Scudéry, in her novel *Artamène ou le Grand Cyrus* (1649–53), follows Herodotus in locating the Amazons in the land of the Sauromates, but presents it as a utopia, to which her heroine, Sapho, retires with her lover Phaon, never to marry.[146] In his *Traité historique sur les Amazones* (1685), Pierre Petit, following Goropius Becanus, claims that the Amazons were never a nation of self-sufficient women. Petit points out (correctly) that although Hippocrates describes the Amazons on horseback, wielding arms, and killing men, he also characterizes them as the wives of the Sauromates.[147] If in the late seventeenth century, improved philology gave rise to skepticism with regard to the historical existence of a tribe composed exclusively of warring women, another skeptical current, which Petit traces back to the Greek geographer Strabo (ca. 58–25 B.C.), dismissed the Amazons as legend because of the impossible inversion they represented: "[I]t is the same as if someone were to say that in those times men were women [and] women, men."[148] A parallel can be drawn between Strabo's dismissal of the Amazons and Weyer's skepticism with respect to witchcraft. More ingenious than Theseus—who risked life and limb battling the Amazons—Strabo deflates the threat posed by warring women by denying the possibility of their historical existence. Analogously, rather than insisting, like the authors of the *Malleus*, on the urgent need to eradicate Satan's helpmeets from the face of Christendom, Theseus-Weyer exposes an alleged army of *sagae*—wise women—as a rag-tag gaggle of raving hags.

---

144 Clarke, *Thinking with Demons*, 132. Bernhard Albrecht, *Magia; das ist, Christlicher Bericht von der Zauberey und Hexerey* (1628), 13.

145 Thévet, 121. Girolamo Mercuriale, *Censura Hippocratis* (1583), cited in Nancy G. Siraisi, "History, Antiquarianism, and Medicine: The Case of Girolamo Mercuriale," *Journal of the History of Ideas* 64 (2003): 231–51, 249.

146 Joan DeJean, *Fictions of Sappho, 1546-1937* (Chicago: The University of Chicago Press, 1989), 107.

147 Pierre Petit, *Traité historique sur les Amazones, où l'on trouve tout ce que les auteurs tant anciens que modernes, ont écrit pour ou contre ces heroines* (Leiden: J.A. Langerak, 1718), 33, 39.

148 Cited in Petit, 16.

Fig. 1.4   Portrait. Johann Weyer, *De praestigiis daemonum* (1583).

De praestigiis daemonum evinces the phenomenon that Stephen Greenblatt calls "Renaissance self-fashioning." In each successive edition of *De praestigiis daemonum*, Weyer reinforces a "distinctive personality, a characteristic address to the world, a consistent mode of perceiving and behaving."[149] He is the cool-headed, warm-hearted Christian physician who works against hotheaded prejudice and cold-blooded injustice that together feed the Devil's insatiable craving for bloodshed. The only known portrait of Johann Weyer figures on the title page of the 1583 edition of *De praestigiis daemonum*, the last Latin edition of the work published during his lifetime.

Weyer peers out of the no-nonsense frame, one eyebrow raised defiantly to meet the gaze of the viewer. The three-quarters angle affords a good look at the balding head and close-cropped beard of the venerable physician. His sober clothes offset the objects in front of him. His left hand rests on a skull, the symbol of his profession, but which can be read more specifically in the context of *De praestigiis daemonum* as a reminder of the vanity of the search for truth in the face of God's will. In the physician's right fist, a scroll registers his authorial pursuits. The choice of the scroll rather than a book, also typical in medical iconography of the time, is significant; what is on display here is less Weyer's learning than his authorship. Both the skull and the scroll tip in toward the physician's open coat; the moral and intellectual qualities that they represent are integrally part of this Christian humanist. The reflexive device that frames Weyer's gleaming head—*vince te ipsum* (conquer yourself)—echoes the inward turn of the objects. The basis of the physician's authority, nourished by his learning, duly digested and incorporated as per the humanist ideal, ultimately rests within the physician himself.

The image of self-containment is, nevertheless, misleading. "Self-fashioning is achieved in relation to something perceived as alien, strange, or hostile," writes Greenblatt. "This threatening Other—heretic, savage, witch, adulteress, traitor, Antichrist—must be discovered or invented in order to be attacked and destroyed."[150] For Weyer, as for the Dominican inquisitors and "bloodthirsty magistrates" he refutes, the Other to be destroyed is the witch. But while the latter are concerned with hunting down Satan's helpmeets and eradicating evil, the physician's destruction—deconstruction, really—happens at a conceptual level. Not only do these women not know anything out of the ordinary, he insists; more important, their imaginations are so afflicted that even the information that they claim to derive from sense experience cannot be taken seriously.

It was Thomas Erastus, a Calvinist physician, who first underscored the impracticality of Weyer's conclusions (How could one do away with torture when confession depended on it?) and identified the principle flaw in his argument (How could Weyer claim exemption from the confusion created by the Devil?). But it was

---

149 Weyer's self-representation in *De praestigiis daemonum* exemplifies the phenomenon that Stephen Greenblatt calls "Renaissance self-fashioning," which he defines in *Renaissance Self-fashioning from More to Shakespeare* (Chicago and London: The University of Chicago Press, 1980) as "an increased self-consciousness about the fashioning of human identity as a manipulable, artful process."

150 Greenblatt, 9.

Jean Bodin, a magistrate, who connected Weyer's argument to the growing problem (as he saw it) of skepticism. For Bodin, there was little difference between Skeptics who suspended judgment, physicians who explained away allegedly demonic phenomena through natural causes, and witches who bartered their bodies for the Devil's knowledge. All were guilty of divine *lèse-majesté*. Witchcraft, which Bodin defined not as heresy but as apostasy, was a crime so heinous that rooting it out required exceptions to regular judicial procedure. Bodin thus revived the associations of women, sex, and secrecy that Weyer had circumvented as well as the rationale for torture that he had condemned. As for the Skeptic and the naturalizing physician, Bodin viewed them as atheists meriting the same fate as witches. Skeptics denied God because they put all truth claims in the balance of doubt, while physicians like Weyer placed nature over God. Just as political order depends upon the wife's obedience to her husband (or so Bodin argues in his *Six livres de la république*), moral order necessitates the submission of a feminized nature to (an anthropomorphized) God. In the next chapter, I reveal the extent to which women bore the brunt of Bodin's response to skepticism.

Chapter Two

The Touchstone of Truth:
Jean Bodin's Torturous Hermeneutics

Jean Bodin (1529–96) was no admirer of women. He identified the subordination of women to men as the defining feature of political order in his *Six livres de la république* (1676). In *De la démonomanie des sorciers* (1580), a work designed to update a vast corpus concerned with the identification and punishment of witches, he attacked women's foibles, particularly their ostensibly insatiable lust. Yet neither Bodin's political theory nor his demonology is really *about* women; misogyny was not what drove him to author these works. Rather, women generally serve as means to an end in Bodin's thought. The wife's natural inferiority to the husband provides an analogy for a nonreciprocal relation of command and obedience that he establishes between the sovereign and his subjects in *De la république*. In *De la démonomanie*, Bodin's portrayal of women as the possessors of unsavory secrets and his characterization of the confessions of witches as fragments of a grandly devilish design create the need for hermeneutical expertise—expertise that he claimed to have. In using women to "think with," the author of *De la démonomanie* had much in common with his opponent, the Lutheran physician Johann Weyer, who protested against the witch trials in *De praestigiis daemonum* (1563). In the first chapter, I showed that by portraying women as naturally susceptible to the distortion of the senses, Weyer enhanced the physician's authority in the context of an epistemology in which he identified common sense as the standard of truth. In this chapter, I bring Bodin's rigid hierarchy of the sexes in *De la république* together with his gendered hermeneutics in *De la démonomanie* to show how he attempted to circumvent the skeptical crisis that Weyer had exacerbated when he underscored the vulnerability of sense perception to devilish manipulation and melancholy. Bodin's struggle against skepticism distinguishes *De la démonomanie* from late medieval demonology; the gender strategies that he deploys to thwart Skeptics thus constitute a central feature of his modern demonology.

Motives on the Margins

In the eighty-page "Refutation des opinions de Jean Wier" that Bodin tacked on the end of *De la démonomanie*, he dramatized his encounter with Weyer's book: "As I finished this work and was on the verge of sending it to press, the Printer [Jacques DuPuys, who had published Grévin's French translation of *De praestigiis daemonum* in 1567] sent me a new book *De lamiis*, by Johann Weyer, a Physician, where he maintains that sorcerers and witches should not be punished."[1] Bodin's purpose in writing *De la démonomanie,* and the root of his exasperation with Weyer, was his earnest, urgent concern that Satan was triumphing (with God's permission) over humankind. A few months before Jacques Chovet published the French translation of the expanded Latin edition of *De praestigiis daemonum* in Geneva (1579), Jean Bodin participated in the trial of Jeanne Harvillier in Laon, where two decades prior, Nicole Aubry's garrulous demons had riled up Catholic fervor against Huguenots (as we saw in the previous chapter). Far from concluding that Harvillier was in the grip of the melancholic humor, as Weyer had urged his readers to do, her confession "sans question ni torture" confirmed Bodin's conviction regarding the reality and danger of witchcraft.[2] Witches were legion—even on the rise, as God punished humankind for its impiety. Weyer, in the added sixth book of *De praestigiis daemonum,* had pleaded for clemency in dealings with witches; Bodin, like the authors of the *Malleus maleficarum,* concludes *De la démonomanie* with a book on the prosecution of witchcraft.

De la démonomanie saw over twenty editions in four languages (French, Italian, German, Latin), most of them within the first twenty years of its original edition.[3] The success of *De la démonomanie* is one of the great enigmas surrounding Bodin. In the 1980s, social historians attributed the appeal of the treatise to concurrent witch phobia and blamed Bodin for re-igniting dormant pyres: "The *Démonomanie* ... more than any other work was responsible for the European witch scare of the late sixteenth century;" Bodin "was the man who was so largely responsible for putting the European witchcraze back on its vengeful course."[4] Yet the claim that *De la démonomanie* became the new *Malleus,* exerting pan-European pressure to rout out witches, is anecdotal and remains unsubstantiated. Alfred Soman has shown through

---

1　　Jean Bodin, *De la démonomanie des sorciers* (Paris: Jacques DuPuys, 1580), 238. "De lamiis liber" was Weyer's response to Thomas Erastus's first dialogue and comprised a condensation of the ideas already expressed in *De praestigiis daemonum.* Oporinus included it, along with Erastus's two dialogues and the added sixth book "On the punishment of witches," containing the physician's most indignant criticisms of inquisitors and magistrates, in the 1577 edition of *De praestigiis daemonum.* Bodin's evident familiarity with all of these pieces indicates that he availed himself either of Oporinus's latest edition or of the even more recent 1579 French edition, which included the sixth book and Erastus's dialogues (but not "De Lamiis liber").

2　　Bodin, *De la démonomanie,* "Preface," [1]. The preface is not paginated and consists of one, relentless paragraph; I give page numbers here starting from the first page of the preface.

3　　Ann Blair, *The Theater of Nature: Jean Bodin and Renaissance Science* (Princeton: Princeton U.P., 1997), 110. On the French éditions of *De la démonomanie,* see Marie-Thérèse Isaac, "De la démonomanie des sorciers: Histoire d'un livre à travers ses éditions," *Jean Bodin: Actes du colloque interdisciplinaire d'Angers, 24 au 27 mai 1984* (Angers: Presses de l'Université d'Angers, 1985), 377–401.

4　　Christopher Baxter, cited in Jonathan Pearl, "Le rôle énigmatique de *La Démonomanie* dans la chasse aux sorciers," *Jean Bodin: Actes du colloque interdisciplinaire d'Angers, 24 au 27 mai 1984* (Angers: Presses de l'Université d'Angers, 1985), 403–10, 403; Brian Easlea, *Witch Hunting, Magic, and the New Philosophy: An Introduction to the Debates of the Scientific Revolution, 1450–1750* (Sussex: Harvester Press, 1980), 15.

research into the witchcraft trials and appeals cases conducted by the Parlement of Paris, by far the largest secular court in Europe, that the two decades that saw the bulk of editions of *De la démonomanie* were the same two decades that witnessed a tightening of standards in the jurisprudence of witchcraft in France. The Parlement of Paris followed up waves of executions sanctioned by provincial courts with crackdowns on abuses in criminal procedure. Indeed, Soman's findings suggest that the Parlement of Paris was as concerned by the lynching of suspected witches (a much cheaper alternative to proper legal avenues) as with witchcraft itself. "The chief problem for the high court was not so much the reality of the crime of witchcraft," he writes, "as it was the maintenance of public order and the imposition of high standards of criminal justice upon a lower magistracy far from easy to control."[5] Far from representing the position of the magistracy as a whole, Bodin and Pierre de Lancre, another hardliner on witchcraft prosecution, were both mid-level judges in provincial courts; they wrote their alarmist treatises against the leniency of their higher placed colleagues. The latter responded with patrician disdain for popular witch phobia. In 1588, Jacques de La Guesle, the king's solicitor general, quipped in reference to the region of Bodin's jurisdiction: "[T]here is a madness in the province of Champagne: they think that nearly everyone there is a witch."[6]

In demonstrating the marginality of Bodin's juridical stance in a treatise that was too erudite and expensive to be accessible to the lynching folk who took the law into their own hands, Soman's insightful conclusions leave us wondering about the evident success of *De la démonomanie*: Who bought and read *De la démonomanie* besides zealous judges eager to eradicate evil? And what was the nature of the appeal of Bodin's treatise if not the fear it fomented? The fact that Michel de Montaigne, a jurist in Pierre de Lancre's jurisdiction (Bordeaux) who shared Weyer's doubts as to the culpability of witches, owned a copy of *De la démonomanie* suggests that its primary point of interest may not have resided in its practical application at all. I argued in the previous chapter that the importance of *De praestigiis daemonum* for future generations lay less in his deployment of the insanity defense on behalf of "witches" than in the epistemological problem that Weyer unwittingly set up. If the devil is so crafty a deceiver, how can we trust our senses to inform us faithfully of the world around us? How could sense experience serve as the basis of knowledge in a universe rife with demonic prestidigitation? The German physician's emphasis on the malleability of the human imagination ultimately reinforced Agrippa von Nettesheim's attack on the validity of sense experience in *De incertitudine et vanitate scientiarum et artium* (1530), a well-known work by 1580. I hope to establish in this chapter that even if Bodin's exhortations to prosecute witchcraft as a *crimen exceptum* went against the grain of contemporary jurisprudence, his response to the

eg witches insane.

---

5   Alfred Soman, "The Parlement of Paris and the Great Witch Hunt (1565–1640)," *The Sixteenth Century Journal* 9 (1978): 31–44, 42. Soman's important articles have been published together in *Sorcellerie et justice criminelle: Le Parlement de Paris (16e-18e siècles)* (Hampshire and Brookfield, Vermont: Variorum/Ashgate Publishing, 1992).

6   Soman, 37–8.

"epistemological malaise" of the late Renaissance had repercussions that reached well beyond witchcraft prosecution.[7]

Bodin's preface to *De la démonomanie* picks up at the point where Weyer's reflection left off. *De praestigiis daemonum* had confirmed to the pertinence of skeptical arguments, such as those published the year before in Henri Estienne's Latin translation of Sextus Empiricus' *Outlines of Pyrrhonism*.[8] Bodin takes full account of these arguments, summarizing and on occasion citing (though never naming) Sextus Empiricus. "Even Philosophers," he remarks, "do not agree as to what comprises the mark of truth that they call [the criterion of truth]." Following an enumeration of various contradictory criteria from the Stoics to Plato and Aristotle (all examples drawn from Sextus), Bodin lays the point to rest with the Skeptics: "The Skeptics, seeing that nothing enters the reasonable soul that was not first in the senses, and that the senses abuse us, held that we can know nothing ... especially because the sense that is the clearest and the sharpest of all is sight, and yet the eyes bear false witness."[9] That Bodin condemns the sense of sight above all others for bearing false witness is not surprising since Sextus does the same; it, nevertheless, has particular resonance in a preface that, although not explicitly refuting Weyer (Bodin saves his personal attack for the "Refutation"), already lays the groundwork for that rebuttal. The sense of sight was precisely what Weyer claimed was corrupted in the women accused of witchcraft, and Bodin, through the evocation of skepticism, implicitly puts Weyer's confident clear-sightedness in question.

Bodin's "rapid, but well-placed" allusion to pyrrhonism serves as a prelude to the articulation of his fideist stance.[10] Since philosophers disagree on how to recognize truth, and given that even the most authoritative philosophers (e.g., Aristotle) have erred, he goes on to argue, we must accept those things that are attested by all peoples in all times with humility and piety. To leave the determination of truth up to some authority (in Bodin's case, the authority of universal consent) was a typical response to skepticism. Yet Bodin's fideism was both specious and partial. First, it depended on an arbitrary distinction between the natural and the supernatural. Bodin squashed rather than addressed the issue that *De praestigiis daemonum* raised, following Pomponazzi: namely, what is natural, what is supernatural, and who has the authority to draw the line between them? Bodin sought to naturalize the natural/supernatural distinction through an equally arbitrary distinction taken from his political philosophy. In the *Six livres de la république*, Bodin claimed that the wife's obedience to the husband's command was the foundation of all political order. In *De la démonomanie*, he anthropomorphizes the natural and the supernatural with the same gender hierarchy. Nature, God's wife, must submit to His will. To privilege her

---

7   Terence Cave, *Pré-histoires: Textes troublés au seuil de la modernité* (Geneva: Droz, 1999), 64. Sophie Houdard comes to the same conclusion: "Et si ce texte a joui, dès sa publication, d'un large succès, c'est sans doute qu'il entre dans un débat plus large que le seul débat judiciaire" in *Les Sciences du diable: Quatre discours sur la sorcellerie* (Paris: Editions du Cerf, 1992), 60.

8   Sextus Empiricus, *Sexti philosophi pyrrhoniarum hypotyposeon libri III*, trans. Henri Estienne (Geneva: Henri Estienne, 1562).

9   Bodin, *De la démonomanie*, "Preface," [13].

10   Cave, 63.

habits over His whim, is to commit *lèse-majesté* no better than witchcraft. As for the witch, she is doubly evil; not only does she commit spiritual and corporeal adultery, but she does so in the aim of playing God—that is, of mastering nature. That brings us to the second characteristic of Bodin's fideism: its partiality. Bodin exempts two figures from the unquestioning piety that he advocates, figures with whom he personally identifies: the prophet and the judge. Bodin structures the first book of *De la démonomanie*, about licit and illicit means of acquiring occult knowledge, around the opposition between the witch and the prophet. The evil inverse of the prophet, the woman who trades with Satan, is an illegitimate rival in the pursuit of occult knowledge. Bodin's claim in the "Refutation" that women cannot be melancholic because melancholy is the condition of genial men confirms that prophecy is a gift that God bestows exclusively on men.

The second figure whom Bodin exempts from unquestioning acceptance of demonological dogma is the judge. The judge, unlike the prophet, does not have access to occult knowledge. He must use reason to discern truth within the evidence provided. In the fourth and final book of *De la démonomanie*, Bodin seeks to answer the question: How in the absence of evidence—witchcraft being notoriously difficult to document— could one establish the guilt of the suspect? Posed in more general terms, this was the question whose answer eluded Bodin's generation: How can we prove what we know? For if we cannot prove what we know, do we really know what we know? The magistrate's pursuit and interpretation of witches' confessions provided a model for a truth-seeking elite at a time when the rise of skepticism had revealed truth even in nondemonological matters to be as slippery to ascertain as the deeds of witches. Bodin's reply to Weyer, the witchcraft skeptic, was also his reply to the skepticism that *De praestigiis daemonum* did much to foster. Against Weyer's naïve confidence in common sense, Bodin viewed everything as a text in need of interpretation. The confessions of witches, like God's law as laid down in the Old Testament, were full of veiled meanings that must be poked and prodded to relinquish the truths they contained. Insofar as Bodin construed the body of the witch as a text full of deeply ensconced secrets, the torture of witches literally embodied his interpretative theory, or what I shall call his "torturous hermeneutics."

Bodin's torturous hermeneutics continued the secrets-of-nature tradition that had infused the *Malleus Maleficarum* (1487), mobilizing the associations of women, sex, and secrecy already present in that work. However, we shall see that in portraying nature as an entity vying impudently with God's authority, Bodin gave a powerful moral cast to the medieval tradition that likened nature's secrets to the inaccessible workings of women's bodies. Both the witch and nature paid homage to God's power but sought to rival his authority; the punishment of their insubordination provided the occasion for knowledge. The pious, natural philosopher partakes in the Creator's rightful role of dominance over creation just as the magistrate, through the aggressive prosecution of witches, fostered the restoration of moral order.

It was not possible to respond to Bodin's hermeneutics without also taking a stand on the gender hierarchy that subtended it. In the closing section of this chapter, I characterize *De la démonomanie* as an intermediary between late medieval demonology and the "new organon" of Francis Bacon, whose inquisitional metaphors regarding the domination of nature have long arrested the attention of feminist historians of science. But the feminization of nature was by no means universal among the individuals whom we now consider representative of the "New Science." To the contrary, most of them rejected Bodin's hermeneutics not so much because they did not believe in witchcraft (although this was perhaps the case for some of them), as because they decried in his work dogmatism masquerading as science. Those who sought not to demonize Skeptics but to overcome pyrrhonism by incorporating their arguments manifested a more open attitude towards women's participation in the search for truth, for Skeptics subverted the gender hierarchy to counter dogmatism. In effect, I will show in Chapter Four that it was in refutation of *De la démonomanie* that Montaigne came closest to imagining gender equality. In Chapter Five, we shall see that an implicit but crucial aspect of French mechanists' rejection of the secrets-of-nature tradition was the repudiation of the keystone of Bodin's system: the political subjection of women and the corresponding exclusion of women from the search for truth.

Modern Demonology?

Bodin scholarship no longer founders on the opposition between "the credulous author of *La démonomanie*" and the forward-thinking theorist of political absolutism.[11] In a spirit closer to the jurist's habits of mind, scholars have turned their attention to the coherence of his opus. Such studies make it possible to think about how the architect of political absolutism also modernized the intellectual universe of the *Malleus Maleficarum*.[12] In his *Six livres de la république* (1576), published by Jacques DuPuys, Bodin responded to civil disorder by theorizing the sovereign's power as absolute, replacing the reciprocal relation implicit in the feudal

---

11   Henri Busson, *Le Rationalisme dans la littérature française de la Renaissance (1533–1601)* (Paris: Vrin, 1957), 546. The author of the article on Bodin in that first empire monument that was Michaud's *Biographie universelle* speculated on the reasons for the oblivion into which the jurist's work had fallen by the end of the Enlightenment: "*La Démonomanie*, another work of Bodin's, may have tarnished the glory that *La République* had earned him." "Bodin," *Biographie universelle, ancienne et moderne; ou, Histoire, par ordre alphabétique, de la vie publique et privée de tous les hommes qui se sont fait remarquer par leurs écrits, leurs actions, leurs talents, leurs vertus ou leurs crimes*, ed. Joseph François Michaud (Paris, 1811–28). Pierre Mesnard, who remains one of the most authoritative Bodin scholars, pointed to *De la démonomanie* as the sign of the decline of a great genius: "*La Démonomanie* is already proof of mental atrophy." Mesnard, "Vers un portrait de Jean Bodin," in Jean Bodin, *Oeuvres philosophiques*, ed. and trans. Pierre Mesnard (Paris: Presses Universitaires de France, 1951), xix.

12   Maxime Préaud points out that *La République* contains some of the "irrational" elements of *De la démonomanie* in "*La Démonomanie*, fille de *La République*," *Jean Bodin: Actes du colloque interdisciplinaire d'Angers, 24 au 27 mai 1984* (Angers: Presses de l'Université d'Angers, 1985), 419–29. See also Nicole Jacques-Chaquin, "*La Démonomanie des sorciers*: une lecture politique de la sorcellerie," in *Jean Bodin: Nature, histoire, droit, et politique*, ed. Yves-Charles Zarka (Paris: Presses Universitaires de France, 1996), 43–70 and Stuart Clark, *Thinking with Demons: The Idea of Witchcraft in Early Modern Europe* (Oxford: Oxford U.P., 1997), 668–82.

oath of homage with a rigid hierarchy comprised of commandment and obedience. In parallel fashion, Bodin in *De la démonomanie* responded to moral disorder by insisting on God's insuperable power and advocating unquestioning acceptance of supernatural effects, the intellectual parallel of political obedience. I will argue in this section that the compulsory tenor of Bodin's fideism was his response to the breakdown of the scholastic understanding of faith or belief (*fides*). We shall see that his fideism foundered on the notion of the supernatural that had been mobilized to confound skeptics.

Bodin's *Six livres de la république* delivered the proverbial coup de grâce to feudalism and confirmed the emergence of the absolutist state. His hierarchical model of political organization entailed a redefinition of relations both among citizens and between citizens and the sovereign. In feudal society, the profession of *fidelitas* was the presumed principle of social cohesion. *Fidelitas* designated the vassal's submission to, but also his trust in his lord; it signaled the reciprocal conviction that whatever commitments had been made would be honored. The feudal oath worked in two directions. The lord offered protection to the vassal in exchange for the latter's "submission, service, and duty."[13] Vassalic fealty was just one permutation in a vast web of human relations. The twelfth-century archbishop Baudouin de Canterbury, in his *Liber de commendatione fidei*, describes *fides* as the basis of human society. Relations between friends, companions, master and servant, chief and warrior, husband and wife, require *fides*, without which there would be no government, no amorous relations, no cities, no families—indeed no human association at any level.[14] Bodin by no means denied the importance of *fides* as a principle of social and political organization. In a long chapter on the bond between vassals and lords, he enumerates six degrees of fealty and analyzes various political problems, including some contemporary ones, arising from the privileges and dependences created through the oath of *fidelitas*.[15] Nevertheless, the distinction that interests Bodin is the one between the prince who is "absolutely sovereign" and others who each depend on "a prince, lord, or protector:" "[T]here is but he who is absolutely sovereign who depends in no way on others; seeing as how the vassal for whatever fief it may be, be he the Pope or an Emperor, owes personal service because of the fief he holds."[16] Absolute power for Bodin specifically designated power that was not attenuated by an oath of fealty. The faith or conviction that commitments will be honored—which Baudouin of Canterbury had identified as the cement of

---

13   Bodin, *La République*, 162. Thierry Pécout, "Féodalisme," *Dictionnaire encyclopédique du Moyen Age*, eds André Vauchez and Catherine Vincent (Paris: Editions du Cerf; Cambridge: James Clarke & Co.; Rome: Città Nuova, 1997), vol. 1, 587. See also Claude Gauvard, "féodalisme," *Dictionnaire du Moyen Age*, eds Claude Gauvard, Alain de Libera, and Michel Zink (Paris: Presses Universitaires de France, 2002), 521.

14   Jean Wirth, "La Naissance du concept de croyance (12e–17e siècles)," *Bibliothèque d'Humanisme et Renaissance* 45 (1983), 13.

15   Bodin goes into great detail explaining why the emperor of the Holy Roman Empire, Charles V, "ne pouvoit prester la foy & hommage lige au Pape sans exception: attendu qu'il estoit homme lige, Pair & subjet naturel du Roy de France, & que le service & hommage est inseparable de la personne." *La République* 176.

16   Bodin, *La République,* 162.

civil society and the basis of institutions—is superfluous to the extent that Bodin envisioned the sovereign exercising the power necessary to enforce law. The subject owed only obedience to the sovereign. "Any Republic, corporation or college and all families are governed by commandment and obedience."[17]

Bodin's articulation of political absolutism rested on a new distinction between public and private spheres.[18] In feudal times, "the totality of social relations rest[ed] on a private bond."[19] At the basis of the power of the feudal lord was a personal oath that bound him reciprocally to each of his vassals. As a result of the fact that political power was established through a personal bond, the heads of aristocratic families acted both as lords and *pères de famille*; they accepted the responsibility for the protection of their vassals. In Bodin's eyes, overlapping public and private spheres conspired to undermine civil order. During the wars of religion, private allegiances of vassalic fealty competed with what Bodin deemed the sole recipe for harmony: the subject's obedience to the sovereign. Envisioning an impersonal structure unimaginable in feudal society, Bodin established an analogy between the natural unit of the family and the artificial unit of the state. "Just as the well governed family is the true image of the republic, and domestic power resembles sovereign power," writes Bodin, "so too is the right government of the home the true model of the government of the republic." An analogy points to a similarity. The king's authority is analogous to the father's authority. But analogy also indicates difference. The father and the king exert authority over distinct domains. The *pater familias* has power over all members of his family and is the owner of the family's property.

Symptomatic of Bodin's rejection of the reciprocity of the vassalic oath of fealty was the way in which he altered one of the metaphors used to describe the king's relation to his subjects. Bodin deploys a marital model of kingship, developed by Lucas de Penna (ca. 1320–ca. 1390) and Charles de Grassaille in *Regalium franciae libri duo* (1538). Borrowing an ecclesiastical metaphor according to which the prelate "marries" his church, de Penna and de Grassaille argued that the king "married" his realm—primarily as a means of underscoring the inalienability of the "dowry" that the *res publica*, as the wife, brought to her royal husband.[20] Bodin, too, adopted this rationale for royal finances. However, he changed the metaphor in one important way. Medieval political theorists emphasized consent—in political terms, the consent of the people to be ruled by their king—as a necessary component of sacramental marriage. Théodore Godefroy, for instance, in *Le Cérémonial de France* (1619), explains how a bishop presents a royal wedding band to the king "as a mark of this reciprocal conjunction," that is, to symbolize the "sweet, gracious, and loving bond of marriage [in which the king is] inseparably united with his subjects."[21] Bodin in contrast ignores the sacramental angle of marriage and the condition of consent

---

17   Ibid., 19.

18   My comments in this paragraph are much indebted to the analyses of Ginevra Conti Odorisio, *Famiglia e Stato nella République di Jean Bodin* (Torino: G. Giappichelli, 1993).

19   Wirth, 13.

20   Ernst H. Kantorowicz, *The King's Two Bodies: A Study in Mediaeval Political Theology* (Princeton: Princeton U.P., 1997), 214–23.

21   Godefroy, cited in Kantorowicz 222, n. 85.

along with it. He posits that heads of family are to their sovereign what wives are to their husbands. In *La République*, the wife obeys the *pater familias* who in turn obeys the sovereign. This relation is neither reciprocal nor voluntary. Drawing from Genesis, Bodin made the wife's divinely decreed subordination to the husband the basis of human society in *La République*: "[T]he power of the husband over the wife ... is the source and origin of all human society." The husband exerts absolute power in his own home, but is powerless in the public arena, where he must simply obey his sovereign. If there is any hint of reciprocity in the subject's obedience to the sovereign, it is that the sovereign guarantees through his law the husband's power over the wife. Without openly advocating the husband's right to kill his adulterous wife, "common to all of Greece as to the Romans," Bodin deplores the attenuation of such customs by the sixth century Emperor Justinian, "a man dazed of sense." In the *Corpus Juris Civilis*, under the influence of his wife Theodora, he "made all the laws he could to the advantage of women, including changing the death penalty to the stigma of infamy ... which seems ridiculous since infamy cannot take away honor from she who has [already] lost it."[22]

In feudal times, the *fidelitas* of wives to husbands was just one manifestation of a web of *fidelitas* that made up civil society—one that did not always prevent women from exercising political power, as numerous Renaissance authors pointed out. In Bodin's absolutism, however, the subordination of wives to husbands is the sine qua non of political order. Not surprisingly, therefore, the exclusion of women from the throne is the very condition of the state's existence. Rule by women amounted to nothing less than the negation of the state. To many historical examples of disastrous female rule, curiously gleaned from catalogues of "illustrious women" in prowomen declamations, such as Agrippa's *De nobilitate et praecellentia foeminae sexus*, Bodin added a more recent one. He laid the blame for civil war not on the schism of Christendom, but on the regency of Catherine de Médicis. Unlike the Protestant Innocent Gentillet, who despised the regent above all for her Florentine birth and Machiavellian ways, Bodin pinned her supposed responsibility for the destruction of the French state squarely on her sex. He compares Catherine to Jeanne I d'Anjou (1326–82), allegedly responsible for the murder of three kings: "We have seen in these last few years tragedies no less strange, and a whole kingdom in combustion for a similar case," Bodin comments.[23] To which "tragedies" he is alluding is not clear, but neither their perpetrator nor their effect—the "combustion" of a nation—is in question. By the 1590s, when the extinction of the Valois line forced a choice between a Huguenot leader or the Spanish Infanta (who would marry a French aristocrat), few Frenchmen condoned female rule. Both of the Hotman brothers— François the *politique* in his *Francogallia* (1573–86) and Antoine the Catholic

---

22 Bodin, *La République,* 11, 20, 24.

23 Bodin, *La République*, 1003. Innocent Gentillet and Henri Estienne, *Discours merveilleux de la vie, actions et deportements de Catherine de Médicis, royne-mère* (1575) (Genève: Librairie Droz, 1995). This is not to say that Bodin embraced Machiavelli. For Bodin's critique of Machiavelli, see Julian Franklin, *Jean Bodin and the Sixteenth-Century Revolution in the Methodology of Law and History* (New York and London: Columbia U.P., 1963), 49.

ligueur in his *Traicté de la loi salique* (1593)—emphasized that the exclusion of women from the throne was one of those "practices and customs of the nation [that] have acquired the force of written law."[24] But Bodin was the only jurist to claim that "Salic law"—an expression that he coined, according to Pierre Bayle—had been a written law.[25] Moreover, "No author, except Bodin," asserts Pierre-Louis Vaillancourt, "dares to maintain that custom and legislation excluded women [from the throne] in all countries. Only Bodin claims 'that there has never been a people so effeminate as to approve gynecocracy'."[26]

Jean Wirth, in an article on the origins of the notion of belief in the Renaissance, contends that in the Middle Ages, the organization of civil society sustained religious notions of belief. He argues that the feudal oath of homage (*fidelitas*) provided an illustration of the religious notion of *fides*, what we might imperfectly translate as "faith."[27] In epistemological terms, according to Wirth, *fides* occupied a distinct space between *scientia,* the knowledge that comes through the acceptance of evidence, and *opinio*, the evocation of uncertain claims. *Fides* designated a paradoxical kind of knowledge: a certitude relative to invisible, probable, or uncertain things. Such knowledge resulted from man's fall from grace: "Fides, the perception of invisible things, allows for the remediation of the defective character of human knowledge, obscured by original sin."[28] For the layperson *fides* and ignorance went hand in hand. Because there were no objective criteria for determining *fides*, one had to rely on the authority of theologians. The link that concretized both the *fidèle*'s trust in God and the reliance of the layperson on the authority of the theologian was precisely feudal *fidelitas*. The vassal's profession of *fidelitas* illustrated religious *fides*: "[F]idelity expressed in the act of faith, in the genuflex and the gesture of prayer, implies an

---

24   François Hotman, *Francogallia*, trans. J.H.M. Salmon (Cambridge: Cambridge U.P., 1972), 275. See Pierre-Louis Vaillancourt "Bodin et le pouvoir politique des femmes," *Jean Bodin: Actes du colloque interdisciplinaire d'Angers, 24 au 27 mai 1984* (Angers: Presses de l'Université d'Angers, 1985), 63–74, 64.

25   Bodin, *La République*, 1011. Pierre Bayle, "Bodin," *Dictionnaire historique et critique*, cited in *Les oeuvres philosophiques de Jean Bodin*, ed. Pierre Mesnard, xxiii–xxxvii. François Hotman refers to "Salic law" in *Francogallia*, so Bayle was wrong in claiming that Bodin coined the expression. The faulty attribution is, nevertheless, indicative of the extent to which Bodin was associated with the hardening of custom into law. François Hotman insists that what people refer to as "Salic law" applied originally only to private law. The idea "that the Salic Law was a part of the public law of the commonwealth and empire, and the law of hereditary succession to the kingdom" is an error, according to Hotman (273).

26   Vaillancourt, 69.

27   My medievalist colleagues assure me that Wirth is mistaken in relating medieval structures of belief to "feudalism"—a word coined in the seventeenth century. I thank Patricia Ingham in particular for pointing out that the quest for origins in Renaissance scholarship often entails the misrepresentation of medieval history. Wirth's argument is thus most pertinent when considered not as an account of medieval society, but as a representation of that society as it would have appeared to sixteenth-century thinkers such as Bodin. In other words, although tracing a shifting relation between conceptions of belief and social structures may not have made sense to Baudouin of Canterbury, it would have made a great deal of sense to Bodin.

28   Wirth, 7–58, 16.

anthropomorphic God, analogous to the feudal lord."[29] Equally important, feudal *fidelitas* expressed a reciprocal commitment illustrative of the Christian economy of salvation. The lord vowed to protect the vassal, providing an easily imaginable example of the invisible good that was the promise of salvation. *Fides* resulted from redemption, and salvation was the fruit of *fides*.

The mission of the Inquisition, founded in the thirteenth century, was to protect *fides* by stamping out heresy. Heinrich Kramer at the outset of the *Malleus maleficarum* (1487) calls "the extermination of the faith" the greatest danger of his time. Innocent VIII gave his blessing to the counter-extermination advocated by Kramer in the Bull *Summis desiderantes affectibus* published along with the *Malleus*. This document, composed in 1484, manifests the same desire to expulse heretics from the wagon-circle of the faithful:

> Desiring with the most heartfelt anxiety … that the Catholic Faith should especially in this our day increase and flourish everywhere, and that all heretical depravity should be driven far from the frontiers and bournes of the Faithful, We very gladly proclaim … those particular means and methods whereby our pious desire may obtain its wished effect, since when all errors are uprooted … a zeal for … our holy Faith will be all the more strongly impressed upon the hearts of the faithful.[30]

To be sure, witches were not alone in threatening the faith. There were the Jews, who denied the prophecies concerning Christ. There were the "Mohammedans" "in the lands of the infidels." And within Christendom, too, were all kinds of infidels: "[I]nfidelity in a person who has been baptized is technically called heresy," say the inquisitors. Kramer, nevertheless, insisted that witchcraft was the worst kind of infidelity and the gravest of all heresies because it entailed an express pact with the Devil. "This heresy, witchcraft, … differs from all other heresy … not merely by a tacit compact, but by a compact which is exactly defined and expressed." The pact is made, he explains, when the Devil appears to the novice in the form of a man, and if he finds her willing to abjure God, "he stretches out his hand, and so does the novice, and she swears with upraised hand to keep that covenant. And when this is done, the Devil at once adds that this is not enough; and … demands the following oath of homage to himself" formalized by the donation of her body and soul.[31]

The Inquisition was founded to save faith from heresy, not from unintelligibility. Yet it hardly seems fortuitous that witchcraft—the *infidelitas* that defined the contours of *fidelitas* more exactly than any other—plagued Europe at a time when feudalism, the social structure that had given meaning to the epistemological construct of *fides*, was disintegrating. In the fifteenth century, the great fiefdoms of France became the property of the crown, evacuating the personal bond between lords and vassals. Vassals simply became subjects of the crown. As the feudal structure crumbled, religious *fides* also lost coherence, becoming a floating signifier, imprecise in

---

29 Wirth, 19.

30 Heinrich Kramer and James Sprenger, *The Malleus Maleficarum*, ed. and trans. Montague Summers, (New York: Dover Publications, 1971), xliii.

31 Kramer, 75–6, 2–3, 20, 100.

meaning and lacking a profile distinct from *scientia* and *opinio*.[32] In the absence of a social analogy that made the paradox of *fides* intelligible, the notion of certitude regarding something invisible seemed increasingly absurd. François Rabelais, chiding the reader's incredulity with respect to the birth of Gargantua in the prologue of *Pantagruel* (1534), ridicules the scholastics' definition of *fides*: "Why wouldn't you believe it? Because (you say) it is not apparent (i.e., it is not plausible—*il n'y a nulle apparence*). I tell you that for that reason alone you should believe it in perfect faith. Because the Sorbonnistes say that faith is an argument of non-apparent (i.e., implausible) things [*foy est arguement des choses de nulle apparence*]."[33] The Inquisition's transformation of the witch-heretic from wayward soul in need of recuperation to monstrous criminal requiring punishment after 1400 was a symptom of the weakening of the concept of *fides*. Late medieval demonology reinforced the intelligibility of *fides*, a notion that had always been difficult to grasp but that had benefited from the once prevalent social analogy of the vassal's oath of fidelity to his lord. The witch's pact conceptualized a kind of bond between the *fidèle* and God that was no longer readily illustrated in social life. Witches in their pact with Satan filled the gap left by vassals and lords, demonstrating what it meant to be faithful through the principle of inversion. Reflective of the reciprocity of the feudal bond, Kramer insists on the mutual dependence of the witch and the Devil, who together with the permission of God, form the unholy trinity of "the three concomitants of witchcraft."[34] The witch cannot carry out her evil deeds on her own; nor can the Devil harm humans without her mediation. It is through the pact that each party expects to realize some future goal.

Yet witchcraft theory, at the same time that it tried to arrest the decline of *fides*, actually hastened that decline. In particular, the effort to establish certain points of dogma through logical proofs and empirical evidence showed a lack of confidence in *fides* and undermined its standing as a distinct epistemological category. The disintegration of *fides* resulted not only from the decline of feudalism, but also from pressure exerted on a mode of knowing reserved for the "noncorporeal but nonetheless true" by the integration of Aristotelian philosophy as of the twelfth century. Walter Stephens, in *Demon Lovers: Witchcraft, Sex, and the Crisis of Belief*, argues that the arrival of Aristotelian *scientia* into the Christian West imperiled faith, and especially belief in noncorporeal things. While the ninth-century *Canon Episcopi*, which contained the most authoritative ecclesiastical statement dealing with witchcraft before the Inquisition, "feared no contradiction in the assertion that Paul, John, and Ezekiel had experiences that were true but contrary to normal experience," the development of the idea of nature (as opposed to Creation) in

---

32   This is Wirth's thesis: "As vassalic fidelity loses its fundamental character, *fides* ceases to be immediately evident and there begins a search for foundations, while the use of the word expands and ceases to obey rigourous definitions. To save the concept and, at the same time, a big part of the religious system, evangelism redefines [*fides*] in terms of the supernatural, rids it of obsolete social implications and leaves it to float with respect to the epistemological system in which it no longer plays any role" 55–6.

33   Rabelais, cited in Wirth, 35.

34   Kramer, 1.

the twelfth century made the paradoxical notion of certitude regarding something imperceptible seem agonizingly deficient.[35] Aquinas entertains the argument that if nature boasts its own causes and effects, then "there is therefore no need to suppose that a God exists."[36] Aquinas went on to refute this claim; nevertheless, according to Stephens, the notion of nature as a potentially autonomous entity created the need to assert the reality of Catholic dogma, that is, to grant the same kinds of evidence to Christian theology as to Aristotelian *scientia*, in which "rigorous logic should prevail over authority and temper sense experience."[37] Articles of faith were simply too precious to risk being left to Rabelais's irreverent designation, "choses de nulle apparence." In the case of witchcraft theory, the "rigorous logic" that supposedly established the truth of witchcraft was the double negative: "Witchcraft cannot not be true." As for sense experience, inquisitors called upon the witch as the only witness qualified to substantiate something that was invisible to the inquisitors themselves. Witches provided evidence of the existence of demons when they confessed (most often under the pressure of torture) their sexual or other corporeal interactions with demons.[38]

Beyond proving the existence of demons, witchcraft helped to prove central points of Catholic doctrine. Kramer, for instance, calls upon *maleficia* to illustrate the sacramental character of matrimony. As a sacrament, marriage was understood as an oath of allegiance instituted by Jesus Christ through which God communicates grace to the faithful. Designating marriage as a sacrament meant that it differed from the vassal's oath of fealty in its spiritual dimension: the Holy Spirit infused the participant in the sacrament with God's grace, enacting an inner transformation invisible to the eye.[39] The sacrament of matrimony was, in other words, subject to precisely the kind of conviction that the scholastics called *fides*. The performative character of grace, which created the marriage, could be neither perceived nor, as a result, ascertained except by negation. The witch could throw spells on soon to be married individuals to prevent the consummation of marriage and thus to destroy "the marriage contract," as Kramer puts it.[40] The possibility of procreation was supposedly a result of the sacrament of matrimony, and so the reality of the sacrament was demonstrated when a witch impeded one aspect of reproduction. In other words, the presence of God's grace was made manifest by its demonically caused absence. Or rather, infertility caused by witches proved that God's grace allowed for fertility. We recognize that the ternary structure of witchcraft—involving a symbiosis between the witch as human intermediary and the devil as possessor of evil powers, but made possible by God—reflects the "three concomitants" of marriage: the vow of fidelity between husband and wife, blessed by the grace of God.

---

35   Walter Stephens, *Demon Lovers: Witchcraft, Sex, and the Crisis of Belief* (Chicago and London: University of Chicago Press, 2002), 131.

36   Aquinas, *Summa theologiae*, 1.2.3, cited in Stephens 131.

37   Blair, 82.

38   Stephens, 143, 26.

39   On the sacrament as the visible sign of a real, albeit spiritual and, therefore, invisible transformation, see Joseph Martos, *Doors to the Sacred: A Historical Introduction to Sacraments in the Catholic Church* (New York: Doubleday, 1981), 71.

40   Kramer, 5, 26, 57.

Bodin had read many demonologists of the fifteenth and sixteenth centuries; he cites not just the *Malleus maleficarum*, but also Pierre Mamoris, Silvestro Mazzolini (*alias* Prierias), Paolo Grillandi, and Barthélemy Faye, to name but a few.[41] His argumentation like theirs rests on the double negative, "witchcraft cannot not be true." Regarding demon-induced mind/body separation, a phenomenon that, after Augustine, he names "ecstasy," Bodin declares: "As for me, I think that this ecstasy is one of the strongest arguments, after God's law that we have for the immortality of the soul."[42] That the immortality of the soul—a doctrine representative of Aristotelian philosophy as well as Judeo-Christian theology—should have to rely on the ecstasy of witches for confirmation might seem surprising to anyone not familiar with late medieval demonology. Also reminiscent of the *Malleus*, Bodin eagerly seeks an empirical basis for what Rabelais facetiously calls "choses de nulle apparence." This project is emphasized in his preface, where he refutes objections that angels and demons cannot act on corporeal entities. Interesting, the problem as Bodin frames it anticipates the major stumbling block of Cartesian dualism: How does an immaterial spirit act upon *res extensa*? Bodin skirts the conundrum by hypothesizing (with the approbation of several authorities) that, in fact, demons are corporeal, made of air. In another move evocative of Descartes, Bodin links *res extensa* to finitude, in order to establish that God alone is incorporeal. Bodin takes the idea of God's infinite unknowability from the esoteric *Sefer ha-Zohar* (ca. 1300) or Book of Splendor, one of the foundational texts for Kabbala in the Renaissance: "[N]othing is as finite as the body, with its circumscribed size and depth: and [since] that which has no limit [*extrémité*] to its surface is infinite, it follows that God alone is incorporeal, otherwise [His] creatures would be infinite like him."[43] For confirmation of things that everybody knows but that no one has seen, Bodin, like Kramer, looks to the witch as to an "expert witness" (to borrow Stephens's expression) who, under the pressure of torture, provides firsthand evidence of the machinations of demons:

> In sum, we [have] the trials against witches in Germany, France, Italy, Spain, ... in writing, and we see every day the infinite testimonies, ... convictions, confessions which persisted until the death of those who were executed—for the most part ignorant people or old women, who hadn't read Plutarch, Herodotus, or Philostratus, nor laws of other peoples, nor spoke with the sorcerers of Germany and Italy to agree so well in all things and on all points as they do.[44]

Bodin insists on women's lack of learning as a guarantee of the empirical value of their testimony.[45] Clearly, literate witchcraft authorities like Bodin felt an urgent need

---

41   Barthélemy Faye, *Energumenicus et Alexicacus* (Paris, 1571); Paolo Grillandi, *Tractatus de sortilegiis* (Lyon, 1536), Pierre Mamoris, *Flagellum maleficorum* (Toulouse, 1485) Silvestro Mazzolini, *De stigimagarum demonumque mirandis* (Rome 1521).

42   Bodin, *De la démonomanie*, 234.

43   Bodin, *De la démonomanie*, "Preface," [5–6].

44   Ibid., [10].

45   Compare to Montaigne: Cet home que j'avoy, estoit home simple et grossier, qui est une condition proper à rendre veritable témoignage ... Ou il faut un home très fidelle, ou si simple qu'il n'ait pas dequoy bastir et donner de la vray-semblance à des inventions fauces,

to see their theories confirmed by those beyond the influence of the written word. Bodin's triumphal insistence on the concurring testimonies of "ignorant people or old women" cannot hide his lurking worry that demonology may be a "self-legitimating discourse." [46] Knowledge that one derives from books is inherently mediated; the witch, like her holy counterpart, the enlightened illiterate (*éclairé illettré*) whose faith the learned Jesuit Jean-Joseph Surin envied, has a purer, more direct, relation to the occult than the humanist/theologian.

Yet Bodin significantly altered the terms of witchcraft theory in *De la démonomanie*, by shifting the energy from preempting heresy to demonizing the atheist, and by trading its central didactic message from a lesson on the efficaciousness of God's grace to a disquisition on His sovereignty. In the *Malleus maleficarum*, the effort to preempt skepticism—in the narrow colloquial sense of a general doubt regarding matters of faith—is omnipresent, but always filtered through the *fidelitas/ infidelitas* opposition. Kramer opens the treatise with the question, "Whether the belief that there are such beings as witches is so essential a part of the Catholic faith that obstinately to maintain the opposite opinion manifestly savours of heresy."[47] Bodin, on the other, hand makes no pretense of defending the faith from heresy. The only heresy he mentions has little to do with witches; significantly, he reserves the superlative label, "the most detestable heresy there ever was," for the Manichean thesis that God and the devil are equal adversaries in a power struggle.[48] Moreover, the crisis of belief manifested in late medieval witchcraft theory reflects the anxious state of mind of learned theologians more than a position in an actual debate. Kramer combats no contemporary adversary; he anticipates skeptical arguments rather than refutes them. He acknowledges that his effort is a new one with respect to the *Canon Episcopi*, an effort necessitated (he says) by the dramatic increase in witchcraft since that time. Bodin, on the other hand, demonizes an intellectual adversary, an adversary who is only foreshadowed in the *Malleus maleficarum*, an adversary whom he seeks to quash through with the tools of the Renaissance humanist. "And not only does [S]cripture, but also all the Academicians, Peripatetics, Stoics, and Arabs agree on the existence of these demons: to such an extent that to doubt it (as the Atheist Epicureans) would be to deny the principles of metaphysics and the existence of God."[49]

The "Atheist Epicureans" went astray because they followed Aristotle too closely, denying "that something is possible that is naturally impossible."[50] The Epicureans had a modern equivalent—those who, developing the very arguments that Kramer had vaguely foreseen and tried to preempt, found natural explanations for effects supposedly caused by demons or God: "Atheists and those who feign

---

et qui n'ait rien espousé," *Essais*, ed. Pierre Villey (Paris: Presses Universitaires de France, 1965), I.31, 205.

46 On demonology as a self-legitimating discourse, see Virginia Krause, "Confessional Fictions and Demonology in Renaissance France," *Journal of Medieval and Early Modern Studies* 35/2 (2005): 327–48, especially 335–8.

47 Kramer, 1.

48 Bodin, *De la démonomanie*, 4.

49 Bodin, *De la démonomanie*, 1.

50 Bodin, *De la démonomanie*, "Preface," [4].

knowledge, not knowing the cause, do not want to confess what they see, for fear of seeming ignorant."[51] The prototype for the modern atheist was Pietro Pomponazzi (1462–1525), a physician and professor of natural philosophy at Padua and Bologna. The natural philosophers of Padua brooked a new compromise between Aristotle and Christian theology by layering the scholastics' epistemological categories of *scientia* (knowledge deriving from evidence) and *fides* (certainty regarding uncertain things) with a distinction between the natural and the supernatural. The supernatural was, in other words, a category invented in contradistinction to Aristotelian nature; while nature is subject to reason, as Aristotle taught, the supernatural can only be apprehended with faith. At a time when *fides* had all but given up the ghost, the natural/ supernatural distinction seemed reassuringly transparent, in sum, intelligible. But as Henri Busson writes, "the separation of the respective domains of reason and faith, advocated by the Paduan school and accepted by many as a safeguard [i.e., faith] for the latter, led before the end of the century to make faith impossible to demanding minds."[52] The danger of this division of labor became apparent in Pomponazzi's *De naturalium effectuum admirandorum causis, sive de incantationibus liber* (On the causes of natural effects, or On Incantations), written in 1520 but published well after his death in 1567 in Protestant Basel. Pomponazzi argued that many supposedly supernatural phenomena including miracles were actually the result of occult forces of nature. What could prevent the realm of the natural from expanding, and thereby from diminishing the domain of the supernatural and ultimately the relevance of faith?

Weyer magnified rather than dismissed the Devil's power, and we have no reason to doubt the sincerity of his belief in Satan's capacities, especially since an omnipresent and nearly omnipotent Devil was consistent with his Lutheranism. The German physician's insistence on the way in which the Devil exploits natural phenomena, such as humors and perception, could, nonetheless, lead some readers to conclude that the Devil was, in fact, superfluous to the strange happenings that witches recounted in their confessions. If the experience of the Sabbath was not real, but a memory fabricated by the Devil through the black ink of melancholy, why couldn't melancholic humors create such perceptions in the absence of Satan's artistry? The Devil, first cause of hallucinations, risked finding himself displaced by the efficient cause, an excess of melancholy or other perceptual disorder.[53] Since Weyer explained the flight of witches through entirely natural means (that is, the unguents they used to propel themselves were naturally hallucinatory), it would seem logical to conclude that any aspect of bewitchment could be attributed to a natural cause. To a reader like Bodin who had read or was at least familiar with Pomponazzi's *De incantationibus,* Weyer's debt to this work would be obvious (it circulated in manuscript well before its official publication). Pomponazzi insisted on

---

51   Ibid., [12].

52   Busson, 544.

53   Jean Céard, "Médecine et démonologie: Les enjeux d'un débat," *Diable, diables, et diableries au temps de la Renaissance*, ed. M.T. Jones-Davies (Paris: Jean Touzot, 1988), 97–112. "Bodin entrevoit le risque d'une thèse qui, à force de ne prêter au diable que les pouvoirs d'un agent naturel, peut conduire à récuser sa présence en la rendant inutile" (104–5).

the power of the imagination to produce corporeal phenomena, citing not only the ancient example of the maternal imagination's marking of the fetus that he derives from Marsilio Ficino's (1433–99) *Theologica platonica de immortalitate animorum* (a text that Weyer's mentor Agrippa had recopied in *De occulta philosophia* and that Weyer knew well), but also the more contentious claim that melancholy could cause the symptoms of possession. In the epilogue to *De praestigiis daemonum*, Weyer seeks to distance himself from those "Pugnacious Peripatetics [who] refer all miracles and monstrosities of whatever kind to natural causes," and he prays for Pomponazzi's salvation: "I would hope ... that before giving up his last breath, Pomponazzi repented, by the singular mercy of God, and that he did not remain an atheist."[54] But to Bodin, Weyer was the new Pomponazzi, all the more dangerous because he applied Pomponazzi's arguments to witchcraft.

Given that the natural/supernatural distinction led so easily to the encroachment of nature on "supernature," it is a curious feature of Renaissance thought that highly orthodox thinkers accepted and even participated in the establishment of separate jurisdictions for faith and reason. While Weyer pushed back the limit of the supernatural, Bodin decreed that this limit was not negotiable. Witches are not mad; instead, "We must consider as mad or senseless those who see the strange actions of witches and spirits, and yet because they cannot understand their cause, or because they are naturally impossible, refuse to believe them." "The most egregious of all errors come from those who, denying the power of spirits and the actions of witches, seek to argue physically about supernatural or metaphysical things, which is an incongruity," Bodin complains. "Each science has its principles and foundations that differ the one from the other."[55] More than once in the "Refutation," Bodin savors the paradox that Weyer "wants to dispute as a natural philosopher [*physicien*] about Metaphysics."[56] Bodin accuses Weyer of mixing up separate sciences, yet he himself assimilates distinct categories. Not only does Bodin conflate the metaphysical and the supernatural, abusively assigning metaphysics (in the Aristotelian corpus, the science of the immaterial, whatever its status) to phenomena that resist natural explanation, he apparently calls upon the physicality of the effects to prove the metaphysicality of the cause. In situations involving demons, Bodin warns, "One should not resist truth, when we see effects, but don't know their cause."[57] Seeing is believing, and when it comes to the workings of witches and demons, explaining what we see is not necessary. "We see with the eye [*on void à l'oeil*] that Demons ... enter the bodies of men and beasts."[58]

At the precise point when Bodin struggles with the arbitrary limit between the natural and the supernatural, he predictably has recourse to skepticism—not the dubiousness regarding witchcraft against which Kramer battles, but the school of thought headed up by Pyrrho, an enigmatic figure whose techniques were recorded by

---

54   Weyer, 581.

55   Bodin, *De la démonomanie*, "Préface," [15].

56   Bodin, *De la démonomanie*, 245, 246, 237. Another formulation of this same charge is that Weyer "conflate[s] heaven and earth" 244.

57   Bodin, *De la démonomanie*, "Preface," [11].

58   Ibid., [15–16].

Sextus Empiricus in the second century A.D. and translated for the benefit of literate (i.e., Latinate) readers by the humanist Henri Estienne in 1562. Less surprisingly still, Bodin makes no effort to transcend intellectual angst by suspending judgment, as Pyrrho's example taught. He argues instead that we must simply accept what experience shows to be true. As both Peter Dear and Ann Blair have observed, experience was a capacious category in the sixteenth century. Bodin's notion of experience was quite different from Weyer's.[59] For Weyer, the original act of eye-witnessing guaranteed the distinction between fact and mere hearsay. In what seems to us a paradoxical move, he uses eyewitness experience as a standard against which to measure the truth-value of texts. Weyer rejects the demons reported by Ficino and his neo-Platonizing friends because they "recorded as known fact many things which they had not seen or ascertained." In contrast, he accepts Moses' statement that God made angels because "(as Scriptural truth attests) God spoke face to face [with him], as with a friend."[60] Bodin, on the other hand, gave no value to individual experience. One of his favorite adverbial expressions, "au doigt et à l'oeil" (to the finger and the eye) evokes the doubly physical perception of feeling and seeing (where feeling was supposed to be somehow less subject to illusion than seeing), yet he deploys this phrase almost exclusively in a metaphoric sense.[61] Bodin wraps up the "Refutation" by lampooning Weyer for disregarding "the experience of all peoples, Kings, Princes, Legislators, Magistrates, Jurisconsults, who have ascertained by finger and eye [*au doigt et à l'oeil*] the execrable impiety and evil deeds with which witches are charged." Needless to say, kings and princes never fingered witchcraft suspects; indeed, this kind of tactile intervention was increasingly reserved for the physician, whose experience Bodin automatically discounts unless it conforms to what everybody else already knows by "common consent," through experience or not.[62]

Bodin's admonition to "lower our heads before God and confess our mind's weakness without getting caught up in the principles and natural reasons that we lack when we try to examine the actions of spirits" calls to mind the oath of *fidelitas* as he describes it in *La République*. The vassal "must doff his sword, gloves, hat, coat,

---

59   According to Blair, Bodin "is on the premodern side of the divide ... between the conception of experience as something known well to all and the single, staged, crucial experiments favored by the mechanical philosophers" (105). She draws this distinction from Peter Dear, *Discipline and Experience: The Mathematical Way in the Scientific Revolution* (Chicago: University of Chicago Press, 1995).

60   Weyer, *De praestigiis daemonum*, 3. Weyer's accreditation of only a narrow group of celestial intermediaries echoes Calvin's restrictive position on angels. Calvin admitted only those intermediary beings discussed in the Bible, "emphasized the total subservience of angels to God[,] and discouraged inquiring into obscure questions concerning the nature and origin of their hierarchies" (Blair, 129). On the new imperative of eyewitness testimony in the Renaissance, see Andrea Frisch, *The Invention of the Eyewitness: Witnessing and Testimony in Early Modern France* (Chapel Hill: University of North Carolina Press, 2004).

61   Bodin, *De la démonomanie*, 251. Other examples: "God's law ... reveals the sorcerer *au doigt & à l'oeil*" (18). He accuses Weyer of allowing his reader "to see and to touch by finger and eye ... what should be consigned to eternal oblivion [*oubliance*]" (54).

62   Bodin, *De la démonomanie*, "Preface," [15].

spurs and kneel, his hands joined between the hands of his Prince … and make the oath."[63] Yet redemption and salvation—what the *fidèle* might hope for in exchange for his fealty—are conspicuously absent from *De la démonomanie*. Bodin's God is that of the Old Testament, a God who has shown his wrath for those who allow the proliferation of witchcraft, a God in need of appeasement: "Irritated, God sent terrible persecutions, as he threatened by his law to exterminate peoples who would tolerate witches to live."[64] Obedience does not bind the sovereign and, analogously, the attitude that Bodin advocates does not presume the two-way obligation implicit in medieval *fides* and in the partnership between the Devil and the witch. Instead, the magistrate attacks impiety, the inverse of *pietas*—from the verb *piare* (to sacrifice, honor, or appease). "There is no less impiety to call into doubt, if it is possible that there are witches, than to question if there is a God," Bodin declares. In his estimation, *De praestigiis daemonum* contains "all the impieties imaginable." And alluding to Weyer's pious demeanor, the jurist warns, "there is no impiety greater than that which is covered with a veil of piety."[65] In the *Malleus maleficarum*, the original mission of the Inquisition to prevent heresy is still apparent, if not in the pursuit of witches, then at least in the effort to fortify the reader's faith through elaborate proofs of the existence of witchcraft. But Bodin, in accepting the Dominicans' recommendation that witchcraft be tried in secular courts, adopts an urgent, combative tone with "master doubters" as well. Weyer built his case on an argument that he took from Erasmus: is it worth the risk of our own salvation to put a person to death if we cannot be entirely sure of her guilt? Bodin takes precisely the opposite tack: those who argue against the extermination of witches stand not to be persuaded, but punished: "[H]e is guilty of the punishment of witches as it is expressly stated in the law, that he who lets witches escape, must suffer the punishment of witches."[66]

The violence of Bodin's fideism reveals the fully arbitrary character of the border between the natural and supernatural. In the absence of a criterion for determining this limit, the magistrate invokes the force of law to enforce an attitude of unquestioning acceptance of God's power and submission to it. If Bodin did not see that his argument rested on intimidation rather than on scientific evidence (either logical or empirical), it was perhaps because his understanding of the natural/supernatural dichotomy rested on the same foundation as his political absolutism, a foundation that he claimed to be natural and divine at once: that of the wife's obedience to the husband's command. Bodin transposes the conjugal symbolism of *La République* to an allegorical plane in *De la démonomanie*, where he personifies and feminizes nature as God's wife.

---

63   Bodin, *De la démonomanie*, 247; *De la République*, 170.

64   Bodin, *De la démonomanie*, "Preface," [4]. Bodin appears to have made up this divine law or extrapolated it quite freely from Leviticus 20: 2, where the crime is that of idolatry and where God does not threaten his people. See Marie-Thérèse Isaac and Roland Crahay, "La 'bibliothèque' de Jean Bodin démonologue: les bases théoriques," *Bulletin de la classe des lettres et des sciences morales et politiques de l'Académie Royale de Belgique*, 73 (1987): 129–71, 160.

65   Bodin, *De la démonomanie*, "Preface," [15], 219.

66   Bodin, *De la démonomanie*, 251.

It is not as if the Hebrews ignored the difference between the works of God and of nature: for Salomon often remarked that when it is said in the allegories that the child is good who obeys the commandments of the father and doesn't forget the law of the mother: he means the commandments of God and the law of nature.

Although Mother Nature exerts some authority over her children, that authority is utterly annulled when it contradicts the commandments of God the Father. Bodin adamantly separates God's capricious yet unlimited powers from nature's more predictable yet circumscribed capacities, inveighing against those who would "make nature into God." Bodin decries a kind of idolatry with respect to nature, encouraged through satanic subterfuge: "Satan makes us adore the celestial bodies, the elements, and the earth, as mother and protectress of men, and of all goods, without looking higher and directing the flight of intellectual contemplation to God, author and creator of all things."[67] The witch who marries Satan perverts the conjugal model twice over: she proclaims her obedience to the wrong husband with the objective of usurping God's prerogative to overrule the laws of nature. The natural philosopher who places nature above God promotes a usurpation instrumental to Satan's triumph; he is no better than a witch.

Bodin's Torturous Hermeneutics

Bodin used skeptical arguments opportunistically. His rapid summary of Sextus Empiricus' main points follows a long development devoted to revealing the errors and blind spots of Aristotelian *scientia*, whose criteria threatened a world of invisible creatures, both demonic and angelic, at the same time as they indicated the means to prove the existence of that slippery spirit world. Alluding to a medal engraved by Valerio Belli (1468–1546) picturing the philosopher on one side and a veiled woman on the other, Bodin concludes: "We can judge that Aristotle did not see the beautiful secrets of nature, which the ancients noticed when they figured behind his medal, a woman with a veiled face named Physis, that is, Nature: meaning that the beauty of nature had been hidden from him and that he only saw her outer vestments."[68]

Bodin's criticism of Aristotle's failure to see behind nature's veil reveals a discrepancy with respect to the unpeeking belief he so sternly advocates. Bodin's desire to show that he knows better than Aristotle (and better than atheists both ancient and modern who would make nature queen) contradicts his advocacy of

---

67   Bodin, *De la démonomanie*, 37, 36, 69.

68   Bodin, *De la démonomanie*, "Préface," [8]. Although Bodin takes Physis' veiled appearance to mean that Aristotle failed to understand nature fully, Ercole Gonzaga in a 1536 letter suggests quite the opposite: "Certainly, if ever a reverse was made that was appropriate and relevant to the head, this one of the Goddess of Nature is most to the purpose, Aristotle having so well reasoned about her that he penetrated her to the core." Cited in Philip Attwood, *Italian Medals, c. 1530–1600* (London: The British Museum Press, 2003), vol. 1, 212. According to Attwood, the female figure is not Physis but the veiled cult statue of Diana of the Ephesians. I thank Mark Blackburn, of the Fitzwilliam Museum, Cambridge for locating the medal for me.

Fig. 2.1   Aristotle and Physis medal. Valerio Belli (c. 1538).

blind acceptance of supernatural causes. This contradiction is not surprising insofar as a two-tiered hierarchy between those who accept and those who know is, after all, typical of most fideist formulas. As we have seen, Catholic theology generally scripted the ignorance of the *fidèle* in a role of submission to the authority of learned theologians. Bodin, too, will identify an intellectual elite responsible for upholding "the honor of God."[69] However, what is truly bizarre and perhaps most troubling about *De la démonomanie* is that this elite is comprised not of theologians but of magistrates. In *La République*, Bodin designates the magistrate or *magister*, whose title denotes the actions "to master and to dominate," as "the officer who has the power to command," a power granted to him by the sovereign whom he must obey.[70] In his dedication of *De la démonomanie* to the *premier président* of the Paris parlement, Chrestofle De Thou, Bodin waxes lyrical over "the splendor and majesty of this beautiful temple of Justice." Yet simple membership in this august corporation does not suffice to grant one the privilege of enforcing God's law. After all, Bodin writes *De la démonomanie* out of extreme annoyance with the laxity of the Parlement of Paris; it will be the fault of de Thou's colleagues, he warns, if God demands retribution for the unchecked proliferation of witchcraft. To truly claim to represent God's law, one must also have been anointed with the gift of prophecy. Paul Rose has argued in his *Bodin and the Great God of Nature* that Bodin's story in the first book of *De la démonomanie* about an anonymous friend who at the age of thirty-seven began to receive counsel in visions and dreams from a benevolent spirit is, in fact, autobiographical. One glimpses in these pages the "details of a conversion to prophetic religion, indeed of the author's own transfiguration as a prophet."[71]

---

69   Bodin, *De la démonomanie*, 218.
70   Bodin, *La République*, 393, 409.
71   Paul Rose, *Bodin and the Great God of Nature: The Moral and Religious Universe of a Judaiser* (Geneva: Droz, 1980), 3. Bodin, *De la démonomanie*, 10–11.

Here I would like to explain how the prophet-magistrate's privileged access to truth depends in two ways on the gender hierarchy that Bodin outlines in *La République*. In particular, I want to show that the witch is essential to the establishment of the authority of the prophet and magistrate. First, the witch demonstrates the transgression involved in any attempt on women's part to pursue occult knowledge, the only knowledge that matters for Bodin. Second, the extraction of the witch's confession allows for the demonstration of the magistrate's hermeneutical prowess, and it is really in Bodin's hermeneutical approach to confessions, texts, and nature— not in his fideist stance—that we find his personal reply to skepticism.

Hermeneutics, in its most basic, transhistorical definition, is the art of interpretation, what Paul Ricoeur calls "the intelligence of the double meaning."[72] Meanings may be derived from utterances and signs, from words on a page or effects of nature. Weyer's stance was antihermeneutical, to the extent that he claimed simply to expose that which had no need of interpretation. The Lutheran physician was a literalist for whom truth was "hidden in the depths" only because Satan had enveloped it in illusion. In contrast, Bodin shared with neo-platonist philosophers of the occult the notion of an essentially recalcitrant truth. Both the doctor and the jurist posited obstructions standing in the way of truth. For Weyer these obstacles lay within the sense organs of the perceiving subject, while for Bodin they were an integral part of the thing to be known. This difference in the location of truth's veiling conditioned their opposing views of torture. Weyer claimed that torture further clouded the faculties of the suspect and obscured truth, while Bodin defined torture as the judge's tool for eliciting truth from a suspect. Bodin, like Weyer, portrayed women as the embodiment of truth. However, whereas Weyer pointed to women's tortured bodies as the cost of a perverse reading into things and as the signs of a grave miscarriage of justice, Bodin argued that women were more obstinate than men in their resistance to torture. Their silent defiance confirmed the suspicion of their hidden secrets, and it tacitly justified corporeal coercion.

"The hostility towards the political power of women, which represents one of the deepest motives of Bodin's philosophy," writes Ginevra Conti Odorisio, "constitutes a unique tie that binds the *République* indissolubly to *De la démonomanie*."[73] In the preface to *De la démonomanie*, among examples of biblical proscriptions against witches, Bodin mentions Jezebel, wife of Ahab, king of Israel. Jezebel was not a witch, but an idolatress who seduced Ahab into worshipping Baal and killing Yahweh's prophets. Jehu avenged the latter by feeding her body to dogs "after having had her thrown from her castle."[74] For Bodin, Jezebel's plunge from the castle-top rectified both moral and political order, reversing her climb to the height of power, an egregious flouting of God's most basic law. Through the fiction of the queen-witch (as Agrippa d'Aubigné would later characterize Catherine de Médicis in the *Tragiques*),[75] Bodin joins two kinds of insubordination with two equally terrible consequences. Rule

---

72   Paul Ricoeur, *De l'interprétation: Essai sur Freud* (Paris: Seuil, 1965), 18.

73   Conti Odorisio, 753.

74   Bodin, *De la démonomanie*, "Préface," [9].

75   See Gisèle Mathieu-Castellani, *Agrippa d'Aubigné: Le corps de Jézabel* (Paris: Presses universitaires de France, 1991), 110–16.

by women leads to the annihilation of the state, while women's knowledge of the occult heralds the decadence of the moral universe. Women were naturally unfit to rule and naturally incapable of knowledge, according to Bodin, for the submission of wives to husbands signifies, "in addition to its literal meaning, the soul's power over the body, and that of reason over cupidity." Bodin draws this nugget of wisdom from Solomon, the sagacious son of David and most powerful king of Israel, who "seems to many people the sworn enemy of women, whom he thought about least when he wrote."[76] Bodin's remark about Solomon makes a fitting assessment of his own work. He thinks so little about women that it is not until the "Refutation" that he makes explicit what he takes for granted throughout the treatise—namely, that although he talks about several male witches and for this reason refers to witches collectively with the masculine "Sorciers," female witches far out number their male counterparts: "for one man there are fifty women."[77] Bodin needs the witch to be a woman—preferably a young marriageable or married woman—for the same reason that Kramer does: the Devil must have sex with someone in order to prove his corporeality, and satanic sex, albeit supernatural, could not be counternatural. The Satan of medieval witchcraft theory was not a sodomite. Witchcraft theorists imagined a devil so dogged in his efforts to increase and multiply evil, that even his sex could not be gratuitous.

Yet Bodin needs the witch to be a woman more than for the purposes of the propagation of satanic progeny; her gender will help distinguish the virtue of his prophecy from the evil of satanic knowledge. In the first book of *De la démonomanie*, Bodin seeks to answer the question, What are illicit and licit ways of acquiring knowledge of occult things? Bodin believed that for the meritorious few, the search for truth culminated in the gift of prophecy. The prophet was the inverse of the witch insofar as he obtained his knowledge from God, while the witch obtained hers from Satan. The prophet received wisdom from God as a reward for the virtuous life he leads, while the witch sought demonic knowledge as a means to an end (poisoning a neighbor or the realization of some other *maleficium*). Refuting Weyer's deployment of the insanity defense, Bodin defined the witch in such a way as to make her accountability perfectly clear: a witch is one "who by diabolical means tries knowingly [*sciemment*] to accomplish something."[78] Engaging in witchcraft was a conscious decision, freely willed. "That is why we used the word 'knowingly' in the definition of the witch."[79] Just as the jurist in *La République* expresses nostalgia for

---

76 Bodin, *De la démonomanie*, 20.

77 Ibid., 224.

78 Bodin is indebted here to Thomas Erastus, who in response to Weyer insisted that witches were criminal not only because they brought harm to others, "but because they learned and professed the diabolical art against God's command." Although Erastus did not deny that the crimes of witches were sometimes a matter of wishful thinking, he insisted on the criminality of the pact itself: "God did not command us to put to death those people for the evil that they may have done had they been able to act on their wishes, but because they learned illicit arts and associated themselves with the Devil" (766, 767).

79 Bodin, *De la démonomanie*, 20. Bodin distinguishes the purposeful pact of the witch from the "tacit or implicit" idolatry that ensues when Satan tricks people into worshiping him under the guise of other gods. "It is not surprising that the people of the Western

the days when husbands could lawfully kill their adulterous wives, Bodin asserts in *De la démonomanie* that, "even if a witch hasn't worked her evil against men or beasts, she still deserves to be burned alive for having renounced God and struck a deal with Satan."[80]

There is simply no place in Bodin's moral universe for occult knowledge in women that is not morally transgressive. So much is clear in his rebuttal of Weyer's claim that women were naturally melancholic and, hence, more prone to falling prey to devilish manipulation. Bodin's personal religion excluded the fall from grace as well as the corollary of redemptive salvation at the hands of Christ. He was a staunch supporter of free will against astrology and endorsed humoral determinism in tepid terms: "It is true that people's minds and morals often follow their humors, as Galen says ... but that is not necessary." He gives as an example the tranquility of the Saturnine melancholic:

> And thus when we read that the holy tongue (by which Adam, as it is written in Genesis, named all things according to their natural properties) called Saturn ..., that is to say "rested" and "tranquil" for the natural inclination of those who have Saturn as the master of their horoscope, who are ordinarily melancholic, rested, and contemplative ... so all of that implies an inclination, but without necessity.[81]

Bodin's association of Saturn and melancholy shows his familiarity with a tradition quite different from the medieval *balneum diaboli* trope that Weyer could have gleaned in the works of the renowned Chancellor of the University of Paris, Jean Gerson (1363–1429).[82] Bodin is alluding here to Ficino, the Florentine humanist

---

hemisphere were bewitched by Satan under the veil of prayers, fasts, sacrifices, processions, and prophecies: because the people of Palestine, of Greece, and of Italy had a religion no different and nothing greater" (42, 16). In this light, Platonists were idolaters: "God seems to have expressly outlawed that we approach his *autel* by degree, but that we come directly to him. Which is what the Platonists failed to understand, who wanted through the means of inferior daemons and half Gods attract the superior gods and finally the sovereign God.... The Platonists and other pagans who by the simplicity of their conscience, and out of ignorance, adored and prayed to Jupiter ... lived very piously, but as idolaters, not as sorcerers" (20).

80   Bodin, *De la démonomanie*, 241, 243. Bodin is picking up here on Kramer's discussion, in the third book of the *Malleus*, of the true nature of the witch's crime. Whereas in book one, Kramer calls the witch a heretic, in the final book on the prosecution of witchcraft, he says that witches are actually not heretics but apostates. The difference, Kramer explains, is that heresy involves "an error in faith," such as denying that the Eucharist is the body of Christ, while an apostate is someone who abjures the faith; abjuration, Kramer notes, "is the essential principles of witches." The stakes of this technical distinction—that appears too late in the treatise not to seem opportunistic—are not trivial; "a heretic is different from an apostate, and it is heretics who are subject to the Court of the Inquisition; therefore witches are not so subject" (195). In defining the witch as an apostate, Kramer places her beyond the authority of the institution he represents; her crimes must be brought to a secular court. In contrast to witchcraft theorists, the Parlement of Paris focused its attention on *maleficia* (the witch's evil deeds against the community--poisoning livestock, thwarting fertility).

81   Bodin, *De la démonomanie*, 34.

82   On Gerson, witches, and melancholy, see Wirth, 33.

and self-diagnosed melancholic, who integrated Plato's theory of divinely inspired furor into Aristotelian melancholy.[83] In his *Problemata*, Aristotle established the melancholic temperament as the physiological commonality of exceptional men: "[W]hy is it," he asks tautologically at the outset, "that all men who are outstanding in philosophy, poetry or the arts are melancholic?"[84] Identifying melancholy as a celestial gift from Mercury, "who invites us to investigate doctrines," and from Saturn, "who makes us persevere in investigating doctrines and retain them when discovered," Ficino somewhat paradoxically characterized melancholy as the shared bodily trait of men prone to transcending the body in a fit of enthusiasm:

> From this [confluence of melancholy with Mercury and Saturn] come original philosophers, especially when their soul, hereby called away from external movements and from its own body, is made in the highest degree both a neighbor to the divine and an instrument to the divine. As a result, it is filled from above with divine influences and oracles, and it always invents new and unaccustomed things and predicts the future.[85]

In her elegant book, *The Gendering of Melancholia: Feminism, Psychoanalysis, and the Symbolics of Loss in Renaissance Literature,* Juliana Schiesari explains that "Ficino not only turned melancholia into an inscription of something extraordinary for men but, more specifically, he made the Saturnine man—the melancholic man—an emblem of the mentally creative man, more specifically of the *literarum studios*[*us*].... What is underscored in Ficino, then, is ... the way the melancholic is poised for the quest for truth."[86]

Ficino's melancholic genius was received with some caution in France. The poets of the Pléiade—among whom numbered Jacques Grévin, the first to translate *De praestigiis daemonum* into French—took care to separate the divine inspiration

---

83   Ficino corrects Plato's view that madness inspires poetry, saying that "even if he perhaps intends divine madness to be understood here, nevertheless, according to the physicians, madness of this kind is never incited in anyone else but melancholics." Marsilio Ficino, *Three Books on Life*, ed. and trans. Carol V. Kaske and John R. Clark (Binghamptom: Medieval and Renaissance Texts and Studies, 1989), 117. Ficino characterized melancholy as the physiological cause (rather than consequence) of greatness. This inversion happens within the text of *De vita* itself. While Chapter Four of Book One is entitled "How many things cause learned people either to be melancholy or to eventually become so," Chapter Six reads: "How black bile makes people intelligent" (113, 121).

84   Pseudo-Aristotle's "Problem XXX, 1" appears under the rubric of "Problems devoted to thought, intelligence, and wisdom." [Pseudo-]Aristotle, *Problems*, trans. W.S. Hett, eds. T.E. Page, E. Capps, and W.H.D Rouse, vol. 2 (Cambridge: Harvard U.P., 1937), 155. Aristotle clearly means "men" in a fully gendered sense, since he establishes a correspondence between melancholy and male sexuality. He explains that "the melancholic are usually lustful" because melancholy "is due to breath," and breath, or wind, is what swells the penis into erection: "The penis proves this, as it quickly increases from small to large because of the breath" (159–61).

85   Ficino, 123.

86   Juliana Schiesari, *The Gendering of Melancholia: Feminism, Psychoanalysis, and the Symbolics of Loss in Renaissance Literature* (Ithaca: Cornell U.P., 1992), 114–15.

to which they laid claim from melancholic madness.[87] Pontus de Tyard (1521–1605), a theoretician of Pléiade poetics, engages in a prolonged didactic distinction between madness that requires medical attention and divinely inspired furor in his *Solitaire premier ou Discours des Muses, et de la fureur Poëtique* (1552).[88] Another cause for ambivalence, which Weyer's psychologization of witchcraft also exacerbated, was the renewed relevance of the medieval critique of melancholy as a *balneum diaboli* as the Pléiade poets followed Henri III's lead in espousing Counter-Reformation piety. As theories of inspiration became more overtly religious, old concerns surfaced regarding the discernment of spirits. The more models of mystical meditation informed Pléiade aesthetics, the more the Devil's bath appeared as a tricky rival to divine inspiration.[89]

The Pléiade's brightest luminary consistently characterized himself as a melancholic *malgré lui*. In his "Discours à P. L'Escot," Pierre de Ronsard (1524–85) describes himself as being

> Maigre, palle, desfait, enclos en la prison
> D'une melancholique & rheumatique estude,
> Renfrogné, mal-courtois, sombre, pensif, & rude,[90]

> [Skinny, pale, unkempt, enclosed in the prison
> Of a melancholic and rheumatic studiousness
> Sullen, discourteous, somber, pensive, and rude,]

while in an elegy to Jacques Grévin (1561), written before his falling out with the Calvinist poet, he brushes a scowling self-portrait:

> Je suis opiniastre, indiscret, fantastique,
> Farouche, soupçonneux, triste & melancolicque
> Content & non content, mal propre & mal courtois.[91]

> [I am stubborn, indiscrete, fantastical
> Savage, suspicious, sad and melancholic
> Happy and unhappy, improper and discourteous.]

---

87   Guy le Fèvre de la Boderie translated Ficino's *De vita libri tres* (1489) into French in 1581. For the reception of Ficino in France, see Jean Festugière, *La philosophie d'amour de Marsile Ficin et son influence sur la littérature française au XVIe siècle* (Paris: Vrin, 1941).

88   Pontus de Tyard, *Solitaire Premier ou discours des Muses et de la fureur poétique*, ed. Silvio F. Baridon (Geneva: Librairie Droz, 1950), 6.

89   Noel L. Brann, "Melancholy and the Divine Frenzies in the French Pléiade: Their Conflicting Roles in the Art of *beaux exercices spirituels*," *Journal of Medieval and Renaissance Studies* 9 (1979): 81–100. See also Olivier Pot, *Inspiration et mélancolie: l'épistémologie poétique dans les Amours de Ronsard* (Genève: Droz, 1990) on Ronsard's ambivalence toward melancholy.

90   Pierre de Ronsard, *Oeuvres complètes*, eds. Jean Céard, Daniel Ménager, and Michel Simonin (Paris: Gallimard, 1993), II: 793, v. 12–14.

91   Ronsard, II: 1112, v. 51–3. Grévin's bitter dispute with Ronsard, Charles IX's most Catholic bard, precipitated his flight to England in 1567. See Lucien Pinvert, *Jacques Grévin (1538–1570): étude biographique et littéraire* (Paris: Albert Fontemoing, 1899).

Discourtesy notwithstanding, the melancholic poet serves as a conduit for the divine—as an "oracle," as Du Perron puts it in his 1585 funeral oration for Ronsard—and derives from his mediatory function a luster of his own: "[I]t did not seem that it was a mortal voice that spoke, but some divinity that made use of his mouth to express his oracles."[92]

Bodin relativized the influence of the humors, manifesting stoic confidence in the power of the will. Yet despite his own ambivalence regarding humoral theory and despite the ambivalent reception of Ficinian melancholy in France, he objected vehemently to Weyer's argument that women mistaken for witches were merely melancholic. The genial condition, Bodin remarks, "behooves [women] as little as the praiseworthy effects of the temperate melancholy humor, that makes man wise, composed, contemplative … these are qualities as compatible with women as fire with water." He claims that "Weyer greatly abused himself in his medical art when he speaks of the melancholy of women." Bodin's interpretation is, in fact, more consistent with Galenic humoral theory than Weyer's vague etiology. When Bodin suggests that the genial effects of the melancholic condition are "as compatible with women as fire with water," he is contrasting the burned blood of the atrabilious madman to the moist and flegmatic female complexion. The kind of melancholy that according to Galen leads to violent madness, and the one that could most convincingly account in Weyer's formula for the behavior of witches, "[proceeds] from excessive heat and dryness as Galen says in *De atra bile*. Now, women are naturally cold and humid, as Galen says, and all the Greeks, Latins, and Arabs agree on this point."[93] Bodin protested that women could not suffer from melancholy, for this was a condition propitious to prophecy, a gift only appropriate to men. Weyer, an ill-informed expert of some of the more subtle points of humoral thermodynamics, characterized the female sex as a whole as temperamentally suited to ignorance. Bodin at least envisioned an exception. Constitutionally incapable of the virtue that led to the gift of prophecy, women, however, could achieve knowledge of the occult in one way: by trading favors with the Devil.[94]

Bodin does not seem to have identified himself as a sufferer of Saturnine tranquility. Through his claim to prophecy, however, he did share with Ronsard the pretense to exclusive access of occult knowledge through allegorical hermeneutics. Ronsard recounts his poetical formation in terms of an apprenticeship to disguise:

> … et de là je vins estre
> Disciple de Dorat, qui long temps fut mon maistre,
> M'apprist la Poësie, et me montra comment
> On doit feindre et cacher les fables proprement,

---

92 Du Perron, *Oraison funebre sur la mort de Monsieur de Ronsard*, in Ronsard, *Oeuvres* (Paris: 1600), 1177, cited in Brann, 86.

93 Bodin, *De la démonomanie*, 226–7. And again, "Weyer is a doctor; he cannot ignore that the humor of woman is directly contrary to adust melancholy, whence proceeds furor" 226.

94 Houdard shows that Bodin demonizes and sexualizes the Pythia, priestess at Delphi, allying her with the witch. A false virgin whose "oracles" derive from demonic infusion via the vaginal orifice, rather than from divine inspiration through immaterial dreams or visions, she makes a mockery of the virtue and purity of the (male) prophet (81).

Et bien desguiser la verité des choses
D'un fabuleux manteau dont elles sont encloses. [95]

[...and from there I became
The disciple of Dorat, who was long my master,
He taught me poetry and showed me how
to feign and hide fables properly
and to disguise the truth of things
with a fabulous mantle in which they are enclosed.]

Whereas Weyer declared the search for truth open to anyone, Bodin describes the search for truth as an arduous quest that confers upon the successful truth-seeker an uncommon aura. This conclusion is what Ann Blair calls the "traditional protreptic function" of allegory, which she traces to Augustine; allegory serves to "valoriz[e] the truth and its divine source by making it difficult of access and reminding us of the weakness of human reason."[96] One should "not stop at the literal meaning," Bodin opines, "since it is true what is said in scripture, *litera occidit spiritus autem vivificat.*"[97] Truth must be merited, and those who attain it demonstrate moral as well as intellectual superiority. Sophie Houdard eloquently emphasizes the exclusive character of Bodin's search for truth: "He falls in with Origen and Augustine to affirm that the double universe or double book, composed by natural and biblical enigmas, should not offer the *sacra mysteria* to the 'vulgar' or to lazy negligents and that the difficulty, the obscurity that envelops them are there to encourage the most learned in the work of interpretation." For this reason, "the 'true intelligence' of things cannot correspond to a literal apprehension of figures; buried beyond the letter, it [the figure] provides access to knowledge, open only to the wise and the experts." Houdard underscores the similarity between the intellectual elitism common to Bodin and to self-proclaimed "magicians" such as Weyer's mentor Heinrich Cornelius Agrippa von Nettesheim whose "impiety" Bodin deplored: "All those who devote themselves to the study of Hebrew, to the Kabbala, but also to the secrets of nature, define themselves as the aristocrats of knowledge."[98] Agrippa and his friends taught that "even the Gospel, like the Mosaic Law, has one meaning on the surface for the more simple, another in its core, which has been separately revealed to the perfect."[99] Bodin despised Agrippa for seeking practical applications (such as the transmutation of ordinary metals into gold) for occult knowledge, and he was not the only one to associate Agrippa's self-serving magic with devilish

---

95   Pierre de Ronsard, "Hynne de l'autonne," in *Œuvres Complètes*, II: 561.

96   Blair, 113. Ronsard presents a very different view of allegory in his "Abbregé de l'Art poetique françoys": "la Poésie n'estoit au premier âge qu'une Théologie allégoricque, pour faire entrer au cerveau des hommes grossiers par fables plaisantes et colorées les secrets qu'ils ne pouvoient comprendre, quand trop ouvertement on descouvrait la vérité" (II: 1175). Here allegory expands access to the truth whereas transparency diminishes it.

97   Bodin, *De la démonomanie*, 64.

98   Houdard, 68.

99   Agrippa, *De triplici ratione cognoscendi Deum*, Chapter Five, cited by Charles Nauert, *Agrippa and the Crisis of Renaissance Thought* (Urbana: University of Illinois Press, 1965), 46.

deals, as the legend of Faust attests. But Bodin's pretense to prophecy led some of his contemporaries to view him with the same suspicions with which he regarded Agrippa. Jacques Auguste de Thou, the son of Bodin's illustrious dedicatee, related that the League preacher, Antoine le Tolosain, set the people of Laon against Bodin, in whose house, he claimed, one was sure to find "censored books," including "books of magic" and sorcery.[100]

Bodin's contemporaries suspected him of Judaism as well as of magic. Pierre Bayle (1647–1706) summed up a century of rumors in his *Dictionnaire historique et critique* (1695–97) when he claimed that the jurist had subscribed to an "amphibian religion" and died a Jew.[101] Such rumors were assuredly closer to the mark than those that made Bodin into a magus, to the extent that the jurist's admiration for the ancient Hebrews is obvious in nearly all of his works.[102] Yet Bodin's reverence for Jewish authors such as Philo Judaeus requires explanation insofar as his claim that literal interpretation kills the spirit of the letter—which he takes from Paul—was in the Renaissance often directed against Jews.[103] Christian complaints about Jewish literalism targeted the failure of the Jews (or of any "judaizing" reader or translator) to decipher allusions to the coming of Christ in the Old Testament. To accuse one's opponent of "judaizing"—and the accusation was common in a time of Biblical scholarship and theological controversy—was either to target rabbinical exegesis that "perverted" the Christological spirit of the Word (this was Luther's view) or to decry the reverence of Christ through "visible things," which amounted to a "new Judaism" reminiscent of the carnal and material preoccupations that characterized Mosaic Law (this was the position of Erasmus).[104] Law, of course, was another field of competing hermeneutics; in this context, too, literal interpretation was disparaged as Jewish. Bodin's fellow jurist, Bartholomaeus Caepolla (c. 1420–77), remarks, "Those who read texts literally and not according to their [true] meaning are said to understand in a Jewish manner, as the Jews understand the Old Testament ... for the Jews refuse to depart from the literal meaning."[105]

---

100 Cited in François Berriot, "Introduction," Jean Bodin, *Colloque entre sept scavans qui sont de differens sentimens des secrets cachez des choses relevees*, trans. anonymous (1923), ed. François Berriot (Genève: Droz, 1984), xx.

101 Bayle, cited in *Les Oeuvres philosophiques de Jean Bodin*, ed. Pierre Mesnard, xxxii. Pierre-Daniel Huet claims (incorrectly) that Bodin was raised by a Jewish mother who taught him Mosaic law. See Mesnard, xi.

102 Judaism for Bodin was more of an ideal than a practicable religion. As the first monotheistic religion, it boasted the prestige and purity of origins. Bodin saw Judaism as the common substratum between warring Protestants and Catholics, and he gleaned from enigmatic Hebrew writings transcendent *sapience*.

103 Blair, 112.

104 Ilona N. Rashkow, "Hebrew Bible Translation and the Fear of Judaization," *Sixteenth Century Journal* 21: 2 (1990), 217–33, 220; Shimon Markish, *Erasmus and the Jews*, trans. Anthony Olcott (Chicago: The University of Chicago Press, 1986), 9.

105 Bartholomaeus Caepolla (Cipolla), *De verborum et rerum significatione doctissima commentaria* (1460–64), cited in MacLean, 142. An edition of Caepolla's work was published in Lyon in 1551.

If Bodin's contemporaries suspected him of Judaism, it was not because he engaged in literal interpretation. Quite the contrary, literalism describes his opponent's approach to witchcraft. As I showed in Chapter One, Weyer denied phenomena that were imperceptible or inaccessible to common sense. Bodin's reputation for judaizing resulted instead from an exegetical practice from which Christ is entirely absent. As Origen explained it, alongside the written law that Moses carried down the mountain, came God's oracles by word of mouth—the Kabbala.[106] Moses was both the purveyor of God's law and the depositary of a secret *sapience*. He was the only one, Bodin points out, to have reached the top rung of the ladder of prophetic knowledge, an image he borrows from Moses Maimonides (1135–1204), the heir of a long line of Talmudic experts. This ladder comprises eleven rungs of human-divine colloquy, all of them mediated through dreams, visions, an so forth, except for the top one, which entails face-to-face dialogue with God. Whereas Weyer proposes the straightforwardness of Moses' conversation with God as a standard for eyewitness evidence, Bodin interprets Moses' mediation between God and His people as an allegory of allegory:

> Moses, having descended the mountain, where he stayed forty days and as many nights, put a veil on his face, to speak to the people: and when he returned to speak with God, he took off his veil, because the people could not look upon his face it was so luminous: that is to say, besides the literal meaning, they could not understand the secrets and allegories carried in several places in the law of God.

The secrets and allegories of the law of God would be reserved ever after for worthy hermeneuts. Bodin defines Kabbala as "knowledge [*sapience*] received from God, by means of his Angels and prophets by word of mouth." He explains that this knowledge "does not reside in characters or figures ... but rather in the secret intelligence of the marvels of God, covered with allegories in scripture."[107]

Bodin's important role in legal reform also contributed to his eschewing of literal interpretation. Indeed, Bodin's legal hermeneutics, which he developed in the *Juris universi distributio* (published by Jacques DuPuys in 1578, probably from a much earlier manuscript),[108] provide an especially instructive parallel to the allegorical orientation of the latter. Bodin participated in a new approach to Roman law known as *mos gallicus*, begun by Andrea Alciati (1492–1550), an Italian disciple of Guillaume Budé (1467–1540) working at the University of Bourges in the late 1520s. The practitioners of *mos gallicus* emphasized that Roman law, as collated and glossed in the Justinian code, belonged to the particular historical and political context from which it had originated, and that it need not be accepted as universally true, as the traditional *mos italicus* taught. As French lawyers relativized the authority of the "torn and scattered limbs of Roman law" through a more contextual study of law, it became possible, even logical, to conclude that right and wrong were culturally contingent categories.[109] Bodin countered the threat of relativism in the *Juris universi*

106 François Secret, *Les Kabbalistes chrétiens de la Renaissance* (Paris: Dunod, 1984), 3.
107 Bodin, *De la démonomanie*, 64, 63.
108 Blair, 10.
109 Bodin, *Juris universi distributio*, cited in MacLean, 27.

distributio by locating the meaning of the law neither in the text that expounded it (*ratio legis*) nor in the intentions of the author that codified it (*mens legislatoris*). Instead, "right reason" established truth by drawing out the universal commonalities behind the great diversity of human laws.[110] According to Julian Franklin, Bodin's *Juris universi distributio* marked "the moment of transition, in juristic method, from the exegesis of authority to a universal basis of critical reflection."[111] "Right reason" and "critical reflection" may seem at the antipodes of allegoresis, but for Bodin they are one and the same. Both involve the Platonic gesture of delving beyond the surface of words to attain some deeper meaning. As Houdard puts it, "Bodin's entire corpus is traversed by the will to see past the casings of things, to get through its thickness to uncover the truth and to reveal the universal principles that lie behind them."[112]

Biblical and legal hermeneutics—the prophet and the judge—converge in Bodin's interpretation of juridical confessions. The judge's method, centered on the extraction and interpretation of confession, epitomizes Bodin's hermeneutical inquiry. So central is confession to Bodin's conception of knowledge that it is as if he imagines Weyer before him in the court of law already being tried for witchcraft: "Moreover it should be noted that Weyer *confessed* that he was the disciple of Agrippa, the greatest sorcerer of his time, and not only was he his disciple, but also his valet and servant, drinking, eating, and sleeping with him after Agrippa had repudiated his wife, as he *confesses*."[113] Bodin charges Weyer with two heresies, without identifying them as such: sorcery and sodomy. Interesting, however, the jurist does not attack the doctor for a third and more obvious heresy; he never mentions Weyer's Lutheranism. All through the 1570s, Juan de Maldonado (1534–83) branded Protestant heretics as demon-worshippers in lectures at the Jesuits' new Collège de Clermont in Paris and in popular Sunday sermons delivered in simplified Latin.[114] The association of the witch-heretic and the Huguenot-heretic was standard by 1580 in Catholic demonology. We saw in Chapter One that *De praestigiis daemonum* had been promoted in France as a piece of Protestant polemic, beginning with Grévin's translation, and censored as such as well. To the extent that Bodin acknowledged his avoidance of the religion question in *La Démonomanie*, quite likely he ignored Weyer's Lutheran polemics deliberately.[115] It is, therefore, doubly interesting that no demonologist should find Weyer's Lutheran literalism more irksome than Jean Bodin.

Bodin singles out with particular annoyance an anecdote in which Weyer "mocks a witch whom Satan ordered to keep his old shoes, as a preservative and counter-charm against other Sorcerers." (I have not located Weyer's version of the story.) For

---

110 MacLean, 61.

111 Franklin, 79.

112 Houdard.

113 Bodin, 240.

114 Jonathan L. Pearl, *The Crime of Crimes: Demonology and Politics in France, 1560-1620* (Waterloo: Wilfrid Laurier U.P., 1998), 68–9.

115 "I don't want to enter into a discussion of the merits of the Religion [i.e., Catholicism], that so many Theologians have amply treated, nor is it my subject here." Bodin, *De la démonomanie*, 245.

Bodin, Weyer's interpretation exemplifies the physician's perverse blindness to the supernatural side of things. According to Bodin, Weyer's evidently flat-footed gloss on the preservation of old shoes misses the point entirely:

> I say that this advice from Satan has a double meaning. The shoes symbolize sins, as shoes are always dragging in filth. And when God told Moses and Joshua 'take off your shoes[;] this place is pure and holy,' he meant, as Philo the Jew says, that we have to cleanse our souls of sin in order to contemplate and worship God. But to converse with Satan, one must be soiled by and mired in perpetual impiety and evil; [those are the conditions under which] Satan assists his faithful servants.[116]

Bodin's reading of Satan's footwear advice nicely illustrates the reversibility of divine and demonic order; for Bodin, belief in the demonic is congruent with a belief in God. On his interpretation, Weyer's refusal to find meaning in Satan's counsel is impious, because if one were to turn the literalist lens the other way, one would read God's request for footwear removal simply as a provident initiative to facilitate holy housekeeping. The failure to interpret is not just a missed opportunity; it is a refusal to read, to see the light. It can lead to grievous consequences: "It has happened that these good literal interpreters, who taking literally the serpent who talks in Genesis, go around saying that animals used to talk back then, have made a million atheists."[117] The "A" word again: the physician who explains demonic effects through natural causes and the "good literal interpreter" who goes no further in his reflection than the words on the page are guilty of the same crimes; both deny the divine, encourage atheism, and offer cover for witches. Allegorical interpretation, on the other hand, allows one to go deeper, to go further, to go beyond the surface without subordinating God's law to nature's habits.

The message that Bodin extracts from his sources is generally uniform. Even witches, when understood correctly, can teach us about properly God-fearing behavior. Because the message is so consistent, the diversity of the "texts" that Bodin interprets hardly registers with the reader. Bodin reads a witch's confession in the same way that he reads the Bible. For him, this makes perfect sense because of the witch's symmetrical correspondence to the prophet; she is Satan's prophet, as it were, and prophets are privy to knowledge of the occult, which is by definition enigmatic. Moreover, most of the confessions in *De la démonomanie,* with the exception of Harvillier's, do come to Bodin in textual form; they have been recorded; in the case of the confession concerning old shoes, they already have been glossed by other commentators. Because of Bodin's bookish approach to the confessions of witchcraft suspects, it is easy to lose sight while reading *De la démonomanie* of the fact that Weyer decries so vividly in *De praestigiis daemonum*: these confessions are, for the most part, the fruit of torture.

Weyer claimed that torture destroyed in the mind of the suspect any sense of distinction between memory and imagination, those two faculties that Albertus Magnus had housed in separate ventricles of the brain. Whereas the memory stored images or *species*, the imagination combined these *species* at will to create chimeras

---

116 Bodin, *De la démonomanie,* 248.
117 Bodin, *De la démonomanie,* 65.

that had never existed. According to Weyer, witchcraft suspects were asked to remember, and having nothing to remember, imagined. Weyer denounces torture for exactly the opposite reason that Elaine Scarry denounces it. According to Scarry, torture destroys language; according to Weyer, torture inspires creative (m)ad-libbing.[118] Jody Enders has established that torture was often likened in ancient times to the aesthetic process of invention, *invenire* meaning to find or discover.[119] Weyer evokes rather the more colloquial meaning of invention: truth, in being invented through torture, was not found but made up. As we have seen, there were precedents for arguments against torture. In ancient Greece, it was illegal to torture Athenian citizens, but it was standard procedure to torture slaves, the vulnerable appendages (collateral?) of the untouchable citizen. Indeed, a slave's testimony was *only* valid under torture, for the Greeks took it for granted that only the rack, the whip, or the wheel could enfranchise the tongue of a slave otherwise bonded by his or her loyalty to the master. By the second century, however, it had become conventional for the defendant's party to point out the fallibility of torture as a truth-finding method, even if Quintilian in his *Institutio oratoria* seems to view this argument as a mark of bad faith.[120] Despite such precedents, Weyer's denunciation of torture was bound to look naïve and even cavalier to many contemporary readers. Confession was the centerpiece of early modern criminal procedure; it confirmed other evidence or presumptions and offered definitive proof of the criminal's guilt. As Edward Peters puts it, "Confession, queen of proof, required torture, queen of torments."[121] Dismissing the provisions made for torture in the Holy Roman Emperor's Caroline Code (1532), Weyer dismissed even voluntary confessions of witchcraft as madness all the while accepting at face value suspects' equally spontaneous denials of witchcraft (such as the old woman from Berg), ignoring the obvious motive that a witch facing imminent death would have for lying.

Yet Bodin's advocacy in favor of expanding the use of torture in the fourth book of *De la démonomanie* was also extreme for its time and place. More than a third of the witchcraft suspects in the cases studied by Soman were not tortured at all. Of those who were tortured, less than one per cent confessed to the crime. Evidently, the judges of the Parlement of Paris did not expect to obtain confessions because they wrote their sentences up even before applying torture. The Paris magistracy, moreover, seems to have regarded the rare fruits of torture with some skepticism. The 1498 Ordinance of Blois stipulates that a suspect could not be tortured twice for the same crime if no further evidence had come to light; the ordinance of Villers-Cotterets (1539) contains similar limitations.[122] Bodin, on the other hand, insisted that witchcraft was an extraordinary crime, to which judges should be able to apply

---

118 Elaine Scarry, *The Body in Pain* (Oxford: Oxford U.P., 1985).

119 Jody Enders, *The Medieval Theater of Cruelty: Rhetoric, Memory, Violence* (Ithaca: Cornell U.P., 1999), 32.

120 See Edward Peters, *Torture* (Philadelphia: University of Pennsylvania Press, 1996), 21.

121 Ibid., 69. Peters reproduces parts of the Caroline Code that are relevant to torture in the appendix to his book, 238–50. For a comparison of the Caroline Code to the Ordinance of Villers-Cotterets with respect to torture, see John H. Langbein, *Prosecuting Crime in the Renaissance* (Cambridge: Harvard U.P., 1974), 17–81 and 239–41.

122 Soman, 40–41.

extraordinary measures. Bodin viewed the crime of witchcraft as so heinous—and so tricky to prosecute—that he held exceptions to normal judicial procedure to be licit, even necessary. He argued that rumor should be considered legitimate evidence and that the testimony of children and women should count as much as that of men (two women's testimony usually counted for that of one man).[123] As for confession, the best kind was, of course, freely given, such as Harvillier's avowal "sans question ni torture." Yet if no confession was forthcoming, the judge was to press for a confession from the suspect "by any means necessary"—through the threat or actual application of torture, usually to the suspect herself, but in some cases to her young daughter, whose "tender age" would make it easy for the judge to persuade her to testify against her obdurate mother (Bodin insists that daughters are often their mothers' apprentices).[124]

Virginia Krause reveals that the rationale behind witchcraft prosecution was as tortuous as the double negative "witchcraft cannot not be true" that underlies its metaphysical motives. Bodin acknowledged that witchcraft was a difficult crime to prove, but never did it appear to him that this was because the crime had not taken place. Instead, witchcraft was difficult to prove because it was the trickiest of crimes. "Satan and witches play their mysteries at night, ... the marks of witches are hidden and covered, ... the sense of sight cannot easily lead its inquisition *au doigt et à l'oeil*, and proof is difficult."[125] Moreover, once the trial is under way, the witch had at her disposal a host of demons to assist her in covering her evil and inuring her to pain. Already the authors of the *Malleus Maleficarum* had alleged a "spell of silence" by which Satan could make his associates invincible to torture. Erastus, too, related that witches cognizant of the risks they run, "hide their evil, and deny it so stubbornly, that even torture cannot pull a single word of truth from their mouths, while they still have strength to endure interrogation."[126] Without citing a single source, Bodin declares, "All agree that witches carry drugs for the purposes of taciturnity, even if it is really the Devil who comforts and assures them."[127] Neither denial nor silence was a viable alternative to confession for the accused in witchcraft cases. To the contrary, explains Krause, "a silent or otherwise resistant person is even *more* guilty than a defendant who confesses easily."[128] Bodin, who seemed to view his mission as the confirmation of the witch's known guilt rather than to find out whether the suspect was, in fact, guilty, thoroughly blurred the line—already a fine one in early modern criminal procedure—between torture that leads to confession and punishment that ensues from that confession. Resisting the judge's questions merely confirmed that the suspect was worthy of punishment. Why, then, should the judge spare her from more torture?

We have seen that Bodin sets the ratio of female to male witches at fifty to one. We have also seen that these statistics rest not on practice but on theory, a theory that

---

123 Bodin, *De la démonomanie*, 177.
124 Ibid., 169.
125 Ibid., 166.
126 Erastus, 776–7.
127 Bodin, *De la démonomanie*, 170.
128 Krause, 333.

in Bodin's case is as political as it is moral. The witch is to God what the adulterous wife is to the sovereign; both commit treason by undermining the very basis of order, the wife's obedience to the husband's command. But even the most systematic of theories needs to be made plausible. As the vicious Vicomte de Valmont advises his imminent victim/pleasure partner Cécile Volanges in Choderlos de Laclos's novel, *Les Liaisons dangereuses* (1782), "verisimilitude is in the details [Ce sont les petits détails qui donnent la vraisemblance]."[129] Joking that verisimilitude in the *Malleus maleficarum* is a matter of "*viri*similitude," Stephens has shown that Kramer added the now infamous litany of women's vices (Part I, Question 6) as an afterthought. The inquisitor realized that he needed to establish women's motives for consorting corporeally with Satan, and he did not have to look further than the misogynistic commonplaces of medieval culture: "[A]ll witchcraft comes from carnal lust, which is in women insatiable."[130] Bodin, too, enhances the plausibility of the divine plot that he purports to uncover in *De la démonomanie* through a character sketch. Even though the jurist was reticent about ascribing temperaments that would curtail free will, he had no scruples about deterministically linking women's bodies, and in particular their "bestial cupidity," to moral traits, above all, to their "undeniable obstinacy."[131] Whereas Kramer linked women's lasciviousness to their "slippery tongues," Bodin insists that women are stubborn, and they are stubborn in keeping secrets.[132] In effect, while Kramer (and Weyer) emphasize women's weakness, Bodin objects that women "are often more stalwart [*constantes*] to withstand la *question* than men, as was shown during Nero's conspiracy, and after the death of Hippias the tyrant of Athens, when women cut out their tongues to thwart any hope of extracting truth [from them]."[133]

Nero's tyrannical ways were sufficiently familiar in the Middle Ages that a legend accrued around him: he had had his mother's womb cut open to see from whence he came. Renaissance humanists knew Nero's story not by legend, but from Publius Cornelius Tacitus (c. 55–120), the great chronicler of Roman history. Tacitus recounts Nero's gratuitous (because unsuccessful) torment of the freed slave Epicharis, who was also a woman:

> [A]ssuming that female flesh and blood must be unequal to the pain, he ordered her to be racked. But neither the lash nor the fire, nor yet the anger of the torturers, who redoubled

---

129 Choderlos de Laclos, *Les Liaisons dangereuses* (Paris: Gallimard, 2003), 230.

130 Stephens, 42, 48; Kramer, 47.

131 Bodin, *De la démonomanie,* 225.

132 Kramer, 44. The association between smoldering sexuality and stubborn secrecy predates *De la démonomanie* of course; it even predates Albertus Magnus' *De Secretis mulierum*. Although it was the slave in ancient Greece whose pain served to guarantee truth and to reinforce "the dominant notion of the Greeks that truth was an inaccessible, buried secret," Page DuBois in *Torture and Truth* (New York and London: Routledge, 1991), argues that another Other was crucial to the construction of buried truth. This was the maternal body, the figurative womb and tomb into which Odysseus descended in his journey to the underworld. It was the body of the Pythia, priestess at Delphi, who contaminated the purity of Apollo's oracles through her corporeality, making truth enigmatic and undecipherable (78–9, 85).

133 Bodin, *De la démonomanie*, 225.

their efforts rather than be braved by a woman, broke down her denial of the allegations. Thus the first day of torment had been defied. On the next, as she was being dragged back in a chair to a repetition of the agony—her dislocated limbs were unable to support her—she fastened the breast-band (which she had stripped from her bosom) in a sort of noose to the canopy of the chair, thrust her neck into it, and throwing the weight of her body into the effort, squeezed out such feeble breath as remained to her.

Tacitus goes on to drive home the moral of the story: an emancipated slave and a woman shielded her compatriots through her silence and thus set a shining example to cowardly freeborn men who betrayed their accomplices behind their backs.[134] This patriotic forbearance would make Epicharis a popular figure among the neo-stoic authors whom we shall meet in the next chapter. But Bodin's point is different. He identifies with the torturers who "redoubled their efforts rather than be braved by a woman," except that where Nero's torturers torment an upstanding patriot in order to perpetuate tyranny, Bodin's judge tortures the witch for the greater glory of God. Bodin's God, in such instances, resembles a tyrant.

Torture, in *De la démonomanie*, is not the (dirty) secret means through which the judge corroborates his demonic fantasms. Torture is the organizing metaphor of Bodin's epistemology. In the Vesalian tradition of Galenic observationalism, Weyer presented common sense as the standard of truth, as I argued in my first chapter. Bodin, more heavily indebted to Aristotle than he admits, puts the onus of truth-finding on reason. After his skeptical deconstruction of various epistemologies, Bodin circles back to one of them, opining, "We must fall in with the opinion of Theophrastus, who has recourse to common sense, which mediates between the senses and the intellect, and reports what we have seen, heard, tasted, and felt to reason, as to a touchstone."[135] Like many of his contemporaries, Bodin looked to Theophrastus for a sensible middle ground between Weyer's naïve celebration of common sense and Agrippa's nihilistic mockery of the uncertainty and insufficiency of sense perception. Theophrastus did not deny that the senses were sometimes deceived, by illness for instance, but he also held that these appearances could somehow be distinguished and dismissed in favor of "better and healthier" ones, "more in accord with the reality of things."[136] Theophrastus' cautious ratification of sense experience in *De sensibus* enjoyed widespread approval among a generation drawn to empirical arguments yet familiar with skeptical ones. Bodin certainly followed Theophrastus in identifying sense experience as the principle of conviction (seeing is believing), but he also underscores reason's responsibility in adjudicating the validity of sense experience. Although common sense is the pivotal point in the cognitive sequence, Bodin emphasizes above all the scrutiny to which sense is subject. Rather than stopping at common sense, as Weyer does, he goes on to liken reason to a "touchstone."

---

134 Tacitus, *Annals*, Cited in Peters, 24.

135 Bodin, *De la démonomanie*, "Préface," [15].

136 Theophrastus, *De sensibus*, 70. To claim that the senses were not as a rule trustworthy was absurd, Theophrastus insisted. This would suggest that nature was faulty, a charge that Bodin, too, would contest, though for religious reasons, in his *Universae naturae theatrum*.

"Touchstone" had two meanings in ancient Greece. Literally, it was the object with which money-changing bankers in ancient Greece distinguished gold from worthless alloys. Like the touchstone (*basanos*), reason allows one to discriminate between "that which is right, that which is wrong, that which is true, that which is false."[137] Figuratively (and we know how much Bodin preferred the figurative over the literal), *basanos* meant torture. The torture of slaves was the touchstone of truth, allowing for the distinction of the true from the false. Because of its truth-finding properties, torture served, in turn, as a metaphor for the search for truth. The verb "basaneo" means to inquire, to research, in fine, to torture.[138] We find this metaphor as early as Thucydides' history of the Peloponnesian war (431–404 B.C.) in which he complains that people accept past traditions without "torturing" them.[139] The testimony of a witness who was not tortured was not reliable. Analogously, a tradition received "without torture" bespoke a lack of critical thinking, revealed woeful credulity. Those scholars who puzzle over Bodin's "credulity" must come to terms with his condemnation of credulity in the *Universae naturae theatrum* (1596), translated into French in 1597 by a physician named François de Fougerolles: "[I]f it is true that there are some who believe this or that because they want to, we must push them for irrefutable demonstrations and interrogate them so to speak under torture to force them to strip down to their naked faith and to acquire science which cannot coexist with … credulity."[140] Here we recognize the complete bankruptcy of medieval *fides*: to put one's confidence in something that is invisible, imperceptible, or otherwise uncertain (Bodin would say "supernatural") is mere whimsy. What is needed is *scientia*—logical proofs, empirical evidence. Through the unveiling of a vast conspiracy between female foolishness and satanic stratagems, Bodin purports to provide the evidence that *fides* lacks.

In sum, Bodin uses skepticism to *prove* that God's power is absolute and that we must obey his command. Bodin's acquisition of this science (or his exposition of this science to his reader) depends on a double application of *la question*: first, the interrogation of witchcraft suspects; second, the stripping down of their confessions and other texts to their naked meanings. So integral is torture to Bodin's hermeneutics that he is willing to create resistance where there is none for the sake of being able to claim to have seen past, to have gotten through. For it is not just witches and atheists who confess their crimes; Bodin pushes even his texts to confess what they know. Aristotle at least complies with his interrogator: angels and demons move the skies and can be moved by them, "as Aristotle *confesses*." But the obstructionist Skeptics resist until the bitter end; they "didn't even want to *confess* that they knew

---

137 Bodin, *Colloquium*, 200.

138 Page DuBois, *Torture and Truth* (London and New York: Routledge, 1991), 9–34.

139 Thucydides, *La Guerre du Péloponnèse*, trans. Jacqueline de Romilly (Paris: Belles Lettres, 1995), I, xx, 1.

140 Jean Bodin, *Universae naturae theatrum* (Lyon: Jacques Roussin, 1596), 512, cited in (and translated into French by) Busson, 542. Fougerolles translates the passage "comme en la torture, par des demonstrations, à se despouiller de leur simple croyance, pour se vestir de la cognoissance de ce qu'ils ignoroyent, et se ranger à la science, laquelle ne peut compatir avec l'opinion et credulité." *Le Théâtre de la nature universelle*, trans. François Fougerolles (Lyon: Jean Pillehotte, 1597), 738, cited in Wirth, 48.

nothing, for in *confessing* that they knew very well that they knew nothing, they would *confess* that something could be known."[141] It is perhaps to begin to read like Bodin to suspect that so much confessing hides a great deal of torturing. Roland Crahay and Marie-Thérèse Isaac, who have "interrogated" the preface of *De la démonomanie* to make it "avow" Bodin's sources, find that his alleged sources are often unrecognizable in his interpretations of them. To check Bodin's interpretations against original texts is at least possible; we can only wonder to what extent Bodin's account of Jeanne Harvillier's confession differs from the words she spoke.

From the Torture of Witches to the Inquisition of Nature

The erudite opus of Jean Bodin, which spanned historiography, economics, political science, demonology, jurisprudence, and natural philosophy, exemplifies Michel Foucault's characterization of the Renaissance as a time of plethoric erudition and philosophical paucity.[142] "There cannot be more than one truth," Bodin insists in the *Universae naturae theatrum*, and, indeed, his hermeneutical lens circled invariably back to the same truth—God's unfathomable power.[143] In his "theater of nature," Bodin insists that truth can and should be found through rational means: "[I]t is not worthy of the *physicus* to preserve by authority those things which he can teach by necessary argument, especially in these times in which everyone wants everything demonstrated to them." And again, "It is on reason, not authority, that we must base our arguments."[144] Yet Bodin's agenda has not changed since *De la démonomanie*. His spokesperson is "Mystagogue" and the general tone of the *Universae naturae theatrum* is irenic; by demonstrating "the greatness and providence of God," Bodin hopes "to restore order and to curb impiety."[145] This project is evident in the order of the book, which proceeds from things most easy to understand, to the most difficult.[146] At some point along the way, the natural philosopher will have no choice but to lift nature's veil, behind which he is sure to always find God's hand. Blair explains: "This kind of invocation of God as *explanans*—the philosophical version of a deus ex machina resolution—was considered inappropriate by philosophers in the Aristotelian vein both before and after Bodin." Bodin was doing just the opposite of what he claimed Weyer had done in *De praestigiis daemonum*. Weyer did not respect the integrity of supernatural phenomena; Bodin, in invoking divine wisdom and providence, "violates the disciplinary boundaries that called for physical explanations for physical phenomena."[147]

---

141 Bodin, *De la démonomanie*, "Préface," [16, 14].

142 Michel Foucault, *Les Mots et les choses: Une archéologie des sciences humaines* (Paris: Gallimard, 1966), 45.

143 Bodin, *Universae naturae theatrum*, cited in Horowitz, 189.

144 Blair notes that such pronouncements generally occur at points when he has already established a conclusion by authority (88).

145 Blair, 3.

146 Blair, 33.

147 Ibid.

Bodin's work was doubly hermetic: hermetic in its obsession with occult subtexts, hermetic in the airtight vision that unified it. His system resulted from an attempt to impose order on disorder (political, theological, epistemological); it was reactionary more than nostalgic. Indeed, we have seen that Bodin's fideism took the form not of a return to medieval *fides*, but of a post-skeptical imperative over which divine and civil law, joined in and embodied by the person of the prophet-magistrate, cast a menacing shadow. I will return in the fourth chapter to Montaigne's response to Bodin's opportunistic use of skepticism and to his coercive approach to persuasion. In concluding the present chapter, however, I want to emphasize the diverse reception of Bodin's hermeneutics by the reformers of science of the next generation.

The reception of Bodin's hermeneutics among French natural philosophers was ambivalent. In *La Vérité des sciences contre les sceptiques ou pyrrhoniens* (1625), Marin Mersenne's "Christian philosopher" criticizes Bodin (and a host of other natural philosophers) for disparaging Aristotle when he had nothing better to offer.[148] Mersenne, however, may have appreciated Bodin's attempt in *De la démonomanie* to gain the upper hand over "master doubters," since that is precisely what his Christian philosopher aims to do. When Descartes trumpeted the novelty of his *Meditationes de prima philosophia*, by daring to overcome doubt through doubt, he was not claiming to have *attempted* something new. He was claiming to have *succeeded* where others had failed. Bodin's use of Sextus Empiricus to stymy doubt with respect to witchcraft (and ultimately, to God's power) was superficial and rhetorical. He invoked skepticism to discredit Aristotle, then silenced the skeptics by arbitrarily declaring the inviolability of the supernatural. Skeptical arguments appeared at a particular step in Bodin's argument and once that step had served its purpose, he moved on to damage control. Virginia Krause likens Bodin's argumentation to "a house of cards" on which Montaigne would hardly have to huff and puff to blow it down.[149]

To continue Krause's metaphor, the ruined foundations that Descartes swept away in the *Discours de la méthode* were not just the last vestiges of scholasticism, but also the failed attempts of late Renaissance reformers (such as Bodin) to come up with something better. From Descartes's point of view, the weakness of Bodin's system lay precisely in his hermeneutics; only God's authority, enforced (or usurped?) by the prophet-magistrate could guarantee the truths revealed in the allegories of the Old Testament, in the secrets of nature, in the sometimes sublime, but usually disappointingly prosaic confessions of witches. Descartes banished metaphor from science, and along with it, eschewed the gender hierarchy through which Bodin naturalizes the arbitrary supernatural/natural distinction in *De la démonomanie*. In Descartes's natural philosophy, nature is not a wife, not even a woman; God is not a commanding husband, not even a man. Carolyn Merchant asserts in *The Death of Nature* that "The mechanists transformed the body of the world and its female soul, source of activity in the organic cosmos, into a mechanism of inert matter in motion." When she further suggests that "The resultant corpse was a mechanical

---

148 Marin Mersenne, *La Vérité des sciences contre les sceptiques ou pyrrhoniens* (1625), 109–10.

149 Krause, 336.

system of dead corpuscles, set into motion by the Creator," she is reading Mersenne, Gassendi, and Descartes, through the hermeneutic lens that they had repudiated.[150] In personifying and feminizing nature (despite her assertion in the 1990 preface that "there are no unchanging, 'essential' characteristics of sex, gender, or nature"), Merchant gives the impression that French mechanists murdered nature, an entity that in their eyes had never existed. Even Descartes's infamous assertion, in the fifth part of the *Discours de la méthode*, that through the application of his method, men might become "the masters and possessors of nature" is but a faint echo of the imperial and explicitly gendered rhetoric coming from across the channel, in the writings of James I's chancellor, Francis Bacon (1561–1626).

An in-depth analysis of Bodin's influence on Francis Bacon, or rather, of Bacon's possible appropriation of elements of Bodin's work, exceeds the scope of this study.[151] An impressionistic comparison of the two men's work, nonetheless, suggests that Bacon espoused Bodin's political absolutism as well as his torturous hermeneutics, and that he envisioned a new synthesis between the two, in which the possession of nature's secrets would enhance the sovereign's power. To be sure, between Bacon's iconoclasm and Bodin's orthodoxy, the distance was great. Bacon's aspirations were practical rather than contemplative, and his efforts to discern causes and in so doing to master effects, would have reminded Bodin, for whom prophecy was an end in itself, of the impiety that he despised in Agrippa.[152] Bacon's rejection of final causes, the very causes that Bodin was so determined to protect, also put his natural philosophy at odds with that of Bodin. Nevertheless, one finds in the *Novum Organum* (1620) (a new tool that would replace the Aristotelian logic-based "Organon"), in *De dignitate et augmentis scientiarum* (1623), and in the *New Atlantis* (1627), resonances with the *Six livres de la république*, with *De la démonomanie*, and with *Universae naturae theatrum*.

Trained in law like Bodin, Bacon was involved early in his career with legal reform devoted to sorting cases into taxonomic categories, which (it was hoped) would allow for a clearer understanding of the principles underlying judgments handed down in particular cases. Bacon proposed a similar method for going about scientific reform. Rather than deducing particulars from general syllogisms, he sought to found axioms by induction, that is, through this systematic study of particulars. To assist this effort, he drew up a table of "prerogative instances": areas of inquiry especially likely to stimulate new knowledge, such as "errors, vagaries, and prodigies of nature wherein nature deviates and turns aside from her ordinary course." Witchcraft, against which James I, Bacon's patron, had authored a *Daemonologie* in 1597, was

---

150 Carolyn Merchant, *The Death of Nature: Women, Ecology, and the Scientific Revolution* (San Francisco: Harper & Row, 1980), 195.

151 Another passage suggestive of Bodin's influence in England is found in Thomas Browne's widely read *Religio Medici* (Menston: Scholar Press, 1970) of 1643: "I have ever beleeved, and doe now know, that there are Witches, they that doubt of these, doe not only deny them, but Spirits, and are obliquely and upon consequence a sort not of Infidels, but Atheists" (67).

152 Peter Dear, *Revolutionizing the Sciences: European Knowledge and its Ambitions, 1500-1700* (Princeton: Princeton U.P., 2001), 64.

just such an instance. In *De dignitate et augmentis scientiarum* (1623), which he addressed to his sovereign, Bacon writes:

> Neither am I of opinion in this history of marvels, that superstitious narratives of sorceries, witchcrafts, charms, dreams, divinations, and the like, where there is an assurance and clear evidence of the fact, should be altogether excluded. For it is not yet known in what cases, and how far, effects attributed to superstition participate of natural causes; and therefore howsoever the use and practice of such arts is to be condemned, yet from the speculation and consideration of them (if they be diligently unravelled) a useful light may be gained, not only for a true judgment of the offenses of persons charged with such practices, but likewise for the further disclosing of the secrets of nature.[153]

Bacon calls for a natural history of supernatural beliefs ("superstitious narratives") in expectation of a practical pay-off: the discovery of witches' secrets might also lead to a knowledge of nature's secrets. Unlike Bodin, therefore, Bacon is not interested in what God is trying to tell his people by permitting witchcraft to proliferate. Taking the place of the prophet-magistrate, the natural philosopher unravels the tricks of nature rather than deciphers the will of God. At the same time, the natural philosopher rivals God in commanding His "wife" when he elicits nature's secrets with force.

Bacon's transformation of witchcraft into a "prerogative instance" completes the "impiety" of the "atheist," natural philosopher against whom Bodin fulminates, but in a way that neither Weyer nor Bodin could have predicted. Bacon does not deny witchcraft; he simply substitutes nature for her divine husband as the center of the witch's confession. As a result, the witch is not the expert witness to a world of spirit that lies beyond the reach of even the most accomplished hermeneut, but a new Prometheus, bettering the lot of humankind at the price of her own pain. Prometheus' eternally pecked liver was the punishment he endured for bringing fire to humankind; the witch's pain is the path to man's mastery over nature.

However foreign Bacon's utilitarian view of witch trials is to *De la démonomanie*, his "inquisition of nature" is, nevertheless, consistent with Bodin's torturous hermeneutics. In privileging "prerogative instances," Bacon values nature's secrets over her freely given, but less pregnant, truths. As we saw with Bodin, the supposition of secrets justifies the use of force. "Nature," Bacon writes, "exhibits herself more clearly under the trials and vexations of art than when left to herself."[154] Peter Pesic insists that "to vex" is not "to torture," and that while Bacon reluctantly supervised torture in cases involving treason, both his legal record and his scientific opus show him drawing a line between forceful inquiry and abusive interrogation.[155]

---

153 Bacon, *De Dignitate et augmentis scientiarum*, cited in Clark, 254.

154 Bacon, *De Dignitate*, cited in Merchant 169. The absence of the metaphor of torturing nature in French sources is all the more striking in that it seems to have become conventional in England by the mid-seventeenth century. In his epistle dedicatory to *The History of Generation examining the several opinions of divers author* ... (London: John Martin, 1651) Nathaniel Highmore (1613–85) lauds Robert Boyle for his determination "to trace Nature in her most intricate paths, to torture her to a confession; though with your own sweat and treasure obtained" [n.p.].

155 Peter Pesic, "Wrestling with Proteus: Francis Bacon and the "Torture" of Nature," Isis 90 (1999): 81–94. On Bacon's metaphors, see also Margaret Osler, "The Gender of Nature

Bill Newman has shown that the metaphor of torturing nature is prevalent in the alchemical tradition, a tradition that informs Bacon's work, but whose torturous methods he also criticizes, according to Pesic.[156] I am not convinced of a significant difference between violence that remains humane and violence that is abusive; those who today justify judicial torture make precisely this rhetorical distinction. The fact remains that Bacon and Bodin shared with the alchemists they criticized (Bodin demonized them) a similar view of the search for truth: attaining what is by nature hidden requires violence; violence, in turn, establishes an elite body of truth-seekers. These are, for Bodin, the prophet-magistrates; for Bacon, they are the "Interpreters of Nature" of his utopian *New Atlantis*. The vision of science in the *New Atlantis* puts an egalitarian corps (not unlike Bodin's "collèges") to work in support of absolute monarchy. Given the inclusive (if still hierarchical) tenor of Bacon's scientific society, it is significant that "Solomon's House" (named for the same wise Solomon whose reputation as "the sworn enemy of women" Bodin had tepidly protested) includes no women. In the *New Atlantis*, Bacon proposes an intellectual utopia without women designed to serve political absolutism which also excludes women: "[I]s not such a preposterous government (against the first order of nature, for women to rule over men) in itself void, and to be suppressed?"[157]

Witchcraft has thus far served as a prerogative instance for my investigation, not into the secret workings of nature, but into the gender strategies through which intellectuals, at a time of intellectual uncertainty, defined the search for truth and asserted their privileged place in it. My contrastive analyses of Weyer, the common-sensical, Lutheran literalist, and of Bodin, the Judaizing prophet-magistrate-hermeneut, allow us to establish one axiom: regardless of the hermeneutics one espouses, the more woman is made to embody truth or nature, or whatever is being searched out, the less she is likely to be considered a legitimate participant in the quest for knowledge. The fact that Bodin's hermeneutics were at the antipodes of Weyer's literalism yet featured a similar gender strategy shows that during the late Renaissance, the exclusion of women from the search for truth was not contingent upon a particular epistemology. To the contrary, it was an eminently malleable tool. My comparison of Bacon's "inquisition of nature" to Bodin's hermeneutics indicates in turn that, regardless of whether one's intellectual investment lay with the natural or the supernatural, the notion of hidden truth went hand in hand with the justification of torture, particularly of women, whose sexualized secrets were usually deemed worthy of punishment. Bacon viewed the interrogation of witches as a special scenario that would yield useful knowledge about nature, while Bodin

---

and the Nature of Gender in Early Modern Natural Philosophy," in *Men, Women, and the Birthing of Modern Science* (DeKalb: Northern Illinois U.P., 2005), 71–85, and Sarah Hutton, "The Riddle of the Sphinx: Francis Bacon and the Emblems of Science," in *Women, Science, and Medicine, 1500-1700: Mothers and Sisters of the Royal Society* (Phoenix Mill Thrupp: Sutton, 1999), 7–28.

156 William R. Newman, "Alchemy, Domination, and Gender," *A House Built on Sand: Exposing Postmodernist Myths about Science*, ed. Noretta Koertge (New York and Oxford: Oxford U.P., 1998), 216–26. Pesic, 93.

157 Bacon, cited in Clark, *Thinking with Demons*, 131.

sought to protect God's dominion through the anti-satanic surveillance afforded by the confessions of witches.

Now it is time to leave the hermeneutical polemics surrounding witches and their secrets, to consider how gender shaped the two major ethical responses to the intellectual crisis of the late Renaissance: neo-stoicism and skepticism. In the next chapter, we shall see how the neo-Stoics of the 1580s and 1590s, and particularly Guillaume du Vair, characterized torture, which Bodin envisioned as a tool for discovering meaning, as the ultimate test of virtue. I will show however that neo-stoic *vertu* was an empty signifier in the absence of its modifier *masle*, and that masculinity in turn was an instable category because it depended upon the will. Thus even though anatomists such as André du Laurens insisted upon the differences of the sexes at the close of the sixteenth century, the neo-stoic emphasis on the will as the determiner of *masle*-ness corroborated a fluid understanding of sex difference that had prevailed earlier in the century. In *De praestigiis daemonum*, Weyer rehearses a number of stories of young women who sprouted beards and exteriorized penises rather than evacuating menstrual blood, "with the intention of proving not only that this change of sex is perfectly real and based upon natural principles, but also that the change occurs only from female to male." While most of Weyer's contemporaries agreed with his claim that "women [are] masculine in potentiality" and held the reverse to be impossible, neo-Stoics warned that a man's failure to control his passions could cause him to revert to femininity.[158] Interestingly, they identified melancholy, the temperament that according to Bodin pertained exclusively to men, as the most emasculating of all passions. The neo-stoic feminization of melancholy corresponded to Henri de Navarre's rise to power, as the *politiques* who supported him sought to gain moral superiority over the Catholic League.

---

158 Weyer, 1991, 345, 346.

Chapter Three

Masle Morale in the Body Politic: Guillaume du Vair and André du Laurens

In *De la démonomanie*, Jean Bodin defined the witch's crime as apostasy or, as Jonathan Pearl aptly puts it, as "divine treason." The metaphor of treason captures a fundamental connection between the jurist's religious and political thought, for in the *Six livres de la république* (1576), "Bodin stressed, over and over again, the absolute obligation of the subject to the master," whether that subject be humankind with respect to God, wife to husband, or subject to sovereign.[1] The witch's pact with Satan was just one particularly egregious case of insubordination. Another was the notion of opposition to tyranny through which Huguenots justified taking up arms. No less reprehensible were the machinations of the Catholic League. As the wars of religion wore on, leaving France, in the gory allegory devised by the militant Huguenot Agrippa d'Aubigné (1552–1630), like a nursing mother pummeled to death by fighting twins, Bodin's notion of an indivisible, absolute sovereign gained ground.[2] Under Henri IV (1553–1610), the theological and epistemological controversies raised by the Reformation were subordinated to a unifying political ideology, and the search for truth became a political program. In an ode to "Truth," the magistrate, diplomat, and architect of the Edict of Nantes, Jacques-Auguste de Thou (1553–1617), blames "unscrupulous zealots" of both stripes for "disorder" and touts the ability to maintain "peace [*repos*]" as a more telling mark of heroism than waging battle.[3] For De Thou, the search for truth was coterminous with the Stoic pursuit of *repos*, and Henri de Navarre embodied the neo-Roman hero—"masle et généreux"—who could ensure the attainment of that blissful state.

In this chapter, I turn to the *politiques*, those French subjects whose loyalty to the monarchy led them to put political before religious considerations in response to religious conflict. Protestant and Catholic, they followed a middling course laid out by Catherine de Médicis' *chancellier*, Michel de l'Hospital (1504–73), between the intransigent *parti* Huguenot and ultramontane extremism. They espoused tolerance of Protestantism as a practical solution to France's ills, and opposed the Catholic League, for whom political order was above all a function of confessional unity. Bodin, who in addition to placing unprecedented emphasis on the absolute power

---

1   Jonathan L. Pearl, *The Crime of Crimes: Demonology and Politics in France, 1560–1620* (Waterloo: Wilfrid Laurier U.P., 1999), 117–19.

2   Agrippa d'Aubigné, *Les Tragiques*, eds. A. Garnier and J. Plattard (Paris: S.T.F.M., 1990), 47.

3   Jacques-Auguste de Thou, "La Verité, Ode" in *Histoire Universelle de Jacques-Auguste De Thou, depuis 1543 jusqu'en 1607*, vol. 1 (London, 1734), 259–63.

of the monarch, advocated tolerance of religious minorities, was not surprisingly reviled as a *politique*. Here I focus on the second generation of *politiques*, those who stood by the monarchy in its weakest moment, when the assassination of the last of the Valois kings in 1589 left the future of France anarchically open. Henri III died with a Protestant cousin from the tiny kingdom of Navarre as his heir.[4] Henri de Navarre was far from ideal as a candidate for the throne, yet the alternative was no better, according to the *politiques*, who feared that the triumph of the League would make France vulnerable to Spanish domination. The *politiques* thus accepted Henri de Navarre's accession to the throne of France as the lesser of two evils (the other being the complete subjugation of France), and promoted his rule as the destiny of France.

This second generation of *politiques* sought to transcend sectarian strife and suppress hermeneutical differences by recourse to a unifying search for truth, ethically defined. The ancient Stoics to whom they turned for inspiration had prided themselves on a coherent philosophy in which the universe, a "rationally organized structure," reflected the *logos* or rational faculty in man.[5] They had construed human capacity for rational thought as the planting of *semina virtutis* (seeds of virtue) and *semina scientiae* (seeds of knowledge) by the divine principle or *logos spermatikos* (seminal reason).[6] The neo-stoic vogue of the 1580s and 1590s owed little to stoic theories of knowledge, however. On the contrary, stoicism was attractive precisely because it allowed for the sidestepping of divisive doctrinal and hermeneutical questions that had arisen from confessional controversy in favor of a unifying ethos. Following Seneca and Cicero, *politiques* of neo-stoic persuasion conflated intellectual activity with moral practice through the identification of the good with the true.[7] We have seen that Bodin, too, associated rational activity with moral judgment. However, Bodin integrated the stoic notion of "right reason" into a Judaic framework, and his Christ-less piety earned him suspicion and censorship. Subsequent *politiques* who cultivated the revival of stoic ethics sought to transcend a fractured faith with an overarching code of conduct. They applied "stoic teachings for the benefit of the ethical and communal conduct of persons who do not agree

---

4   As of the 1520s, the kingdom of Navarre included only territories north of the Pyrenees. In 1557, Antoine de Bourbon (father of the future Henri IV) requested a Protestant minister from Geneva. Like his son, he would go back and forth between Catholicism and Protestantism, but Navarre would remain a Protestant stronghold. For a succinct account of Henri de Navarre's relations with the French court, see Michel de Waele, *Les Relations entre le Parlement de Paris et Henri IV* (Paris: Publisud, 2000), 97–117.

5   A.A. Long, *Hellenistic Philosophy: Stoics, Epicureans, Sceptics* (Berkeley and Los Angeles: University of California Press, 1974, 1986), 108.

6   Maryanne Cline Horowitz, *Seeds of Virtue and Knowledge* (Princeton: Princeton U.P., 1998), 6.

7   Anthony Levi, S.J., explains in *French Moralists: The Theory of the Passions, 1585-1649* (Oxford: Clarendon Press, 1964) that for the neo-Stoics, "not only is the good necessarily intelligible, but what is true, or 'according to reason,' is itself moral." Consequently, in "the practical sphere, rational activity becomes one and the same as virtue" (71).

on theology."[8] The "Truth" sought after by De Thou and his fellow *politiques* connoted an attitude rather than a doctrine, while *sagesse*, or wisdom, referred specifically to the attainment and exercise of moral virtue. Despite its pagan origin, stoicism enhanced Christian piety with an aura of manliness, and neo-stoic authors emphasized, to varying extents, the compatibility of the moral code they promoted with the basic teachings of Christianity. "Around 1600, especially in the France of Henry IV and in the Netherlands," Gerhard Oestreich writes, "stoicism became the ideology, almost the religion of educated men."[9]

Testing Masculinity

The shift from conflicting interpretation to ethical unity may be glimpsed in the change of value ascribed to torture. In Chapters One and Two, we saw that torture had to do with meaning; the application of pain either violated truth (Weyer) or elicited it (Bodin). As the *politiques* sought to cultivate a common ground in ethics, the focus moved from the act of torture to the appropriate response to torture. Epicharis, the notoriously taciturn woman whom we met in the last chapter, set the standard in this regard for aspiring Sages. Louis Le Bermen, author of *Le Bouclier des Dames* (1621), emphasizes the pain-defying patriotism of the Roman woman,[10] while Tristan L'Hermite places her suffering center stage in his tragedy, *La Mort de Sénèque* (1644):

> Les lieux où souffrira cette fille constante
> Serviront de Theatre à sa gloire éclatante,
> Les gesnes qui rendront son beau corps abbatu
> Ne feront seulement qu'exercer sa Vertu,
> Et parmy tant de maux sa parole estoufée
> Fera de sa Constance un eternal Trophée.[11]

---

8   Horowitz, 169. According to Long, there was little place for belief in the stoic theory of knowledge; Zeno of Citium (ca. 300 B.C.), who ruminated while ambulating in the Painted Colonnade at Athens—the *Stoa*, hence the name "Stoic"—classified belief as acts of "weak assent" to something, as a recognition of what really is the case, yet more akin to ignorance than to knowledge (109, 129).

9   Gerhard Oestreich, *Neostoicism and the Early Modern State*, eds. Brigitta Oestreich and H.G. Koenigsberger, trans. David McLintock (Cambridge; New York: Cambridge U.P., 1982), 37.

10   "Epichare libertine romaine monstra l'amour qu'elle portoit à sa patrie en ce qu'estant descouverte d'une conjuration contre Neron fut si constante que par aucunes sortes de supplices et de tourmens qu'on luy eust sceu presenter ne descouvrit jamais les complices de la conjuration." Louis Le Bermen, *Le Bouclier des Dames*, (Rouen, 1621), 251–2. Cited in Marie de Gournay, *Oeuvres complètes*, eds. Jean-Claude Arnould, Evelyne Berriot, Claude Blum, Anna Lia Franchetti, Marie-Claire Thomine, and Valerie Worth-Stylianou, vol. 2 (Paris: Champion, 2002), 980, n. H. It seems that Le Bermen is confusing Epicharis' status as an "affranchie"—freed slave—with libertinism.

11   Tristan L'Hermite, *La Mort de Sénèque: Tragédie*, ed. Jacques Madeleine (Paris: Nizet, 1984), p. 37, v. 417.

[The place where this steadfast girl suffers
Will serve as a Theater to her dazzling glory,
The torment that racks her body
Will only exercise her virtue,
And amidst so much pain, her smothered speech
Will make of her constancy an eternal Trophy.]

Constancy, virtue, and eternal *gloire* amidst bodily dismemberment: the truth revealed by means of torture was not the content of a secret, as it was for Bodin, but the valor of the person who refused to give it away. Subjected to torture, Epicharis revealed only her true mettle, her virtue (*virtus*), in sum, her manliness.

In Chapters One and Two, I showed that Johann Weyer and Jean Bodin promoted particular forms of interpretation (literal, allegorical) by reading women's words and bodies; at the same time, they ensured their own privileged access to the knowledge derived from such reading by excluding women from its pursuit. In this chapter and the next, I turn to the question of how gender categories served to define the search for truth when truth connoted an ethical outcome rather than something to be known. These chapters juxtapose the stoic and skeptic search for truth, two schools of thought that humanists revived in the 1560s following the first round of fighting between French Catholics and Huguenots and that reached their *apogée* during the 1580s and 1590s in the pivotal juncture that spanned Henri III's recognition of Henri de Navarre as his legitimate successor (1584), Navarre's siege of Paris, (second) abjuration of Protestantism (1593), coronation (1595), and proclamation of the edict of Nantes (1598). To the extent that Stoics and Skeptics alike aspired to serenity, there was considerable overlap between them. Both schools of thought appealed to those of *politique* persuasion, typically members of the magistracy, and syntheses between them were common.[12] It would be difficult, however, to imagine a perfectly balanced combination of stoicism and skepticism. Not only had the ancient Skeptics specifically targeted the Stoics as the most formidable sect of dogmatists, establishing a relation of antagonism between them; practically speaking, stoicism and skepticism were incompatible. The path for stoic pursuit of apathy (a-*pathos*) and the course charted in the Skeptic's search for *ataraxia* or tranquillity took their travelers in opposite directions. The Stoics advocated mastering the imagination in order to preempt and quell the passions, while the Skeptics proposed a series of "modes" leading to the suspension of judgment. Both Stoics and skeptics modeled an intellectual exercise that involved the self-conscious manipulation of ideas, images, or "facts" (customs and laws), but to different ends. The Stoic sought to subdue rebel passions that subverted virtue; he therefore associated Truth with attainment and closure. The Skeptic, on the other hand, subverted normative truth claims as a means of perpetuating a *skepsis* or search characterized by indeterminacy and openness.

---

12   Pierre-François Moreau notes: "On a beaucoup étudié, dans la culture de la Renaissance, les conflits et 'concordances' entre Platon et Aristote, mais le même phénomène, moins aperçu, se produit aussi pour les philosophies hellenistiques" in "Les trois étapes du stoïcisme moderne," *Le Stoïcisme au XVIe et XVIIe siècle: Le retour des philosophies antiques à l'âge classique*, ed. Pierre-Francois Moreau (Paris: Albin Michel, 1999), 14.

Nowhere is the difference in spirit between the open-ended search of the Skeptic and the destination-driven quest of the Stoic more salient than in the use each made of gender categories. As we shall see in the next chapter, the Skeptic relativized sexual customs, inverted gender roles, and subverted sex difference as a means of undermining truth claims commonly taken for granted. Montaigne, the most thorough of skeptics, took this technique further than any of his predecessors (and, for that matter, further than his continuators) through a personal identification with the feminine. In contrast, the Stoics based their ethical prescriptions on a rigid set of gender distinctions. The governing refrain of the stoic ethos was explicitly masculinist: one should "praise those who in adversity face fortune, and oppose a male and generous courage to their afflictions."[13] *Sagesse* was the preserve of virtuous men, while opinion and the passions that it fomented were the lot of women, children, and the vulgar.

Perhaps because it is so obvious, the gender ideology that frames the Stoic pursuit of *repos* has not inspired much scholarly commentary. But the caricatural masculinity of the neo-stoic Sage was far from static. The stoic ethos defined masculinity as an essence that could only be revealed through action. Virtue had to be tested and proved—hence the ubiquity of torture in stoic narrative. According to Guillaume du Vair (1556–1621), the most influential among French neo-Stoics, "It would be a huge task to cite examples of those who not only waited courageously for torture [*le tourment*], but persuaded by reason sought it out, and withstood it with a degree of pleasure."[14] The Stoics condemned tyrants like Nero who resorted to torture. Nevertheless, torture had undeniable value for the Stoics: it separated the boys from the men, as it were, and once in a great while, confirmed the virtue of an exceptional woman. Bodin had pointed to Epicharis as an example of women's greater ability to withstand pain; her silence typified the secrecy that Bodin ascribed to women. Authors writing in a stoic vein, on the other hand, flagged the exceptionality of her feat, for it was expected that women would bend under the pain and pressure of torture.[15] Torture was thus a touchstone of truth, where truth was synonymous with virtue, and virtue equivalent to virility. Considering the silence of Epicharis in terms of J.L. Austin's philosophy of speech utterances, nevertheless, suggests the tenuousness of the essence revealed through action. The Roman woman's eloquent silence participates in the category of utterances that Austin dubs "performative." Her refusal to speak "is the performing of an action," the enunciation, one might say, of her loyalty to her fellow conspirators or simply of her unyielding courage in the face of pain. In order for a performative utterance to be "felicitous," that is, in order that it accomplish the action that it purports to instantiate, it must fulfill

---

13 Pierre de l'Estoile, *Registre-Journal du regne de Henri III*, eds. Madeleine Lazard and Gilbert Schrenck, vol. 6 (Geneva: Droz, 2003), 196.

14 Guillaume du Vair, *Les Oeuvres de Messire Guillaume du Vair, Evesque et Comte de Lisieux, Garde des seaux de France* (Paris: Sébastien Cramoisy, 1641; Geneva: Slatkin Reprints, 1970), 327. All subsequent citations of Du Vair's works are taken from this volume.

15 A coconspirator in Tristan L'Hermite's tragedy apostrophizes Epicharis as "Genereuse Amazone, Esprit tout heroïque" (p. 37, v. 417).

several conditions. The final criterion in Austin's checklist requires that the person who makes the utterance "must actually so conduct themselves subsequently."[16] In other words, no performative is felicitous unless the intentions it expresses are upheld—or at least not denied—by further utterances or actions. This would suggest that resisting torture through silence is not a definitive indication of virtue, only an indication of virtue in that moment; the essence revealed through action remains contingent on the situation that produced it and, consequently, this essence must be perpetuated through the continual iteration of virtuous action. In such circumstances, tranquility looks fleeting indeed.

What is striking about the pursuit of masculine virtue, for men or women, is the work that it entailed. The *politiques* aspired to *repos* in the face of visceral passions, and they adopted the Stoics' scorn for opinion as a means of transcending conflict. Yet the attainment that de Thou calls "Truth" was never final. The specter of regression created a psychological situation necessitating constant self-discipline. neo-stoic authors expressed the tension between the attainment and evanescence of virtue in gendered terms. *Politiques* such as Du Vair insisted on inflexible gender polarities, emphasizing the prudence with which one must preempt the passions to prevent their feminizing contagion. At the same time, though, their preoccupation with the surprisingly slippery subject of sex difference suggested that one's belonging to a particular gender could not be taken for granted. Quite unexpectedly, the *masle* morale promoted in the neo-stoic campaign of the 1580s and 1590s perfectly illustrates Judith Butler's claim that "the action of gender requires a performance that is *repeated*," that "gender is an identity tenuously constituted in time, instituted in an exterior space through a stylized repetition of acts."[17] In designating the place of Epicharis' torture a "Theater," Tristan L'Hermite not only calls attention to the fiction of the drama at the very moment when the truth (Epicharis' virtue) is to be revealed, he also highlights the Roman woman's performance in the scripted role of the sage. Stoics referred to the "Theater" as fortune's stage; "cities, kingdoms, and empires change thus and grow up from each other's ruins;" says Du Vair, "the acting changes constantly, and nothing remains stable except the Theater."[18] The role of the Sage is to remain constant in the face of whatever fortune might deal him.[19] Epicharis' successful enactment of that role—one that a number of her co-conspirators disdained—demonstrated that men had no particular purchase on *masle vertu*, nor women on cowardice. Stoic moral philosophy rested on rigid gender oppositions, but they were roles in the final analysis, and the establishment of rigid distinctions between the feminine and the masculine in no way precluded an individual's passage from one to the other. Women evinced virility when they stood firm in the face of torture, and men displayed their womanly nature when they

---

16   J.L. Austin, *How to Do Things with Words* (Cambridge: Harvard U.P., 1962), 6, 14–15.

17   Judith Butler, *Gender Trouble: Feminism and the Subversion of Identity* (New York and London: Routledge, 1999), 178–9.

18   Du Vair, 332.

19   Jacqueline Lagrée, "La vertu stoïcienne de constance," *Le Stoïcisme au XVIe et XVIIe siècle: Le retour des philosophies antiques à l'âge classique*, ed. Pierre-Francois Moreau (Paris: Albin Michel, 1999), 94–116.

"fail[ed] to repeat" the performance of virtue.[20] Paradoxically, the ethical retreat from doctrinal and hermeneutical conflict in the name of *repos* produced an energy drain of its own, because the neo-Stoics made moral value contingent upon the continual enactment of masculinity. Insofar as the ontology of gender remained momentary at best in the mind-over-matter mentality cultivated by the *politiques*, the gender-bending aspect of Montaigne's skepticism was less a refutation of stoic dogma, than the magnification and exacerbation of an ambiguity already implicit in the neo-stoic campaign.

The Neo-Stoic Feminization of Melancholy

Humanists began to prescribe stoicism—combined in greater or lesser degree with general Christian precepts—as an antidote to contemporary woes in the early 1580s.[21] The most cosmopolitan of the late sixteenth-century neo-Stoics was the Flemish humanist professor, Justus Lipsius (1547–1606). In *De Constantia libri duo qui alloquium praecipue continent in publicis malis* (1584), Lipsius staged a dialogue between a young man who has fled his troubled country (designated as Lipsius) and an older man (Langius) who advocates endurance and constancy in the face of *publicis malis*, which, he insists, are omnipresent and, therefore, inescapable. Langius encourages Lipsius to recognize that his troubles will subside only once he has vanquished sorrow through constancy. The French translation of *De Constantia*, published in Leiden in 1584, went through twelve printings before Henri IV's death and inspired many French imitations. In *La tranquilité de l'esprit* (1588), Louis Le Caron, a pro-League lawyer, portrays the good subject and Christian as one who

---

20 Butler, 179.

21 The first humanist editions of stoic writings date from much earlier. Poliziano's translation of Epictetus' *Enchiridion* was published in his *Opera omnia* (Venetiis: Aldo Manuzio, 1498). Erasmus edited Seneca's works in *L. Annaei Senecae Opera, et ad dicendi facultatem, et ad bene vivendum utilissima, per Des. Erasmum ex fide veterum codicum, tum ex probatis, postremo sagaci non nunquam divitatione, sic emendata, ut merito priorem aeditionem, ipso absente, nolit haberi pro sua ...* (Basel: Froben, 1529). Calvin published a commentary on Seneca's *De Clementia* in *L. Annei Senecae, romani senatoris, ac philosophi clarissimi, libri duo De clementia, ad Neronem Caesarem* (Paris: Ludovicum Cyaneum, 1532). Cicero's *De finibus* was edited in Paris by Petrus Johannes Olivarius in *Mar. Tull. Ciceronis De finibus bonorum & malorum libri quinque, cum brevibus annotationibus Petri Ioanis Olivarii Valentini* (Paris: Simon de Colines, 1537). But Pierre-François Moreau insists that before the 1580s, stoicism was a philosophy that humanists evaluated and critiqued along with others (that is, Epicureanism) to which it was compared ("Les trois étapes," 16–20). This trend persisted in Henri III's fleeting *Académie du palais* (1576 to 1580), where the dominant frame of reference remained Aristotelian. Philippe Desportes (1546–1606) alludes to the "Stoitiens" when addressing strategies for mitigating fear in a cycle of lectures on the moral virtues, but does not apply this to current events. Robert J. Sealy emphasizes the isolated character of the Palace Academy in *The Palace Academy of Henry III* (Geneva: Droz, 1981): "[T]his intellectual activity, although it took place openly and at the heart of the operation of the French court, had no influence on the events which surrounded it nor did the debates mirror in any way the great or small happenings of government" (167).

accepts that the generation and corruption of all things is God's will, and who can, in turn, muster sufficient detachment to see that what seems bad now might be for the best in the long run. Presenting the rise and fall of empires as a providential feature of history, Le Caron insists that it is not up to the created to dispute the plans of its creator. [22] But it was above all Du Vair who shaped French neo-stoicism and tied it irrevocably to the *politiques*. He was the most published Catholic author between 1588 and 1615 and would ensure the fortune of his printer, Abel L'Angelier.[23] Acclaimed for his speeches during the League's occupation of Paris, author of a *Philosophie morale des stoïques* (1585) and a *Manuel d'Epictète* (1585), Du Vair applies the moral philosophy of the Stoics to daily life in war-torn France in *La Constance et consolation ès calamitez publiques* (1595), a work that would see more than a dozen editions by the end of Louis XIII's reign. Like Lipsius, Du Vair stages a conversation between a downcast narrator and his friends. However, where Lipsius' inculcation takes place in Langius' lush gardens, Du Vair's three friends—all of them representing prominent *politiques*— plead their cases against the backdrop of Henri de Navarre's 1590 siege of Paris. A mother who hangs herself, unable to feed her children; a family reduced to cooking up their dog with meager flames from moldy straw; rumors of soldiers kidnapping and cannibalizing children—these are all snippets of the gruesome reality that Du Vair's interlocutors manage to neutralize by recourse to the wisdom of the Stoics.[24]

The ancient Stoics advocated a conditioning of the imagination in which sense impressions that would normally provoke fear, sadness, disgust, desire, or any number of passions are objectified, subjected to scrutiny, and opposed to imagined alternative impressions. Through this controlled imagining, one could moderate the negative effects of harmful sense impressions and overcome deeply ingrained aversions, fears, or desires. A crucial part of this reconditioning of mental reflexes

---

22   Loys Charondas Le Caron, *De la tranquilité de l'esprit, livre singulier. Plus un discours sur le proces criminel faict à une Sorcière condamnee à mort par Arrest de la Court de Parlement, & executee au bourg de la Neufville le Roy en Picardie, avec ses interrogatoires & confessions. Traictez grandement necessaires pour le temps present : extraicts des discours Philosophiques de L. Charondas le Caron Parisien* (Paris: Jacques du Puys, 1588), 20, 41. As the title indicates, *La tranquilité de l'esprit* was published along with Le Caron's commentary on a witch trial by Jacques Dupuys, the printer responsible for Jacques Grévin's translation of Johann Weyer's *De praestigiis daemonum* as well as Bodin's *De la démonomanie*. Le Caron begins his *Discours sur le proces criminel* with an allusion to the Weyer/Bodin debate, siding with the latter: "Aucuns ont estimé que les ensorcellmens que font les sorciers & sorcieres, & communication qu'ils ont avec les diables, ne sont qu'illusions procedans de l'imagination de l'esprit, qui se les forge en la fantasie: ou par subtilité les fait apparoistre aux autres. Mais ceste opinion a esté refutée par plusieurs excellens autheurs, & par nous au premier livre de la divine Philosophie" 159.

23   Gilles Banderier, "Du Vair et Du Perron: Deux vies parallèles," in *Guillaume du Vair: Parlementaire et écrivain (1556–1621)*, *Colloque d'Aix-en-Provence 4–6 Octobre 2001*, eds Bruno Petey-Girard et Alexandre Tarrête (Genève: Droz, 2005), 108; Jean Balsamo, "Guillaume du Vair, Malherbe, et les Epistres Amoureuses et morales de François de Rosset," *Guillaume du Vair*, 231. On the L'Angelier business, see Jean Balsamo and Michel Simonin, *Abel L'Angelier et Françoise de Louvain (1574-1620)* (Geneva: Droz, 2002).

24   Du Vair, 61.

was resistance to abstraction; to avoid being carried off by speculation or projection that would only amplify the negative effects of dangerous sense impressions, one must stick to the actual, the present, the concrete. Epictetus (50–ca.125 A.D.) likened the conditioning of the imagination to athletic training, while Marcus Aurelius Antoninus (161–80 A.D.), in his philosophical diary, imagined disgusting bodily phenomena—hairy armpits, halitosis, gangrene—to practice controling sense impressions by breaking them down into their constituent parts and defusing them.[25] The reflective de-dramatization that Du Vair's interlocutors prescribe in *La Constance et consolation* reflects the stoic practice of imagining. Du Vair's interlocutors dismantle the hardships that he apprehends, namely "banishment, poverty, the loss of honor, children, friends, and life."[26] They tell him that death is inevitable, that all we really fear is the moment of its occurrence, and that usually it delivers us from pain or illness. The horrific anecdotes pertaining to the siege that Du Vair recounts in *La Constance et consolation* ground stoic precepts in concrete experience and implicitly refute the charge that philosophy's arguments are weak in "the school of Fortune."[27]

Stoicism offered coping mechanisms for unfortunate individuals of whom there were many in the 1590s in France. Yet it is unlikely that the Stoa would have enjoyed such a revival had its message not been politically opportune as well as individually applicable. One of the most important functions served by stoic moral philosophy in the 1590s was to undermine the moral authority of the Catholic League. As sectarian strife proliferated and political order disintegrated in the 1580s and 1590s, feelings of dread and the concomitant urge to repent were especially intense among Catholics in Paris, where Henri III's depressed religiosity vied with the eschatological anxiety cultivated by the League. Appropriating the apocalyptic expectations that had transformed Luther into a prophet of Christ's return, ultra-Catholic printers warned that humanity had sunk to unprecedented depths of depravity and exhorted repentance, lest God unleash his wrath on the new Jerusalem that was Paris.[28] Astrological almanacs fomented the fear of the messiah's second coming through the prediction of a planetary conjunction identical to that which had preceded his birth.[29] The assassination that Henri III had ordered against the Guise brothers in

---

25 I am paraphrasing John Lyons, *Before Imagination: Embodied Thought from Montaigne to Rousseau* (Stanford: Stanford U.P., 2005), 5–22.

26 Du Vair, 320.

27 Ibid., 312.

28 On Luther as prophet of the second coming and the development of apocalyptic thinking during the Reformation, see Andrew Cunningham and Ole Peter Grell, *The Four Horsemen of the Apocalypse: Religion, War, Famine and Death in Reformation Europe* (Cambridge U.P., 2000), 19–91. On Paris printers' relation to the League, consult Denis Pallier, "Les Réponses catholiques" in *Histoire de l'édition française*, eds Henri-Jean Martin, Roger Chartier, Jean-Pierre Vivet, vol. 1 (Paris: Promodis, 1982), 327–47, esp. 342–7.

29 Denis Crouzet, "Henri IV, King of Reason?" trans. Judith K. Proud, *From Valois to Bourbon: Dynasty, State, and Society in Early Modern France*, ed. Keith Cameron (Exeter: University of Exeter Press, 1989), 74–8. Also by Crouzet, "La représentation du temps à l'époque de la Ligue: 'Le clouaque et esgoust des immondices des autres [siècles] passez'," *Revue historique* 270 (1984): 297–388 and *Les Guerriers de Dieu: La violence au temps des troubles de religion* (Seyssel: Champ Vallon, 1990).

1588 brought messianic mysticism to a fever pitch. Parisians responded to their murder with an outpouring of collective contrition. Mournful processions throughout the city marked the zenith of the League's compelling causal connection between the spiritual state of the individual and the political state of the state. *Ligueurs* hailed the murder of Henri III at the hands of the Dominican monk Jacques Clément as an act of God. Until Denis Crouzet's work on the subject, historians had for the most part neglected the religious motivations of those Catholics who adhered to the League. They viewed the millenarian dread and flamboyant spirituality cultivated by its leaders and members as a façade for political ambition. Ann Ramsey has shown that this long-standing view of the League is the legacy of the *politiques*–Catholics for the most part, but Gallican Catholics–who were eager to deprive the League of its powerful religious appeal. Stressing the danger that uncontrolled passions posed to both the individual and the state, the *politiques* rejected "the exteriorized and somatic qualities of Leaguer piety" as ultramontane imports and as masks for purely political motives. Furthermore, they denied that demonstrative displays of piety had valid religious motivation.[30] An important aspect of the *politique* critique of League spirituality that has received surprisingly little attention was the neo-stoic feminization of melancholy. The *politiques* of the 1590s conflated mourning and melancholy and opposed the effeminate lamentation of the melancholic to the *masle vertu* of the stoic Sage.

Just as *politiques* denied the League's religious content, reducing the expression of spiritual angst to a politically motivated performance, they also denied the melancholic's exclusive privileges. Lipsius dismisses disposition to prophecy claimed by Bodin in *De la démonomanie* as enthusiasm and rejects the allegorical hermeneutics that he championed: "They are, God help me, a dangerous species of men, but they are too numerous amidst this civil strife. They refer almost everything to this age alone. Yes, they even play the prophet instead of the reader: and they do not extract meaning from my text, but bring it to the text, and affix some intentions according to their own ideas."[31] Trapped in the self-referentiality of the present, self-proclaimed oracles prescribe radical remedies that spell the death of the body politic. "The *res publica* [*chose publique*]," Du Vair opines, "has perished more because of the remedies applied to it than through its own malignancy."[32] Instead of advising purging (in the case of feverish violence), ablation (in the case of gangrenous Protestantism), or euthanasia (in the case of moribund government), Du Vair evokes the turning wheel of fortune and, recalling a topos dear to historiographers of the day, underscores the regenerative potential of crises:

> It is a famous maxim in medicine that in acute illnesses, predictions are never certain. If [a high fever] causes a doctor to lose his judgment, what wise man shall dare assure anything regarding the outcome of our civil furors…? It would be rash to promise the health/salvation [*salut*] of our State, but so is it uncertain to predict its ruin. How many

---

30 Ann W. Ramsey, *Liturgy, Politics, and Salvation: The Catholic League in Paris and the Nature of Catholic Reform, 1540–1630* (Rochester: University of Rochester Press, 1999), 59.

31 Justus Lipsius, *Six books of Politics or Political Instruction*, ed. Jan Waszink (Assen: Royal Van Gorcum, 2004), 241.

32 Du Vair, 371.

cities, states, empires have there been that great and horrible accidents have shaken and crumbled, such that those who witnessed them expected their certain death, and yet that were strengthened by the shock and came back more powerful and flourishing than ever before?"[33]

Du Vair urges circumspection and restraint despite an apparently desperate situation and insists on the responsibility that the physician has towards his patient. Placing Christian charity at the bedside of the suffering state, Du Vair makes the "wise man" a nurse to his country: "In matters of state, as in medicine, one should not intervene [*mettre la main*] in terminal illnesses [*maladies désespérées*].... Even were our ruin ineluctable, ... is it not the duty of good children and true friends to tend to the hopelessly ill and to make their death as sweet as possible since they cannot spare them from it?"[34] In the worst case, a positive attitude will soften an inevitable death. In the best case, it will support the patient on her rebound to health. In any case, pessimism is of no help to anybody, and prophecies dispensed by those eager to mourn are of the self-fulfilling kind. Du Vair shared Montaigne's ironic view that those expert in prophesying have above all mastered the subtle art of turning ambiguous "jargon" to their purposes and thus "of finding, in any writings, whatever they want."[35]

Of all the passions, the neo-stoic *politiques* considered none more "seditious" than sadness—tristitia or *tristesse*. For Du Vair, *tristesse* is pure pathology: "[W]izened *tristitia*, ... penetrates all the way to the marrow of our bones, fades our faces and wilts our soul at the same time, such that nothing agreeable is left in us. ...It is pitiful to see us then: we go around our heads hanging down, our eyes cast on the ground, our mouths wordless, our limbs motionless; our eyes serve only to cry."[36] Pierre Charron (1541–1603), who plagiarized Du Vair's discussion of *tristesse* in his great but confusing synthesis of fideist and skeptic currents in *De la sagesse* (1601), defines the passion as "a languor of the mind, and a discouragement engendered by the opinion that we have of being afflicted by great hardships: it is a dangerous enemy of our repose...[and] unworthy of the wise, according to the doctrine of the Stoics."[37] It is, moreover, "an attack against God." "For what is [*tristesse*]," he asks, "if not an insolent and outrageous complaint against the lord of the universe and the common law of the world that holds that all things under the heavens of the Moon are mutable and perishable?"[38] Under the spell of *tristesse*, Du Vair explains, gravity overwhelms the body, while tears, the body's sole excretion, atrophy it. The

---

33 Ibid., 73.

34 Ibid., 308.

35 Michel de Montaigne, "Of Prognostications," *The Complete Essays of Montaigne*, trans. Donald Frame, 3 vols. (Garden City: Doubleday, 1960), I: 37–8. Montaigne, Essais, ed. Pierre Villey (Paris: Presses Universitaires de France, 1965) 1.11, 44.

36 Du Vair, 329.

37 Pierre Charron, *De la sagesse* (Paris: Fayard, 1986), 195. Charron established his royalist credentials around the same time as Du Vair in a *Discours chrestien, Qu'il n'est permis ny loisible à un sujet, pour quelque cause que ce soit, de se liguer, bander et rebeller contre son Roy* (1594).

38 Charron, 197.

man who succumbs to *tristesse* is like Niobe, the mourning mother whose endless flow of tears turned her to stone. Pulling the erect body into a servile slump and fossilizing its organic vitality, debilitating *tristesse* takes its toll on virility. "One might as well dress men as eunuchs, indeed castrate them completely," Du Vair insists, "rather than let them succumb to that *tristesse* that takes away all that they have that is male and generous and leaves [them] with the countenances and all the infirmities of women."[39] Du Vair touts *tristitia* as a gender marker more essential than anatomy—depressed men might as well be castrated—and more telling than any accoutrement. Dismissing mourning as women's work, he relates that the Thracians dressed mourning men in women's clothes to instill shame in them and encourage them to abandon "effeminate countenances."[40] "But what was the use of clothes for that? For it seems to me that their faces and all of their actions provided sufficient warning that they were no longer men."[41] Neither anatomy nor dress, but outlook and action: these are the defining elements of manhood according to Du Vair. Du Vair points approvingly to the legislation of natural maleness in Roman law, deploring men who, giving themselves over to *tristitia*, "corrupt nature, prostitute [their] virility, and make a mockery of themselves and others." In contrast, he admires "the first Roman laws, male and generous, [that] prohibited men from engaging in such effeminate lamentation, finding it horrible to denature oneself and to flout virility in this fashion."[42] These are precisely the kinds of laws that would serve Paris well, by squelching the morose mood imported from modern-day Rome.

Historians typically point to the Gallican magistracy as the seedbed of *politique* sentiment and of French neo-stoicism. Du Vair was a *maître de requête*, while de Thou, a *président à mortier*, was the son and grandson of past presidents.[43] Since medieval times, however, the Parlement of Paris had been a staunch ally of the medical faculty, and the reciprocity of this relationship is evident in Du Vair's *Constance et consolation*, not only in his florid medical metaphors but also in his choice of interlocutors.[44] Orphée represents Jacques Houllier, son of the physician by the same name. Musée represents Du Vair's friend Henri de Monantheuil (1536–1606), professor of medicine and mathematics at the elite Collège de France, who delivered a panegyric of Henri IV there in May 1594.[45] That year also saw the publication of André du Laurens's *Discours des maladies mélancholiques* (1594). A native of Arles, Du Laurens had completed part of his training in Paris under the supervision of Houllier's colleague, the Hippocratic disciple Louis Duret (1527–86)

---

39   Du Vair, 329.

40   Ibid.

41   Ibid.

42   Ibid.

43   There were eight *présidents à mortier* in the Paris Parlement. After the *chancellier* and the *premier président*, they were the highest ranking officials within that body. The *mortier*, a kind of hat, was worn or held by all of these dignitaries during particularly ceremonious occasions. Antoine Furetière, "Mortier," *Dictionaire universel* (Paris: S.N.L.-Le Robert, 1978).

44   Laurence Brockliss and Colin Jones, *The Medical World of Early Modern France* (Oxford: Clarendon Press, 1997), 235.

45   Henri de Monantheuil, *Panégyric de Henri IV, Roy de France et de Navarre, treschrestien, tres-invincible, tres-clement* (Paris: Fréderic Morel, 1594).

and succeeded Laurent Joubert in his post as professor of medicine (and chancellor) at Montpellier. Du Laurens's *Discours des maladies mélancholiques*, which Allen Thiher has identified as "the first medical treatise on mental health written in the vernacular,"[46] has not been interpreted in a political light. Yet his later publications show a keen propensity for making medical doctrine serve a political agenda. In *De mirabilis strumas sanandi vi regibus Galliarum christianis divinitus concessa* (1609), Du Laurens lends medical authority to the Bourbon revival of medieval thaumaturgy by explaining "the admirable power [vertu] to heal scrofula by touch alone, divinely conceded to the very-Christian Kings of France alone."[47] Du Laurens's *politique* leanings are already palpable in the *Discours des maladies mélancholiques*, which he addressed to the wife of the duc d'Uzès, one of the crown's most loyal servants, and which was published by Jamet Mettayer, who kept up a constant stream of accounts of Henri IV's military campaigns during the interregnum.[48] Although it would be imprudent to claim that Du Vair had read Du Laurens's *Discours des maladies mélancholiques* before writing *La Constance et consolation* (the conditions of the siege severely limited the circulation of books, particularly those published by a royalist printer like Mettayer), no doubt Du Laurens participated in the development of the neo-stoic ethic spearheaded by Du Vair. The passion that Du Vair called *tristesse*

---

46   Allen Thiher, *Revels in Madness: Insanity in Medicine and Literature* (Ann Arbor: The University of Michigan Press, 1999), 73.

47   André du Laurens, *Discours des escrouelles divisé en deux livres,* in *Les Oeuvres de Me André Du Laurens, Sieur de Ferrieres, Conseiller, & premier Medecin du Tres-Chrestien Roy de France & de Navarre, Henry le Grand, & Chancelier en l'Université de Montpelier.* Trans. Théophile Gelée (Paris: Michel Soly, 1646), 92. On this work, see Brockliss and Jones, 239.

48   Like Joubert, who dedicated his *Erreurs populaires* to Marguerite de Valois, Du Laurens wrote the *Discours de la conservation de la vue: des maladies melancholiques: des catarrhes: & de la vieillesse* (1594) in the vernacular and addressed it to a noblewoman, Louise de Clermont-Tallard duchesse d'Uzès, comtesse de Tonnerre (1504–96). Each of Du Laurens's four discourses corresponds to an indisposition from which the ninety-year-old *comtesse* chronically suffered: poor eyesight, melancholy, colds, and old age. A favorite of Catherine de Médicis, a correspondent of Elizabeth, queen of England, and the confidant of Marguerite de Valois, the comtesse de Tonnerre was one of the most learned ladies of the French court. The eleven-year-old Charles IX sent her a personal invitation to his coronation, in which he expresses regret that she, his "vieille lanterne," had not been present to shed light on the recent visit of an ambassador from a country whose language no one had understood. Thanks to her high standing at court, the comtesse obtained a bishopric for herself (!) as well as important military and diplomatic functions for her husband, Antoine de Crussol, whom Charles IX would name duc d'Uzès in 1565. De Crussol boasted a *curriculum vitae* that many a *politique* might envy. As an elite member of the Chevaliers de Saint Michel who was buried in the cemetery of the Cordeliers in Uzès, de Crussol was unambiguously Catholic. The Protestants of his native Languedoc, nevertheless, elected him as their top military officer. His distinguished career reflected above all his loyalty to the crown, whether that meant pacifying the Languedoc or laying siege to La Rochelle. For detailed information and excerpts from letters written to or by de Crussol, consult Georges Mathon, "Antoine de Crussol, comte de Crussol, duc et Pair de France, Premier duc d'Uzès," at www.nimausensis. com/personnages/AntoineCrussol.htm. As of 1596, Mettayer published the *Discours des maladies melancholiques* on its own.

was the primary symptom of the malady that Du Laurens called melancholy. Just as Du Vair underscored the pathological symptoms of *tristesse* by feminizing them, Du Laurens qualified melancholy as a disease that he associated with women.

Du Laurens's *Discours* is a fairly straightforward synthesis of Greek and Arab medical tradition pertaining to melancholy.[49] The defense of the imagination with which *Discours* opens nevertheless situates the author's discussion of the malady within a stoic framework.[50] Those who fail to distinguish between imagination and common sense, Du Laurens says, "are heavily abused," because common sense "receives species at the same time as the exterior senses ... but imagination receives them and retains them in the absence of the object." We may recall that Johann Weyer had placed common sense at the center of his empirical epistemology, while characterizing the imagination as an obstacle to knowledge about the world around us. Du Laurens had read *De praestigiis daemonum*, and he, like Weyer, says that common sense synthesizes sensual information, whereas imagination recalls and manipulates images stored in memory. But whereas Weyer focuses only on the imagination's corruptibility, Du Laurens initially foregrounds its subservience to the will. Metaphor, the transference of one thing's properties to another, results from a willed combination of images: "[T]he imagination composes and joins species together, for instance, from gold and mountain it feigns a mountain of gold, which common sense cannot do."[51] Common sense depends on the presence of a stimulus, but the imagination's freedom to conjure up images at will makes it doubly useful and unique to humans: "[M]an's imagination serves both for practice and for contemplation. The imagination of animals can feign no image, except insofar as it is present; man has the freedom to conceive what he wishes, and even though he has no objects before him, he can find them in the treasury which is memory." As in stoic imagining, this contemplative function, rendered habitual, allows us to control our affective responses. We do not fear a painted lion, Du Laurens explains, because reason is accustomed to distinguishing between the "feigned" images of the imagination and the actual stimuli represented by common sense.

Du Laurens's valorization of salutary imagining sets the stage for his dramatization of the havoc wreaked by melancholy. Du Laurens acknowledges that the melancholic humor makes some individuals "philosophize, poetize, and prophesize, such that it [melancholy] seems to have something divine about it." Yet these melancholics are exceptional:

> Aristotle in his Problems writes that melancholics are the most ingenious, but one must understand this passage sanely [*sainement*], for there are several kinds of melancholy; ... The one that is cold and terrestial, makes men stupid and slow in all of their actions of

---

49   Du Laurens's first published work, an *Apologia pro Galeno* (1593), is a defense of Galen's account of the workings of fetal cardiopulmonary vessels, then standard in the schools.

50   Du Laurens was familiar with the philosophy of the Stoa. In his *Historia anatomica humani corporis et singularum ejus partium* (1595), he points out the Stoics' debt to medicine, claiming that it was from Hippocrates' characterization of Nature as "foresightful [*prévoyante*]" that they gleaned their notion of "providence" (*Oeuvres*, 336).

51   Du Laurens, 100.

mind and body, timid, lazy, and without understanding; it is called asinine melancholy. The one that is hot and burned makes men furious and incapable of any responsibility. It is thus only the one that is mixed with a little blood that makes men ingenious and that makes them excel over others.[52]

And because the melancholic complexion remains "within the bounds and limits of health," it is not the physician's concern. Instead, Du Laurens devotes the bulk of the *Discours* to explaining three forms of truly medical melancholy, following Paulus of Aegina's classification of morbus hypochondriacus—a disease label mentioned by Galen—as a type of melancholy in the seventh century.[53] Du Laurens distinguishes a first form of melancholy that affects the brain. The individual afflicted with this form of the disease suffers from sadness [*tristesse*], worry, insomnia, "visions peopled with a million phantoms and hideous specters." He stutters and is, moreover, "without courage, always fearful and trembling, scared of everything, even of himself, like the beast that sees its reflection." This melancholic enjoys scaring himself, returning to his hideous reflection like a beastly Narcissus: "[I]n sum, [the melancholic] is a wild animal, irritable, suspicious, solitary, an enemy of the sun, whom nothing can please except the sole displeasure of forging a thousand false and vain imaginings."[54] The cerebral melancholic greatly resembles the pathetic man overcome by the passion of *tristesse* described by Du Vair and Charron. Misapplying the uniquely human capacity to forge images, he entertains imaginative creations that exacerbate rather than mitigate the passions. Indeed, more than once in the *Discours*, Du Laurens refers to melancholy as a "passion," blurring the line between the moral and the medical.

Du Laurens does not berate the cerebral melancholic for his effeminacy, as Du Vair does the wimpy man overcome with *tristesse*. He does, however, further pathologize the entire disease label by modeling one of the forms of melancholy on the female disease, suffocation of the womb. After briefly mentioning a second form of melancholy that implicates the whole body, Du Laurens goes on to describe the third kind which he calls "hypochondriacal," meaning that it emanates from the hypo-chondres, the organs below the diaphragm.[55] Typically, these organs include the liver, the spleen, and the uterus, which Du Laurens singles out for its notable furiousness: "Hippocrates and several other physicians recognize a hysterical hypochondria, that comes from the womb through the retention of menstruation or other matter: it produces the same effects as the others, and is very often more furious as a result of the marvellous sympathy that the womb has with all the other parts of the body."[56] By the late sixteenth century, the hysterical hypochondria to which Du

---

52 Ibid., 113, 115.

53 G.A. Ladee, *Hypochondriacal Syndromes* (Amsterdam, London, and New York: Elsevier Publishing Company, 1966), 7.

54 Ibid., 110.

55 According to Du Laurens, "[l]'une vient par le vice propre du cerveau, l'autre vient par sympathie de tout le corps, quand tout le temperament & toute l'habitude est melancholique ; la derniere vient des hypochondres, c'est à dire des parties qui y sont contenuës, mais sur tout de la rate, du foye, & du mesentere. La premiere s'appelle absoluëment & simplement melancholie, la derniere avec addition se nomme melancholie hypochondriaque" (119).

56 Du Laurens, 177.

Laurens alludes was better known as "suffocation of the womb," a disease label that, as Helen King has shown, resulted from an error in humanists' translation of a Hippocratic aphorism.[57] Ambroise Paré explains that "uterine stifling" results when rotting substances in the womb produce vapors or "ventositez" that, like helium in a balloon, cause the uterus to swell and rise, while Jean de Varanda (d. 1617), who served in Du Laurens's stead as vice-chancellor of the faculty of medicine in Montpellier while he was at court, envisions the ligaments that anchor the uterus as the cords of a slingshot, elastic enough to propulse the vapors that putrify within throughout the body.[58] Insofar as the organ best known for becoming "stuffed and filled with a humor" and for causing "an oppression in the chest that makes them breathe twice as fast [as usual]," the heart to palpitate, and the face to flush, was neither the liver nor the spleen, but the womb, it seems fairly clear that Du Laurens models hypochondriacal melancholy as a whole on the etiology of suffocation of the womb.[59] Louise Bourgeois (1563–1636), for whom Du Laurens secured a court

---

57   Helen King argues that the disease label "suffocation of the mother" only came into existence during the sixteenth century. In ancient Greek medicine, according to King, the womb's wandering signaled that the woman's moisture level had dropped below a critical point; it did not constitute a disease in its own right. As a symptom, uterine migration shared its cure with other symptoms. "Since all disorders of women ultimately result from their soft and spongy flesh and excess blood," writes King, "all disorders of women may be cured by intercourse and/or childbirth.... [T]here is thus nothing special about the prescription of [marriage and pregnancy] in cases of movement of the womb" (24). That changed in the 1540s, according to King, when philologists translated the Hippocratic texts into the vernacular. The original Hippocratic aphorism 5.35 reads, "In a woman suffering from hysterika ... a sneeze is a good thing." In his commentary of the aphorisms, *In Hippocratis Aphorismi*, Galen of Pergamum (A.D. 129–ca. 200) proposes substituting the original "hysterika" ("diseases of the womb") with "hystereké pnix" ("stifling coming from the womb"), a symptom mentioned elsewhere in the Hippocratic corpus. Leonhart Fuchs (1501–66), Guillaume de Plancy (1514–68), Claude Champier (fl. 1556), and Jacques Houllier (1510–62) took Galen's suggested translation of aphorism 5.35 to heart (60). Henceforth, Latin and vernacular renditions of the aphorism read: "In a woman suffering from suffocation of the womb, a sneeze is a good thing." Consequently, when physicians began to author their own accounts of diseases addressed by the ancients, they, too, spoke of "suffocation of the mother" as a disease in its own right with a precise panoply of symptoms, causes, and cures (sneezes not among them). By the sixteenth century, sexual intercourse was no longer the universal panacea of soggy women, as it was in ancient Greek medicine; it was thought specifically to cure the unhinged uterus. Helen King, "Once upon a Text: Hysteria from Hippocrates," in *Hysteria Beyond Freud*, ed. Sander Gilman (Berkeley: U of California Press, 1993), 3–90.

58   Ambroise Paré, *Œuvres* (Paris: veuve Gabriel Buon, 1598), 973. Jean de Varanda, *De morbis et affectibus mulierum libri tres* (Lyon: Pierre Myteau, 1619), 168.

59   Du Laurens, 175, 177. When not actually conflating melancholy and suffocation of the mother, historians of hysteria have been content to evoke the possible cross-pollination in the elaboration of their respective etiologies. Etienne Trillat in his *Histoire de l'Hystérie* (Paris: Seghers, 1986) suggests that melancholy and "hysteria" were, in fact, related. "C'est la mélancolie qui intéresse tout particulièrement l'histoire de l'hystérie, parce qu'il existe entre l'une et l'autre une filiation sinueuse" (37). Similarly, Jeffrey Boss points to, but does not develop, a lacuna in histories of hysteria when he writes, "the possible influence of ideas on melancholy on those about hysteria still lacks historical analysis," in "The Seventeenth-

appointment as midwife to Marie de Médicis, portrays the spleen and the uterus as rivals in her *Observations diverses sur la stérilité, perte de fruit, foecondité, accouchements, et maladies des femmes et enfants nouveaux naiz* (1609), evocative of a takeover of melancholy by a female malady.[60]

The plural *melancholies* mentioned in the title of the *Discours* registers Du Laurens's effort to synthesize—or at least to account for—the multiple traditions pertaining to melancholy.[61] Du Laurens respects Bodin's insistence on the exclusivity of genial melancholy that lies beyond the physician's authority while recognizing an essentially female form of melancholy, thereby satisfying Weyer's claim that women are naturally melancholic. Yet Du Laurens's hierarchy of melancholies, articulated at the upper end by male genius and at the lower end by female flatulence (hypochondriacal melancholy is "always accompanied by windiness"),[62] does not corroborate Juliana Schiesari's thesis that "the melancholic position ... dominates Western thought as a special prerogative for representing the alienated and creative individual, whereas for women it is normative, thus reducing women to the category of an essentialized and therefore inconsequential lack."[63] The genial melancholic hardly dominates Du Laurens's *Discours*. To the contrary, he is literally off the charts, pushed out of the picture by the winds of a more medically pertinent form of melancholy, which Du Laurens modeled on the female disease *par excellence*. The pathologized melancholic, the melancholic whose symptoms were borrowed from

---

Century Transformation of the Hysteric Affection, and Sydenham's Baconian Medicine," *Psychological Medicine*, 9 (1979): 224.

60   "The spleen, neighbor of the womb and seat of melancholic blood, swollen and overburdened with this humor, pushes on the womb, an organ that likes to push, but that does not want to be pushed, and as a result, [the womb] takes offense and does just as the prideful [*le glorieux*] does in a crowd, for in swelling, she inflicts strange suffocations." Louise Bourgeois, *Observations diverses sur la stérilité, perte de fruit, fécondité, accouchements, et maladies des femmes et enfants nouveaux-nés* (Paris: Côté-femmes, 1992), 161. Du Laurens first heard about Bourgeois in 1601 from one of his patients, Marie de Brabançon, the wife of the *politique* de Thou. Perkins speculates that de Thou's support for the future Henri IV against the Catholic League in the 1580s and 1590s, was influential in Bourgeois's appointment at court (21). Bourgeois "studied in the works of Paré," passed an exam entitling her to a license in 1598, and in addition to the *Observations*, published a compendium of recipes for remedies drawn from amateur and professional healers, the *Receuil des secrets* (1636).

61   Du Laurens styled himself as a peacemaker in many of his works, adjudicating, for instance, the dispute between the "biting" iconoclasm of Vesalius and the "harsh" traditionalism of Sylvius. Style, not substance, is the focus of Du Laurens's assessment: "Vesalius and Sylvius flourished in the same time, but the former was too biting and prompt to calumny, and the latter too harsh and vehement in his defense of Galen." Du Laurens faults Vesalius not for his methods and findings, but for his aggressive demeanor. "Andreas Vesalius, in my judgment, wrote the most exactly of all, and some hold that he omitted nothing from what belongs to the science of dissection and the action and usage of the parts. But many criticize him for having transcribed almost everything from Galen, and yet for continually attacking and correcting him, spurred on by I know not what spur [*aiguillon*] of ambition or impulse to contradict" (19).

62   Du Laurens, 172.

63   Juliana Schiesari, *The Gendering of Melancholia: Feminism, Psychoanalysis, and the Symbolics of Loss in Renaissance Literature* (Ithaca and London: Cornell U.P., 1992), 75.

the female disease suffocation of the womb, tainted the prestige of the melancholic whose condition placed him inside the "bounds of health" and outside of the doctor's authority. The poet Marc Antoine Girard de Saint Amant (1594–1661) mocked the melancholic's intestinal travails; his irreverent caricature resembles Du Vair's and Du Laurens's pitiable creature more than Ronsard's uncivil but divinely inspired poetic persona whom we encountered in the last chapter.[64] On stage, the melancholic's delusions and scatological symptoms provided a storehouse of farcical scenarios from Jean Rotrou's *L'Hypocondriaque ou le mort amoureux* (1631) to Molière's *Malade imaginaire* (1673).[65] And Descartes, when pondering the reasonableness of putting sense experience in doubt in the first Meditation, dismisses out of hand "those *insensez* whose brains are ... muddied and obfuscated by the black vapors of bile.... They are madmen, and I would be no less extravagant were I to model myself on their examples."[66]

The depreciation of melancholy resulted in part from the increased popularity of melancholy as a medical diagnosis. Pointing out that Galen's *De atra bile* went through twenty-two editions in the sixteenth century, H.C. Erik Midelfort concludes:

> A result of this "rise of Galenism" in the sixteenth century, therefore, was that melancholy was more widely regarded as a disease, and as a common disease, in 1600 or 1620 than it had been in 1500. The doubt and ferment around the melancholy humor and the melancholy temperament had arisen, not from any new anatomical discoveries or scientific approaches, but from the improved philological abilities and from the improved and much more plentiful texts now available to learned physicians and to the classically educated layman.[67]

As the first medical treatise on mental health written in the vernacular for the nonmedical reader, *Discours* accelerated the "doubt and ferment" surrounding melancholy. Indeed, it could be said that the first vernacular treatise on melancholy spelled the demise not only of the melancholic genius, but also of melancholy as a medical diagnosis. His synthesis was a symptom of the disintegration of a disease label fraught with contradictions: temperament or disease? hot or cold? male or female? prophecy or madness? Du Laurens's imitators in the seventeenth century would further expose the unwieldy disparities wrought by the amalgamation of divergent moral and medical traditions.

But Du Laurens was also responding to a political context with his *Discours des maladies mélancholiques*. Like the author of *La Constance et consolation*,

---

64   Marc Antoine Girard de Saint Amant, "Les visions, à Damon," which begins: "Le Coeur plein d'amertume, et l'Ame ensevelie / Dans la plus sombre humeur de la melancolie, / Damon je te descris mes travaux intestins . . ." *Oeuvres*, vol 1. (Paris: Nizet, 1971), 125.

65   For a full analysis of melancholy in seventeenth-century French theater, see Patrick Dandrey, *Les Tréteaux de Saturne: Scènes de la mélancolie à l'époque baroque* (Paris: Klincksieck, 2003).

66   René Descartes, *Oeuvres de Descartes*, eds. Charles Adam et Paul Tannery (Paris: Vrin, 1964), vol. 9, pt. 1, 14.

67   H.C. Erik Midelfort, *A History of Madness in Sixteenth-Century Germany* (Stanford: Stanford U.P., 1999), 163.

Du Laurens faced a choice in 1593 between the Catholic League, whose unifying premise was that "moral order in society began with the king's commitment to uphold religious uniformity," and the just-converted former leader of the *parti Protestant*, Henri IV, whose determination to extirpate Protestantism was doubtful.[68] His *Discours des maladies mélancholiques,* published a year later, would have been read by his contemporaries as a declaration of his loyalty to the king. Du Laurens's portrayal of the melancholic as "so depraved that there is nothing human/manly left in him [*qu'il n'a plus rien de l'homme*]," participated, like Du Vair's overtly stoical critique of *tristesse*, in discrediting the spiritual manifestations of the League and breaking down the moral authority that it enjoyed as a result of its seamless assemblage of religious conviction and political aspirations. Against this backdrop of seditiously sad enthusiasts, Henri IV was well-poised to emerge as the king of reason. Although scholars have not tended to recognize Du Laurens's *Discours* as a political gesture; what mattered to him was that Henri IV certainly did. Called to the court in 1600, Du Laurens would become Marie de Médicis's first physician in 1603, and in 1606, Henri IV named him *premier médecin du roi.*

"From a Girl Became a Boy": Guillaume du Vair and the Fortunes of the *Politique*

Besides feminizing the League through the critique of *tristesse*, the development of the moral philosophy of the Stoics served to transform the connotations pertaining to the *politique*. In the last decades of the sixteenth century, the *politique* underwent a significant image makeover. For the *politiques* were disparaged not just as "lukewarm Catholics," as the Jesuit Martin del Rio (1551–1608) put it in his immensely successful demonological treatise, *Les Controverses et recherches magiques* (1599), but also as Machiavels.[69] Good Christians condemned "those fake and dissembling politics, who make play of religion, and turn it and move it according to the weathervane of the times;" they designated this impious play with a neologism: "*machiaveliser*"— "to Machiavelize."[70] First among Machiavelli's pupils, according to her Catholic and Protestant detractors, was Catherine de Médicis (1519–89), the Florentine mother of the child-king Charles IX (1550–74). She sought to safeguard the crown by playing the Huguenot Bourbons against the very Catholic, very ambitious dukes of Lorraine. As a result, Catholics held her responsible for putting a Protestant in line for the throne of France. Furthermore, the Huguenots had no doubt that she had commissioned the assassination attempt on the admiral Coligny, a prelude, as

---

68   Michael Wolfe, *The Conversion of Henri IV: Politics, Power, and Religious Belief in Early Modern France* (Cambridge: Harvard U.P., 1993), 33.

69   Cited in Pearl, 71. Del Rio was a student of Maldonat at the Collège de Clermont, and unlike Bodin, he linked witchcraft to Protestantism. He was one of Montaigne's nephews.

70   Le Caron, 65, 66, 38. The fact that Le Caron advocates religious concord and political tolerance suggests that even those committed to what others would recognize as the position of the *politiques* were skittish about a label that identified them with manipulative Machiavels. On the relation between the alternating aims of religious concord and political tolerance, see Mario Turchetti, "Religious Concord and Political Tolerance in Sixteenth- and Seventeenth-Century France," *Sixteenth Century Journal* 22 (1991): 15–25.

Fig. 3.1   *Politique*-siren. Pierre de L'Estoile, *Les Belles figures et drolleries de la Ligue.*

it turned out, to the Saint Bartholomew's day massacre (1572), during which some two thousand Protestants perished. A satirical engraving from the 1570s likens the *politique*'s persuasion to a siren call: "What is this monster and what is its name?" asks the opening verse accompanying the engraving. "The Greeks called it Siren ...; in our century today, we call it a *Politique*," goes the didactic reply. The catechumen in the satirical engraving of the *politique*-siren goes on to ask, "So tell me, why is he female?" To which the instructor replies, "His greatest virtue is to flatter everyone and to steal the heart and courage of the strongest."[71]

Sirens had figured in the *Ballet comique de la Reine* on the occasion of the Duc de Joyeuse's marriage to the reigning queen's sister in 1581. There, they fulfilled the positive function of singing the praises of the king. But the connotations surrounding these mythical creatures made it easy to construe the *politique*'s praise as flattery. The satirical poem accompanying the engraving explains that the double fish's tail represents the *politique*'s slippery overtures to both sides; the bottle, his debauchery; and the trumpet, his hatred of the sovereign.[72]

Stoicism provided moral fiber to those Frenchmen who, disillusioned with Henri III, nevertheless, threw their lot in with Henri IV. In addition to supplying a compelling moral base that could bridge the confessional gap, stoicism allowed them to distance themselves from the queen regent and her alleged tutor Machiavelli. It provided a credo to an objective; consequently, De Thou could refer to the accomplishment of peace—the very outcome that Catherine de Médicis

---

71   Cited in Frances Yates, *The French Academies of the Sixteenth Century* (London: The Warburg Institute, 1947), 329.

72   Yates, 241, 262.

Fig. 3.2   Henri IV, Sceptre de milice. Léonard Gaultier (1602).

had pursued—not as an unholy compromise, but as the attainment of "Truth."[73] As for countering the charge of "machiavellian rhetoric," the *politiques* devised two different strategies.[74] Many *politiques*, sensitive to the charge of Machiavellism, simply pretended to disdain rhetoric. The first Bourbon made a great show of plain speaking, *franchise* or frankness, the heritage of the Franks, implicitly severing his discourse from Florentine dissimulation.[75] A famous portrait of Henri IV shows him about to slice a spaghetti-like mass suspended from somewhere on high: the Gordian knot of rhetoric.

For the magistracy, however, it was not possible to do away with persuasion without also undercutting its authority. Du Vair thus sought to rehabilitate persuasion in *De l'éloquence française* (1594) by replacing connotations of feminine seduction with those of masculine conquest. We have seen how the moral philosophy of the Stoics was instrumental in feminizing the League; we shall now see how it served to masculinize the *politique*.

In an arresting passage of *La Constance et consolation*, Du Vair describes his triumph over *tristesse* in terms of a female-to-male sex change. He refers to this spectacular transformation as a matter of a change of fortune, that notoriously unpredictable entity against which the Sage exercised his constancy: "I swear to you, after having heard them out, it seemed as if my fortune had changed [*j'avais change de fortune*], and that like Caenis, who from a girl became a boy, so too from pusillanimous and effeminate, I had become constant and courageous, and where once miserable, was now almost happy."[76] Caenis, the daughter of the Thessalian Elatus, became a man subsequent to being raped by Neptune. Nestor relates the story of Caenis' transformation in Ovid's *Metamorphoses*:

---

73   For Catholic Parisians' growing hatred of Catherine de Médicis and an account of the Saint Bartholomew's Day massacre, see Barbara Diefendorf, *Beneath the Cross: Catholics and Huguenots in Sixteenth-Century Paris* (New York and Oxford: Oxford U.P., 1991), 90–91; 93–106. In an anonymous *Discours sur les moyens de bien gouverner* (1576), the Huguenot Innocent Gentillet deplored the foreign tyrants who had implemented Machiavelli's strategy of sowing dissension among subjects as a means to preserve power. The author of the Latin translation of Gentillet's book, published a year later, claimed that it was through Catherine de Médicis that the Devil had chosen to spread Machiavelli's amoral and atheistic spirit throughout France. See Friedrich Meinecke, *Machiavellism: The Doctrine of Raison d'Etat and its Place in Modern Europe*, trans. Douglas Scott (London: Routledge, 1957), 51.

74   On the uneasy awareness regarding the power of rhetoric and its potential for misuse, see Victoria Kahn, *Machiavellian Rhetoric from the Counter-Reformation to Milton* (Princeton: Princeton U.P., 1994).

75   The *politique* rejection of rhetoric was disingenuous, of course. Henri de Navarre's conversion to Catholicism demanded exceedingly careful preparations on all fronts. Jean Louis Guez de Balzac relates the following anecdote about the converted Calvinist and bishop of Evreux Jacques Davy Du Perron (1556–1618)—responsible, among other things, for negotiating Henri IV's reconciliation with Rome: "The Pope Paul [V], seeing the incomparable Cardinal who had reconciled the King with the Church, enter his room, had the habit of saying, 'Let God inspire the man whom I see, for he is sure to persuade us of whatever he wants.'" Guez de Balzac, *Oeuvres diverses*, ed. Roger Zuber (Paris: Champion, 1995), 171.

76   Du Vair, 188.

When Neptune had tasted the joys of his new love, he said: "make now your prayers without fear of refusal. Choose what you most desire." ... Caenis said: "The wrong that you have done me calls for a mighty prayer, the prayer that I may never again be able to suffer so. If you grant me that I be not woman, you will grant me all." She spoke the last words with a deeper tone which could well seem to be uttered by a man. And so it was; for already the god of the deep ocean had assented to her prayer, and had granted her besides that she should be proof against any wounds and would never fall before any sword. Atracides [i.e., the Thessalian, Caeneus, the transformed Caenis] went away rejoicing in his gift, spent his years in manly exercises, and ranged the fields of Thessaly.[77]

As Caenis recognized, rape underscores a power differential, drawing a crude line between who has power and who does not. Sexual violence has as its subtext women's disenfranchisement or, in the case of men, their feminization, as we see in Du Vair's discussion of penetrating *tristesse*. In choosing to become a man, Caenis seeks to escape the powerlessness instituted by rape. Her utterance of that wish is performative in that it adumbrates her transformation; Nestor reports that she speaks it "with a deeper tone." Reversing the usual dynamic of disempowerment, Neptune's rape of Caenis results in the transmission of *virtus* and its attributes. Not only will Caenis, as Caeneus, be invulnerable to rape; s/he will be, furthermore, invulnerable in battle. Erasmus explains the adage "Invulnerabilis ut Caeneus:" "You are invulnerable like Caeneus. Said of those who cannot be hurt. It is stated in the poets' tales that Caeneus, by Neptune's help, could not be injured by any missile."[78] Literalizing the metaphor of divine insemination that is at the heart of stoic epistemology; Neptune plants the seeds of virtue in Caenis' soul.[79]

Many of Du Vair's contemporaries would have recognized that the story of his emergence from *tristesse* is also the story of his shifting political allegiance. Du Vair's comparison of his newly Stoical outlook to a female-to-male sex change describes his abandonment of the League and his newfound loyalty to the crown in the person of Henri IV. In 1587, Renaud de Beaunes, archbishop of Bourges, delivered a funeral oration for Mary Stuart (1542–87). Written by Du Vair, then thirty-one years old and a clerk in the Parlement, it was an unambiguous piece of League propaganda, for Mary Stuart's mother was Marie de Guise, sister of François I de Lorraine, duc de Guise (1519–63), who had set off the first war of religion by ordering the massacre of Protestants at Wassy.[80] Raised at the French court, Mary Stuart was heir to the throne of Scotland and queen of France during the very short reign of her first

---

77 Ovid, *Metamorphoses*, trans. Frank Justus Miller, vol. 2 (Cambridge: Harvard U.P., 1984), 195.

78 Erasmus, *Adages*, trans. Margaret Mann Phillips, ann. R.A.B. Mynors, vol. 5 (Toronto; Buffalo: University of Toronto Press, 1982), 16 (III, iv, 25).

79 Du Vair alludes to the seminal transmission of virtue in his treatise on eloquence: "[T]o children is passed the seeds of their fathers' generosity or rudeness of courage ... which is what Homer duly noted when speaking of Telemachus, son of Ulysses, he said, 'the virtue of your father has flowed [*s'est découlée*] into you'" (400).

80 On the complicated history of the publication of the "Oraison" and its attribution, consult René Radouant's chapter on it in *Guillaume du Vair: L'homme et l'orateur jusqu'à la fin des troubles de la Ligue (1556-1596)* (Paris: société Française d'imprimerie et de librairie, 1907), 105–29. On the enduring mystique of Marie Stuart as an emblem of the Counter-

husband, François II (1559–60). Upon his death, she returned to Scotland where she emerged as a dangerous rival for Elizabeth I, who imprisoned her and eventually had her executed on charges of treason. At the time of her death, her cousins the duc de Guise (Louis II) and his brother, the Cardinal Henri de Lorraine, were at the zenith of their popularity in Paris, a state of affairs duly noted by the author of the "Oraison funèbre sur la mort de la Reyne d'Escosse." To conjure up the valiant feats of the "illustrious house of Lorraine" from the graves of ancestors is superfluous, declares Du Vair, "since the will to vanquish and triumph, hereditary in the lineage, ... stands out so prominently in our day in the descendents of the race." Mary Stuart's death enhanced Guise *gloire* with the "tragic prestige" of martyrdom, for every preacher in Paris rushed to canonize her.[81] Du Vair, too, plays the hagiographer to Mary Stuart, relating the details of her execution:

> [Then], like Iphigenia, fated to appease the storms and tempests of the sea, she was sacrificed to the rage of her ennemies, who thought that calm would be restored through her death; and they had her head chopped off with a big ax. And that majestic head that had worn the crowns of two kingdoms, was shown to the people all bloody, the mouth open, eyes sealed, and her hair all white and horribly and piteously sparse from her long imprisonment.

It was a given that the death of Mary Stuart would not quell the storm of sectarian strife, and Du Vair foments vengeance against Elizabeth: "Christian Princes," he exclaims, "God called you before to wreak vengeance against her abuse, and because you have been negligent in [doing so], he allowed all of you to be violated in the person of this queen so as to rally you to the common cause of avenging her death."[82] Du Vair's indignant account of the presentation of Mary Stuart's prematurely hoary, hacked-off head recalls the display of a defiled female body that founded the Roman republic. According to the legend recounted by Livy in his *History of Rome*, Lucius Junius Brutus incited a popular uprising against the tyrannical Tarquins by parading around the body of his cousin Lucretia, who, reputed for her chastity, had killed herself after being raped by Sextus Tarquinius.[83] Du Vair calls upon Christian princes, not the Parisian people, to take up "torches" to avenge Mary Stuart, yet it is clear that these sovereigns are accountable to the people. Du Vair's exhortation is also an accusation; Henri III has been negligent in pursuing the Protestant monarch. The contrast between the conquest-driven Guise clan and the negligent, violated monarch hints rather ominously at Henri III's precariousness.[84]

Reformation *vanitas* topos, see Didier Course, *D'or et de pierres précieuses: Les paradis artificiels de la Contre-réforme en France, 1580-1685* (Lausanne: Payot, 2005), 121–31.

81   Radouant, 105.

82   Du Vair, "Oraison funèbre sur la mort de la Reyne d'Escosse," *Oeuvres*, 752–3.

83   On the fortunes of this legend during the Renaissance, see Stephanie Jed, *The Rape of Lucretia and the Birth of Humanism* (Bloomington: Indiana U.P., 1989).

84   Even unwavering royalists were thoroughly exasperated by Henri III's passivity. In eighteen anti-League sonnets, circulated "more boldly than prudently" by Pierre de l'Estoile (1540–1611) in 1589, the imprisoned Lieutenant Rapin exhorts his king to take heart and chides those who fail to stand up to the League as being less courageous than women and girls. Cited in Pierre de l'Estoile, 166.

Less than two years later, the duc de Guise, the Cardinal de Lorraine, and Henri III were dead. The one remaining Guise, Charles de Lorraine, the marquis de Mayenne, vied for control of the League with "the Sixteen," representatives of the sixteen neighborhoods of Paris.[85] The republican turn taken by the League that Du Vair anticipates in his funeral oration for Mary Stuart was in the end not to his taste.[86] He consummated his conversion to the *politique* cause in 1593, when he delivered before the Parlement a passionate defense of Salic law opposing a stratagem to place the Spanish Infanta on the vacant throne of France. Warning that the Spanish aspired "to establish a servitude and captivity … more cruel than in the Indies," Du Vair urges the Parlement to ensure that "the domination of a woman would never be approved in France." Despite the *politique* sentiment that animates the "Suasion de l'arrest donné au parlement, pour la manutention de la loy Salique," it shares a common feature with the League-friendly funeral oration for Mary Stuart: a woman becomes the catalyst for collective action on the part of men. Whereas the execution of Mary Stuart brings Catholics together against Protestants, the prospect of Phillip II's daughter on the throne of France causes Frenchmen to unite against Spain. It is not that Spain is a particularly objectionable nation. To the contrary, Du Vair confesses his admiration for the unbending *vertu* of the colonial super-power: "Truth be told, the nation of the Spaniards is brave and generous; their discovery of mines of silver and gold, of heaps of pearls and precious gems in their conquest of the Indies has not softened their mores, bastardized their courage, relaxed their vigor, contrary to almost all other peoples of the world, who in acquiring riches, have lost their virtue." But those riches divide French Catholics, Spanish troops inflict their virile vigor on French daughters, and the rule of a woman would irrevocably seal the destruction of the integrity and sovereignty of France. On the other hand, Du Vair promises that the defense of Salic law, which for "twelve hundred years has conserved this kingdom whole," combined with a little patience, will allow for the coalescence of a divided kingdom. "The king of Navarre is on the verge of becoming Catholic…. The Spanish see there the death of all their hopes," and rightly so, Du Vair opines, for "[i]f the king of Navarre becomes Catholic, the others will undoubtedly follow, and there will be a stampede [*presse*] to determine who will get there first."[87] Peace and religious concord,

---

85 On this group, see Robert Descimon, *Qui étaient les Seize? Mythes et réalités de la Ligue parisienne (1585–1594)*, Mémoires de la Fédération des Sociétés Historiques et Archéologiques de Paris et de l'Ile de France, vol. 34 (Paris: Klincksieck, 1983).

86 Louis-Georges Tin comments on Du Vair's opportunism in "Ambiguïtés de la vie civile au XVIe siècle," in *Guillaume du Vair*: "Du Vair semble l'un des derniers penseurs de ce temps à croire aux vertus de la vie publique, à une époque où le repli sur soi paraît l'attitude ordinaire des penseurs et des humanistes. Mais surtout, fait curieux, il ne précise nullement ce en quoi consiste la vie civile à laquelle il engage son interlocuteur [dans son *Exhortation à la vie civile*], et encore moins pour quel parti il faudrait s'engager. En cela, il ressemble quelque peu à ceux dont parle Montaigne, ceux qui attendent l'issue des événements pour se ranger du côté de la fortune" (273). Radouant asserts que Du Vair must have composed his *Exhortation à la vie civile* before 1594, in other words, before both *De l'éloquence française* and *La Constance et consolation* (270).

87 Guillaume du Vair, "Suasion de l'arrest donné au parlement, pour la manutention de la loy Salique," *Oeuvres*, 606.

he feels, are just around the corner, if only the Parlement will do its job and uphold the law of the land. Du Vair wraps up his very long "Suasion" with a call to arms. "Let us not waste time with lengthy speeches"; rather, he urges his listeners, to compose an *arrest* (pronouncing the Parlement's opposition to any violation of Salic law) "before the hour is up and we rise from our seats." [88]

Du Vair's closing remarks in the "Suasion" play on the opposition between words and action, commonplace during the wars of religion. "In France," Du Vair notes in *De l'éloquence française* (1594), "eloquence has always been scorned by our Princes and our landed nobility: they had convinced themselves that it was better to do well than to say well."[89] As we have seen in the League's critique of Machiavellian rhetoric, there were good reasons for preferring actions to words. Words were suspicious because always potentially duplicitous; one could say one thing, but do another. Compared to deeds, furthermore, words were uttered in vain if they were not backed by force. Throughout the "Suasion," Du Vair recalls the impotence of words during the terror of the Sixteen. With a hagiographical pathos that exceeds that of his funeral oration for Mary Stuart, Du Vair rememorates the murder of President Brisson, whose words were powerless against the aggression of the Sixteen:

> Do we not remember that it was the counsel of the Spaniards, who with the hands of the thugs of this city tore [our fellow members of Parlement] out of their seats, dragged them into prisons, wounded them, and made a spectacle of them in the street? The only President remaining in this Parlement, whom we could rightly name the marvel of letters, the ornament of France, the wonder of all foreign nations that have some taste for knowledge, while coming to the Palais [de Justice], was seized, dragged, beaten down, imprisoned, condemned by private [i.e., not representative of the public] and irreputable scelerates; tortured [*bourrelé*] and exposed like a trophy to the eyes of the people, such that neither his children nor his other family members dared even look at his body to give it an honorable burial. And what was his crime, sires? He was French, eminent in dignity, famous in erudition.[90]

In light of such humiliation, Du Vair's final call to action in the "Suasion," where action consists in the composition of a legal document, rings like a reaffirmation of the performative power of words. In the funeral oration for Mary Stuart, Du Vair's words were propaedeutic to action (taking up torches); the orator acts as the helpmeet to men of arms. In the "Suasion," on the other hand, Du Vair elevates the Parlement,

---

88   Compare this rhetoric to that of Demosthenes (384–22 B.C.) in his third *Olynthiac*, vol. 1 (Cambridge and London: Harvard U.P., 1984), 51: "You have among you, Athenians, men competent to say the right thing; no nation is quicker-witted to grasp the meaning of speech, and you will at once be able to translate it into action, if you only do your duty." Du Vair is warning his compatriots against Philip II of Spain just as Demosthenes warned war-weary Athenians against the imperial ambitions of Philip II of Macedonia (382–36 B.C.), father of Alexander the Great. Demosthenes was famed for his eloquence; Cicero consecrated his reputation as the most brilliant Attic orator.

89   Guillaume du Vair, *De l'éloquence française et des raisons pourquoy elle est demeuree si basse*, in *œuvres*, 400.

90   Du Vair, 612.

whose words *are* deeds, to a near sacerdotal function. The prudence of the Parlement along with its "legitimate authority, [will] be the principal tools with which God [will] operate the conservation of religion and the restoration of the state." It was no doubt in hopes that Henri IV, bound by gratitude, would recognize the Parlement's authority, that many of Du Vair's *ligueur* colleagues followed through with his recommendation to uphold Salic law, implicitly legitimating the not-yet-converted Huguenot as the king of France.

Beyond simply supporting Henri IV in the "Suasion de l'arrest donné au parlement, pour la manutention de la loy Salique," Du Vair sought to define a newly powerful role for the magistrate under Bourbon rule. His rehabilitation of persuasion in *De l'éloquence française* reads like a charter for this initiative. The treatise consists in an introduction which is part manifesto, part history, followed by Du Vair's French translation and critique of the most famous of Cicero's orations, the *Oratio pro Milone*. Noting Du Vair's admiration for Cicero, Marc Fumaroli, in his great study, *L'Age de l'éloquence: Rhétorique et 'res literaria' de la Renaissance au seuil de l'époque classique*, observes that Du Vair's rhetorical tastes differed from those of other neo-Stoics, notably the famously lapidary Lipsius. "While Christian Stoicism in Flanders with Justus Lipsius had as a logical corollary an 'anti-ciceronian' style, in France, with Du Vair, it resulted in the rehabilitation of Cicero, badly mistreated until then."[91] In the solitude of retreat, Lipsius, and Montaigne, too, distilled dense moral messages in *sententiae* taken from the ancients, producing a "rhetoric of citations" conducive to private contemplation. Du Vair, on the other hand, dreamed of galvanizing public action, and his nostalgia for the orator as the de facto ruler of the *civitas* led him naturally to Cicero (106–43 B.C.), filtered in the following citation through Tacitus' *Dialogus de oratoribus* (ca. 81 A.D.):

What is more royal in this world, than to respond to the prayers of the afflicted, to save them in their calamity, to deliver them from danger, to procure their salvation, and to be the safe harbor of the innocent and oppressed? What is more magnificent than to see that those who are wealthy seek out your friendship, honor and revere you as the defender and protector of their good fortune? What is more august than to see, when you stand up to speak, that everyone quiets down, cocks their ears attentively, and fixes their eyes on you; than to observe the desires and inclinations of the people turn with your words, [and] the opinion of judges and the counsel of the senate bend under your voice?[92]

---

91 Marc Fumaroli, *L'Age de l'éloquence: Rhétorique et 'res literaria' de la Renaissance au seuil de l'époque classique* (Geneva: Droz, 1980), 500, 502.

92 Du Vair, 395. Marcus Aper in Tacitus' *Dialogue of the orators* defends the advantages of eloquence over those of poetry: "I come to the pleasures procured by the eloquence of an accomplished orator ... what is more sweet than to see oneself solicited ... by the most considerable people? To know that it is neither to one's money, nor to one's lack of direct heirs, nor to the management of some public responsibility, that these services are rendered, but to one's self? ... What a procession of citizens when you go out! ... What respect in the tribunal! What joy to stand to speak ... when all faces are turned towards you! To see the public come together, circle round, and share all the emotions that it pleases the orator to transmit!" Cornelius Tacitus, *Dialogue des orateurs*, ed. Henri Goelzer, trans. Henri Bornecque (Paris: Les Belles Lettres, 1947), VI, 28–9. Du Vair is concerned with many of the questions that preoccupy Tacitus in the *Dialogus*, especially the question of the decadence of eloquence, its

Giving full reign to the fantasm of omnipotence through eloquence, Du Vair fancies himself as the savior of the afflicted, friend of the opulent, and master of the "senate." Du Vair is speaking here for his colleagues as well as himself, for jurists intent on affirming the Parlement's great dignity and authority often compared it to the Roman senate. Just as Roman senators had been considered in the *Corpus Juris* as bearers of majesty along with the emperor, French lawyers insisted that the Parlement was *pars corporis principis* or *regis*, a part of the prince's body politic, and thus his peer.[93] In Du Vair's prose, the sovereign becomes superfluous when surrounded by orators exerting a function so "royal,""magnificent,"and "august."

Of course, Du Vair was not unaware of the suspicions with which his contemporaries regarded persuasion, and he takes care to counter them. To be sure, he concedes, lies can be made to look like truth. "To what is men's understanding bound but to the true?" He muses, "[f]alsehood itself is only ever received under the name of truth."[94] Du Vair also acknowledges that as a result of its power to disguise the false as true, eloquence poses a proven public danger. "Many bad men have misused eloquence, [and] subverted its use to the ruin of their country." Those who, "imbued with feverish austerity," spurn eloquence "as dangerous to the government of States" and fear that evil men will use it to "overthrow laws and trouble the *repos* of the country" are not entirely misled. Nevertheless, Du Vair argues that eloquence is an inherently neutral tool that can be deployed to honorable or infamous effect, and he views Plato's contention that truth speaks for itself as dangerously naïve.[95] Had Du Vair been writing during the Augustinian moment of the Catholic reformation a century later, he might have pointed to man's fall from grace to explain that the artificiality and mediation inherent in rhetoric were part of man's "second nature"— a necessary evil, as it were, in a fallen world. Instead, he alludes in more scholastic fashion to the habits of Providence. "To take away [Truth's] strength and leave her naked in this combat, would be, it seems to me, quite imprudent; and to esteem her more without arms than armed is contrary to Providence, which is never so unjust when it comes to its works, as to prefer what is weak [*imbecille*] to what is strong and powerful."[96]

No lance-lobbing Amazon, truth is like a naked woman in a battlefield, whom eloquence masculinizes by arming "her." Du Vair draws on the Aristotelian distinction between imbecility (weakness) and strength, commonplace in late sixteenth-century

---

change over time, and its relation to political structures. The optimism of Marcus Aper, who defends the eloquence of the "moderns," is palpable in Du Vair's prose. At the same time, the observation of another interlocutor (Secundus) that eloquence has no place in the state when the people have no power corresponds to Du Vair's explanation of why eloquence does not flourish in a monarchy. Du Vair's failure to signal his debt to Tacitus corresponds to the natural aesthetic he promotes. He criticizes his contemporaries for loading their speeches with erudite allusions and advocates a more integrated style, where the wisdom one gleans from others has been digested to the point of becoming one's own.

93   Julian Franklin, *Jean Bodin and the Rise of Absolutist Theory* (Cambridge: Cambridge U.P., 1973), 7–8.

94   Du Vair, 381.

95   Ibid., 397.

96   Du Vair, 398.

accounts of female-to-male spontaneous sex changes, to claim that eloquence perfects its user. The most famous story of this kind was that of Marie Garnier, who at the age of fifteen allegedly experienced an abrupt anatomical change while leaping over a ditch. Recalling his ocular inspection of the newly christened Germain Garnier, Ambroise Paré asserts, "Nature tends always towards what is most perfect, and not …to make what is perfect become imperfect."[97] Applying Nature's *telos* to the use of rhetoric, Du Vair genders the strength imparted by eloquence. The ideally dosed oration bolsters defenseless Truth; her vulnerable body acquires tone and tension: "[T]his fashion of oration is like a beautiful, healthy body, which is neither swollen nor bloated, and in which … the nerves do not show, nor the bones pierce the skin, but which is full of blood and spirits, corpulent, with muscles apparent, polished skin, and a reddish color."[98]

The comparison of eloquence to a healthy, well-proportioned body was not Du Vair's invention. He lifted the metaphor from Tacitus' *Dialogus de oratoribus*, in which Marcus Aper criticizes the "hard and dry" style of Asinius: "A speech, like the human body, is not really beautiful when the veins stick out and when we can count the bones, but when pure and healthy blood fills the members and covers the muscles, and that the nerves themselves have colors that hide them."[99] Quintilian (ca. 30–100) had recourse to similar language in the *Institutio oratoria*, where he combats Seneca's suspicions of rhetoric. Seneca complains about dry textbooks that "expose the bones—which must of course be there, and be bound together by the proper sinews, but which also need to be covered by the flesh."[100] And Montaigne, who promoted an eloquence of nonchalance in "De l'Institution des enfants" that clearly influenced Du Vair's ideal of natural eloquence, likewise compares well-woven discourse to an adequately fleshy body: "I do not like weavings where the seams show, just as in a beautiful body, we should not be able to count the bones and the nerves."[101]

Du Vair's expression of a discursive esthetic by means of a corporeal metaphor was thus conventional or at least not original. However, while Tacitus, Quintilian, and Montaigne describe their preferred style of oration by comparison to a beautiful body whose gender they seem to take for granted, Du Vair was alone in envisioning a dynamic involving the transformation of truth from weak to strong, from imperfect to perfect, from feminine to masculine. Fumaroli reads the muscular, sanguin body described by Du Vair as that of a *femme forte*.[102] Yet health for the neo-Stoics was a

---

97 Ambroise Paré, *Des Monstres et prodiges*, ed. Jean Céard (Paris: Droz, 1971), 30.

98 Du Vair, 409.

99 Tacitus, 21, p. 48. Fumaroli says that Du Vair lifted this sentence from Louis Le Roy's French translation of the *Dialogus* (512, n. 191).

100 Quintilian, *The Orator's Education*, ed. Donald Russell, vol. 1 (Cambridge and London: Harvard U.P., 2001), 63.

101 Montaigne, 1.26, p. 172. For a comparison of the positions of Montaigne and Du Vair with respect to eloquence, see R. Crescenzo, "Le traité *De l'éloquence française* de Du Vair (1594): Une réponse à la position de Montaigne sur l'éloquence?" in *Montaigne et Henri IV*, Actes du colloque international (Bordeaux-Pau), ed. Cl.-G. Dubois (Biarritz: J. & D. éd., 1996). I thank Eric MacPhail for pointing out this passage in Montaigne to me.

102 Fumaroli, 512, 514.

feature of masculinity, as we saw in Du Vair's feminization of *tristesse*. In Du Vair's manifesto, truth is clearly best served by a healthy male body, a body one might readily glimpse in a battlefield.

In *De l'éloquence française*, Du Vair completes the equivalence between words and action begun in the "Suasion." League propaganda had portrayed the *politique* as a siren who compensated for her inherent weakness with words—flattery and manipulation. Du Vair, in contrast, depicts truth as a fragile, feminine entity, and armors her in eloquence, so that weapons themselves become superfluous. "What greater honor can we imagine in this world, than to command without arms and without forces those with whom we live? To be master not only of their persons and of their belongings, but of their will?" Where many of his contemporaries, including those who forged their prose in the crucible of the stoic revival, depicted eloquence dressing and dissimulating truth with tantalizing sartorial artistry and bedeviling jewels, Du Vair imagines eloquence endowing truth with the sinewy muscles and sanguin flesh of a body that any warrior might envy, a body that is "invulnerable like Caeneus."

"[F]rom a girl became a boy": in *La Constance et consolation*, the narrator's flagging morale is b(u)oyed by a remedial lesson in the control of the imagination; in *De l'éloquence française*, feminine, naked truth, assumes an invincible male form thanks to eloquence. In both cases, the dynamic of masculinization masks a more fundamental transformation. We readily read Du Vair's autobiographical *Constance et consolation* as a *mea culpa*, as an attempt to account for his salutary conversion to the *politique* platform after his early flirtation with the League. Du Vair invites us to view him acceding from one stable category to another, from girl to boy, from *ligueur* to *politique*. But this is an illusion. The neo-stoic *politique* was anything but the firmly masculine entity that Du Vair makes him out to be. Du Vair portrays stoicism as a kind of constant to which he, the wishy-washy one, eventually returns, as if the *politique* had always been a Sage, as if the *politique* had not initially been feminized as a manipulative Machiavel. Du Vair's story of personal transformation distracts from the metamorphosis that he actually instantiates: the reification of the *masle vertu* of the *politique* and the erasure of all traces of the *politique*'s ties to the reviled Florentine disciple of Machiavelli, Catherine de Médicis. Similarly, in *De l'éloquence française*, Du Vair pretends to endow truth with the strength and perfection of a male body, but what he is really doing is masculinizing persuasion, denigrated all through the wars of religion as the feminine and inferior counterpart to masculine action. The narrative of masculinization allows Du Vair, paradoxically, to present that which he is in the process of creating—the impeccable courage of the *politique*, the magnificence of the eloquent magistrate-orator—as if he were merely describing stasis. One easily forgets, when reading these texts, that the *politique* had once been a siren, that persuasion was still disparaged as feminine flattery. In Du Vair's performative prose, Neptune's wish-granting powers join forces with Henri IV's policy of *oubliance*: it is as if Caeneus had always been Caeneus.

Invulnerable Like Caeneus?

Through his allusion to Caenis' metamorphosis in *La Constance et consolation*, Du Vair dramatized his personal transformation from melancholic Leaguer to steadfast royalist. At the same time, he bestowed a kind of moral authority on the *politique*, previously scorned as a manipulative machiavel. Du Vair's comparison of his changing state of mind to the bodily disposition of Caenis/Caeneus encapsulated the function served by stoic moral philosophy; it allowed the *politiques* to reverse the values devolving from gendered associations. Even though Henri IV based many of his policies on those of his despised mother-in-law, the second generation of *politiques* found in stoicism an advantage that Catherine de Médicis had not had: the means to discredit Catholic extremism and to valorize political pragmatism. By becoming spokesmen for the wisdom of the Stoa, the supporters of Henri IV argued that the womanish Leaguer made France vulnerable to Spanish predation, while the upstanding *politique*, manifesting his *masle vertu* through action-inspiring words, ensured France's continued invulnerability.

The illusion of masculine attainment was not an easy one to maintain, a fact that is curiously evident in the myth to which Du Vair alludes. The continuation of Caeneus' story undermines the very masculinization for which Du Vair deploys it. Erasmus devotes most of his gloss of the adage "invulnerable like Caeneus" to narrating Caeneus' death: "Finally, when he went to the help of the Lapiths against the Centaurs he was taken alone by surprise, overwhelmed by a multitude of enemies, and killed without any bodily wound."[103] Since one might be "invulnerable like Caeneus" but get killed anyway, we are entitled to wonder: Was the expression "invulnerable like Caeneus" uttered with tongue in cheek? Early modern editions of Ovid's *Metamorphoses* that immortalize Caeneus' final moment pictorially invite the same question. The Italian engraver Antonio Tempesta (1555–1630) portrays Caenis/Caeneus before and after her/his transformation.[104] He depicts Caenis along the water's edge, in conversation with Neptune. We might expect the after image to portray Caeneus ranging the fields of Thessaly in "manly exercises." Instead, Tempesta portrays Caeneus in the arms of a Centaur, about to be dashed to the ground. Were it not for the inscription below the engraving, "Caeneus in Perithoi nuptiis a Centauris interficitur" (Caenus killed by the Centaurs at the wedding of Pirithous), one might mistake Caeneus for a woman being ravished by a Centaur. Caeneus' rounded jaw is beardless; his billowing toga covers pillowy thighs and a fullsome bosom. Tempesta's engraving points towards an ironic undertone in the adage "invulnerable like Caeneus."

---

103 Erasmus, vol. 5, 16–17. I am indebted to Eric MacPhail for signaling this adage to me.

104 Ovid's *Metamorphoses* were among the most frequently and heavily illustrated books in the sixteenth and seventeenth centuries. Woodcuts by Bernard Salomon in *Metamorphose figurée* (Lyon, 1557) and Johannes Spreng in *Metamorphoses Ovidii* (Frankfurt, 1563) influenced Tempesta's etchings, which were, in turn, reworked by Jean Mathieu in Nicholas Renouard's *Les Métamorphoses d'Ovide, Traduites en Prose Françoise, et de nouveau soigneusement reveuës, corrigées en infinis endroits, et enrichies de figures a chacune Fable* (Paris: veuve Langelier, 1619 and 1637).

Fig. 3.3   Caenis and Neptune. Antonio Tempesta, *Metamorphoseon sive transformationum ovidianarum libri quindicem, aeneis formis ab Antonio Tempesta Florentini incisi, et in pictorum, antiquitatisque studiosorum gratiam nunc primum exquisitissimis sumptibus a petro de Iode Antverpiano in Lucem editi.*

An effeminate Caeneus in the arms of a creature reputed for sexual predation calls to mind the particular form of vulnerability which Caenis had been eager to escape by becoming a man. In effect, in Nestor's eyewitness account of Caeneus' demise (as related by Ovid in the *Metamorphoses*), the Centaurs are determined to undo his masculinity. "You too, Caenis, shall I brook[,]" taunts one of them. "For woman shall you always be to me, Caenis shall you be. Does not your birth remind you, do you not remember for what act you were rewarded, at what price you gained this false appearance of a man?"[105] The Centaurs fail to reenact the rape figuratively by penetrating Caeneus with their weapons, but they eventually succeed in crushing the breath out of him by piling tree trunks upon him. The fragility of the neo-Stoics' masculinist ethos is implicit in the very myth to which Du Vair compares his mastery of *masle vertu*.

In terms of legitimating Henri IV and ensuring the future of the French monarchy, the stoic revival served its purpose. The king was well suited to incarnate *masle vertu*; he was undeniably masculine, if not always virtuous. Even the love affairs

---

105 Ovid, 215.

Fig. 3.4   Caeneus. Tempesta, *Metamorphoseon ...* (1606).

on which he squandered considerable energy (much to the despair of his spiritual advisors) would be viewed by posterity as indices of his innate virility rather than as marks of weakness. In contrast, Du Vair's fantasy of bending the will of the people through words was never realized. Henri IV, once back in Paris, viewed the Parlement's pretensions with impatience. The "Suasion" that had assured his acceptation by the Parlement and that was meant to demonstrate the new function of the orator/magistrate was to be the last of its kind. In contrast to the honors he bestowed upon the more circumspect Du Laurens, Henri IV quickly made Du Vair the president of the Parlement of Aix-en-Provence, a distinction that doubled as an exile.[106] Ironically, he who had ensured Henri IV's legitimation by the Parlement by convincing his peers that "the domination of a woman would never be approved in France" had to wait for Marie de Médicis' regency to assume the office for which he had been preparing his whole life: Keeper of the Seals, with, in addition, "all functions of the authority of chancellors, and even to preside in all the courts of Parlement and other royal companies, and of those and of all other justices have the oversight and superintendence like a chancellor."[107]

---

106 Fumaroli, 512.

107 Cited in Alexandre Tarrête, "La Querelle qui opposa Du Vair au duc d'Epernon (1618) et le pamphlet de Guez de Balzac," *Guillaume du Vair*, 125.

Even then, disillusionment was almost inevitable. We have seen that the rigorous masculinity prescribed by the neo-Stoics paradoxically multiplied opportunities for effeminate "regression," and analogously, the dogged optimism promoted by Du Vair during the darkest days of the Paris siege prepared his subsequent slip into *tristesse* as peace diminished occasions for the fusion of words and action that he had engineered. Du Vair's poet-grammarian friend, François de Malherbe (1555–1628), points to a discrepancy between the Keeper of the Seals' doctrine and his doings, when he suggests that Du Vair has been nourishing a black humor. Malherbe attributes Du Vair's illness to the "melancholic humors in which he seems to take pleasure in remaining. It is possible to think of the public without neglecting oneself; these are not contrary cares."[108] In the nascent ethic of *honnêteté*, it was henceforth the spectacularly suffering Stoic—the one who, as Du Vair says in *La Constance et consolation*, withstands torture "with a degree of pleasure"—who would be guilty of complacency.[109] The *Garde des sceaux*'s activist care of the state had led to an unseemly neglect of the self. In 1618, Jean-Louis Guez de Balzac (1595–1694) attacked Du Vair, then in conflict with Balzac's patron, the duc d'Epernon, suggesting in an anonymous pamphlet that his stoic sagacity was but a charade. Taking aim at Du Vair's widely admired *vertu* and eloquence, Balzac reveals the Keeper of the Seal's vulnerability to the passions—to tyrannical irascibility above all—and exposes the orator's elocutionary infelicities.[110]

Balzac would soon emerge as the arbiter of a new French eloquence, more pliant in its application and more universal in appeal than the rousing *arrests* of the venerable *politique*. Balzac navigated seamlessly between the patronage of Richelieu, woman-dominated salons, and Roman grandeur, while Du Vair's gallican, erudite cohort retreated into the cabinet Du Puy, pursuing their researches as citizens of the Republic of Letters.[111] The majestic role dreamed by Du Vair for the Parlement was not to be. On the one hand, as part of the bargain for his absolution, Henri IV invited the Jesuits back to France, legitimating the magistracy's most formidable rivals in the realm of rhetoric; they set their sights on the entire kingdom, from the ladies of the court to the savages in Canada. On the other hand, the command by which the first Bourbon ordered the Parlement to register the Edict of Nantes set the tone for the increasingly peremptory *lits de justice* against which it would rebel during the Fronde, while the secret articles that accompanied the edict presaged the frankly Machiavellian doctrine of reason of state, in which the Parlement would not participate.[112]

To be sure, the magistracy would enjoy throughout the *ancien régime* a mystical, if vague prestige owing to the venerability of the institution, as well as to the hereditary

---

108 Radouant, 405, n. 3.

109 Du Vair, 327.

110 Tarrête, 123–39.

111 I am summarizing Fumaroli's eloquent conclusion, especially 695–706. See also Fumaroli 545, 589–90.

112 On the Bourbons' increasingly authoritarian treatment of the Parlement, see Waele, 387–416; Sarah Hanley, *The lit de justice of the Kings of France: Constitutional Ideology in Legend, Ritual, and Discourse* (Princeton, Princeton U.P., 1983); Orest Ranum, *The Fronde: A French Revolution, 1648–1652* (New York: W.W. Norton, 1993).

character of its offices. Yet a *conseiller* in the Norman parlement, Jean Dupré de la Porte hints at "the disaffection of young talent" for the Bar in *Le Pourtraict de l'éloquence française* (1621), an unsubtle imitation of Du Vair's *De l'éloquence française*.[113] The frontispiece, engraved by Michel Lasne, features the Henri II d'Orleans, duc de Longueville (1595–1663), and Du Vair balanced on either side of the column that supports Eloquence. Fumaroli observes that the apparent symmetry of these two figures and of their devices ("honey is in his mouth, iron in his hand;" "honey is in his mouth, the law in his hand") masks an uneven face-off between them. Longueville, a descendant of Jeanne d'Arc's loyal companion in arms Jean de Dunois (whom Jean Chapelain celebrated in his ill-fated epic *La Franciade*), had by the age of twenty distinguished himself as an able military captain. During the regency of Marie de Médicis, he fought in open battle against her despised Italian counselor, Concino Concini, maréchal d'Ancre. The aristocrat was a man of action; the Keeper of the Seals, a man of words, but this is not the distinction that concerns Dupré.

Whereas Du Vair incarnated an eloquence that is "good, straight, and simple," aristocrats like the duc de Longueville preferred Jesuitical eloquence, which Dupré disparages as hermaphroditic because unclear in its intentions. The eloquence currently in vogue, Dupré complains, "has more trouble being recognized than [one has with respect to] the Hermaphrodite in judging which sex dominates."[114] Dupré is unable to put his finger on what is so objectionable about the new style, except for its ambiguity. For one aspiring to the fusion that Du Vair achieved in his "Suasion de l'arrest donné au parlement, pour la manutention de la loy Salique" between moral message and *masle* medium, eloquence with no intrinsic moral content was threatening; it could go either way, any way. Conversely, to those young aristocrats brought up on the flexible rhetoric of the Jesuits, the action-inciting eloquence that Du Vair had compared to a muscular male body in *De l'éloquence française* must have looked somewhat stiff. In Lasne's engraving, the young duc de Longueville steps confidently forward, meeting the gaze of the viewer, while the aging Du Vair, cramped in his *robe longue*, sets his sights on some indeterminate space behind the viewer, suggestive of nostalgia.

Neo-Stoicism and the Nature of Gender

We can draw two conclusions regarding neo-stoic notions of gender from the metaphor of sex change that Du Vair deploys in *La Constance et consolation* and in *De l'éloquence française*. First, just as natural eloquence was for Du Vair the fruit of tremendous labor and erudition,[115] the idea of nature on which the Stoics grounded gender categories was already a product of stoic ethics. The Stoics insisted on the conformity between their ethics and nature; for them, to pursue virtue was to live in accordance with nature. Cicero in *De finibus* explains, "the Stoics say that that has value which is either itself in accordance with Nature or such as to

---

113 Fumaroli, 538.
114 Cited in Fumaroli, 538.
115 On Du Vair's notion of nature in eloquence, see Fumaroli, 508 and 512, n. 191 bis.

bring about that state of affairs."[116] However, one of the standard complaints lodged by Christian humanists against the Stoics was that the impracticable virtue they prescribed was anything but natural. Calvin, who had written a commentary on Seneca's *De clementia* (1532), opposes the passion of Christ and the patience of the Stoic in the last chapter of *L'Institution de la religion chrétienne* (1536, trans. 1541), concluding not only that the Stoics had little to gain through their stony indifference, but moreover that such patience (or suffering) was not within man's potential:

> the Stoic philosophers foolishly described in times past a magnanimous man, who having stripped off his humanity, was no more affected by adversity than prosperity, by sad things than joyous ones, or rather that he was without feeling, like a stone. And what did they gain from this lofty wisdom ? They depicted a simulacrum of patience, which has never been found among men and [never will be].[117]

Similarly, Le Caron, despite the generally stoic tenor of *De la tranquilité de l'esprit*, reassures his reader that he is "not of the opinion of the Stoics who claim to deliver the human mind from all affection and seek to force nature itself."[118] Meanwhile, Du Vair and Charron decry the effeminacy of those vanquished by *tristesse* with expressions such as "corrupting nature" and "denaturing oneself," but their longing for a law that would make masculinity compulsory suggests that what the Stoics called "nature" required a certain amount of dressage. *Tristesse* is a formidable trickster precisely because "she insinuates herself under the name of nature," according to Du Vair. Although the verb "insinuates"—in French "se couler"—would seem to indicate that *tristesse* pours in from an outside source, Du Vair goes on to explain that this interloper is of native fabrication. "Her strikes are all the more difficult to parry in that she is a domestic enemy, nourished and tended to in us, and that we have ourselves engendered."[119] Recovering one's natural virility thus entails the paradoxical task of reforming or purging a part of oneself that claims natural status. Du Vair and Charron invert the ancient Stoics' claim that to live virtuously was to follow nature; they insist that living up to one's nature as a man means pursuing *masle vertu*.

Second, one's gendered nature was not grounded in the body, but a result of the will. In *La Constance et consolation*, the narrator recovers his masculinity through the banishment of *tristesse* and adoption of *masle vertu*. In *De l'éloquence française*, truth grows the sinuous, sanguine flesh of a young male body upon melding with the musculature of eloquence. To be sure, the body is important as a marker of masculinity, as it is of femininity. However, Du Vair construes the body as the expression or incarnation of a nature that exists before the body, but that depends entirely on the strength of the will (in the case of masculinity) for its actualization. Consequently, the neo-Stoics espoused a paradoxical view of gender: essentialist

---

116 Cited in Long, 187.

117 Jean Calvin, cited in Pierre-François Moreau, "Calvin: fascination et critique du stoïcisme," *Le Stoïcisme au XVIe et XVIIe siècle*, 59. Petrarch made a similar point. See Moreau, "les trois étapes," 16.

118 Le Caron, 139.

119 Du Vair, 317, 330.

because grounded in nature, fluid because a function of the will, performative because only realized through action. Of course, to say that for the neo-Stoics, one's nature as a gendered entity depended on the will, does not mean that Du Vair claimed that one could will oneself to be a man or a woman. Will went only in the direction of the deepening voice of Caenis. Masculinity demanded reinforcement from the will, while the weak-willed defaulted to femininity. Femininity, in this view, is less a distinct nature than an unaccomplished one. The parallel between Du Vair's story of truth that becomes male in donning eloquence and physicians' narratives of girls who become boys by jumping over fences is striking: in both cases, the passage from female to male is construed as the teleological tending toward the more perfect, toward nature, toward what was meant to be.

I turn in this final section to the relation between neo-stoicism and notions of sex difference in late sixteenth-century anatomy. What are we to make of the fact that the same year that Du Vair imagined himself as Caenis metamorphosizing into a man in *La Constance et consolation*, Du Laurens, in his *Historia anatomica humani corporis et singularum ejus partium* (1595), argued against the widely accepted claim that one sex could change into the other? Winfried Schleiner notes that Du Laurens's insistence on the difference between male and female bodies at the end of the sixteenth century contravenes Thomas Laqueur's influential thesis in *Making Sex: Body and Gender from the Greeks to Freud,* according to which woman was seen as a variation on man until the mid-eighteenth century when the "one-sex body" ceded to a truly dimorphic view of the sex difference.[120] Katharine Park and Robert Nye, in their review of Laqueur's book, object that he imposes an anachronistic view of sex difference on his early modern sources, failing to recognize that the body did not carry as much weight then as it does today: "The problem is that Laqueur seems unwilling to accept that the metaphysical categories and distinctions of classical and Renaissance writers were just as real to them as our more material ones are to us. He insists on collapsing their rich world of analogies into notions of identity, in keeping with our modern outlook."[121] Although Park and Nye do not address neo-stoicism, the sex changes imagined by Du Vair—changes due to attitudinal reform rather than anatomical shifts—nicely corroborate their claim that anatomy is just one aspect of the Renaissance construal of sex difference. Michael Stolberg, in a richly researched article on late sixteenth- and early seventeenth-century anatomists' assertions of sexual dimorphism with regard to skeleton, asks: "[W]hat else apart from growing attention to empirical detail, could have prompted sixteenth- and seventeenth-century medical authors, across political and confessional divides, increasingly

---

120 Winfried Schleiner, "Early Modern Controversies about the One-Sex Model," *Renaissance Quarterly* 53 (2000): 180–91; Thomas Laqueur, *Making Sex: Body and Gender from the Greeks to Freud* (Cambridge and London: Harvard U.P., 1990). Also on Du Laurens's refutation of the "one-sex body," see Ian Maclean, *The Renaissance Notion of Woman: A Study in the Fortunes of Scholasticism and Medical Science in European Intellectual Life* (Cambridge: Cambridge U.P., 1980), 33; and Evelyne Berriot-Salvadore, *Un Corps, un destin: La femme dans la médecine de la Renaissance* (Paris: Champion, 1993), 36–7.

121 Katharine Park and Robert Nye, "Destiny is Anatomy," *The New Republic* 24 (1991): 54.

to insist on anatomical sexual difference?"[122] He proposes several explanations specific to medicine: through anatomical discoveries, physicians could aspire to fame and fortune, and they had a particular interest in defining gynecology as a distinct specialty in order to attract female patients. Moreover, anatomy detracted from the humoral system, and physicians felt the need to explain sex difference in terms of structures rather than humors. Stolberg also considers broader cultural factors: anatomical discourse of the late sixteenth century reflected a larger emphasis in natural philosophy on the perfection of nature, and may also have resulted from a newly positive view of women. This last suggestion seems to me to be questionable for precisely the reason given by Park and Nye. Anatomy, in the prevailing moral philosophy of the time, was certainly not destiny. Neo-Stoics like Du Vair did not locate gender identity in the body but rather in the will. Thus, I will show that while the new emphasis of female difference was on occasion evoked for pro(to)feminist purposes, its effects on the uneven value accorded to masculinity and femininity was slight at best.

Galen provided the classic formulation of what Laqueur calls "the one-sex body" in *De usu partium*, translated into French in 1566 by Jacques Dalechamps as *De l'usage des parties du corps humain*: "All the generative parts that are in man are also found in women and there is but one difference. ... [I]n woman they are hidden and nestled within the body while in males they are thrust out and prominent near the crotch [*l'entrefesson*]."[123] Coldness, the great impediment to action, prevented the exteriorization of the genitals in women: "Because of the weakness of natural heat, [her parts] were not able to be pushed and chased out."[124] Temperature aside, male and female organs were identical to the point of being reversible; Galen invites his reader to "consider in your mind whichever you choose first, either the organs of women turned inside out, or those of men inverted and withdrawn, you will find them all the same."[125]

Natural philosophers began to object in the latter third of the sixteenth century to the idea (actually argued by Aristotle) that woman was a "mutilated, imperfect, and impotent animal"—in short, that she was a "defect of nature"—on theological grounds.[126] Confessional polemics throughout the sixteenth century had drawn attention to aberrations in nature. Monstrous births were apocalyptic portents; anomalous illnesses, harbingers of doom. Often divisive, portents and prodigies—multiplied, magnified, and mangled through the medium of print—had the unintended result of drawing attention to disorder in nature. Placards of creatures representing

---

122 Michael Stolberg, "A Woman Down to her Bones: The Anatomy of Sexual Difference in the Sixteenth and Early Seventeenth Centuries," *Isis* 94 (2003): 274–99, 291. He is refuting the claim that the difference between male and female skeletons was first emphasized in the eighteenth century made by Londa Schiebinger, "Skeletons in the Closet: The First Illustrations of the Female Skeleton in Eighteenth-Century Anatomy," *Representations* (1986)14: 42–82.

123 Galen, *De l'usage des parties du corps humain*, trans. Jacques Dalechamps (Lyon, 1566), 833.

124 Ibid., 836.

125 Ibid., 834.

126 Jean Liébault, *Trois livres des maladies & infirmitez des femmes,* ed. Lazare Pe. (Rouen: Jean Berthelin, 1649), 2.

an amalgamation of species invited passers-by to dwell on the monstrosity of God's creation, while oracular interpretations of nature's aberrations dramatized the haphazard habits of a reckless and vengeful divinity. The Protestant gentleman and member of Henri III's fleeting palace academy, Pierre de la Primaudaye, chastizes his contemporaries for attributing so many mistakes to God: "I would like to know, if when God created the first woman, he made an imperfect work or not; did he not create her perfect in her degree for which he created her, like man in his?"[127] Likewise, the specialist of female maladies, Jean Liébault, asks if one should judge ontologically different things according to a single set of criteria: "Would we say that there is imperfection in the works of nature and its creatures because they are not all of one nature and species, but of different natures, and that some are more excellent than others?"[128] To Johann Weyer's emphasis on the infirmity of women, Nicolas Rémy objects: "[T]o argue in this way is to bring a very heavy charge against Nature, who is on the contrary wise in all she does."[129]

The eighth "anatomical controversy" that Du Laurens addresses in Book Seven of the *Historia anatomica humani corporis*—"Whether the genital parts of women differ from those of men only by position, as the ancients have thought; and whether a woman can be changed into a man"—is inspired by the same concerns as the questions posed by La Primaudaye, Liébault, and Rémy.[130] In the introduction to the *Historia anatomica humani corporis*, Du Laurens underscores the bond between creation and its Creator, calling man "a mirror of God's creation," "God's book," "the image of the Creator himself." He condemns "Calumniators of Nature" and decries the "obnoxious audacity of those who call Nature *maratre* and cruel." He refutes Epicurus' claim that "men are made by chance [and] from the fortuitous concourse and confused assemblage of atoms" and roundly rejects Pliny's point that man's nudity, unique among animals, indicates his inferiority. Quite the contrary, he insists, man's difference from other animals exemplifies nature's divine wisdom as "mother and governess of the Universe." He challenges "even you, Atheist" to resist succumbing to the wonderment inspired by "Pallas' sacred fort" (the brain), the delicate structure of the eyes, the amazing artistry of the hand.[131]

It was this emphasis on the perfection of God's creation that allowed Du Laurens to see the reproductive organs of women as fundamentally different from those of

---

127 Pierre de la Primaudaye, *Suite de l'Academie Françoise en laquelle il est traicté de l'homme & comme par une histoire naturelle du corps & de l'ame* (Paris: Guillaume Chaudiere, 1580), 11.

128 Liébault, 2.

129 Nicolas Rémy, cited in Brian Easlea, *Witch Hunting, Magic, and the New Philosophy: An Introduction to Debates of the Scientific Revolution 1450–1750* (Sussex: Harvester Press; New Jersey, Humanities Press, 1980), 32.

130 Du Laurens, 357.

131 Marin Mersenne, in his 1624 attack against atheists, advises his reader to read "the anatomy of the human body that Du Laurens has done, and I assure you that you will laugh wholeheartedly at the ignorance of those who accuse physicians of libertinage." Marin Mersenne, *L'Impiété des deistes, athées, et libertins de ce temps, combatuë, & renversee de point en point par raisons tirees de la Philosophie, & de la Theologie* (Paris: Pierre Bilaine, 1624), 136.

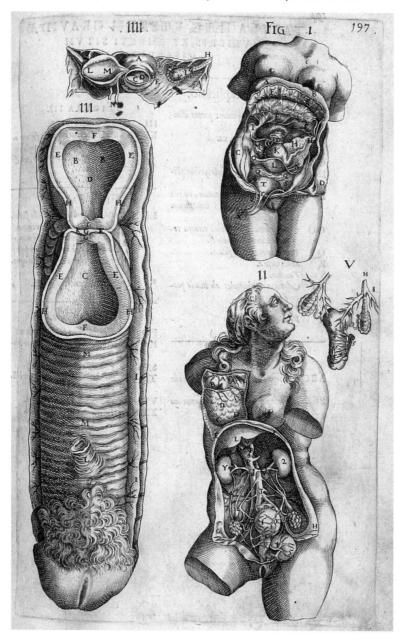

Fig. 3.5   Female genitalia. André Du Laurens, *Historia anatomica humani corporis et singularum eius partium multis & observationibus novis illustrata* (1600).

men (even though the engraving of the penile vagina that he pilfered from Vesalius's *De humani corporis fabrica* significantly undermined his communication of this way of seeing to the reader).

In a manisfesto-like tone reminiscent of Vesalius, Du Laurens refutes Galen's claim that women's sex organs are identical to those of men:

> I have always highly valued the Ancients. However, not being obligated as if by oath [*comme par serment*] to follow the opinions of others, but guided by sense and reason, which are the instruments that philosophers rely upon to determine natural causes, I will say here in few words my opinion on the matter. The genitals of the two sexes are different not only by location, but also by number, form, and structure.

The profession of the natural philosopher does not involve professing an oath of fidelity to the ancients, Du Laurens insists; sense and reason plainly show that the difference between male and female bodies is not merely a matter of placement of the reproductive organs inside or outside the body. As for Paré's corollary claim that women sometimes "degenerate" into men, "I consider that monstrous and difficult to believe." Du Laurens recognizes that spontaneous female-to-male sex changes are cited as proof of the identity between male and female organs of generation: "[I]t is often alleged that several women were changed into men by the sole force of heat, pushing out the genitals that were hidden inside, because of [the heat's] weakness [*imbecilité*]; and it is said as a result that they do not differ in form, but only by location." But he dismisses this logic as circular and argues that alleged changes mask ongoing ambiguity. From the beginning, he argues, these individuals present a mix of incompatible features; they are hermaphrodites.[132]

Du Laurens's researches appear to have been quite influential. Jacques Ferrand, citing Du Laurens, refers to Galen's convertible body as a theory that "our modern Anatomists deny."[133] Insofar as Du Laurens's discovery stemmed from his participation in a natural philosophical trend that like stoicism, promoted positive thinking and peaceful ways, it is not surprising that at least one seventeenth-century author enlisted Du Laurens's anatomical discovery for his prowoman polemic. The German physician Johann Peter Lotichius, in his *Gynaicologia: De nobilitate et perfectione sexus feminei* (1630), refutes the usual claim that the male sex, more perfect than the female in its anatomical realization, is superior in other ways: "André du Laurens has exposed such comparisons as futile and less than anatomical."[134]

It is indeed unlikely that Du Laurens would have drawn any conclusions about the general worth of women based on an anatomical comparison of men and women. He would not have argued that women were less worthy than men because their bodies

---

132 André du Laurens, *Les Œuvres de Me. André du Laurens, Sieur de Ferrières, Conseiller & premier Medecin du Tres-Chrestien Roy de France & de Navarre, Henry le Grand, & son Chancelier en l'Université de Montpelier*, trans. Théophile Gellée (Paris: Michel Soly, 1646), 357–8.

133 Jacques Ferrand, *De la maladie d'amour ou mélancholie érotique* (Paris: Denis Moreau, 1623), 10–12. Helkiah Crooke lifts his argument against comparability from Du Laurens in his *Mikrocosmographia: A Description of the Body of Man* (1615).

134 Cited in Schleiner, 189–90.

were imperfect, nor would he have sought to establish the perfection of women based on the claim that the female body was perfect in its own right. In the *Discours des maladies mélancholiques*, he comments, "It is true that Galen attributes more to temperament than to conformation, and devotes a whole book to maintaining loud and clear that the mores of the soul follow the temperament of the body. I do not however want to attribute so much to temperament or to conformation, that they can entirely force our soul."[135] Du Laurens is probably responding here to Juan Huarte, a physician from Navarre (in the Spanish Pyrenees) who in his *Examen de ingenios para las ciencias* (1575)—translated into French as *Anacrise, ou parfait jugement et examen des esprits propres et naiz aux sciences* by Jacques Chappuys in 1580 and reedited frequently in France throughout the seventeenth century—took humoral determinism further than any Renaissance physician. Huarte purported to advise parents on their boys' career options based on their humoral complexions, taking the proverb "Nature fait habile" as his motto.[136] No temperament was more *habile* or talented than that of the melancholic, whose solitude Huarte identifies with the austerity of Counter-Reformation Spain.[137] In contrast, the temperament that characterizes the female sex is propitious for generation, but useless for learning: "[T]he first woman did not have a mind as great as Adam's, because God made her cold and humid, which is the temperament necessary to be fertile and to engender, yet that contravenes knowledge."[138] In effect, "all physicians reject coldness, as useless to all of the workings of the rational soul."[139] If some girls manage to learn Latin, Huarte says, it is not thanks to their intelligence, but to their receptive memories; girls only absorb knowledge sponge-style and reproduce it by rote. Refuting Galen (and implicitly, Huarte), Du Laurens argues that neither temperament nor "conformation"—that is, the features that one is formed with, including anatomy—determines the actions of the soul. However, accepting the stoic view that the mind uses the body "as an instrument," he says that "acquired mores" can correct innate tendencies.[140] The soul maintains a measure of autonomy, not enough perhaps to actually transform the body, as in Caenis' performative pronunciation of her wish to be invulnerable, but enough certainly for a woman like Epicharis to overcome whatever womanish weakness Nero might have hoped to exploit while torturing her.

In sum, it seems that for a physician imbued with the moral philosophy of the Stoics, as Du Laurens certainly was, the question of the form, number, and placement

---

135 Du Laurens, 111.

136 Juan Huarte, *Anacrise, ou parfait jugement et examen des esprits propres & naiz aux sciences*, trans. Gabriel Chappuis (Lyon: François Didier, 1580), 22, 24.

137 Fumaroli paraphrases Huarte via Gérard de Nerval: "Le soleil noir de la mélancolie ... brille sur l'Espagne et sur ses théologiens. 'L'obscure clarté' de Saturne soutient l'orgueil de l'Espagne, pays chaud et sec, à mi-chemin du septentrion et des tropiques, élu pour la mélancolie. Et cet *ingenium* mélancolique de l'Espagne trouve dans la 'sévérité solitaire' de ses théologiens, dépositaires par excellence de la vérité catholique, sa plus haute manifestation" (130).

138 Huarte, 19.

139 Huarte, 62.

140 Le Caron, 49.

of the sex organs was irrelevant to the evaluation of the intellectual capacity of the individuals in whose bodies they resided. The Stoic regarded the body, whether monstrous or "perfect in its degree," as an instrument of the will. We glimpse in Du Laurens's distaste for Galenic determinism a glimmer of things to come: Descartes's claim that mind and body are distinct substances and his reconstrual of the body in mechanistic terms. Yet stoicism led to conclusions no less sexist that those of the Galenist Huarte, because the Stoics construed the soul's ability to impose its will as a manifestation of *masle vertu*. In his rebuttal of Huarte's *Examen*, entitled *Examen de l'examen des esprits*, Jourdain Guibelet mocks Huarte for subscribing to "the old opinion" that women are deformed men. Yet in comparison to Huarte's dismal assessment of girls' capacity for knowledge, he makes the no more flattering assertion that women are like animals: "[T]hey have no reason to reign in their appetites; they let themselves be carried away by their imagination's movements."[141] Huarte had relied on the mind/body homologies of Galenic humoral theory to justify the exclusion of women from the pursuit of knowledge. In Guibelet's misogyny, we recognize the circular nature of the Stoics. The failure to control the imagination and to reign in the passions reveals the lack of *masle vertu*.

My analysis of Du Laurens's discovery suggests that the voluntarism of the Stoic ethic provided an important (and overlooked) alternative to Galenic determinism in the late sixteenth century. There can be no doubt that late sixteenth-century neo-stoicism paved the way for Cartesian dualism and corresponding mechanism. However, no Stoic would arrive at the conclusion reached by some pro(to)feminist Cartesians—"l'esprit n'a point de sexe" ("the mind has no sex")—because they viewed sex as the body's reflection of a noncorporeal nature that was already gendered. Before moving on to assess Descartes's debt to stoicism, we must first address the *Essais* of Michel de Montaigne, whose skepticism thoroughly exposed the contingency of neo-stoic masculinity.

---

141 Jourdain Guibelet, *Examen de l'examen des esprits* (Paris: Michel Soly, 1631), 706.

Chapter Four

The Suspension of Difference: Michel de Montaigne's Lame Lovers

Debate about the moral worth and intellectual capacity of women pervaded early modern intellectual life. In France, this debate became known as the *Querelle des femmes*. A wide variety of discourses are said to participate in the antifeminist side of the *Querelle*, from romance (Jean de Meun's *Roman de la rose*) to demonology (the *Malleus maleficarum*). On the prowoman side, there is more homogeneity; indeed, it seems likely that the "querelle" referred originally only to pro(to)feminist argument. A "querelle," according to Antoine Furetière in his *Dictionnaire universel* (1697), denotes either "contestation, dispute, combat" or a controversial position that one defends on behalf of another: "Friends support their friends' *querelle* under all circumstances. That author wrote an apology of the work; he took on the *querelle* of he who wrote it."[1] Thus, an exchange of poems in the 1540s among Bertrand de la Borderie, Charles Fontaine, and Antoine Héroët became known as the *Querelle des amies* because each expounded the philosophy of love of a different (fictitious) "Amie" or female friend.[2] Those who defended the cause of women in general usually did so not through poetry but in mock debate or pointed declamations, following the conventions of the paradox, a "formal defense, organized along the lines of traditional *encomia*, of an unexpected, unworthy, or indefensible subject."[3] Hence Charles Estienne declares in his *Paradoxes* (1553), a highly successful adaptation of Ortensio Lando's *Paradossi cioè, sententie fuora del comun parere* (1543), "That the excellence of woman is greater than that of man." Estienne proclaims women's superior purity, prowess, courtliness, intelligence—all for the benefit of male readers, whom he addresses in frequent interjections ("as I was saying, *messieurs*").[4]

Since the point of the paradox was "to show off the skill of an orator and to arouse the admiration of an audience, both at the outlandishness of the subject and the technical brilliance of the rhetorician," critical analyses of the pro-woman side of the *Querelle* often focus on the question of the author's sincerity.[5] Not surprisingly,

---

1   Antoine Furetière, "Querelle," *Dictionnaire universel* (The Hague and Rotterdam: A. and R. Leers, 1590).

2   Lawrence D. Kritzman, "The Neoplatonic Debate," *A New History of French Literature*, ed. Denis Hollier (Cambridge and London: Harvard U.P., 1989), 188.

3   Rosalie L. Colie, *Paradoxia Epidemica: The Renaissance Tradition of Paradox* (Princeton: Princeton U.P., 1966), 3.

4   Charles Estienne, *Paradoxes*, ed. Trevor Peach (Geneva: Droz, 1998), 225. The *Paradoxes* saw three editions in 1553 alone, followed by four more in 1554. Trevor Peach, "Introduction," Charles Etienne, *Paradoxes*, 8.

5   Colie, 3.

women's voices tend to be more compelling than those of men when viewed in these terms. It was only after a lengthy trial to rescind her vows that Gabrielle Suchon wrote her *Traité de la morale et de la politique* (1693), in which she argues in favor of the liberty, knowledge, and authority of women; she lived in poverty and published at her own expense.[6] Suchon's determination lends to her understated vindications a poignancy unmatched by the rhetorical skill of any (male) humanist. As Albert Rabil Jr. puts it, "a woman writing was in herself a statement of women's claim to dignity."[7]

The notion of a *Querelle* brings to light the enduring relevance of "the woman question." Moreover, it gives visibility to little-known texts authored by women. At the same time, however, placing four centuries of pro(to)feminist discourse within the parentheses of a *Querelle* imposes artificial homogeneity on the various and varied authors who spoke about women, while severing "the woman question" from the political, economic, and intellectual contexts that made it compelling to the people of the time. Sensitive to this problem, Tjitske Akkerman and Siep Stuurman divide the *Querelle* into two phases:

> [The] first [phase] spans late-medieval and Renaissance times and ends somewhere in the seventeenth century; and a second one … more or less coincides with the Enlightenment. The feminism of the first period is fairly well represented by the genre of the *Querelle*, which was above all a discourse on morality and manners with philosophical concerns occasionally intruding. Enlightenment feminism, however, was exemplified by an altogether different mode of discourse, underpinned by a few key philosophical notions, such as reason, progress and above all, equality.[8]

Pro-woman discourse in the Renaissance (if it was sincere) aimed mostly to inspire respect and admiration for women. Enlightenment feminism had political objectives. The seventeenth century, according to Akkerman and Stuurman, was a transitional period between these two forms of pro(to)feminist discourse. In effect, only after Descartes laid out his grand blueprint for the search for truth in the *Discours de la méthode* did the idea of progress implicit in late Renaissance historiography come to be seen as something that individuals could shape.[9] Men and women could reform existing institutions to improve the quality of human life. They began in the seventeenth century with instruction: François Poullain de la Barre proposed a new curriculum for women's education. They continued in the eighteenth century with

[handwritten marginal note: Eg up until that point no change ? epistem ?]

6   On Suchon's *Traité de la morale et de la politique*, see Linda Timmermans, *L'Accès des femmes à la culture (1598-1715): Un débat d'idées de Saint François de Sales à la Marquise de Lambert* (Paris: Champion, 1993), 777–82.

7   Albert Rabil Jr., "Editor's Introduction to the Series," Henricus Cornelius Agrippa, *Declamation on the Nobility and Preeminence of the Female Sex*, trans. and ed. Albert Rabil Jr. (Chicago and London: University of Chicago Press, 1996), xxii.

8   Tjitske Akkerman and Siep Stuurman, *Perspectives on Feminist Political Thought in European History* (New York: Routledge, 1998), 10.

9   On the idea of perfectibility in late Renaissance historiography see George Huppert, *The Idea of Perfect History: Historical Erudition and Historical Philosophy in Renaissance France* (Urbana: University of Illinois Press, 1970).

political demands: the Marquis de Condorcet and then Olympe de Gouges extended the discourse of rights to women during the Revolution.[10]

Doubtlessly, Renaissance and Enlightenment participants in the *Querelle des femmes* had different objectives, and it is useful to distinguish them. Nevertheless, Stuurman's claim that "early-modern feminism was a literary genre rather than a definite philosophical current" merits reconsideration.[11] Differentiating between a Renaissance "genre" to which philosophical concerns were largely peripheral, and an Enlightenment current grounded in "key philosophical notions" reflects a Cartesian bias. One of Descartes's accomplishments was to redefine as literature what in the Renaissance had certainly counted as philosophy. According to Hasan Melehy, "the cogito [marked] a moment of separation of the institutional realms of philosophy and literature."[12] Most important for Descartes's purposes, rejecting metaphor in the *Regulae ad directionem ingenii* (*Rules for the Direction of the Mind*, first published in 1684 in Dutch) and disdaining humanistic erudition in the *Discours de la méthode* (1637) worked to discredit skepticism, that ancient school of thought whose revival in the second half of the sixteenth century had done so much to exacerbate the anarchy of knowledge that he deplored.[13]

This chapter is about the intertwining development of pro-woman polemic and the rise of skepticism in Renaissance France.[14] It is not fortuitous that two of the most outspoken interlocutors in the *Querelle des femmes* had strong connections to skepticism.

---

10 On Olympe de Gouges, see Joan Scott, *Only Paradoxes to Offer: French Feminists and the Rights of Man* (Cambridge: Harvard U.P., 1996).

11 Siep Stuurman, *François Poulain de la Barre and the Invention of Modern Equality* (Cambridge: Harvard U.P., 2004), 53. Ginevra Conti Odorisio makes this point at the end of *Famiglia e Stato nella* République *di Jean Bodin* (Torino: G. Giappichelli, 1993): "Il dibattito sui rapport tra I generi e quindi anche sul ruolo e la funzione della donna, lungi dall'essere una querelle come generalmente viene considerate, oziosa, letteraria, consituisce invece uno degli elementi fondamentali del dibattito ideologico che accompanga ogni fenomeno di trasformazione sociale ed e indispensabile per comprendere il modello cultural su cui la società si fonda e i valori in cui si identifica" (128).

12 Hasan Melehy, *Writing Cogito: Montaigne, Descartes, and the Institution of the Modern Subject* (Albany: State University of New York Press, 1997), 14.

13 Whenever people notice some similarity between two things, they are in the habit of ascribing to the one what they find true of the other, even when the two are not in that respect similar." René Descartes, *The Philosophical Writings of Descartes*, trans. John Cottingham, Robert Stoothoff, and Dugald Murdoch, vol. 1 (Cambridge and New York: Cambridge University Press: 1985), 9.

14 As far as I know, there has been no sustained analysis of the connection between skepticism and the *querelle des femmes*. Constance Jordan, in *Renaissance Feminism: Literary Texts and Political Models* (Ithaca: Cornell U.P., 1990), alludes only briefly to pyrrhonism in her analysis of Marie de Gournay (286). In *Hermaphrodites in Renaissance Europe* (Burlington: Ashgate Publishing Company, 2006), Kathleen Perry Long analyzes gendered themes in the sourcebook for Renaissance Skepticism, Sextus Empiricus' *Outlines of Pyrrhonism*. The most thorough treatment of gender in Montaigne's *Essays* is Richard Regosin, *Montaigne's Unruly Brood: Textual Engendering and the Challenge to Paternal Authority* (Berkeley: University of California Press, 1996). I am much indebted to Regosin in this chapter, although I focus more explicitly on skepticism than he does.

Heinrich Cornelius Agrippa von Nettesheim's refutation of Aristotle's claim that men are more courageous, wiser, and nobler than women in *De nobilitate et praecellentia foeminei sexus* (1529) foreshadows his condemnation of scholastic presumptuousness in his *De incertitudine et vanitate scientiarum* (1530).[15] Marie de Gournay, author of *De l'égalité des hommes et des femmes* (1626), was Montaigne's *fille d'alliance* (covenant daughter), and skeptical arguments permeate her work, including *De l'égalité des hommes et des femmes*. The titles of Agrippa's and Gournay's responses to "the woman question" reveal a different approach, however, an approach that reflects the development of skeptical thought over the course of the sixteenth century: Agrippa argues for the superiority of women over men, while Marie de Gournay argues for women's equality with men. In *François Poullain de la Barre and the Invention of Modern Equality*, Siep Stuurman credits the Cartesian Poullain de la Barre for inventing the notion of equality in *De l'égalité des deux sexes* (1674). While Descartes's dualism certainly provided the content for the argument that "the mind has no sex" and, therefore, that sex difference could not be used as a basis for excluding women from the search for truth, I argue that the notion of the equality of the sexes is not of Cartesian origin. Instead, I contend that Marie de Gournay drew the idea of equality from her reading of Montaigne's *Essays*. Granted, neither those *Essays* nor their author typically figure in accounts of the *Querelle des femmes*.[16] Montaigne was no pro(to)feminist. Nevertheless, the *Essays* are full of the essaying (weighing, balancing) of received ideas pertaining to men and women, masculinity and femininity. The flattening of gender hierarchy and the suspension of gender difference, both privileged expressions of Montaigne's skepticism, laid the groundwork for Marie de Gournay's invention of equality.

Fideism versus Skepticism

In order to understand how skepticism transformed "the woman question," it is useful to differentiate Montaigne's "modern skepticism" from the fideist application of the skeptical critique of knowledge.[17] Early modern interest in ancient skepticism

---

15   Albert Rabil, Jr., "Agrippa and the Feminist Tradition," Henricus Cornelius Agrippa, *Declamation on the Nobility and Preeminence of the Female Sex*, 17.

16   Maïté Albistur and Daniel Armogathe in their *Histoire du féminisme français du moyen âge à nos jours* (Paris: Des Femmes, 1977), include Montaigne's *Essays* in their list of "literary landmarks" pertaining to the *Querelle des femmes*. They note the ambiguities in Montaigne's disparate thoughts on women, concluding, "How are we to understand the fact that the old gentleman was so close to she who was to become the first feminist of the seventeenth century? How do we reconcile the paltry opinion he had of women with the sudden alliance with she who took up the defense of the female sex?" (118).

17   I take the term "modern Skepticism" from Sylvia Giocanti, *Penser l'irrésolution: Montaigne, Pascal, La Mothe le Vayer. Trois itinéraires sceptiques* (Paris: Champion, 2001), 31. Giocanti is most categorical in her identification of Montaigne as a skeptic. She argues that the suspension of judgment is an end in itself in the *Essays*; the radical skepticism one encounters therein is moreover inimical to faith. In contrast, Ann Hartle in *Michel de Montaigne: Accidental Philosopher* (Cambridge and New York: Cambridge U.P., 2003) contends that

stemmed initially from an apologetic agenda. Christian (usually Catholic) apologists incorporated the skeptical suspension of judgment into fideist developments: human reason acknowledges its limitations and accepts the impenetrability of revealed truths. By the early 1500s, many believers had become impatient with the clergy's devotion to the faith-numbing task of ironing out the wrinkles in the great amalgam between Aristotelian natural philosophy and Catholic theology begun by Thomas Aquinas in the thirteenth century. Heinrich Cornelius Agrippa von Nettesheim's assault on the presumptuousness of human claims to knowledge in *De incertitudine et vanitate omnium scientiarum et artium liber* (1530) represents "the culmination of a current of discredit" suffered by scholastic philosophy.[18] The epistle to the reader consists in a facetious comparison of the author to Hercules: Agrippa meets with "greate labours, and with no lesse daunger, beynge of no lesse travaile, then peril to overcome these monsters of Studies and Schooles."[19] After a very long catalog of the blows he expects to receive at the hands of insulted readers, he sounds the battle cry: "These then so unadvised Giantes, and enemies of the Holie Scriptures, are to be assalted, and their Fortresses and Castles ransacked." His mission is

> to declare howe greate the blindenesse of men is, with so many Sciences and Artes, and with so many Maisters and Authours, always to erre from the knowledge of the Truethe: and how greate a rashenesse, and presumptuous arrogancie it is, to preferred the schooles of Philosophers, before the Church of Christe: And to set before, and make equivalent, the opinions of men, with the Woorde of God.[20]

Agrippa's sense of playfulness and provocation is equally evident in *De nobilitate et praecellentia foeminei sexus*, a declamation he pronounced in 1509 at the University of Dôle in Burgundy in honor of Margaret of Austria. In his preface

---

Montaigne "takes up the most fundamental philosophical questions in a profoundly original, comprehensive and coherent way" and denies that Montaigne pursued imperturbability as the supreme good; instead, she asserts, he believed that "there is indeed truth and it resides in God" (1, 16). It seems to me that Montaigne's "accidental philosophy," as Hartle fittingly calls it, is not incompatible with skepticism, if we understand skepticism to be a practice rather than a doctrine.

18   Jean-Paul Dumont, *Le Scepticisme et le phénomène: Essai sur la signification et les origines du pyrrhonisme* (Paris: Vrin, 1972) 33.

19   Heinrich Cornelius Agrippa, *Of the Vanity and Uncertaintie of Artes and Sciences*, trans. James Sanford (1569), ed. Catherine M. Dunn (Northridge: California State U.P., 1974), 3. Agrippa may compare himself to Hercules in reference to the Academic skeptic Carneades. According to Montaigne, "Clitomachus said of old that Carneades had surpassed the labors of Hercules, in having torn away from man the habit of assent—that is to say, opinion and rashness in judging." Michel de Montaigne, *The Complete Essays of Montaigne*, trans. Donald Frame (New York: Doubleday, 1960), III: 276; *Essais*, ed. Pierre Villey (Paris: Presses Universitaires de France, 1965), 1035. I will henceforth cite the Frame translation as DF, Villey edition as PV.

20   Agrippa, *Of the Vanity*, 10. Agrippa's encompassing critique of human knowledge complemented his interest in magic. The occult defied explanation, confirming the weakness of human reason. See Charles G. Nauert, Jr., *Agrippa and the Crisis of Renaissance Thought* (Urbana: University of Illinois Press, 1965), 141.

to Maximilian Transilvanus composed twenty years later, Agrippa refers to the work as to "trifles of my youth" and promises to produce works "on more profound and serious topics."[21] But *De nobilitate* is no more frivolous than *De vanitate*, and the question of Agrippa's sincerity is inadequate to grasping his purpose. Agrippa's defense of the paradox of women's superiority "exhibits serious intent: the need for such outlandish arguments to maintain an extreme opinion is meant to reflect on the outlandishness of the argument that would be necessary to maintain the opposite extreme."[22] Whether or not Agrippa believed that women were more virtuous than men (his dealings with Margaret of Austria certainly would not have confirmed this thesis), without a doubt, he scorned complacent self-satisfaction characteristic of men in relation to women:

> If one says with Aristotle that, among all living beings, the males are more courageous, wise and noble, the apostle Paul, who was a more excellent teacher than he, responds in these words: "God has chosen foolish things of the world to confound the wise, God has chosen the weak of the world to confound the strong; and God has chosen vile things and those that are despised, things which are not, in order to reduce to nothing things which are."[23]

Agrippa's contrast between Aristotle and Paul in *De nobilitate* prepares his opposition of faith to knowledge in *De vanitate*. In *De nobilitate*, women confound "superior" men. In *De vanitate*, the ass trumps the learned. Agrippa devotes the last chapter of *De vanitate* to praising the ass as a model of Christian humility.[24] Women, asses: the parallel is certainly not flattering. But the point in both cases is to compel (learned) men to humility. *of human nature*

Agrippa's use of skepticism in *De vanitate* follows the typical fideist paradigm: he berates knowledge in order to introduce the necessity of faith.[25] Like Erasmus,

---

21   Agrippa, *De nobilitate*, 40.

22   Linda Woodbridge, *Women and the English Renaissance: Literature and the Nature of Womankind, 1540–1620* (Urbana: University of Illinois Press, 1984), 42.

23   Agrippa, *De nobilitate*, 65; he refers to I Corinthians 1:27–8.

24   Agrippa, "Ad encomium asini digresso" [In praise of asses]. Despite all the persecutions the ass endures, "his simple mind, incapable even of discerning lettuce from thistles," responds "with an innocent heart, lacking in bitter humor, peaceable with respect to all animate beings, bearing with patience all the burdens applied to his back." Cited in Jean-Paul Dumont, 38.

25   Agrippa alludes only briefly to the two schools of Hellenistic skepticism: "the Academikes ... saide that nothinge might be affirmed: ... the "Pirronikes ... affirmed nothinge." The Academics, above all Arcesilaus of Pitane (c. 315–240 B.C.) and Carneades (214–129 B.C.), aggressively dismantled stoic epistemology. Commentaries by Lanctantius (260–325) and by Augustine on Cicero's (106–43 B.C.) *Academica* familiarized medieval readers with the doctrine of the Academic Skeptics. Augustine opposed skepticism in *Contra academicos* (ca. 386). On Augustine, see Dumont 29–32. In *Sextus Empiricus: The Transmission and Recovery of Pyrrhonism* (New York: Oxford U.P., 2002) Luciano Floridi emphasizes that neither Lanctantius nor Augustine dealt with pyrrhonism (13). The Pyrrhonists followed Pyrrho of Elis (c. 360–c. 270 B.C.) in his quest for tranquility through the "suspension of judgment." Ambrogio Traversari translated Diogenes Laertius' chapter on Pyrrho of Elis in

he follows Lanctantius, who in his *Divinae institutiones* viewed the skeptical attack on positivist philosophy as a preliminary step to faith. In contrast to Agrippa's anti-intellectualism, Montaigne's *skepsis* grants value to the life of the mind, broadly construed. It is by giving full reign to the search for truth that one is led to suspend judgment, and to stumble into a wonder all the more transcendent because utterly unexpected. Paradoxically, the modernity of Montaigne's skepticism resulted from his greater fidelity to ancient sources and particularly to his careful reading of Sextus Empiricus' *Pyrrhonianae hypotyposes* (Outlines of Pyrrhonism). Known only to a handful of humanists in the early sixteenth century, this second-century Greek physician would come to overshadow Cicero and Diogenes Laertius as a historian of Hellenistic skepticism in the second half of the sixteenth century, and the influence of his *Hypotyposes* would outstrip that of Agrippa's *De vanitate*.[26] Henri Estienne's 1562 translation of Sextus Empiricus' *Hypotyposes* from Greek into Latin furthered Agrippa's extension of skeptical thought from theology to philosophy, but its impact was more profound than Agrippa's diatribe. The *Hypotyposes* differed from *De incertitudine et vanitate scientiarum* in the same way a how-to manual differs from a manifesto. One could approve or condemn Agrippa's disquisition against all forms of human knowledge; a moralizing text invites moral judgment. Sextus, in contrast, had no moral message to offer; the second-century Skeptic defines pyrrhonism as a practice—a mode of inquiry, a form of argument—through which the establishment of equipollence leads to the suspension of judgment. "Only Sextus," write Julia Annas and Jonathan Barnes, "provides us with the lifeblood of Sceptical practice— argument against the Dogmatists: argument, argument, argument."[27] The *Outlines*, as the name implies, reads like a textbook, an inventory of formulas complete with illustrative examples. Dry, even tedious in parts, the *Outlines* lacks the grand, quotable *sententiae* of *De vanitate* and the moral spark and smarting metaphors that made

---

the *Lives of Eminent Philosophers* from Greek to Latin in the early fifteenth century. Diogenes Laertius enumerates the various offshoots of Pyrrho's "noble philosophy": "All of these were called Pyrrhoneans after the name of their master, but Aporetics, Sceptics, Ephectics, and even Zetetics, from their principles, if we may call them such—Zetetics or seekers because they were ever seeking truth, Sceptics or inquirers because they were always looking for a solution and never finding one, Ephectics or doubters because of the state of mind which followed their inquiry, I mean, suspense of judgment, and finally Aporetics or those in perplexity." Diogenes Laertius, *Lives of Eminent Philosophers*, trans. R.D. Hicks, vol. II (London and Cambridge: Harvard U.P., 1931), IX: 70, p. 483. François Rabelais reveals the extent of Diogenes Laertius' influence in the *Tiers livre* (1546), where Gargantua observes, "now the most learned and most prudent philosophers are not ashamed to be seen entering in at the porches and façades of the schools of the Pyrrhonian, Aporrethic, Skeptic, and the Ephetic sects" (cited in Floridi, 35).

26   Gianfrancesco Pico della Mirandola (1469–1533), author of *Examen vanitatis*, wrote about Sextus Empiricus in correspondence to Jacques Lefèvre d'Etaples. Floridi, 32. It seems likely that Agrippa's source in *De vanitate* was neither Cicero, nor Diogenes Laertius, but Sextus. Cicero ignored Pyrrhonists, Diogenes Laertius ignored Academics, yet Agrippa speaks of both in *De vanitate*. Sextus distinguishes between Pyrrhonists (with whom he identifies) and Academics (whom he decries as closet dogmatists).

27   Julia Annas and Jonathan Barnes, "Introduction," *Sextus Empiricus: Outlines of Scepticism* (Cambridge: Cambridge U.P., 1994), ix.

Agrippa such the fiery, Faustian, personality. Though pedantic in his explanations and smug in his examples, Sextus struck a deep chord with Renaissance authors.

For Montaigne, and for others like him who did not read Greek fluently, Estienne's Latin translation of Sextus' *Outlines* (published along with Diogenes Laertius' "Life of Pyrrho") provided a detailed record of the techniques and *topoi* of the ancient Skeptics. Montaigne had many of Pyrrho's expressions carved into the beams of his study: "I determine on nothing;" "I suspend judgment;" "inclining to neither side;" "to every opinion an opinion of equal weight is opposed," and so forth.[28] Moreoever, of his *Essays*, published in 1580, 1588, and 1595, he devoted the longest one, the "Apologie de Raymond Sebond," to a theoretical exposé on skepticism.[29] The "Apologie de Raymond Sebond" was the *honnête homme*'s introduction to pyrrhonism all throughout the seventeenth century and has dominated scholarly analyses of Montaigne's skepticism ever since. Yet Pyrrho's lessons pervade even those essays in which the actual subject of skepticism seems to concern their author the least. Pascal, in his conversation with Monsieur de Saci, calls Montaigne a "pure pyrrhonian: his entire discourse and all of his *Essays* revolve around this principle; and it is the only thing he claims to establish, although he does not always draw attention to his intention."[30] Indeed, as Sylvia Giocanti puts it, "The skeptic is a skeptic in that he essays his irresolute thought, not in that he exposes it with resolution."[31]

Montaigne's inversion of the values that other philosophers assigned to masculinity and femininity is among the most thorough expressions of his skepticism. Few grasped more fully than Montaigne the extent to which the premise of men's superiority over women shaped the dogmatic philosophies of his time. He destroys stoic ethics, the dominant moral philosophy of his day, by underscoring the extent to which the Stoics conflated tranquility and masculinity, and by revealing how weak masculinity is as a basis for tranquility. He mocks Johann Weyer's empiricism by valorizing the impressionable imagination that, according to the physician, prevented women from accessing truth. He counters Jean Bodin's torturous hermeneutics by

---

28   Floridi, 41–7.

29   Through the "defense" of Sebond's thesis that we can know the truth about ourselves and about God through the study of the book of nature, Montaigne in fact argues the opposite. Ostensibly in reply to those who object that Sebond's reasons are weak and unpersuasive, Montaigne sets out to discredit reason's claim to know anything. But the defense cannot fail to encompass the original thesis; through recourse to Pyrrho, and particularly the impossibility of establishing a standard of truth, Montaigne casts doubt on human claims to know anything. In *Le Scepticisme de Montaigne* (Paris: Presses Universitaires de France, 1997), Frédéric Brahami argues: "C'est dans la fréquentation intime de la *Theologia Naturalis* que Montaigne a…formulé et explicité son scepticisme. Entre Montaigne et Sextus ou Cicéron, il y a la modification chrétienne, la médiation humaniste de Sebond. Cette médiation donne la raison essentielle de la différence radicale entre le scepticisme nouveau qui voit le jour dans les *Essais*, et qui fécondera les formes ultérieures de la pensée sceptique, et celui de la pensée antique" (13).

30   Blaise Pascal, "Entretien avec M. de Saci," *Œuvres complètes*, ed. Louis Lafuma (Paris: Seuil, 1963), 293.

31   Giocanti, 12.

overturning the gender hierarchy that the jurist places at the base of his political philosophy. But in dismantling positive claims to knowledge, Montaigne does not leave a gap that only God can fill. Unlike Agrippa's wrecking ball, Montaigne unseats dogmatic deployment of gender to foster the suspension of judgment that leads to tranquility.

The subversion of normative gender for Montaigne is a means to an end—one that has little to do with championing women, much less reforming institutions. Skepticism entails an individual ethic and cannot serve as the basis for collective action. Paradoxically, however, the solipsistic character of Montaigne's *skepsis* gives him a freedom that pro-woman writers of the day did not have. The latter sought (ostensibly) to persuade their readers of the worth of women; to do so they had to accommodate their readers' sensibilities. Charles Estienne suppresses one chapter from his French adaptation of Lando's *Paradossi*: "Non esser cosa detestabile ne odiosa la moglie dishonesta" (the unfaithful woman is not detestable); one could go too far, even if it was clear that one did not mean what one said. Understandably, women writers were often more circumspect than the men who championed them. Gabrielle Suchon does not ask that women be admitted to the Sorbonne; she recommends simply that women be allowed to live outside the cloister and wedlock as "Neutralists." In contrast, since Montaigne has no pretensions to accomplish anything (except perhaps self-knowledge), and, indeed, announces his disregard for the reader, his thought experiments are limited only by his imagination, whose vastness he fathoms through the subversion of gender identity. To be sure, imagining things differently does not commit one to pursuing their realization. In "Of Idleness," probably one of the first essays that he wrote, Montaigne describes the products of his imagination as "chimeras and fantastic monsters."[32] Yet certainly impetus for change is impossible without the capacity to imagine things other than how they are. "Fortis imaginatio generat casum" (a strong imagination creates the event), Montaigne says at the outset of "Of the Power of the Imagination." It was in the name of reason that Cartesian feminists and their Enlightenment successors would vindicate women's access to knowledge and eventually political representation. But the imagination had its role to play as well, and few early modern imaginations played so freely with gender identity as that of Montaigne.

I focus in each of the following three sections on a different facet of Montaigne's skeptical gender-bending. His attentiveness to gender as a feature of dogmatic philosophy resulted in large part from his familiarity with the masculinist ethos of the Stoics. In the first essay, "By Diverse Means We Arrive at the Same Ends," he inverts the value system of stoic ethics, questioning the virtue of *masle vertu* and valorizing the defect of womanly pity. These effeminate ethics distinguished him from *politiques* such as Du Vair who promoted stoic self-control and discipline as the ticket to peace and political order. Characterized by pride, obstinacy, and an over-abundance of masculine vigor, stoicism appears in the opening chapter of the *Essays* as a cause rather than a solution to violence. In "Of the Power of the Imagination," Montaigne again targets stoicism, this time by highlighting the will's failure to control the imagination. Stories involving spontaneous female-to-male sex

---

32 DF I: 26; PV, 33.

change lead the Skeptic painlessly to the tranquility that eludes the Stoic, because their very *invraisemblance* encourages the suspension of judgment. In "Of Cripples," Montaigne's destabilization of gender identity leads directly to *ataraxia*; he achieves the suspension of judgment by relativizing masculinity and femininity to the point of suspending gender difference. "Of Cripples" is a critique of Jean Bodin's *De la démonomanie*, a critique that encompasses not just the demonologist's punitive pursuit of witches, but also the compulsory character of his fideism. Montaigne reveals that Bodin's "touchstone of truth" is nothing more than violence; violence, too, sustains the arbitrary power of one sex over another.

Montaigne seized the potential of gender-bending from the outset, and was indebted throughout the long evolution of his *Essays* to Sextus Empiricus's relativist comments regarding sexual practices and gender roles. Indeed, we shall see that Montaigne gleans his critique of stoic manliness as well as the point that the maintenance of gender hierarchy depends on violence from a single passage in the *Outlines of Pyrrhonism*. However, Montaigne's incorporation of gender became increasingly bold and increasingly direct over the course of his gradual composition of the *Essays*. What began as a critique of stoic ethics became a privileged vehicle for the practice of skepticism by the time Montaigne composed the third book of the *Essays*. We may view Montaigne's suspension of gender difference in "Des boyteux" as the culmination of his skeptical deployment of gender. But the Skeptical search for truth is not teleological; it keeps going. While the dogmatists say "that they have discovered the truth," Skeptics, according to Sextus, "are still investigating."[33] Gournay's reflection begins where Montaigne's ends.

Montaigne's Effeminate Ethics

"Sceptics do not start from a position of their own," explain Annas and Barnes. "They do not have a set of beliefs, nor even a view as to how philosophy ought to be done. Rather, they follow the going practice of philosophy, and work from within to undermine it."[34] As Pascal would put it in his *Pensées*, "This sect fortifies itself more through its enemies than through its friends."[35] The Hellenistic Skeptics readily acknowledged that their fortifying enemies of choice were the Stoics. Diogenes Laertius reports an anecdote to this effect. Chrysippus, the most influential of the Hellenistic Stoics, had declared, "If Chrysippus had not lived, there would have been no Stoa." Carneades, his skeptical contemporary, quipped in rejoinder, "without Chrysippus there would have been no Carneades."[36] In Montaigne's day, it was Chrysippus' Roman heirs, above all Seneca, who provided the quarry for skeptical fortification. They were mainly interested in ethics (rather than epistemology) and accentuated the practical orientation of Hellenistic stoicism. Seneca in particular

33   Sextus Empiricus, *Outlines of Scepticism*, trans. Julia Annas and Jonathan Barnes (Cambridge: Cambridge U.P., 1994), 3.

34   Julia Annas and Jonathan Barnes, "Introduction," Sextus Empiricus, *Outlines of Scepticism*, xii.

35   Blaise Pascal, *Pensées*, fragment 34 [Lafuma], *Œuvres complètes*, 503.

36   Diogenes Laertius, cited in Long, 94.

organized stoic moral philosophy around the poles of masculinity and effeminacy: "[T]here is as great a difference between the Stoics and the other schools of philosophy as there is between males and females," Seneca declares at the outset of *De Constantia*, "since while each set contributes equally to human society, the one class is born to obey, the other to command."[37] Seneca aligns the superiority of stoicism with the dominance of men, pointing Montaigne towards a skeptical response: he discredits *masle vertu*, valorizes feminine foibles, and recuperates these shortcomings as advantages. Thus, just as Carneades' skepticism would have looked very different had he not had Chrysippus as an interlocutor, so we might say, "Without Seneca, there would have been no Montaigne."

Since Augustine, Christian apologists had objected to the stoic ethic as an inhuman and prideful hubris. In his facetious preface to *De vanitate*, Agrippa feigns fear that Stoics, angered by his attack on all arts and sciences, will turn him to stone. Montaigne, too, plays with the mineral theme in his second essay, "On Sadness." Montaigne begins with a stoic commonplace—"It is always a harmful quality, always insane; and, as being always cowardly and base, the Stoics forbid their Sages to feel it." He proceeds to illustrate the harmful effects of *tristesse* through the inevitable Niobe, whose excessive tears over the loss of her seven sons and seven daughters turned her to stone. Yet Montaigne hardly approves stoic impassibility in "Of sadness." Niobe calcifies herself through weeping, but a German captain by the name of Raisciac comes to the same stony end as a result of his effort to contain his tears as he grieves for his son. The smothering of emotion leads not to tranquility, but to the extinction of life.[38]

If Montaigne's critique of stoic apathy (a-pathos) grew out of a long Christian tradition, it seems likely that his attention to the gender ideology that underlies stoic ethics originated in his reading of Sextus Empiricus. In the discussion that he devotes to "the ethical part of philosophy," Sextus Empiricus asks, "Is anything by nature good, bad or indifferent?" Sextus surveys the customs of people in different times and places in search of an answer. He applies the tenth mode of opposition, "the one depending on persuasions and customs and law and beliefs in myth and dogmatic suppositions." Besides cannibalism, many of Sextus' oppositions have to do with gender and sexuality, including incest, cross-dressing, and "manliness":

> Cowards and men who throw away their shields are in many places punished by law; which is why the Spartan woman, when she gave her son his shield as he left for war, said: "Either with it, or on it." But Archilochus, as though boasting to us about having thrown away his shield and fled, says about himself in his poems: "Some Saian gloats over the shield which by a bush I left behind unwillingly, unblemished armour: myself, I escaped death's end." The Amazons used to lame the male children they bore, to make them unable to do anything manly, and they looked after warfare themselves; but among us the opposite has been deemed fine. The Mother of the Gods accepts effeminate men;

---

37   Seneca, *Moral Essays*, trans. John W. Basore, vol. 1 (Cambridge: Harvard U.P., 1928), 49.

38   DF I: 42–3; PV, 11–12.

and the goddess would not have made this judgment if being unmanly were by nature bad. There is much anomaly about how fine it is to be manly.[39]

In an implicit attack on stoic ethics, Sextus suggests that manliness is nothing more than martial valor: bearing arms and using them. In Sparta, even mothers—those who are supposedly most prone to pity and compassion—indoctrinated their sons to become unflinching warriors. Yet Sextus opposes the authority of the Spartan mother to that of a higher maternal power: Cybele, the mother of the Gods. Her acceptance of "effeminate men" suggests that unmanliness is natural. Along the same lines, the Amazons' laming of male children indicates that manliness is simply the attribute of whoever is willing to use violence to gain power over another. Sextus suggests that the dominance of men in a patriarchal society rests on a similarly arbitrary mechanism: "[A]mong us the opposite has been deemed fine." Under such circumstances, Archilochus's pragmatism makes good sense: Is not cowardice more salutary than temerity?

Montaigne follows up on Sextus' critique of stoic manliness in the very first chapter of the *Essays*, where his intertext is clearly Seneca's *De clementia* (On mercy). In "By Diverse Means We Arrive at the Same Ends," Montaigne compares the effects that diverse attitudes of vanquished enemies have on their victorious assailants. "The most common way to soften the hearts of those whom we have offended, when having vengeance in hand, they hold us at their mercy, is to move them by submission to commiseration and pity. And yet, bravery, constancy, means entirely contrary, have sometimes had the same effect." Montaigne offers an explanation for why it is that a captor might remain indifferent to supplication while capitulating to bravado:

> It may be said that to subdue your heart [*courage*] to commiseration, is the act of easygoing indulgence and softness [*mollesse*], which is why the weaker natures, such as those of women, children, and the common herd, are the most subject to it; but that, having disdained tears and prayers, to surrender simply to the reverence for the sacred image of valor [*vertu*], is the act of a strong and inflexible soul which holds in affection and honor a masculine and obstinate vigor.

The victorious party that does not want to appear weak, womanish, or ordinary, should only acquiesce to the valor that it would like to claim for himself. The rest of Montaigne's short essay consists in historical anecdotes which support this observation. In his assault of Guyenne, Edward Prince of Wales was unmoved by the pleas of the Limousins, yet out of respect for three French noblemen who put up a hopeless fight, was led to grant them armistice. The emperor Conrad III, having besieged his enemy the duke of Bavaria, ordered the noblewomen in the duke's court to leave with anything they could carry. When the women tried to load up their husbands, children, and even the duke upon their backs, the emperor was so moved by their "magnanimous courage" that he spared them all.[40]

---

39   Sextus Empiricus, 37, 191, 200. Montaigne approves of the cross-dressing of Aristippus in "On the Education of Children," DF I: 171; PV, 167.

40   DF I: 1–2; PV, 8.

Standing up valorously to one's conqueror sometimes produces a favorable result. Other times it backfires, however, sparking the fury of the more powerful party. The 1580 version of the essay ends with a puzzler; while Pompey pardoned the entire city of Mamertia, thanks to the virtue and magnanimity of Zeno who offered to expiate the city's offense himself, a similar display of virtue in the city of Peruse gained no pardon whatsoever for Sylla or for his fellow citizens. The theme of the essay increasingly shifts from diverse means leading to the same end to similar means leading to different ends. The question as to how the victor will respond to the valor of the vanquished grows in the 1588 and 1595 editions of the *Essays*. In 1588, Montaigne adds a gruesome story "directly contrary to my first examples." Alexander has finally defeated the city of Gaza along with its commander, Betis. Piqued by Betis' valiant resistance (he had received two wounds in combat), Alexander warns Betis that he will not die as he wished (in heroic combat). Betis "stood without saying a word to these threats," and Alexander, "seeing his proud and obstinate silence" has his heels pierced and attached to a cart and has him dragged around until he is shredded to death. In 1595, Montaigne inserts another unsavory tale. Dionysius, conqueror of the city of Rhegium, gloats to Phyton, his freshly vanquished opponent, that he has had all of the members of Phyton's family drowned. Phyton only expresses impatience for his own death, which Dionysius decides to draw out as long as possible. But Phyton foils Dionysius. Under lashing whips, Phyton "kept his courage steadfast [*constant*] ... and with a firm countenance persisted in recalling loudly the honorable and glorious cause of his death." Phyton's "rare valor [*vertu*]" moved Dionysius' soldiers to the point of mutiny, so Dionysius cut short the travails of his prisoner and had him quietly drowned like the rest of his family. The display of valor is no foolproof path to clemency.[41]

Seneca condemned cruelty as inhuman and unbefitting for a king.[42] But Montaigne suggests that the cultivation of *masle vertu* in fact predisposes one to the sadism abhorred by Seneca. If one ascribes value to suffering, it makes sense that one would want to measure the worth of one's opponent by subjecting him to torture. David Quint reads "By Diverse Means" as Montaigne's commentary on the values of his noble contemporaries, and in particular as an attack on "the stoic drive for ethical self-sufficiency linked with the code of personal honor of the sixteenth-century warrior noble."[43] Contemporary readers of the *Essays* would certainly have understood his opening essay as an allusion to the cycles of violence

---

41 DF I: 3–4; PV, 9–10.

42 In *De Clementia*, Seneca remarks: "Cruelty is an evil thing befitting least of all man, and is unworthy of his spirit that is so kindly; for one to take delight in blood and wounds and, throwing off the man, to change into a creature of the woods, is the madness of a wild beast....The reason why brutality is most of all abhorred is this: because it transgresses first all ordinary, and then all human, bounds, searches out new kinds of torture [*supplicia*], calls ingenuity into play to invent devices by which suffering may be varied and prolonged, and takes delight in the afflictions of mankind; then indeed the dread disease of that man's mind has reached the farthest limit of insanity, when cruelty has changed into pleasure and to kill a human being now becomes a joy" (423–5).

43 David Quint, *Montaigne and the Quality of Mercy: Ethical and Political Themes in the Essais* (Princeton: Princeton U.P., 1998), 3.

that pitted Protestants against Catholics. The first edition of "By Diverse Means" showcases mainly magnanimous winners who correspond to Seneca's portrait of the ruler in *De clementia*. One discerns in these edifying anecdotes an oblique lesson for the reigning Catholic sovereign; he should, like Pompey, act magnanimously towards rebellious Protestants, granting them clemency. But with the additions of the two subsequent editions of the essays, vengeance overshadows clemency, and the value of honor itself is on the line. The vanquished become more obstinate while the victors outdo themselves with cruelty. Betis answers Alexander's threat of torture "with a look not only confident but insolent and haughty." Phyton receives Dionysius' taunting with calculated apathy. Betis and Phyton bring upon themselves the full wrath of their captors by following the unbending virtue recommended by Seneca in *De Constantia*. Alexander, usually "the boldest of men and so gracious to the vanquished" is moved to sadism by Betis' silence: "I'll conquer your muteness [*taciturnité*] yet; and if I cannot wring a word from it, at least I'll wring a groan."[44] Dionysius forgoes his torture of Phyton only because he sees that he needs to silence him more quickly. These vanquishing heroes resemble the tyrannical Nero, who disregarded the constant Seneca's exhortations to clemency and commanded his suicide.

In "By Diverse Means" Montaigne echoes Sextus Empiricus' critique of stoic manliness when he points out that the opposition that structures the moral philosophy of the Stoics—*masle vertu* versus effeminate *mollesse*—fails to account for the diversity of human experience. Great men (Alexander) do not always act great; ordinary people (Dionysius' soldiers) respond magnanimously to displays of valor; valiant women (the Bavarian ladies) as well as men inspire clemency: "Truly man is a marvelously vain, diverse, and undulating object. It is hard to found any constant and uniform judgment on him." But Montaigne parts paths with Sextus when he asks himself what *he* would do were he in the position of Dionysius or Alexander. At the same time as he casts doubt on the value of *masle vertu*, Montaigne states his inclination for the womanish attributes that the Stoics abhorred. Imagining himself as a victor, he decides that either supplication or confrontation on the part of the vanquished enemy "would carry me away, for I am wonderfully lax in the direction of mercy and gentleness." On second thought, he speculates that tears would move him *more* than bravado and that he "would surrender more naturally to compassion than to esteem." Montaigne inclines towards pity, the "vicious passion" which Seneca describes as "the failing of a weak nature that succumbs to the sight of others' ills," which is "most often seen in the poorest types of persons"—above all, "old women and wretched females."[45]

Significantly, Montaigne ties his effeminate leanings to the larger project of the *Essays* through his use of the verb "essayer." "Essayer" appears twice in "By Diverse Means." In the last paragraph, the Thebans, in a losing struggle against Alexander's army, "essay" vengeance, that is, they consume their last breath of willpower in the effort of avenging their loss. "No one was seen so beaten down with wounds as not to try [*n'essaiast*] even in his last gasp to avenge himself, and with the weapons of

44   DF I: 3–4; PV, 9–10.
45   Seneca, *De Clementia*, 439.

despair to assuage his death in the death of some enemy." The willful, valiant, but futile "essaying" of the wounded Thebans contrasts neatly with the connotations the verb has when Montaigne applies it to himself. He puts himself in the shoes of a victor "assailed and essayed" by the piteous supplication of his victims or by their martial valor. Through the passive use of the verb—to be "essayed" by something— Montaigne places himself on the receiving end. His stance is one of receptivity, of *mollesse*. *Mollesse* was the trait that, as Montaigne points out, the Stoics attributed to "weaker natures": children, the elderly, but above all, women. In effect, we have seen that it was not just the Stoics who scorned *mollesse* as a feminine trait. The Dominican authors of the *Malleus Maleficarum* claimed that women were naturally more susceptible than men to the influence of the devil because of their impressionable bodies and minds. Although the physician Johann Weyer ridiculed many of Heinrich Kramer's claims, he, too, asserted that women were more impressionable than men: he speculated on the possibility of an etymological link between *mulier* (woman) and *mollier* (soft).[46] Only the students of the Stoa, however, seem to have worried about *mollesse* in men. I showed in the last chapter why this was so: gender for them did not inhere in temperament or complexion. *Masle vertu* was instead a function of the will; it was something one must achieve through disciplined training and exposure to spectacularly unfortunate circumstances. The prestige of the Sage came from his exceptionality, even among men. But Montaigne, particularly in the second and third editions of the *Essays*, equates *masle vertu* with prideful obstinacy, similar to Sextus, who reduces "manliness" to martial valor in the *Outlines of Pyrrhonism*. Moreover, Montaigne suggests through the closing example of the Thebans essaying to avenge their quickly approaching deaths that the voluntarism so prized by the Stoics has become the rule.

Montaigne does not make a virtue out of *mollesse* in "By Diverse Means." Receptivity, Sextus points out in his critique of stoic ethics, is not something that one can shape into a virtue.

> The Stoics ... say that goods in the soul are certain kinds of expertise, namely the virtues. They say that an expertise is a compound of apprehensions which have been exercised together, and that apprehensions come about in the ruling part. But how there might come about in the ruling part (which according to them is breath) a deposit or accumulation of enough apprehensions for an expertise to develop it is impossible to conceive; for each succeeding imprinting erases the previous one, since breath is fluid and is said to be affected as a whole by each imprinting.

Sextus identifies two problems. There is the technical issue of how apprehensions can amount to anything since the part of the soul that receives them, namely breath, is characterized by *mollesse*, with the result that each new apprehension, rather than adding to the previous one, would dissipate it. The underlying question concerns the passage from passion to action: How can impressions (the reception of an apprehension) in an evanescent medium be transformed into the capacity to act?

---

46 See Chapter One.

Sextus concludes that this is impossible and denies that the soul is morally good; indeed, he asserts, "nothing at all is by nature good."[47]

Montaigne's deconstruction of stoic ethics leads to a different conclusion: in the context of a surfeit of action, passivity has moral worth. The desire for vengeance is driven by memory, and memory is precisely what Sextus identifies as the missing link between the reception of apprehensions and the formation of virtue practiced by the Stoics:

> Since ... the soul and its ruling part are, as they say, breath or something subtler than breath, you will not be able to conceive of an imprinting on it ... (of the sort we see on seals) . . .. For it could not contain memory of the numerous theorems which make up an expertise, since those already there would be erased during the subsequent alterations.[48]

In a perpetually soft medium—contrary to wax, which hardens into the shape of the seal—, an impression stays only as long as it not effaced by a new one. Montaigne's profession of *mollesse* in the very first essay is consistent with his claim that "I do not portray being; I portray passing ... from day to day, minute to minute" (III.2) as well as with his emphasis on his "excellent forgetfulness" (I.17). If memory is the site where the experience of violence molts into the desire for vengeance, then *mollesse*, which prevents the hardening of impressions, favors the collective amnesia mandated by Henri IV in the Edict of Nantes: "The memory of all past things will remain dormant and extinguished, as if they had never come to pass.... We forbid all of our subjects from reviving the memory, from attacking, injuring, or provoking one another with reproaches over what happened for any pretext or cause."[49] Thus, *mollesse*—to allow oneself to be essayed by something without being provoked to action—can serve as the basis of an ethics at a time when the attributes that the Stoics derided as womanly had become the exception rather than the rule. Paradoxically, through his identification with women's pity, compassion, and commiseration, Montaigne places himself above those hardened victors who deny clemency to pitiable captives for fear of resembling women.

Imagining Sex Change Skeptically

Immediately following his opening comparison of other philosophers to women in *De Constantia*, Seneca develops a medical metaphor:

> Other philosophers, using gentle and persuasive measures, are like the intimate family physician, who, commonly, tries to cure his patients not by the best and the quickest method, but as he is allowed. The Stoics, having adopted the heroic course, are not so much concerned in making it attractive to us who enter upon it, as in having it rescue us

---

47   Sextus Empiricus ,194.

48   Ibid., 85.

49   Decrusy, Isambert, Jourdan, *Receuil général des anciennes lois françaises*, vol. 15 (Paris : Berlin-Le Prieur, 1829), 172–73.

as soon as possible and guide us to that lofty summit which rises so far beyond the reach of any missile as to tower high above all fortune.[50]

The "heroic course" prescribed by Seneca for the attainment of tranquility may not be pleasant but it is, he claims, effective. Montaigne begs to differ in "De la force de l'imagination," where he questions the will's ability to master the imagination. Disciplined imagining was crucial to the Stoics' cultivation of *masle vertu* and thus for the tranquility that was supposed to ensue from it. In addition to denying the efficaciousness of the stoic method, Montaigne proposes a skeptical alternative. He happens fortuitously across the tranquility that eludes the Stoic in the process of deconstructing stoic imagining. The imagination's *mollesse*—and particularly the credulity fostered by such *mollesse*—paves the way to a form of tranquility that is far more accessible than the lofty impassibility prescribed by the Stoics.

I noted above that Montaigne diverged from the neutral demeanor that Sextus maintained throughout the *Outlines* when he asked himself what he would do were he a victorious commander essayed by the pathetic supplications or vigorous obstinacy of his vanquished enemies.[51] John Lyons discerns in Montaigne's self-scrutiny a profound and enduring debt to the Stoics. Montaigne's focus on the self, which distinguishes his skepticism from Sextus' impersonal inquiry, reveals his incorporation of the stoical practice that Lyons calls "embodied imagining." The Roman Stoics prescribed a kind of mental conditioning in which the will commands the imagination to conjure up grueling trials in great detail. This training by imagination was supposed to prepare the Sage for any unsavory turn of fortune, to create in him the habit of anticipating and neutralizing passions. In "That to philosophize is to learn to die," Montaigne showcases this function of the imagination:

> Let us rid [death] of its strangeness, come to know it, get used to it. Let us have nothing on our minds as often as death. At every moment let us picture it in our imagination in all its aspects. At the stumbling of a horse, the fall of a tile, the slightest pin prick, let us promptly chew on this: Well, what if it were death itself?[52]

By keeping death constantly in mind, by imagining how the slightest mishap might unravel into death, one domesticates death and removes the suspense that surrounds it. A by-product of this "premeditation" is an unusual level of self-consciousness. According to Lyons, "Montaigne's exceptional and deep attention to the minute

---

50   Seneca, "De Constantia Sapientis," *Moral Essays*, 49.

51   He may have taken his cue here from Agrippa, who explains in his dedicatory epistle to Margaret of Austria that in composing *De nobilitate* he had to battle his own pride, for "to accord women preeminence over men seemed the height of shame, almost the sign of an emasculated spirit" (41).

52   DF I: 80. PV, 86. Hartle points out that even in I.20, Montaigne eschews the elitist fraternalism of the Stoics (99). He begins in stoic fashion by distinguishing the philosopher from unreflective common man: "[T]he remedy of the common herd is not to think about it." In the end, however, the premeditation of the philosopher produces the same result as the nonchalance of the common herd: "We must strip the mask from things as well as from persons; when it is off, we shall find beneath only that same death which a valet or a mere chambermaid passed through not long ago without fear" (DF I: 77; PV, 84, 96).

changes in his own body and to the physical detail of the things around him as they change over the years actually confirms the author's assimilation of basic stoic concepts. Things become interesting to observe when we are not afraid of them, and change is more clearly perceptible when we have a standpoint—a core stability of consciousness—from which to measure it."[53] Following Kyriaki Christodoulou's observation that stoicism gave Montaigne "the materials necessary for the construction of the *arrière-boutique* [back shop], a retreat fiercely defended by a *moi* devoted to attaining the *ataraxia* of the soul," Lyons argues that Montaigne's notion of an interior space resulted from his habit of stoic imagining. [54]

I would modify Lyons's thesis somewhat: Montaigne's attention to the self reveals his *skeptical appropriation* of stoic imagining. Montaigne does not just *separate* the stoic practice of embodied imagining from the normative prescriptions of stoic ethics (self-control, mastery of passions, constancy, and so forth). He furthermore *undermines* the willed imagining of the Stoics in the essay that follows "That to Philosophize Is to Learn to Die." The adjacent position of "Of the Power of the Imagination" to the most stoical essay and its thematic proximity to "By Diverse Means" establish an oblique dialogue with stoicism. Montaigne opens "Of the Power of the Imagination" by evoking his *mollesse*, here a feature of the imagination. "I am one of those who are very much influenced by the imagination. Everyone feels its impact, but some are overthrown by it. Its impression on me is piercing [*son impression me perce*]." Whereas in I.1, *mollesse* has therapeutic value for a society suffering the atrophy of hyper-masculinity, in "Of the Power of the Imagination," the impressionable imagination appears initially as a liability for the health of the individual: "The sight of other people's anguish causes very real anguish to me.... A continual cougher irritates my lungs and throat.... I catch the disease that I study and lodge it in me [*et le couche en moi*]."[55] As in I.1 and I.2, Montaigne begins by rehearsing a stoic thesis: an undisciplined imagination precludes the healthy psychological state to which the Stoics aspire, for when the will fails to control the imagination, it is impossible to attain tranquility. Ultimately, however, Montaigne underscores the will's failure to control the imagination and points to the vulnerability of the stoic quest for masculine attainment.

The eroticization of contagion—("son impression me perce," "[je] le couche en moy") anticipates the main theme of I.21: sexuality.[56] Montaigne devotes the longest

---

53   John Lyons, *Before Imagination: Embodied Thought from Montaigne to Rousseau* (Stanford: Stanford U.P., 2005), 45.

54   Kyriaki Christodoulou, "Montaigne et la vertu stoïque," *Le Parcours des Essais de Montaigne, 1588–1988*, eds Marcel Tetel and G. Mallary Maters (Paris: Aux Amateurs de livres, 1989), 175–85, 176. The *arrière-boutique* to which Christodoulou alludes comes from "Of Solitude" DF I: 244; PV, 241. Lyons does not claim that Montaigne adhered to stoic doctrine. He echoes Gustave Lanson's assessment *Les Essais de Montaigne: Etude et analyse* (Paris: Librairie Mellottée, 1929) of Montaigne as "an athlete of philosophy" whose mind "reveals its originality precisely in the difficulty it experiences ... in cleaving to the principal positions of this philosophy" (124–5).

55   DF I: 92; PV, 97–8.

56   For a rich analysis of Montaigne's use of the verb "coucher," see Todd Reeser, "Re-reading Platonic Sexuality Sceptically in Montaigne's 'Apologie de Raymond Sebond,'"

portion of the essay to anecdotes concerning the will's impotence in the face of an unresponsive penis. "I know of one man, whom I can answer for as for myself, … having heard a friend of his tell the story of an extraordinary impotence into which he had fallen at the moment when he needed it least, and finding himself in a similar situation, was all at once so struck in his imagination by the horror of this story that he incurred the same fate." The mere thought of another's impotence is enough to produce de facto castration on the spot. No less embarrassment ensues when the penis' untoward enthusiasm overrides the will. "People are right to notice the unruly liberty of this member, obtruding so importunately when we have no use for it, and failing so importunately when we have the most use for it, and struggling for mastery so imperiously with our will, refusing with so much pride and obstinacy our solicitations, both mental and manual."[57] Seneca claims that no missile can reach the towering heights inhabited by the stoic Sage. Montaigne points out that the Sage's lackadaisical member may be enough to bring him down.

Not all of the imagination's effects are unwanted, however. Montaigne also evokes unwilled, yet felicitous effects of an indomitable imagination, including nocturnal emissions—"boiling youth, fast asleep, grows so hot in the harness that in dreams it satisfies its amorous desires"—and sex change. "Pliny says he saw Lucius Cossitius changed from a woman into a man on his wedding day. …And through his and his mother's vehement desire, Iphis the boy [*puer*] fulfilled vows made when he was a girl." Montaigne is referring to Ovid's well-known story of Iphis, the girl whose mother had disguised her as a boy to prevent her father from killing her, and who on her wedding day became a man out of sheer desire for her betrothed. Isaac de Benserade adapted Ovid's tale to the stage in *Iphis et Iante* (1634), maximizing the titillation of Iphis' love for Iante by situating the metamorphosis after the wedding (rather than before it as in Ovid's story) so that Iphis is still a woman on her wedding night:

> Mais la possession me ravissait aussi
> Et quoique mon ardeur nous fût fort inutile,
> J'oubliais quelque temps que j'étais une fille …
> D'un baiser j'apaisais mon amoureuse fièvre
> Et mon âme venait jusqu'au bord de mes lèvres …
> Je lui baise le sein, je pâme sur sa bouche,
> Mais elle s'en émeut aussi peu qu'une souche.

> [But possession ravished me too
> And although my ardor was quite useless to us
> I forgot for a moment that I was a girl …
> With a kiss I quenched my amorous fever
> And my soul came to the edge of my lips …
> I kiss her breast, I swoon over her mouth
> But she was as moved (by my efforts) as a tree stump.]

---

in *Masculinities in Sixteenth-Century France*, ed. Philip Ford and Paul White (Cambridge: Cambridge French Colloquia, 2006), 103–26.

   57   DF I: 94, 97, 98; PV, 99, 102.

Fig. 4.1   Iphis. Johann Wilhelm Baur, *Ovidii Metamorphosis, oder Verwandelungs Bücher* (Nuremberg: Rudolph Johan Helmers, 1703).

One wonders if Benserade had Montaigne's impotent friend in mind when he dramatized Iphis' frustrated desire!

In the end, Isis intervenes to transform Iphis so that he can legitimately possess the beautiful Iante. The gonad-granting goddess is cranked down from on high in a grand deus ex machina dénouement, in which Iphis narrates her/his body's metamorphosis:

> Miracle ! Je suis homme, une mâle vigueur
> Rend mes membres plus forts aussi bien que mon cœur
> Mon corps devient robuste en un sexe contraire,
> Et je marche d'un pas plus grand qu'à l'ordinaire.[58]

> [Miracle ! I am a man, a masculine vigor
> Makes my limbs stronger as well as my heart
> My body becomes robust in a contrary sex,
> And I walk with a longer stride than usual.]

In Benserade's play as in Ovid's original recounting of the story, Isis' intervention occurs at the climax of the narrative. Johann Wilhelm Baur (1600–40) chose to portray the same moment for his engraving of the story. The billowing smoke evokes the "thunder" (a euphemism for the creaking and groaning of cog and wheel as the goddess makes her mechanical descent) that the wedding party in Benserade's play claim to hear before the appearance of Isis. Again privileging the moment of divine intervention, Benserade's fellow playwright Pierre du Ryer (1605–58) puts a Christian spin on Iphis' metamorphosis in his 1660 translation of the *Metamorphoses*. Albeit reluctant to call Iphis' transformation a "Miracle!" as Benserade's Iphis does, Du Ryer, nevertheless, sees the perseverance of Iphis' mother (she prays for the masculinization of her daughter) as an edifying example of the good there is to be gained through piety.[59] Montaigne, on the other hand, leaves Isis out of his brief account. In the context of the essay, the reader is led to conclude that Iphis' metamorphosis results solely from the strength of an imagination overheated by forbidden same-sex desire.

The happily-ever-after *dénouement* of Iphis' story, particularly in Montaigne's deity-less recounting of it, differs from that of another girl-becomes-boy plot in Ovid's *Metamorphoses*: Caenis, the nymph to whom Guillaume du Vair compares himself in *De la Constance et consolation*. The story of Caenis' transformation into

---

58 Isaac de Benserade, *Iphis et Iante*, ed. Anne Verdier (Vijon: Lampsaque, 2000), 112–13, 122.

59 Pierre du Ryer, "Explication d'Iphis metamorphosée en garçon," *Les Métamorphoses d'Ovide traduites en François par M. Du-Ryer de l'Académie Françoise, Avec des explications à la fin de chacune fable* (Paris: Veuve Cochart, 1694): "Let us not neglect to say too that this change in Iphis is a reward for the mother's piety, who always had recourse to the gods in her worry, and never ceasing hoping in them. For even if we set aside miracles, God always rewards good people by things that nature does on his command, and that carries out these orders only at the moment dictated by Providence: wanting to show in this way that people who are extraordinarily virtuous, will not fail to receive in the greatest misery extraordinary consolation" (cited in Benserade, 140–41).

the invulnerable man, Caeneus, provides Du Vair with an analogy for his passage from the vulnerability of *tristesse* to the impenetrability of the stoic Sage. Whereas in Iphis' case the love plot creates the narrative pull—will she be able to possess her betrothed?—Caenis's story turns on the wish granted by Neptune: will Caeneus prove to be invulnerable? Iphis' story ends with her acquisition of "masculine vigor"; s/he is able to consummate her/his marriage vows and lives happily ever after with Iante. Caenis' masculinization is just the beginning of her/his story. Caeneus develops and confirms his reputation for invulnerability through subsequent adventures involving plenty of opportunities for being exposed to penetrating weapons. This testing makes him an excellent exemplar for stoic imperviousness (on condition that we ignore that he is eventually squashed to death). The calculated character of stoic masculinization contrasts neatly with Montaigne's final example of spontaneous sex change. Interpolated into the second edition of the *Essays*, this one pertains to his contemporary, the famous Marie Germain:

> Passing through Vitry-le-François, I might have seen [*je peuz voir*] a man whom the bishop of Soissons had named Germain at confirmation, but whom all the inhabitants of that place had seen and known as a girl named Marie until the age of twenty-two. He was now heavily bearded, and old, and not married. Straining himself in some way in jumping, he says, his masculine organs came forth; and among the girls there a song is still current by which they warn each other not to take big strides for fear of becoming boys, like Marie Germain.[60]

Marie Germain's sex change is accidental and thus nonteleological. It is the unpremeditated result of an effort directed toward an unrelated outcome: straining to reach the other side of a ditch. Whereas Benserade's Iphis "walk[s] with a longer stride than usual," thanks to Isis' intervention, the song to which Montaigne alludes warns that big strides can *cause* girls to change into boys. In other words, Marie Germain's carelessness causes the eruption of her "male vigueur." That masculinity could result from carelessness is entirely at odds with the Stoics' careful climbing beyond the range of the "missiles" of passion. And that is precisely the point.

Just as Caeneus's long record of impenetrability exemplifies the stoic quest for tranquility, Marie Germain's impromptu passage to manhood embodies the skeptical pursuit of *ataraxia*. This becomes clear if we compare Montaigne's account of Marie Germain's spontaneous sex change to one of the few allegories recounted by Sextus Empiricus:

> They say that [Apelles] was painting a horse and wanted to represent in his picture the lather on the horse's mouth; but he was so unsuccessful that he gave up, took the sponge on which he had been wiping off the colours from his brush, and flung it at the picture. And when it hit the picture, it produced a representation of the horse's lather. Now the Sceptics were hoping to acquire tranquility by deciding the anomalies in what appears and is thought of, and being unable to do this they suspended judgment. But when they suspended judgment, tranquility followed as it were fortuitously, as a shadow follows a body.[61]

---

60   DF I: 93; PV, 98–9.
61   Sextus Empiricus, 10–11.

Apelles eventually represents the elusive lather at the mouth of the horse, but only by accident when he throws in the proverbial towel (sponge). The long-desired yet still unexpected lather recalls the *jouissance* of Montaigne's close friend, whose semen spills out only once he has officially given up on getting it up: "[B]y admitting this weakness and speaking of it in advance, he relieved the tension of his soul, for when the trouble had been presented as one to be expected his sense of the responsibility diminished and weighed upon him less."[62] The horse symbolized valor and virility. "You stake your valor ... on that of your horse" Montaigne asserts in "Of War Horses" (I.48).[63] The first Bourbon took this recommendation to heart; the *vert galant* had himself immortalized astride a horse near his newly constructed Pont Neuf. Apelles' straining to represent so virile a subject epitomizes the skeptical critique of the pursuit of *masle vertu*: it does not lead to tranquility but to frustration. The froth of the horse results from Apelles' uncontained anger and, in a sense, symbolizes it. The Skeptic experiences tranquility-inducing wonderment precisely at the point of the Stoic's greatest anxiety: in the acceptance of the failure of masculine attainment. Attaining tranquility is, therefore, less painstaking (and less painful) for the Skeptic than for the Stoic.

My analysis of I.21 so far might suggest that the Skeptic, like the Stoic, equates the attainment of tranquility with the securing of masculinity. Montaigne's "friend" vanquishes his impotence, Iphis enjoys *his* wedding night, and Marie Germain develops by accident the virility for which the Stoic deliberately strives. Montaigne even asserts, somewhat tongue-in-cheek, that girls would be disingenuous not to welcome a newly-sprouted penis as a wish granted. Their imaginations are "so continually and vigorously fixed on this subject [the penis] that in order not to have to relapse so often into the same thought and sharpness of desire, it is better off if once and for all it incorporates this masculine member in girls." It is clear that in the economy of "Of the Power of the Imagination," female-to-male sex change is a privileged trope. But this is because Montaigne, true to the skeptical practice of fortifying his position with the ruins of the enemy, is playing a game of one-upmanship with the superb Stoics. For du Vair, the story of Caenis' manly metamorphosis represents the stoic search for truth. Caeneus' invulnerability embodies the stoic identification of tranquility with masculinity. For Montaigne, the masculinity of Marie Germain is only an *analogy* for tranquility, borrowed from stoic moral philosophy. Masculinity has no intrinsic interest for the Skeptic. Far more important than the form taken by Marie Germain's body is the fortuitous way about which it comes. As an accident waiting to happen, skeptical tranquility is less predictable than its stoic counterpart. Froth emerges not from the deliberate touches of Apelles' brush, but from the great mess of colors he used on the entire canvas. Similarly, the Skeptic can find what she is looking for in the material she already has at her disposal, and perhaps especially in the material of which she is about to dispose. We should not be fooled in "Of Idleness" when Montaigne likens the imagination's offspring to "a hundred thousand kinds of wild and useless weeds" that teem in a fallow but fertile land or when he compares them to the "shapeless masses and lumps of flesh" that women produce

---

62   DF I: 95; PV, 100.
63   DF I: 291; PV, 289.

without the form-giving properties of male seed.[64] That Apelles represented the most subtle part of his painting through paint he was about to discard indicates that the Skeptic's most fertile quarry is found in useless, aberrant excess.[65] In "Of the Power of the Imagination," the colorful mess that instantiates tranquility consists of the stories he relates to illustrate the power of the imagination.

As Thomas Laqueur recognizes, Montaigne's allusion to Marie Germain cannot be taken at face value as evidence of the widespread, early modern belief that women and men shared the same genital apparatus (what Laqueur famously terms "the one-sex body"). Whereas Ambroise Paré glosses the anatomical shifts by which Marie Germain's inner genitals were exteriorized, Montaigne attests only to the fact that when he saw Marie Germain (if indeed he did see him—the imperfect subjunctive leaves it open to doubt), he was "heavily bearded, old, and not married." "Whatever Montaigne thinks really happened to the girl who jumped the fence, the essay resolutely obscures," notes Laqueur; "it simply refuses to come to rest on the question of what is imaginative and what is real."[66] In effect, Montaigne goes on to suggest that belief in the imagination's power to effect spontaneous sex changes may itself be a product of the imagination: "It is probable [*vray semblable*] that the [principal] credit of miracles, visions, enchantments, and such extraordinary occurrences comes from the power of imagination, acting principally upon the minds of the common people which are softer [*plus molles*]."[67] We have seen such arguments before: Johann Weyer claimed that women are easily tricked into believing they have seen things that have not actually taken place because of their impressionable imaginations. Montaigne echoes Weyer when he says of the "common people": "Their belief has been so strongly seized that they think they see what they do not see." In a related passage in "It Is Folly to Measure the True and False by Our Own Capacity" (I.27), Montaigne paraphrases another physician. The chancellor of the medical faculty of Montpellier, Laurent Joubert, explains that unformed minds (minds lacking formal education) are also those most susceptible to error. In the preface to his *Erreurs populaires*, published by Millanges (who also published the *Essays*) in 1578, he writes:

Just as insipid water receives all tastes indifferently, and white wool all colors, so we can fashion the soul with all qualities, and happy is the one that meets good masters [early on] so that it is not engraved, colored, soaked, or scented with bad lines, colors, humors, or smells, wrong, corrupted, and vicious from the start.[68]

---

64   DF I: 25; PV, 32.

65   In *Idle Pursuits: Literature and Oisiveté in the French Renaissance* (Newark: University of Delaware Press, 2003), Virginia Krause writes, "Montaigne's rhetoric of uselessness, so often associated with idleness in the *Essais*, becomes a paradoxical form of plenitude" (156).

66   Thomas Laqueur, *Making Sex: Body and Gender from the Greeks to Freud* (Cambridge: Harvard U.P., 1990) 128–9.

67   DF I: 94; PV, 99.

68   Laurent Joubert, *La Première et seconde partie des erreurs populaires, touchant la medecine & le régime de santé* (Paris: Claude Micard, 1587), 5.

Montaigne seems to have the *Erreurs populaires* in mind when he says:

> [I]t seems to me I once learned that belief was a sort of impression made on our mind, and that the softer and less resistant the mind, the easier it was to imprint something on it ...The more a mind is empty and without counterpoise, the more easily it gives beneath the weight of the first persuasive argument. That is why children, common people, women, and sick people are most subject to being led by the ears.[69]

Montaigne agrees with Weyer and Joubert: the imagination's *mollesse* fosters credulity. Weyer claimed to see through illusion in implicit opposition to the melancholic women he defended, and Joubert flaunted his university credentials in explicit contradistinction to the credulity of popular practitioners. But Montaigne had nothing but scorn for the medical establishment, and he dismissed their self-serving distinctions: "[I]t is foolish presumption to go around disdaining and condemning as false whatever does not seem likely to us [ce qui ne nous semble pas *vray-semblable*]; which is an ordinary vice in those who think they have more than common ability."[70] To the extent that it may not be in our power to know the truth, those who base their judgments on what seems to them to be true operate under subjective criteria, which in the case of doctors are distorted by an overinflated ego. Developing the idea of the "weight" of persuasion, Montaigne quotes Cicero: "As the scale of the balance must necessarily sink under the weight placed on it, so must the mind yield to evident things." [71] Ostensibly, those who lack learning will acquiesce more easily to persuasion, since they lack a counterbalance. But Montaigne points out that the learned act in precisely the same manner, acquiescing to whatever they believe to be evident, or *vray semblable*, since they have no counterweight to their own presumption.

Montaigne's "rationalist" hypothesis regarding credulity in I.21 ("It is probable [*vray semblable*] that the [principal] credit of miracles, visions, enchantments, and such extraordinary occurrences comes from the power of imagination, acting principally upon the minds of the common people which are softer [*plus molles*]") rings hollow in light of his excursus on the *vray-semblable* in 1.27. We discern the inflection of a pompous physician in the impersonal "It is probable that...." The physician's normative notion of verisimilitude is at the antipodes of Montaigne's project to tell "what can happen" in the way that history differs from poetry or fiction: "There are authors whose end is to tell what has happened. Mine, if I could attain it, would be to talk about what can happen."[72] Marie Germain may not have changed from woman to man, but who is to say that such a change could never take place, that it is *invraisemblable*? Far be it from Montaigne to claim to judge what is and is not possible. Does he not begin the essay by drawing attention to the *mollesse*

---

69 DF I: 182; PV, 178.

70 DF I: 182; PV, 178. Montaigne mocks medical empiricism in "Of Experience" (3.13): "Experience really is on its own dunghill in the subject of medicine, where reason yields it the whole field" (DF III: 325–6; PV, 1079).

71 DF I: 182; PV, 178.

72 DF I: 102; PV 105–6.

that he shares with common people and women? Just as manliness is a two-edged sword fostering noble acts of clemency and the worst acts of sadism, so effeminate *mollesse* has its good and bad side. To be sure, *mollesse* leaves one vulnerable to the penetrating imaginations of others and thus to illness, impotence, even death. But it also creates the openness that fosters the suspension of judgment. "Montaigne's credulity is his skepticism," comments Ann Hartle. Montaigne reads human history—true or false, true-seeming or *invraisemblable*—as a telling reflection of human potential: "Whether it has happened or no, in Paris or Rome, to John or Peter, it is still a measure of human potentiality, and is instructive to me. I see it and profit from it just as well in shadow as in body." To profit from the shadow of things, so did the Skeptics first happen upon tranquility. Giving up on resolving tricky questions, they suspended judgment. "But when they suspended judgment, tranquility followed as it were fortuitously, as a shadow follows a body."[73]

The Stoics condemned effeminacy as an illness to be purged; they emphasized the constant discipline of the will, for even the Sage could regress to feminine *mollesse*. Montaigne, on the other hand, evokes the mutability of gender as a measure of the potential of human imagination, whose vastness and unpredictability conduce to wonder.[74] He privileges stories involving sex change because, in typical skeptical fashion, he is appropriating stoic materials the better to undermine stoical doctrine. Marie Germain is Montaigne's Apelles, an allegory of tranquility that occurs unexpectedly, as one is in the midst of something else. Her stretching to straddle a ditch represents the leap of faith, the credulity that Montaigne recommends with respect to stories dismissed as *invraisemblable* by the presumptuous. The brief interval in which she/he hovers airborne between the banks of the ditch corresponds in turn to the suspension of judgment. The externalization of her genitals, finally, is an analogy for the tranquility that follows the suspension of judgment.

Laqueur speculates that Marie Germain and the fence-hopping Marie/Marin le Marcis fueled "male anxiety about effeminacy or about the acquisition of masculine traits by women." He sees in Montaigne's impotence (he takes Montaigne's "friend" to be Montaigne himself) a potential cause of such anxiety: "Perhaps Montaigne's penis is at stake.... [H]e settles into the only sustained topic of the essay: impotence and the power of the imagination, and of women, to cause it."[75] Montaigne's manifest

---

73   Sextus Empiricus, 10–11.

74   Giocanti evokes "Of the power of the Imagination" when she says: "[S]kepticism leads to a valorization of the inventive capacity of reason called imagination that allows us to transform our existence by perceiving reality in a literary mode, based on the fictions of the mind" (18). Hartle, too, emphasizes the positive role that Montaigne assigns to the imagination: "His rich imagination allows him to be open to the unfamiliar and thus not subject to the presumption of the learned who dismiss as false whatever seems impossible to them" (5). Neglecting Montaigne's critique of stoic voluntarism, Dora E. Polachek reads Montaigne's imagination negatively in "Montaigne and Imagination: The Dynamics of Power and Control" in *Le Parcours des Essais de Montaigne, 1588-1988*, eds. Marcel Tetel and G. Mallary Masters (Paris: Aux Amateurs de livres, 1989), 135–45. "By acknowledging that the locus of control is an inner one, the formerly imagination-imprisoned reinstates himself as subject," she argues (145).

75   Laqueur, 129.

anxiety about his body does not really explain why stories regarding sex change were popular in the late Renaissance. Either Montaigne's impotence-inspired anxiety is a personal one, in which case we would need to ascertain that other authors who address Marie Germain's transformation had similar issues, or anxiety regarding impotence is universal among men, in which case stories of spontaneous sex change should be a historical constant. Most critics are understandably loath to identify Montaigne as the representative of a particular philosophical tradition. "One cannot really call [Montaigne] a Stoic, an Epicurean, or even a pure Skeptic," opines Hugo Friedrich.[76] But this reluctance to label Montaigne leads to another form of reductionism: a cult of individuality in which the author himself becomes the answer to any question opened by his work. Montaigne's interest in spontaneous sex change may, indeed, stem from anxiety surrounding his own malfunctioning penis, but surely there is more to the story than this.

I have argued that Montaigne's interest in spontaneous sex change is philosophical; he exposes the peril implicit in the stoic conflation of tranquility with *masle vertu*. Just as he demonstrates the impotence of stoic voluntarism by calling attention to penile malfunction, he points to the externalization of Marie Germain's genitals to show how much more effective the Skeptic's *skepsis* is than the teleological quest of the Stoic. Openness to the possibility of stories at the limit of *vraisemblance*—an attitude enabled by effeminate *mollesse*—is far more propitious to tranquility than stoic straining toward *masle vertu*. Stories involving spontaneous sex change are particularly useful to Montaigne, because they provide him with an in-kind reply to the stoic narrative of masculinization. Yet any story deemed incredible by the presumptuous can foster the suspension of judgment: "How many things of slight probability there are, testified to by trustworthy people, which, if we cannot be convinced of them, we should at least leave in suspense!"[77] Indeed, Montaigne relates many other commonplaces that have nothing to do with sex change, including a sequence of stories pertaining to the maternal imagination's power to shape the fetus. Thus, although sexuality and especially masculinity are central to the theme of "Of the Power of the Imagination," unseating gender identity is not what *causes* the suspension of judgment in the essay. It is not *because* Marie Germain is of indeterminate gender that Montaigne suspends judgment (in fact, he describes her quite unequivocally as a man). Rather, it is the *invraisemblance* of her metamorphosis that helps the Skeptic.

Montaigne fully intended Marie Germain's story to provoke the reader's doubt; the counterpoint of credulity and ensuing suspension of judgment require this initial reaction. He clearly identifies the transformation allowed by a one-sex body as a popular belief when he evokes the song that girls sing to warn one another of the perils of leaping. Furthermore, as his secretary relates in his *Journal de voyage en Italie* (1580), Montaigne's "authority" regarding the veracity of Marie Germain's transformation (and most likely for many of his other stories as well) was Ambroise Paré, an unlettered surgeon whose *Des monstres et prodiges* (1573) was hardly taken

---

76   Hugo Friedrich, *Montaigne*, ed. Philippe Desan, trans. Dawn Eng (Berkeley: University of California Press, 1991), 57, 66.

77   DF I: 184; PV, 180.

seriously by learned physicians.[78] We saw in the previous chapter that one such physician, André du Laurens, concluded against female/male homology in 1597 and deemed spontaneous sex change "monstrous and difficult to believe." Du Laurens explained female-to-male transformation away by suggesting that male and female organs were present together from the outset, but that male organs became more prominent with puberty.[79] As for Marie/Marin le Marcis, whose alleged transformation had legal consequences since s/he had taken up residence with (another?) woman, her/his trial would give rise to Jacques Duval's *Traité des hermaphrodites* (1612), in which, based on manual "visitation," he concludes that Marie/Marin was indeed of ambiguous sex, a "gunanthrope," or woman inflected with masculine organs.[80] But for Montaigne's purposes, making Marie Germain out to be a hermaphrodite would take the *invraisemblance* out of the story, foreclosing the opportunity to suspend judgment. In the oscillation between one thing and another, the Skeptic suspends judgment, not in the establishment of a third identity that resolves tranquility-inducing irresolution.

Sextus Empiricus explains how the movement from one entity to another (and sometimes back again) is integral to skeptical thought. To establish a thing's identity, we first have to relate it to another thing: "That other thing would first have to be established, in relation to the first thing or to yet another thing," Kathleen Perry Long explains, resulting "in a process of circular reasoning or in regress *ad infinitum*," which leads to the suspension of judgment. Long astutely observes that in targeting circular reasoning and identities speciously established through infinite regress, skepticism "create[d] a potential basis for questioning cultural constructs of gender in early modern Europe, for the definition of 'female' in relation to the concept 'male'... calls either for circular reasoning or infinite regress in the search for some foundational identity."[81] Montaigne does not question gender identity in his telling of Marie Germain's transformation; to the contrary, the implausibility of her leap from one gender to another depends upon the assumption that male and female are distinct entities. Her/his momentary hovering between two sexes only hints at the possibility that these entities cannot be taken for granted. In "Of Cripples," however, Montaigne applies the skeptical concept of circular reasoning directly to deconstruct gender identity. Gender emptied of essence—what I call the suspension of difference—provides the occasion for the suspension of judgment.

---

78   Montaigne, *Journal de voyage en Italie*, ed. Pierre Michel (Paris: Livre de poche, 1974): "Ils disent qu'Ambroise Paré a mis ce conte dans son livre de chirurgie" (24).

79   André du Laurens, *Les Œuvres de M. André du Laurens, Sieur de Ferrières, Conseiller & premier Medecin du Tres-Chrestien Roy de France & de Navarre, Henry le Grand, & son Chancelier en l'Université de Montpelier*, trans. Théophile Gellée (Paris: Michel Soly, 1646), 357–8.

80   Jacques Duval, *Traité des hermaphrodites* (Paris: Lisieux, 1880), 376. On Duval, see Kathleen Perry Long's third chapter, "Jacques Duval on Hermaphrodites: Culture Wars in the Medical Profession" in *Hermaphrodites in Renaissance Europe* (Burlington: Ashgate, 2006), 77–108.

81   Kathleen Perry Long, "Hermaphrodites Newly Discovered: The Cultural Monsters of Sixteenth-Century France," *Monster Theory: Reading Culture*, ed. Jeffrey Jerome Cohen (Minneapolis: University of Minnesota Press, 1996), 183–201, 184.

Ourselves, *par deça*: The Amazons

In "Of Cripples" Montaigne relates how, at the insistence of "a sovereign prince" eager to overcome his incredulity, he visited a dozen women held prisoner on charges of witchcraft. After speaking with them and witnessing various confessions and proofs, he concludes, "In the end, and in all conscience, I would have prescribed them rather hellebore than hemlock."[82] Pierre Villey identifies Andrea Alciati as the probable source for Montaigne's famous remark, but the moral that Montaigne draws from his inspection reveals an unmistakable debt to the Erasmian logic deployed by Johann Weyer in *De praestigiis daemonum*: "[I]t is putting a very high price on one's conjectures to have a man roasted alive because of them." Weyer claimed that the confessions of witches were nothing but the mad ramblings of a deranged imagination, and Montaigne concurred. "The witches in my neighborhood are in mortal danger every time some new author comes along and attests to the reality of their visions." This "new author" is none other than Jean Bodin, against whom Montaigne defends the doubt that Weyer casts on the various "marvels" alleged by witches in their confessions. "[W]e may be pardoned for disbelieving a marvel, at least as long as we can turn aside and avoid the supernatural explanation by nonmarvelous means. And I follow Saint Augustine's opinion, that it is better to lean toward doubt than toward assurance in things difficult to prove and dangerous to believe."[83]

The doubt that Montaigne recommends along with Augustine—in a rare allusion to patristic authority—seems to contradict the credulity that he defends in earlier essays.[84] In "Of the Power of the Imagination" and especially in "It Is Folly to Judge the True and False by Our Own Capacity," he had staked a position quite similar to that of Bodin: the supernatural is beyond man's purview, and he is presumptuous to try to bring it down to his level. Bodin cited Theophrastus (372–287 B.C.), Aristotle's disciple and successor as head of the Peripatetic School, to lend antique luster to this position. In *De sensibus*, Theophrastus emphasized the limit of human inquiry with respect to first and final causes. Montaigne explains the appeal of Theophrastus' position: "Theophrastus said that human knowledge, brought about by the senses, could judge the causes of things to a certain degree, but that in approaching first and final causes, it had to stop and blunt itself." Humans are entitled to empirical knowledge, but the divine motives enveloped in first and final causes are off limits.

---

82 DF III: 273. PV, 1032.

83 Scholars have long recognized "Of Cripples" as Montaigne's critical reply to Jean Bodin's *De la démonomanie*. See, for instance, Terence Cave, *Pré-histoires: Textes troubles au seuil de la modernité* (Geneva: Droz, 1998), 80–84. Cave's analysis focuses on the question of whether or not Montaigne is more "liberal" than Weyer. Discussions presenting "Of Cripples" as the third installment of the Weyer-Bodin-Montaigne trilogy generally do not account for the implications of Montaigne's evocation of the Amazons.

84 In *De civitate Dei*, Augustine evokes wonders in the context of a discussion of the torments suffered in hell in the aim of sobering Skeptics of their folly, a project that hardly seems congenial to Montaigne's message in "Of Cripples." However, Augustine also emphasizes that wonders are in fact all around us, even within the things we take for granted; Montaigne would have found this idea more appealing. See Lorraine Daston and Katharine Park, *Wonders and the Order of Nature, 1150-1750* (New York: Zone Books, 1998), 39–40.

Montaigne concedes that this position is an agreeable one: "It is a moderate and sweet opinion, that our own sufficiency can lead us to the knowledge of some things and that it has certain measures of power, beyond which it is temerarious to apply it."[85] Indeed, he makes a similar claim in "Of Cripples": "The knowledge of causes belongs only to Him who has the guidance of things, not to us who have only the enduring of them, and who have the perfectly full use of them according to our nature, without penetrating to their origin and essence." Moreover, like Bodin, he scorns the "folly" of those who put themselves on a par with God: "[R]eason has taught me that to condemn a thing thus, dogmatically, as false and impossible, is to assume the advantage of knowing the bounds and limits of God's will and of the power of our mother Nature; and there is no more notable folly in the world than to reduce these things to the measure of our capacity and competence."[86]

The pious tenor of Montaigne's attack on human presumption cannot, however, mask his fundamental disagreement with Bodin. Whereas Bodin advocates unquestioning submission to "miraculous" effects, Montaigne advises suspending judgment. In the final analysis, Montaigne finds Theophrastus' sensible compromise between the overly inquisitive and the anti-intellectual circular and propitious only to skeptical irresolution: "[If man] admits, along with Theophrastus, ignorance of first causes and principles, let him boldly abandon the rest of his science: if the foundation is lacking, his [*discours*] is on the ground; the disputation and the investigation has no other aim or end than principles; if this stops his course, he is thrown into infinite irresolution."[87] Thus although Montaigne condemns physicians like Weyer who have ready-made explanations for everything, he speaks of Bodin as well when he comments, "Vainglory ... forbids us to leave anything unresolved and undecided."[88] Bodin's fideism is not just dogmatic, but dangerous: "It is unfortunate to be in such a pass that the best touchstone of truth is the multitude of believers, in a crowd in which the fools so far surpass the wise in number."[89] In Chapter Two we saw that Bodin, following Theophrastus, identified reason as the touchstone of truth; the senses should report their findings "to reason, as to a touchstone." But Montaigne perceives that far from championing a rational epistemology, Bodin argues from authority, an authority grounded in the "experience" of peoples everywhere—in sum, an authority composed of received ideas. Moreover, Montaigne observes that the faith-by-numbers formula championed by Bodin relies on coercion: "Where the ordinary means fail us, we add command, force, fire, and the sword." Montaigne objects to Bodin's compulsory fideism in much the same way that Pierre Bayle would object to the *compelle intrare* logic behind Louis XIV's revocation of the Edict of Nantes. What kind of faith, Bayle asked, could be fostered through violence? "Thank God," Montaigne wrote a century earlier, "my belief is not controlled by anyone's fists."[90]

---

85   DF II: 255; PV, 560.
86   DF I: 183; PV, 179.
87   DF II: 256; PV, 561.
88   DF I: 186; PV, 182.
89   DF III: 268; PV, 1028.
90   DF III: 270-71; PV 1031.

Montaigne portrays Bodin's aggressive approach to witchcraft as the epitome of an epistemology in which proving the truth begs the question of what the truth of the matter is. Bodin sounded a refrain in the Preface to *De la démonomanie*: "[W]e should not resist truth when we see the effects, but do not know their causes." Montaigne, too, condemns the search for causes: "I see ordinarily that men, when facts are put before them, are more ready to amuse themselves by inquiring into their reasons than by inquiring into their truth. They leave aside the cases and amuse themselves treating the causes." Yet Montaigne points out that Bodin, despite his claim to pay attention only to effects, is as guilty of this presumption as anyone, since in asserting that a cause is divine rather than natural, he has already established the cause. Intent upon exerting his torturous hermeneutics, the prophet-magistrate searches for God's intentions before "searching for truth." According to Montaigne, he forgets to ask if the effects that inspire his penetrating feats of exegesis ever really took place. People, Montaigne observes, "pass over the facts, but they assiduously examine their consequences. They ordinarily begin thus: 'How does this happen? What they should say is: 'But does it happen?'" As an illustration of human predilection for reason-searching, Montaigne glosses an Italian proverb:

> Apropos or malapropos, no matter, they say in Italy as common proverb, that he does not know Venus in her perfect sweetness who has not slept with a cripple [*la boiteuse*]. Fortune, or some other particular incident, long ago put this saying into the mouth of the people; and is said of males as of females. For the Queen of the Amazons replied to the Scythian who was inviting her to make love: 'The lame man [*le boiteux*] does it best!'

Montaigne enumerates competing physiological explanations as to why limping lends itself to better lovemaking than an even gait. The lame make love better: a) because their "irregular movement" brings uncommon pleasure; b) because the blood that would normally go to the legs accumulates in the genitals that consequently gain in vigor; c) because, deprived of physical exercise, they give themselves "more entire to the sports of Venus." Thankfully, he gives his reader one final option: d) none of the above. "Do not these examples confirm what I was saying at the beginning: that our reasons often anticipate the fact, and extend their jurisdiction so infinitely that they exercise their judgment even in inanity and nonbeing?"[91]

By treating a popular proverb as a truth supported by universal assent, Montaigne mocks the touchstone of truth that he ascribes to Bodin. Despite its "inanity," the theme of lameness and its effects on love-making are central to his critique of Bodin's dogmatism. More than a pleasure principle, lameness stands for the violence at the heart of Bodin's political, moral, and epistemological system. Violence enforces women's subjection to men, just as the Amazons' violence ensures their dominance over the male members of their "feminine commonwealth." In *Les Six livres de la République*, Bodin placed the wife's obedience to the husband at the foundation of political order on the grounds that women's subjection to men was ordained by God and determined by nature, waxing nostalgic for ancient Rome when husbands were entitled to kill their adulterous wives. The conjugal hierarchy at the basis of political

---

91 DF III: 274–5; PV, 1034. Montaigne also criticizes the enthusiasm for explaining causes in "Des coches" (III.6).

order founds a power differential in the moral order as well: nature is God's wife, thus subordinate to him. As a result, those who place nature over God upset moral order and are guilty of a kind of divine *lèse-majesté* almost as heinous as witchcraft. Witchcraft, finally, involves the witch's obedience to the wrong husband. The interrogation used to determine whether a woman is a witch anticipates punishment for the crime. Should she respond to such interrogation with silence, she is as damned as if she confesses, for her silence reveals her stubbornness, a trait that predisposes women to becoming witches. The magistrate confirms his exceptional prerogative as hermeneut of the supernatural when he extracts the witch's secrets through torture and strings together inchoate snippets into an interpretable whole.

Because of Montaigne's attentiveness to the dependence of stoic ethics on a gendered value system, he critiqued *masle vertu* and professed effeminate *mollesse*. So, too, it is because Montaigne perceived that Bodin relied on the dogma of women's natural and divinely instituted subordination to men to mask the circularity of a self-affirming system that he turns to the Amazons in "Of Cripples." Montaigne gleaned the proverb "the lame man makes the best lecher" (II, ix, 49) from Erasmus's *Adages*:

> The story goes that the Amazons in the old days had a custom of making their male offspring lame by damaging shin or hip. And so, when they were engaged in a war with the Scythians, and the Scythians were trying to induce them to come over to their side, saying that thus they would have fit men for their husbands and not lame and mutilated, Antiara the Amazon leader replied with the words "the lame man makes the best lecher."

Erasmus explains that the adage is "customarily used when someone prefers his own lot, though it may be far from grand, to another man's though it seems preferable."[92] Thus, the Amazon does not mean that the lame man makes love better than the able-bodied Scythian man who propositions her. Instead, she means that she would rather have a lame lover—she would rather dominate her lover—than be dominated by the Scythian. According to Sextus Empiricus, "The Amazons used to lame the male children they bore, to make them unable to do anything manly, and they looked after warfare themselves; but among us the opposite has been deemed fine."[93] Sextus exposes the hypocrisy of those who decry the cruelty of the Amazon practice of crippling their male children. It is a preemptive measure; if the Amazons did not lame their boys, they would be subject to similar treatment at the hands of their sons. Institutionalized violence keeps women on top in their matriarchy, just as in patriarchal society, male dominance over women is a matter of force: "[A]mong us,

---

92   Desiderius Erasmus, *Adages*, trans. Margaret Mann Phillips, ann. R.A.B. Mynors, vol. 4, *Collected Works of Erasmus* (Toronto and Buffalo: University of Toronto Press, 1982), 108. Montaigne takes one of his explanations from Erasmus: "The same thing has been observed in our own day: those who have deformed legs or lack some other limb are often sexually more effective than the rest of men, presumably by way of some natural compensation. A reason why a lame man should be more lecherous than others is given by Aristotle in the *Problems*, section 10, problem 26: in his case 'less nutriment passes downwards owing to his defective lower limbs, and more makes for the parts above them and is turned into semen.'"

93   Sextus Empiricus, 200.

the opposite has been deemed fine." Montaigne synthesizes Sextus' remarks with those of Erasmus: "In that feminine commonwealth, to escape the domination of males, they crippled them from childhood—arms, legs, and other parts that gave men an advantage over them—and made use of them only for the purpose for which we make use of women over here [*par deça*]."[94] The lame man makes the best lover simply because he is crippled in all other aspects of his life. Being crippled makes him a sex slave to the Amazon and ensures that he will do no more than what "the feminine republic" requires of him: produce progeny. Like Sextus, Montaigne acknowledges that things work in precisely the same way "over here," except that the terms of the hierarchy are inverted.

The exotic barbarity of the Amazons concludes on a familiar note. The roles are inverted, but we recognize them easily. There are those who command and those who obey. The brutality of the Amazons with respect to their male progeny merely makes obvious that the subjection of women "over here" is arbitrary and maintained through violence. Montaigne's use of the Amazons is one of the most powerful examples in the *Essays* of what Ann Hartle describes as the "dialectic" movement of Montaigne's thought: "[T]he moment of openness to the possible allows him to find the strange in the familiar."[95] It does not matter whether the Amazons existed. The opening of the essay, on the subject of calendar reform, leads him to muse about the incertitude of history: "Here we are in fine condition to keep a record of past events!"[96] Real or fictitious, the tactics used for conserving power in the "feminine commonwealth" of the Amazons allow us to see what is taken for granted "over here" in a new—and newly strange—light. In my analysis of Marie Germain's transformation, I argued that Montaigne needed to take gender identity for granted in order to inspire the dialectic of doubt and credulity that is the ticket to tranquility in "Of the Power of the Imagination." However, re-reading Marie Germain's metamorphosis in light of "Of Cripples" and in particular of the Amazons' matriarchal strategy invites a cultural interpretation of the femininity Marie forwent when she hopped over a ditch: girls take smaller strides because they are crippled. Their lameness does not result from their interiorized genitals, but rather from their unwitting internalization of the violence that maintains their subjection to men *par deça*—an internalization that Bodin hoped to make so total that they would not even dare to venture in Marie Germain's unfettered footsteps.

In Sextus Empiricus' *Outlines of Skepticism*, the surprising resemblances of Amazonian matriarchy to patriarchy *par deça* participate in the tenth mode of opposition, "the one depending on persuasions and customs and law and beliefs in myth and dogmatic suppositions." We would identify the tenth mode of opposition—the Skeptic's response to the question "Is anything by nature good, bad or indifferent?"—with cultural relativism.[97] Sextus points out that we cannot condemn

---

94   DF: 274; PV 1033.

95   Hartle, 3.

96   DF III: 265; PV, 1026.

97   Sextus Empiricus 37, 191. On Montaigne and relativism, see Zachary Sayre Schiffman, *On the Threshold of Modernity: Relativism in the French Renaissance* (Baltimore and London: The Johns Hopkins U.P., 1991), 53–77.

the Amazons for their barbarity because "we" do the same thing "over here." But Sextus does not just invite his reader to refrain from judging the Amazon's barbarity; he does this in the context of a deconstruction of masculinity. "Manliness" is simply the dominant position one occupies in society, thanks to the use or threat of force; women can be masculine provided they dispose of enough power to maintain that position. Similarly, Montaigne exposes the supposedly natural categories of woman and man—the foundation of Bodin's dogmatism—as an egregious case of circular reasoning, in which one thing is defined in terms of another and vice versa, so that an ostensibly intrinsic core is, in fact, wholly constructed by reference to something extrinsic to it.

Montaigne amplifies the relativity of gender through the image of the buskin, also called Theramenes's shoe after the Athenian orator who according to Erasmus was so versatile in his argumentation that he was said to switch stools to please opposite parties: "There is nothing so supple and erratic as our understanding: it is the shoe of Theramenes, good for either foot. And it is double and diverse, and matters are double and diverse." Richard Regosin mines Erasmus's adage pertaining to Theramenes to underscore the relativity and instability of gender in Montaigne's *Essays*:

> Because it is a form without a specific content, the buskin can be simultaneously both this or that and this and that. In the separation of form and content that it performs, in the absence of a fixed identity or essential meaning, Erasmus extends the buskin as a protean figure, like the Ulysses he evokes, "playing any part to perfection." In this display of words and figures changing sides, turning, as it were, inside out, Erasmus includes Suidas's comment that the buskin was of a kind that both men and women could wear. In itself the reference multiplies the idea of versatility—just as the shoe fits either the right or left foot so it fits either a masculine or feminine foot—but it can also serve as a suggestive reminder that the concepts of masculine and feminine themselves can fit either "foot" or sit, to use Erasmus' figure, on one stool and then the other, and on both as well. Masculine and feminine in the *Essais* are also *cothurni*, versatile, double, like the buskin and like the concepts of right and left themselves, whose meaning, we might say, is contextual, differential, relational rather than referential.[98]

The establishment of relative value through opposition—the only kind of value that masculinity and femininity have—is the function of the touchstone. Montaigne was surely familiar with Herodotus' allusion to the touchstone in his narration of the king of Persia's ill-fated decision to invade Greece. To the temerarious ambition of Xerxes (486–465 B.C.), one prudent voice objected. His uncle, Artaban, speaks out in opposition to the plan. To justify his unsolicited intervention, Artaban reminds his nephew of the utility of "contrary opinions" in the quest for truth. "O King," exclaims Artaban, "contrary opinions have not been expressed, it is not possible to choose the best to adopt it, and we must go with the only one that has been expressed; but if they have been it is possible; it is as with pure gold; we cannot recognize pure gold by considering it on its own, it is in rubbing it on the touchstone next to another gold

---

98   Regosin, 222–3.

that we recognize the best."[99] The Skeptic, too, appreciates opposing arguments, but only to empty them of their difference. The lengths to which the Amazons go to diminish the strides of their men mirror the crippling of women crucial to the preservation and propagation of patriarchal society; differences reveal the artifice common to any society organized around a hierarchy of the sexes. "Ogni medaglia ha il suo riverso" [Every medal has its reverse], remarks Montaigne.[100] Two sides of a (symbolically circular) coin are made of the same material; they give the same mark when scraped against a touchstone. So, too, extremes defended by opposing parties in "the school of philosophy" meet to reveal equal imbecility.

> The pride of those who attributed to the human mind a capacity for all things caused in others, out of spite and emulation, the opinion that it is capable of nothing. These men maintain the same extreme in ignorance that the others maintain in knowledge; so that it cannot be denied that man is immoderate in all things, and cannot be stopped except by necessity and inability to go further.[101]

The essay breaks off on that ineffable note: silence signals the *jouissance* that follows the suspension of judgment "as a shadow follows a body."

If there is anything to learn from this rapturous concatenation of dizzying doubles, collapsing cores, and imploding poles that lead from crippled legs to shoes, from buskins to Janus-faced medals, from numismatics to philosophical schools, it is that the touchstone that is supposed to essay these infinitely regressing pairs is not the hard and immutable object that reflects gold marks like the stony will of the Stoic deflects passion. The touchstone is, instead, as relative to the metals that mark it as those metals are to one another. Characterized by *mollesse*, the human mind is "deformed" by the ideas it essays, changing as it tries them on. Thus the Montaigne writing "Of Cripples" is clearly not the same as he who writes "That to Philosophize Is to Learn to Die." John Lyons perceives "a core stability of consciousness" in the stoical Montaigne.[102] That core, we learned from Sextus Empiricus in his critique of stoic epistemology, is comprised of virtues: "The Stoics ... say that goods in the soul are certain kinds of expertise, namely the virtues."[103] The presence and vigor of these virtues (and thus of the touchstone-like core they ostensibly form) are ascertained through the trials that essay them; thus only the continual performance of virtue confirms the continual presence of a core. In "Of Cripples," Montaigne's most purely pyrrhonic essay, there is no core, only monstrosity and deformity. "I have seen no more evident monstrosity and miracle in the world than me. We become habituated to anything strange by use and time; but the more I frequent and know myself, the more my deformity astonishes me, and the less I understand myself."[104] Just as the monster does not comprise an alternative to natural order but the negation

---

99 Herodotus, *Histoires,* trans. Ph-E. Legrand (Paris: Les Belles Lettres, 1951), 7.10. I thank Eric MacPhail for signaling this passage to me.
100 DF III: 276; PV, 1035.
101 Ibid.
102 Lyons, 45.
103 Sextus Empiricus, 194.
104 DF III: 269; PV, 1029.

or frustration of that order (and we know that Aristotle characterized women as deformed, hence monstrous, men), effeminate *mollesse* does not represent a feminine essence so much as the lack of a (masculine) core. Montaigne's appreciation for feminine or effeminate defects—his valorization of womanly pity, his identification with women's supposed credulity—does not result from an essentialist notion of what women are, as opposed to men. What he appreciates in femininity is precisely its potential for atomizing the very notion of essence, an essence that the Stoics defined tautologically in terms of masculinity.

Montaigne thumbs his nose at the rigid belief prescribed by Jean Bodin through a virtuosic demonstration of the suppleness of thought in "Of Cripples." Pyrrho's techniques allow Montaigne to relativize gender hierarchy and deconstruct gender identity for the sake of subverting the compulsory spirit of Bodin's fideism. He demonstrates the reversibility of the husband's arbitrary power over the wife, which is the foundation not just of Bodin's notion of political and social order, but which also structures his idea of intellectual order. The natural philosopher's expertise extends only to God's wife, nature. Consequently, it is not he but the prophet who is able to discern God's will; it is the prophet who determines the boundaries between the natural and the supernatural. Mirroring the conjugal hierarchy at the basis of moral order, the natural philosopher, interpreter of nature, must obey the prophet, hermeneut of "her" divine husband. Montaigne mocks natural philosophers, but decries self-proclaimed prophets, particularly those who derive their prognostications from a tortu(r)ous hermeneutics: "[T]hose who are trained in this subtle trick of tying and untying knots would be capable of finding, in any writings, whatever they want. But what gives them an especially good chance to play is the obscure, ambiguous, and fantastic language of prophetic jargon, to which their authors give no clear meaning, so that posterity can apply to it whatever meanings it pleases."[105] Whereas natural philosophers are ineffectual in their attempts to explain nature's workings, prophets are dangerous because they aim to apply God's will, according to their interpretation of it. In "Of Cripples," Montaigne warns as much against the practical application of ideas in general as against the dogmatic nature of Bodin's ideas in particular.

It would, therefore, be to misunderstand Montaigne's critique of Bodin to impute a pro(to)feminist program to "Of Cripples." One who takes another to task for playing God with human lives cannot turn around and claim to improve upon God's institution of human society. Following the relativist tenor of the Pyrrhonist's tenth mode of opposition, Montaigne presents a mine of conflicting sexuality and gender norms in I.23, "Of Custom and Not Easily Changing an Accepted Law." For instance: "There are places where there are public brothels of males, and even marriages between them; where the women go to war alongside their husbands, and take their place not only in the combat but also in command."[106] Montaigne does not say where or when male brothels and same-sex marriage were customary. The warrior women to whom he alludes here may be the Amazons. They serve the same function in any case: female rule in faraway nations exposes the arbitrary character of masculine command *par deçà*. But the point of "Of Custom" is not to judge

---

105 DF I: 37–8; PV, 44.
106 DF I: 109; PV, 112.

customs. Framing his oppositions with indeterminate designations ("Here ... x; there ... y" or "some ... a; others ... b"), Montaigne reduces all human practices to an indistinguishable mass, over which no culture or individual can claim any particular prerogative. Leveling human customs sets the stage for the condemnation of novelty and apology of orthodoxy, wherein any attempt to override or ameliorate an existing custom is only to introduce a new one. The flight from extremes—the suspension of judgment between two contrary customs—can condition a personal ethic but does not furnish a basis for social reform.

At the same time, Montaigne's "social conservatism" does not negate the possibility of a pro(to)feminist recuperation of his stunning deconstruction of gender hierarchy in "Of Cripples." Thus far, I have shown how Montaigne exploited the instability of gender identity as a means of advancing a *skepsis* without term. In the final section, I turn to Montaigne's covenant daughter, Marie le Jars de Gournay, showing how she seized upon the potential of equipollence achieved through the suspension of gender difference to make a case for women's equality with men.

From Equipollence to Equality: Marie de Gournay

Marie le Jars de Gournay (1565–1645) read the *Essays* in 1585 at the age of twenty. She sent Montaigne a letter during her stay in Paris in 1588, prompting him to pay a visit to the Gournay family (she and her widowed mother and five other sibling) in Paris and again at their homestead in Gournay-sur-Aronde. This was the start of Marie de Gournay's career as a *femme de lettres*, which would continue to revolve around Montaigne and the *Essays* after his death in 1592. In 1594, she published the *Proumenoir de M. de Montaigne* (1594), a curious novel developed from a story she had one day recounted to Montaigne and that she subsequently decided to put in writing ("coucher ... par escrit") to send to him as well as a translation and a collection of poems. Gournay supervised the publication of the 1595 edition of the *Essays*, published by L'Angelier as the *Proumenoir* had been, and, indeed, was responsible for more than a half dozen editions until 1635. Gournay worked from a transcription commissioned by Madame de Montaigne of the Bordeaux copy, Montaigne's annotated copy of the 1588 *Essays* in view of a new edition. Until the rediscovery of the Bordeaux copy in 1802, Gournay's editions remained authoritative.[107]

Although her editorship of the *Essays* remained her most important contribution to French letters, Gournay was a prolific writer—by necessity, since she strove to live by her pen alone. Many of her works were topical, occasioned by events or subjects of particular interest to potential patrons. One of these was a pamphlet-length piece, *De l'égalité des hommes et des femmes* (1622), dedicated to Anne of Austria. Akkerman and Stuurman point to *De l'égalité des hommes et des femmes* as a case in point of the coexistence of pro-woman literature and feminist philosophy in the seventeenth century: "[I]t is impossible to assign her work in an unequivocal way

---

107 Alan M. Boase, *The Fortunes of Montaigne: A History of the Essays in France, 1580–1669* (London: Methuen, 1935), 48–76.

to either the *Querelle* literature or the genre of egalitarian-rationalist feminism."[108] I think that we can attribute a more precise role to Gournay in the articulation of a modern feminism. The hand-picked guardian of Montaigne's textual progeny, she found in the equipollence he essayed the first philosophical model for the equality of men and women.

Equality was not a new idea, of course. With the authority of Augustine behind him, Agrippa calls upon Genesis, a text typically used to justify the subjection of women (as we saw with Bodin), in order to establish the soul as a gender-neutral entity.

> God most beneficent, Father and creator of all good things, who alone possesses the fecundity of the two sexes, created humans in his image, male and female he created them. Sexual distinction consists only in the different location of the parts of the body for which procreation required diversity. But he has attributed to both man and woman an identical soul, which sexual difference does not at all affect. Woman has been allotted the same intelligence, reason, and power of speech as man and tends to the same end he does, that is, eternal happiness, where there will be no restriction by sex.[109]

However, Agrippa's opening affirmation of the identity of souls seems posited the better to exclude it. Whereas misogynists set aside the Augustinian doctrine of the equality of the soul in order to speak of women's inferiority, Agrippa abandons it in order to demonstrate their superiority: "But, setting aside the divine essence of the soul in humans, in everything else that constitutes human being the illustrious feminine stock is almost infinitely superior to the ill-bred masculine race."[110] Curiously, this champion of the female sex begins his demonstration speaking about the beauty of the female body, the inverse of those who insist on the debility of the female body to justify her subjection.

In *De l'Egalité des hommes et des femmes*, Gournay justifies her approach at the outset: she will focus only on equality of the sexes rather than proclaim, as Agrippa had done, the superiority of women. This equality is not based on a theological framework, although she buttresses it with patristic and scriptural authority. Instead, equality is very clearly the product of skeptical *epochè*: "Most of those who take up the cause of women, against the prideful preference that men attribute to themselves, give them back the same coinage, for they return the preference to [women]. As for me, who flee all extremities, I content myself with equaling them to men: Nature opposing also in this regard superiority as well as inferiority."[111] The affirmation of the equality of the sexes resembles the suspension of judgment sought by Skeptics. To lean either in favor of men or of women, like boasting that we know everything or nothing, evinces only "the inability to go further," as Montaigne puts it in "Of

---

108 Akkerman and Stuurman, 10.

109 Henricus Cornelius Agrippa, *Declamation on the Nobility and Preeminence of the Female Sex*, trans. and ed. Albert Rabil Jr. (Chicago and London: University of Chicago Press, 1996), 43.

110 Agrippa, *De nobilitate*, 44.

111 Gournay, "De l'égalité des hommes et des femmes," *Œuvres complètes*, eds. Jean-Claude Arnould et al.(Paris: Champion, 2002), 965.

Cripples." Indeed, Gournay's mention of "coinage" echoes the Italian proverb that Montaigne cites in that essay—"every medal has its reverse"—as well as its implicit message that opposing things become equal in their extremity.[112] Pierre Charron (1541–1603), another of Montaigne's disciples, states in *De la sagesse* (1601): "[A]ll things have two handles [*anses*] and two faces."[113] The notion of doubleness that allows for equipollence is evident in Gournay's title; specifying "the equality of men and women" rather than "the equality of the two sexes" as Poullain de la Barre would do, she draws attention to sameness in difference; "men" and "women," whom Bodin imagines according to a vertical hierarchy are here aligned horizontally, the one balancing the other. Gournay affirms the fundamental likeness between men and women with a *quolibet*—an expression characterized by spontaneity and originality—reminiscent of Montaigne's familiar style:

> Furthermore, the human animal is neither man nor woman, to consider it well; the sexes are not made to constitute a difference of species, but only for propagation: And if it is permitted to laugh on the way, the gibe [*quolibet*] will not be out of season that teaches us that nothing looks more like a male cat [*le chat*] sunning itself on a window sill than a female cat [*la chatte*].[114]

By comparing species—cats to "human animals"—Gournay minimizes sex difference. Gournay implicitly invites us to imagine, through the kind of reversal that Montaigne practices in the "Apologie," that cats, if they could speak, might tell us that nothing looks more like a male human sitting on a doorstep than a female human.

In insisting on equality rather than superiority, Gournay is more a student of the skeptical Montaigne than of the fideist Agrippa. However, she does share with Agrippa the fideist turn to authority, judging reason too pliable a thing to be trustworthy: "And if I judge well, either of the dignity, or of the capacity of Ladies, I do not claim here to prove it through reasons, because the stubborn can debate them, nor by examples, because they are too common, but only by the authority of God Himself, the Fathers, pillars of his Church, and of the great Philosophers who have served as lights to the universe."[115] The Church fathers are certainly the most important to annex to her position because she blames male ecclesiasts for denigrating women for reasons of self-interest. Like Agrippa, she perceived that the justification of prejudice against women on theological or religious grounds

---

112 DF III: 276; PV, 1035.

113 Pierre Charron, *De la sagesse*, ed. Barbara de Negroni (Paris: Fayard, 1986), 400. Charron became friendly with Montaigne while serving as vicar-general of Bordeaux. That Charron bequeathed most of his fortune to Montaigne's sister, Léonor de Camain, indicates the extent of his sense of indebtedness to Montaigne, even if he never signaled his extensive borrowings in print. According to Gournay, Charron was a "perpetual copier of [Montaigne], except for the excesses where he gets carried away sometimes." Cited in Boase, 63.

114 Gournay, 978. In the context of a disputation, *quodlibeta* were impromptu questions on any subject whose initiative lay with the audience. Brian Lawn, *The Rise and Decline of the Scholastic "Quaestio Disputata"* (Leiden, New York, Köln, 1993), 15–16.

115 Gournay, 967.

was the root of the problem.[116] Pointing out that women have been allowed, in the absence of qualified men, to baptize dying infants, Gournay suggests that it is not that the "ancient Fathers" did not believe women to be worthy of such tasks, but that "they outlawed women from communicating the other Sacraments, only to maintain ever more entirely the authority of men: either because they were themselves of the masculine sex, or so that, rightly or wrongly, peace was better assured between the two sexes as a result of the weakness and disparagement of one of them."[117] Here is a precise example of the crippling that Montaigne says is practiced "over here," in a mirror image of the Amazons' mutilation of their men. The "peace" engineered by male ecclesiasts comes at a terrible price, only we do not see it because it is so customary.

In a 1594 poem entitled "Des Amazones desarmées au mesme temps de guerre," Gournay envisages the transcendence of sectarian strife in France on the eve of Henri IV's accession to the throne of France through the Amazon's reform:

> Nous avons surmonté la superbe insolence,
> De mille nations par le fer de la lance:
> Thesée et le Thebain nous avons combatus,
> Quand douze Monstres fiers ce Brave eut abbattus.[118]

> [We have triumphed over the haughty insolence
> Of a thousand nations by the iron of our spears:
> Against Theseus and the Thebean we have fought,
> Where twelve proud monsters this hero would have felled.]

The rest of the poem portrays the Amazons enjoying the fruits of peace and recommending them to the war-weary French. Curling their hair instead of scalping their enemies, adorning their breasts with fancy fabrics rather than with compresses (an allusion to the mastectomy allegedly practiced by the Amazons to facilitate throwing the javelin), the feminization of the Amazon signals her emergence from barbarity. Gournay articulates this transformation through a geographical rapprochement from "far-flung zones" to the center of civilization that is, of course, the Paris of Henri IV.[119] While the political message is clear, the disarmament of the Amazons is ambivalent insofar as it concerns a feminist agenda. In disarming, have the Amazons given something up? Gournay returns to the pre-peace Amazon in *De l'égalité des hommes et des femmes*. In verses taken from Seneca (translated by Ronsard) and from Homer (translated by Gournay), she waxes lyrical about the formidable warrior women's terrorization of the Greeks and their fabled victories over Theseus and Hercules.

---

116 Boase, 58.

117 Gournay, 982–3.

118 Gournay, 1777. The brave Thebean to whom Gournay alludes is Hercules. Christine de Pizan recounts an engaging version of the same story in her *Livre de la cité des Dames* (1405). Christine de Pizan, *The Book of the City of Ladies*, trans. Earl Jeffrey Richards (New York: Persea Books, 1982), 40–51.

119 "Voyez doncques icy les fortes Amazones: / Nous quittons Thermodon et nos lointaines Zones / Pour vous dire, ô François, Peuple illustre et guerrier, / Combien la paix est belle à l'ombre du laurier" (Gournay, 1778).

Predictably, among the great philosophers Gournay cites in *De l'égalité* is Montaigne, distinguished member of the "Triumvirate of human wisdom and moral philosophy" along with Plutarch and Seneca. Commenting on Montaigne's remark in "Of the Affection of Fathers"—"[I]t seems to me, I know not why, that no kind of mastery is due to women over men except the maternal and natural"—Gournay asks, "Is that not to put [women] in a particular instance in the equal counterbalance of men and to confess that if he does not put them there in general he is afraid to be wrong?"[120] She reads Montaigne's noncommittal "je ne sçay comment" as a questioning of what others (Bodin) confidently present as a feature of divine and natural order. Interestingly, Gournay suggests that Montaigne could have found an explanation for women's lack of authority if he had only considered the role of custom: "He could have explained his restriction through the poor and disgraceful manner in which the Sex is nourished."[121] That is, Montaigne could have said that women were only ever in a position of authority over men as mothers—a natural form of authority—because they were deprived of authority received through education. For no other author does Gournay provide a hypothetical argument of this sort, perhaps because she feels entitled, as Montaigne's chosen heir, to speak for him. And indeed, it is not a total travesty, for Gournay is pointing out, as Montaigne does when he compares "our" society to that of the Amazons, that the inequality of the sexes is a matter of custom.

The difference is that whereas Montaigne is content to relativize custom as a means of achieving tranquility, Gournay condemns it. And whereas Montaigne respects the customs he has shown to be arbitrary (for to innovate would be to stray even further from the truth than to follow established tradition), his covenant daughter seeks to correct those that produce inequality:

> If women attain, less often than men, the heights of excellence, it is a marvel that this deprivation of good education, … does not do worse, and keep them from getting there at all. If one must prove it: is there more difference between men and women, than between women and other women according to the upbringing [*institution*] they received, depending on whether they are raised in cities or villages or in different nations? And consequently, why would not their instruction in the affairs and letters equally with men, fill up the empty distance that one observes ordinarily between men's and women's heads?[122]

Gournay visualizes the difference between the content of men's and women's minds in spatial terms; an "empty distance" separates them. I showed that "Of Cripples" ends with a kind of universal polarization, wherein any two opposing things are stretched so far along an axis that they collapse back in on one another, indistinguishable in their extremity. In fact, this is true of the *Essays* as a whole; the more perfectly two entities are opposed—the Skeptic and the credulous woman, for instance—they more they are likely to end up resembling one another. Gournay wants to turn the difference between men and women into likeness, to close the gap, as it were, but this is a deliberate movement that travels only in one direction

---

120 DF II: 72.
121 Gournay, 973.
122 Gournay, 971.

toward an end whose value is not relative: "Why in truth would not the good way of nourishing them succeed in filling the interval that is found between their minds and those of men?"[123]

In her desire to see women fill in the empty spaces separating their minds from those of men, Marie de Gournay diverges from the purer pyrrhonism of her father, ascribing positive value to the learning with which he fueled his never-ending subversion of dogmatic thought. However, her characterization of the distance separating women from men as an empty space points to a question mark in the early seventeenth-century Republic of Letters: with what, precisely, should anyone try to fill their head? The Skeptics had wreaked havoc on the traditional teaching in the schools; knowledge itself, some complained, was in a state of anarchy. A humanist through and through, Gournay would have had a ready recommendation: fill those young ladies' minds with the wisdom of the Ancients. We can only wonder what she must have thought of the philosopher who fifteen years later prescribed precisely the opposite regimen. Methodically emptying out his mind of the humanist heritage that Gournay would have wanted each woman to have, but whose utility he questioned, he found not an empty space, but the ineluctable presence of his own thought. If Marie de Gournay applied the skeptical notion of equipollence to articulate the first philosophical—that is, non-theological—theory of equality as it concerned men and women, it was René Descartes who deployed the Skeptic's subversive techniques to found a rationalist epistemology that would provide new and enduring content to the idea of the equality of women and men.

---

123 Ibid., 972.

Chapter Five

"Even Women:"
Cartesian Rationalism Reconsidered

Feminist (cultural) historians and philosophers generally concur that Cartesian rationalism proved a double-edged sword for women: while Descartes attacked existing obstacles preventing women from participating in the pursuit of knowledge, he also (unintentionally) laid the foundation for new exclusions all the more difficult to overcome. Feminist assessments of Cartesian rationalism focus on Descartes's dualism, on his claim that mind and body are separate, radically distinct substances. On the one hand, François Poullain de la Barre extrapolated from Descartes's assertion of the universality of good sense and separateness of the mind from the body to declare, "the mind has no sex," thereby annulling the homology between mind and body assumed in Galenic humoral theory. On the other hand, as Erica Harth puts it, "if an identical disembodied mind in men and women alike is made to be the principle of sexual equality, what can be made of embodied difference?"[1] Minds may be equal in the abstract, but experience shows that minds do not exist (equally) in the abstract. Some minds are more affected by their embodiment than others, as the Princess Palatine, Elizabeth of Bohemia (1618–80), pointed out in a 1645 letter to Descartes: "[M]y body is imbued with many of the weaknesses of my sex"; these weaknesses made it difficult for her to accept the mind-over-matter

---

1   Erica Harth, *Cartesian Women: Versions and Subversions of Rational Discourse in the Old Regime* (Ithaca and London: Cornell U.P., 1992), 9. Alluding to Foucault's *Les Mots et les choses*, Harth states that "the age of Descartes witnessed the displacement of an older discourse of 'resemblance' or 'patterning' by one of ordered analysis" (6). Tempering the drastic rupture between the late Renaissance and "the age of Descartes" posited by Foucault, Harth argues that the metaphor persisted in the language of the "Cartésiennes," and that this figurative mode participated in the critique of masculinist objectivity that they detected in Descartes's writings. It is doubtful, however, that Descartes's female enthusiast-critics had any community of interest with the occult authors from whom Foucault takes most of his examples, because the metaphors favored by these marginal figures were manifestly antifeminist, as shown by William R. Newman, "Alchemy, Domination, and Gender," in *A House Built on Sand: Exposing Postmodernist Myths about Science*, ed. Noretta Koertge (New York and Oxford: Oxford U.P., 1998), 216–26. Eileen O'Neill also takes issue with the contention that metaphoric language acts in and of itself as a critique of the implicit masculinism of scientific discourse in "Women Cartesians, 'Feminine Philosophy,' and Historical Exclusion," *Feminist Interpretations of René Descartes*, ed. Susan Bordo (University Park: Pennsylvania State U.P., 1999), 232–57. O'Neill points out that Descartes's personification of the earth as a woman in his only extant poem "The Birth of Peace" (1649) "has not been taken to be a rejection of mechanism by Descartes late in his life" (244). René Descartes, *Œuvres*, eds. Charles Adam and Paul Tannery, 11 vols. (Paris: Vrin, 1969), V, 265.

cure he proposed to rid her of her melancholy.[2] There was, therefore, the danger that Poullain de la Barre's felicitous phrase could be construed in a prescriptive rather than descriptive mode: "[T]he mind *should* have no sex," with men more capable of meeting that requirement than women. Women—known as "le Sexe" in the gallant language of seventeenth-century salon culture—were, in a sense, more visible as gendered beings than men, and as a result, their inclusion in the search for truth could not be taken for granted. Alleging differences in the contexture of male and female brain fibers, the Cartesian enthusiast Nicolas Malebranche devised a sexual division of intellectual labor in *De la Recherche de la vérité* (1674). Malebranche cast women as aestheticians, as fashioners of monstrously profuse surfaces, and men as the penetrators of deep, important questions. Genevieve Lloyd concludes that Cartesian dualism "proved crucial for the development of stereotypes of maleness and femaleness, and it happened in some ways despite Descartes's explicit intentions."[3]

Feminist critiques of Descartes tend to adopt a common perspective; according to Stanley Clarke, they "formulate [Descartes's] views mainly by starting from the context of his writing and its historical and cultural influence."[4] Lloyd, for example, states that Cartesian dualism was bound to be read in a certain way: "[I]n the context of associations already existing between gender and Reason, his version of the mind-body relationship produced stark polarizations of previously existing contrasts."[5] Londa Schiebinger remarks that prevalent beliefs went unchallenged since Descartes did not openly advocate for on behalf of women: "What might appear to be a 'neutral stance' in effect left traditional male prerogative—both social and intellectual—unchallenged."[6] Nancy Tuana points out that Descartes's "definition of the rational person is in tension with the traditional view of woman as being more influenced by the body and the emotions than man."[7] These scholars reveal the tension between gender-neutral Cartesian rationalism and the existing

---

2   All French quotations from Descartes or his correspondents will be taken from René Descartes, *Œuvres*, eds. Charles Adam and Paul Tannery, 11 vols. (Paris: Vrin, 1969). I will refer to them henceforth as AT. English translations of Descartes, excepting the correspondence with Elizabeth that I translate myself, come from René Descartes, *The Philosophical Writings of Descartes*, trans. John Cottingham, Robert Stoothoff, Dugald Murdoch, 2 vols. (Cambridge and London: Cambridge U.P., 1984). I reference this translation as CSM. I have consulted Lisa Shapiro's translation of the Descartes/Elizabeth correspondence in *The Correspondence between Princess Elisabeth of Bohemia and René Descartes*, ed. and trans. Lisa Shapiro (Chicago: The University of Chicago Press, 2007).

3   Genevieve Lloyd, "Reason as Attainment," in *Feminist Interpretations of René Descartes*, ed. Susan Bordo (University Park: Pennsylvania State U.P., 1999), 70–81, 71.

4   Stanley Clarke, "Descartes's 'Gender'," in *Feminist Interpretations of René Descartes*, ed. Susan Bordo (University Park: Pennsylvania State U.P., 1999), 82–102, 83.

5   Lloyd, 76.

6   Londa Schiebinger, *The Mind Has No Sex? Women in the Origins of Modern Science* (Cambridge: Harvard U.P., 1989), 171.

7   Nancy Tuana, *Women and the History of Philosophy* (New York: Paragon, 1992), 39. Tuana ends her analysis of Descartes's contribution to the "maleness of reason" with Heinrich Kramer's claim that "all witchcraft comes from carnal lust, which is in women insatiable," as if the *Malleus maleficarum* was not only contemporary to Descartes but mainstream in its ideas as well.

sexist context through narrative, showing that after an initial period of excitement and openness—what Harth calls "the Cartesian moment"—women saw the doors of scientific inquiry close in their faces. The example of the itinerary of Christian Huygens (1629–95), a correspondent of Descartes, and later of the foremost anatomists in Europe, Nicolas Hartsoeker and Antoni van Leeuwenhoek, illustrates the gradual exclusion of women from scientific discourse. While in Paris in 1660 and 1661, Huygens frequented the Cartesian salon of Madame de Bonneveaux and her assistant, Madame de Gueudreville. Albeit a Dutchman, Huygens was inducted into the all-male enclave of the Parisian *Académie royale des sciences*, and no evidence indicates that he attended Bonneveaux's salon after that time. The founding of the Académie des Sciences (1666) thus deprived scientific spaces comprised of both sexes of their most talented interlocutors, and if Molière's *Femmes savantes* (1672) is in any way representative of real-life *salonnières*, their trivial preoccupations reflect the impoverishment of all public scientific discourse after 1666. Philaminte's plan to found an academy just for women registered real exclusion:

> Car enfin je me sens un étrange dépit
> Du tort que l'on nous fait du côté de l'esprit,
> Et je veux nous venger, toutes tant que nous sommes.
> De cette indigne classe où nous rangent les hommes,
> De borner nos talents à des futilités,
> Et nous fermer la porte aux sublimes clartés. [8]

> [For in short I feel quite bitter
> About the wrong that is done to our minds
> And I want to avenge us all, as long as we are
> Of the unworthy class to which men consign us;
> They limit our talents to superfluities
> And hide sublime lights behind closed doors.]

It was not at Saint-Cyr, the academy for the daughters of impoverished military officers founded in 1686 by Louis XIV's morganatic wife, Françoise d'Aubigné, Marquise de Maintenon (1635–1719), that girls would be encouraged to pursue the lofty course of study envisioned by Philaminte. After a quietist epidemic swept a mystical lethargy across the academy, Maintenon centered her curriculum around Catholic virtue, aristocratic etiquette, bourgeois frugality, and practical skills, even though she in her younger salon days had read and admired Descartes's early works, like any *précieuse*.[9] Charles Perrault, a great admirer of Descartes and the intrepid champion of the moderns in the *Querelle des anciens et des modernes*, waxed lyrical over the domestic virtues of women in *L'Apologie des femmes* (1694), a rebuttal to Nicolas Boileau Despréaux's satire of women. Marie de Gournay had still deployed the conventional *femmes fortes* of the *Querelle des femmes* literature in 1621: Achilles' victory over Penthesilea, Queen of the Amazons, was his crowning glory.

---

8   Jean-Baptiste Poquelin de Molière, *Les Femmes savantes*, in *Oeuvres complètes*, ed. Robert Jouanny, 2 vols. (Paris: Garnier, 1962), II, 716, Act III, scene 2, verses 851–6.

9   John J. Conley, *The Suspicion of Virtue: Women Philosophers in Neoclassical France* (Ithaca and London: Cornell U.P., 2002), 154, 126.

Furthermore, did not Epicharis prove that women are capable of "that other Triumph of magnanimous force, that consists in constancy while suffering the bitterest travails?"[10] But Perrault's defense of women anticipates the sentimental *tableaux* of the eighteenth-century *drame bourgeois*. A father describes the charm of married life to his gynophobic son:

> Entre dans les Reduits des honnestes familles,
> Et vois-y travailler les meres & les filles
> Ne songeant qu'à leur tâche & qu'à bien recevoir
> Leur pere ou leur époux quand il revient le soir.

> [Enter into the abodes of upstanding families,
> And see mothers and daughters working there
> Thinking only of their task and of warmly welcoming
> Their father or their husband when he comes home in the evening.]

Perrault congratulates conciliatory women who bring their gluttonous husbands back to moderation through frugal cuisine, while admiring others who, in turning a blind eye to adultery, reform their libertine husbands by example. Perrault seems to have intuited that his picture of domestic bliss might fall below some women's aspirations; in his preface, he anticipates that several "will not like these mothers and daughters who work in the house.... They will find these manners very *bourgeois*."[11] Observing the closing doors lamented by Philaminte and the increasing emphasis on the bourgeois value of female domesticity, several historians of feminism have argued that the late seventeenth-century "great enclosure [*grand renfermement*]" described by Michel Foucault with respect to madness had a gender dimension as well.[12] While the notion of a *grand renfermement* of women (as of the mad) may be an overstatement, it is undeniable the virile *femme forte* celebrated during the regency of Anne d'Autriche had surrendered her arms by the early eighteenth century. Anne-Thérèse Lambert in her *Réflexions nouvelles sur les femmes* (1727) accepts Malebranche's limitation of female intelligence to matters of taste.[13]

The emphasis on a cultural context in feminist evaluations of Cartesian philosophy reflects a commitment to address social and material considerations typically neglected in the study of philosophy. Evelyn Fox Keller explains the appeal of structuralist historiography in these terms. In the *Structure of Scientific Revolutions* (1962) Thomas Kuhn challenged "the view that science is autonomous and absolutely progressive—approximating ever more closely a full and accurate

---

10   Marie de Gournay, "De l'égalité des hommes et des femmes," in *Œuvres complètes*, eds. Jean-Claude Arnould et al. (Paris: Champion, 2002), 980–81.

11   Charles Perrault, *L'Apologie des femmes* (Paris: Jean-Baptiste Coignard, 1694), 7, 12, "préface," [n.p.].

12   See Maïté Albistur and Daniel Armogathe in their *Histoire du féminisme français du moyen âge à nos jours* (Paris: Des Femmes, 1977), 135–9, and Linda Timmermans, *L'Accès des femmes à la culture (1598–1715): Un débat d'idées de Saint François de Sales à la Marquise de Lambert* (Paris: Champion, 1993), 619.

13   Faith E. Beasley, *Salons, History, and the Creation of Seventeenth-Century France: Mastering Memory* (Aldershot and Burlington: Ashgate, 2006), 36.

description of reality 'as it is'." According to Keller, feminists embraced Kuhn's picture of science that left room for "political and social forces affecting the growth of scientific knowledge."[14] Susan Bordo, in turn, credits Michel Foucault (as well as Keller) for reforming an "anticultural attitude [that] runs very deep in philosophy."[15] The commitment to understanding a text with respect to the culture of its time has contributed to the flowering of new research that addresses the institutions and social circles that fostered early modern science, including some illuminating work on early modern women.[16] Nevertheless, it is a partial approach to allow "cultural context"—often conflated with reception history—to set the parameters for interpreting Descartes's work. To determine how contemporary and subsequent Cartesians and anti-Cartesians promoted, adapted, or mocked Descartes's ideas certainly helps to understand how he came to be known as one of the "fathers of modern epistemology."[17] By the same token, it helps explain why feminists continue to regard him with suspicion. But François Azouvi and Stéphane Van Damme have shown that the reception and use of Descartes's writings is often more revealing of the preoccupations of those who claimed to be its heirs than of that philosophy itself.[18] Positing Descartes as the originator of a paradox that still plagues us— an affirmation of the gender-neutral essence of reason, which in its blindness to

---

14   Evelyn Fox Keller, *Reflections on Gender and Science* (New Haven and London:Yale U.P., 1985), 5.

15   Susan Bordo, *The Flight to Objectivity: Essays on Cartesianism and Culture* (Albany: State University of New York Press, 1987), 3. Bordo's use of the term "culture" is problematic. She claims to step back "from the text, to survey the culture in which the text is located and given body" (3). Yet the cultural matrix that informs her reading is one of her own fabrication; adopting as her "hermeneutic tools" the "psychological (and often psychoanalytic) categories of 'anxiety,' 'dread,' 'denial,' and 'escape'," she defines the Cartesian quest for certitude as a "flight from the feminine" (4). Bordo's notion of seventeenth-century (presumably European) culture comes from the popular feminist historiography; she credits Carolyn Merchant, Barbara Ehrenreich, Dierdre English, and Adrienne Rich for revealing "the years between 1550 and 1650 as a particularly gynophobic century." She cites the *Malleus Maleficarum*, Francis Bacon's metaphors of domination, and "the gradual male takeover of birthing" as evidence of this ostensibly pervasive feature of early modern European culture (108–9).

16   See for example the rich collection of articles in *Women, Science, and Medicine, 1500–1700: Mothers and Sisters of the Royal Society*, eds. Lynette Hunter and Sarah Hutton (Thrupp, Stroud, Gloucestershire: Sutton, 1997), as well as the following monographs: Anna Battigelli, *Margaret Cavendish and the exiles of the mind* (Lexington: U.P. of Kentucky, 1998) and Susanna Akerman, *Queen Christina of Sweden and her Circle* (Leiden: Brill, 1991).

17   Schiebinger, 170.

18   According to François Azouvi in *Descartes et la France: Histoire d'une passion nationale* (Paris: Fayard, 2002), there is not much of Descartes's philosophy left in many of the subsequent uses made of his name: "On trouvera dans cet ouvrage le récit de quantité d'épisodes auxquels le nom de Descartes est associé, et qui n'ont pourtant plus de rapport avec la philosophie proprement dite" (11). Similarly, Stéphane Van Damme writes that Descartes "fut par le passé un janséniste pour les uns, un protestant pour les autres, l'éminent représentant de la philosophie républicaine, voire dans l'immédiate après-guerre, un penseur petit-bourgeois" in *Descartes: Essai d'histoire culturelle d'une grandeur philosophique* (Paris: Presses de Sciences Po, 2002), 13.

difference, reinscribes the search for truth as an implicitly masculine endeavor—should, therefore, be carefully distinguished from the investigation of what his writings have to say about women and/or gender. For even if Perrault's ode to female domesticity was suggestive of an emerging ideology of separate spheres and the Enlightenment discourse of universality contained an egregious gender bias, what this reveals about Descartes is not clear. Locating in Descartes's writings the seeds of later development begs the question of the faithfulness of these interpretations. Did Poullain de la Barre and Malebranche hew in equal measure to the spirit and the letter of Descartes's written legacy? Such a judgment can only be made by comparing Descartes's stance on a particular matter—in this case women's place in the search for truth—to what his followers said about it. Grasping Descartes's position on a subject should be a prerequisite to the study of the reception of his philosophy; we cannot retrace what his position was through the study of the influence of his philosophy.

In this chapter, I explain the originality of the gender implications of Descartes's philosophy in terms of his engagement with the dominant epistemological and ethical positions of the late Renaissance. Two questions concern me in particular. First, to what extent was Descartes's rationalist epistemology an egalitarian one? Second, does Cartesian philosophy sanction the reform of sexist institutions? To consider these questions from the perspective of the intellectual traditions that Descartes inherited hardly seems groundbreaking. Yet those who study Descartes's debts to various schools of thought (Richard Popkin, Edwin Curley, Roger Ariew) have not been interested in how his engagement with them oriented his attitudes towards gender. Those who study the ramifications of Cartesian philosophy for women (Lloyd, Bordo, Harth) have not typically done so from Descartes's perspective of the problems that he thought he was solving. As a result of Descartes's amalgamation and transformation of skeptical and stoical strands, I contend, his philosophy not only legitimated women's full participation in the search for truth, but also was the first to provide the philosophical justification for the reform of institutions that produced and maintained inequality between men and women. Thus, whereas many feminist critiques have tended to infer the limitations of the gender neutrality of Cartesian philosophy through its reception at the hands of a sexist society, I reverse the line of inquiry to show that Descartes provided the wherewithal to question the "persuasions and customs and law and beliefs in myth and dogmatic suppositions" that Sextus Empiricus relativized in his tenth mode of opposition and that Montaigne and Gournay linked to self-preserving violence.[19] My analysis will progress in a loosely chronological fashion, from the *Discours de la méthode* (1637) to the *Passions de l'âme* (1649), which will enable me to show that while Descartes seems to have been committed to providing a gender-neutral epistemology from the beginning, the egalitarian implications of his rationalist epistemology emerged most fully in his later moral philosophy. This should in itself illustrate the point that human experience, including interaction with others, is a crucial component of the Cartesian search for truth.

---

19   Sextus Empiricus, *Sextus Empiricus: Outlines of Scepticism*, trans. Julia Annas and Jonathan Barnes (Cambridge: Cambridge U.P., 1994), 37.

The Dangers of Doubt

Descartes's most important interlocutors, epistemologically speaking, were the Skeptics.[20] As I showed in Chapter Four, skepticism was the school of thought most consistently associated with the pro-woman side of the *Querelle des femmes* in the sixteenth and early seventeenth centuries, and it was from the Skeptics that Descartes adopted, among other things, an egalitarian stance. "Good sense," he asserts in the opening sentence of the *Discours*, "is the best distributed thing in the world: for everyone thinks himself to be so well endowed with it that even those who are the hardest to please in everything else do not usually desire more of it than they possess. In this it is unlikely that everyone is mistaken. It indicates rather that the power of judging well and of distinguishing the true from the false—which is what we properly call 'good sense' or 'reason'—is naturally equal in all men."[21] Few readers could have ignored that Descartes gleaned this wry observation from one of Montaigne's *Essays*, which Marie de Gournay published in their entirety the year before Descartes's birth. The allusion is to "Of Presumption": "It is commonly said," muses Montaigne, "that the fairest division of her favors Nature has given us is that of sense; for there is no one who is not content with the share of it that she has allotted him. Is that not reasonable? ... I think my opinions are good and sound; but who does not think as much of his?"[22] Montaigne deduces the equal distribution of sense from the equal presumption with which people assume that their opinions are reasonable. In the skeptical economy of the *Essays*, equality is measured on a negative scale: men have no more purchase on truth than women do. Descartes's observation begins with the same note of irony; what "everyone" thinks to be true can hardly be considered a valid criterion of truth in a text devoted to the demolition of received ideas. Nevertheless, he will go on to ratify this presupposition. The premise of basic epistemic equality is central to his argument since the universality of reason reflects the basic unity of the sciences whose truths may all be discovered through a single method (as opposed to scholastic philosophy, which assigned different methods for each science). He makes the point explicitly in the *Regulae ad directionem ingenii (Rules for the direction of the mind)*, a work he composed around 1628 but never published: "Distinguishing the sciences by the differences in their objects, they think

---

20   "Much criticism of Descartes," comments Edwin Curley in *Descartes against the Skeptics* (Cambridge: Harvard U.P., 1978), "stems from a failure to see his work in the context of the late Renaissance skepticism against which it is so largely directed" ix. Merchant notes that skepticism was an impetus for the founding of mechanical philosophy in France, but does not link this observation to a reflection on gender (194–5). Bordo speaks of the cultural relativism in Montaigne's Essay "Of Coaches" as part of an intellectual crisis in the late Renaissance that sets the stage for Descartes's reordering of knowledge from the inside out; she is interested in how Descartes does (or does not do) away with skepticism, but neglects what *topoi* he may have gleaned from the skeptics (38–43). Unfortunately, Bordo neither defines nor historicizes "feminist skepticism" in "Feminist Skepticism and the 'Maleness' of Philosophy," in *Women and Reason*, ed. Elizabeth Harvey and Kathleen Okruhlik (Ann Arbor: University of Michigan Press, 1992), 143–62.

21   AT, VI, 1–2; CSM, I, 111.

22   PV, 657; DF, II, 365. On the relation of good sense to taste later in the seventeenth century, see Beasley 32.

that each science should be studied separately, without regard to any of the others. But here they are surely mistaken. For the sciences as a whole are nothing other than human wisdom, which always remains one and the same, however different the subjects to which it is applied."[23] Because the unity of science depends on the basic resemblance of all people, Descartes means "men" in its general sense of "humans" when he claims in the *Discours* that good sense or reason is equal in all "men." In this light, sex difference is one of the contingencies among individuals of the same species that he would place under the scholastic rubric of an "accident" as opposed to a "form"—not an essential difference, in other words.[24]

One need not look beyond the *Discours*, however, to see that Descartes carefully hedged his establishment of epistemic equality. Already in the second part of the *Discours*, Descartes qualifies his initial assertion regarding the equal distribution of sense. He is commenting on the appropriateness of his example for various readers, following his resolution to purge all received ideas. "The simple resolution to abandon all the opinions one has hitherto accepted is not an example that everyone ought to follow. The world is largely composed of two types of minds for whom it is quite unsuitable." The first sort who should not try Descartes's experiment includes those clever types who, over-confident in their judgment and over-eager to exercise it, lack the requisite patience "to direct all their thoughts in an orderly manner." Shaking off the shackles of the known would precipitate these readers into an anarchic never-never land, for once they have strayed "from the common path, they could never stick to the track that must be taken as a short-cut, and they would remain lost all their lives." The second sort of people not fit for a total reformation of the content of their minds consists of "those who have enough reason or modesty to recognize that they are less capable of distinguishing the true from the false than certain others by whom they can be taught; such people should be content to follow the opinions of these others rather than seek better opinions themselves."[25] These two categories come straight from "Of Presumption," where Montaigne says that the world is divided between two types: learned men obsessed with doctrine and "common, ordinary minds."[26] We have seen that Montaigne usually includes women in the latter category, and to judge by letters concerning the *Discours* during the year following its initial publication, the same is true for Descartes.

One of the chief objections voiced by the first readers of the *Discours* was that Descartes had shortchanged what should have been *la pièce de résistance* of his development—namely, the proof of God's existence. This was the complaint lodged by Père Vatier, a professor at the prestigious Collège de la Flèche. Descartes responded to the Jesuit on 22 February 1638, in an effusive and deferent letter in which he takes special care to reassure his interlocutor regarding his awareness of the problem. "It is true," Descartes concedes, "that I have been too obscure in what I wrote about the existence of God in this treatise on Method, and I admit that although it is the most important part, it is the least worked out section in the whole work."

---

23   AT, X, 360; CSM, I, 9.
24   AT, VI, 2–3; CSM, I, 112.
25   AT, VI, 15; CSM, I, 118.
26   PV, 657; DF, II, 365.

He goes on to allege two reasons for this obscurity. First of all was the issue of time. Descartes wrote the *Discours* at the last minute, when the printer was pressing him for the manuscript, as the accompanying *Essays* were already in press. "But the principal reason for its obscurity," Descartes goes on, "is that I did not dare to go into detail about the arguments of the sceptics … for these thoughts did not seem to me suitable for inclusion in a book which I wished to be intelligible … even to women." skeptical doubt, he explains to Vatier, was the crucial prelude to establishing God's existence: "The certainty and evidence of my kind of argument for the existence of God cannot really be known without distinctly recalling the arguments which display the uncertainty of all our knowledge of material things."[27] But a full development on the uncertainty of material things was not suitable for a female readership. In response to a similar objection by Marin Mersenne in March 1637, Descartes had already insisted on the centrality of skepticism to the establishment of his metaphysics: "I had no better way of dealing with this topic [the proof of the existence of God] than by explaining in detail the falsehood or uncertainty to be found in all the judgments that depend on the senses and the imagination, so as to show in the sequel which judgments depend only on the pure understanding, and what evidence and certainty they possess." He insists that the overly cursory development leading to the proof of God's existence was no oversight, but a deliberate act of self-censure. He omitted it "on purpose and after deliberation, mainly because I wrote in the vernacular [*en langue vulgaire*]. I was afraid that weak minds might avidly embrace the doubt and scruples which I would have had to propound, and afterwards be unable to follow as fully the arguments by which I would have endeavoured to remove them [*les en tirer*]."[28]

Descartes fears that he would so successfully school "weak minds"—a category with which "even women" is evidently synonymous—in the techniques of doubt, that when it came time to lead them to certain knowledge, he would be unable to do so, and they would remain in an abyss of doubt that could degenerate into atheism and moral relativism. The same rationale in response to the same concern figures almost identically in a third letter to an unnamed interlocutor, probably Jean de Silhon (1596–1667),[29] and he comes back to it in the Latin *Meditationes de prima philosophia* (1641), dedicated to the theologians of the Sorbonne, in which he delivers a fuller proof of God's existence via the ostensibly treacherous path of all-out doubt. Whereas in the *Discours*, Descartes mildly resolves to "pretend that all the things that had ever entered my mind were no more true than the illusions of my dreams," in the *Meditationes* he supposes that there is "not God, who is the supremely good and the source of truth, but rather [that] a malicious demon of the utmost power and cunning has employed all his energies in order to deceive me."[30] And while in the *Discours* he proves God's existence in the space of a paragraph, in the *Meditationes* he devotes an entire Meditation to it. These differences, he explains in the preface to the reader, reflect the intended audience of each work. "[T]he route which I follow

27 AT, I, 560; CSM, III, 86.
28 AT, I, 350; CSM, III, 53.
29 AT, I, 353–4; CSM, III, 55–6.
30 AT, VI, 32; CSM, I, 127; AT, IX, 17; CSM, II, 15.

to explain [the existence of God and the human soul] is so untrodden, and so remote from the ordinary road, that I thought it would not be helpful to give a full account of it in a book written in French and designed to be read by all and sundry, in case weaker intellects might believe that they ought to set out on the same path."[31]

Descartes distinguishes between readers who are unequally equipped to search for truth, and there is some indication (in his letter to Vatier) that he aligns these distinctions with gender difference. This conviction would be consistent with Montaigne's practice of identifying women with the common herd, except that Montaigne often subverts conventional hierarchies in his *Essays*, so that he speaks with condescension of "common souls" in "Of Presumption," but elsewhere he identifies with these souls, notably valorizing the effeminate *mollesse* of impressionable women. Descartes, in contrast, maintains a consistent hierarchy between those he deems fit for finding or "inventing" truth and those who are only equipped to recognize the validity of a previously discovered truth. The *Discours de la méthode* thus begs the question: To what extent does the assertion of an equal *distribution* of reason commit him to a democratization of the search for truth? Descartes's letter to Vatier would seem to indicate that the search for truth is an elite enterprise from which women are excluded, except as assenting spectators. How we interpret Descartes's cautious overture to women readers in the *Discours* depends, however, on how we understand his use of skepticism and the scruples with which he surrounded his deployment of skeptical arguments. Descartes's pessimistic assessment of women's ability to overcome skeptical doubt does not necessarily indicate that he thought that women were *esprits foibles*, only that he recognized that the prized component of his readership thought that this was so.

Descartes's letters to Vatier, Mersenne, and Silhon, as well as his preface to the *Meditations*, show that he had a keen sense of audience and that he carefully packaged his ideas with different readers in mind. This is evident not only in his choice of language—French for the common reader who might be led astray by doubt, Latin for the experienced *savant*—but also in the *Essays* to which the *Discours* served as a preface. Each of these *Essays* took on an uncontroversial subject for the benefit of a slightly different audience.[32] Together, the *Discours de la méthode* and the *Essays* served as a prospectus of his work—a general outline containing the highlights of a great opus to come followed by some samples of the fruits of his method. He had chosen to proceed with this sampling because "certain considerations kept [him] from publishing" a treatise on the world that he had completed four years earlier; he wanted to avoid the ecclesiastical condemnation endured by Galileo Galilei as a result of his *Dialogo sopra i due massimi sistemi del mondo, Ptolemaico e Copernico* (1632). Thus, although Descartes sought to reach as wide an audience as possible with the *Discours*—"even women," as he says—his overriding concern was to win the good graces of the theologians. He did not want to alienate Catholic polemicists like Florimond de Raemond or the Père Garasse who in *L'Histoire de la naissance progrez et decadence de l'Heresie de ce siecle* (1605) and *Doctrine curieuse des beaux esprits de ce temps, ou pretendus tels* (1623), respectively, fulminated against

---

31 AT, VII, 7; CSM, II, 7.
32 Pierre Mesnard, *Essai sur la Morale de Descartes* (Paris: Boivin, 1936), 43.

women who read the Bible and theology.[33] He especially wanted to cultivate the support of more open-minded, yet orthodox men like Vatier, Mersenne, and Silhon, who were far more worried about the deleterious effects of skepticism than he was.

Doing battle with the skeptics had become almost a rite of passage among Descartes's scientific, yet deeply Catholic coterie. This ritual was necessitated because skepticism in the early seventeenth century had become associated with *libertinage* or free-thinking, in large part as a result of Pierre Charron's peculiar repackaging of Montaigne's skepticism in *De la sagesse* (1601).[34] Typical of other fideists, Charron rejected human claims to knowledge; "[T]ruth," he says, "is not an acquisition nor a thing that allows itself to be grasped and handled, and even less possessed by the human mind. It lodges in God's breast."[35] Yet Charron was concerned with ethics rather than truth in *De la sagesse*, and he establishes ethics as an independently human sphere so that the pursuit of "preud'homie" or the accomplishment of actions that are "simply, naturally, and morally good" is a strictly human endeavor; grace is a gift of God, and there is no point in devoting "long discourses or teachings" to it.[36] Whereas Montaigne had simply revealed customs to be relative and, therefore, arbitrary, Charron's establishment of a wisdom independent from divine *sapientia* and alongside grace—a practical ethic reminiscent of the stoic Sage—could lend itself to the *libertin* conclusion that religion was superfluous to morality. Moreover, as a result of Charron's opposition between custom and the wisdom of the sage, Montaigne's *arrièreboutique* becomes in *De la sagesse* a space of duplicity, where one can take off the mask with which one dissimulates in public: we must "separate ourselves from our public office; each one of us plays two roles and two personas."[37]

---

33 Florimond de Raemond, *L'Histoire de la naissance progrez et decadence de l'Heresie de ce siecle* (1605), Livre 7, 875–6; François Garasse, *Doctrine curieuse des beaux esprits de ce temps, ou pretendus tels* (1623), livre V, section 5, 498–505.

34 Charron's borrowings from Montaigne, combined with Descartes's silence with respect to his sources, make it difficult to discern when one is confronted with a Montaignian passage in a Cartesian work, whether Descartes is citing the *Essays* or *De la sagesse*. The question is salient, because Montaigne's thorough-going pyrrhonism is far more subversive of gender hierarchies than Charron's fideist "wisdom." Symptomatic of this difference, much of Charron's discussion of the inequality of husbands and wives in "Du mariage" (Book I, Chapter 41) comes from Bodin, notably the closing passage : "le pire a esté que l'adultère demeure presque par tout sans peine de mort, et seulement y a divorce et separation de compagnie, introduit par Justinien, homme du tout possedé de sa femme, qui fit passer tout ce qu'elle peut à l'advantage des femmes" Pierre Charron, *De la sagesse* (Paris: Fayard, 1986), 312. Charron's borrowings from Du Vair (see my Chapter Three) also make it very difficult to perceive any feminist potential in *De la sagesse*. Alan Boase remarks that "In Charron, a 'simplist' type–psychology is allowed to take the place of a truly individual psychology" (99); on this score, Descartes is much closer to Montaigne.

35 Charron, "Petit traicté de sagesse," in *De la sagesse*, ed. Barbara Negroni (Paris: Fayard, 1986), 860.

36 Charron, 861. As I showed in Chapter Two, Bodin's fideism had a mystical valence, and Charron in his first published work, *Les Trois Vérités* (1593), recycles some of the main themes of *De la démonomanie*: God is infinite, hence unknowable, demons provide evidence of invisible but nonetheless omnipresent spiritual powers.

37 Charron, 415.

In generalizing from Montaigne's quip that he played the mayor in public but himself at home, Charron unwittingly infused the role-playing involved in deferring to custom with a confessional as well as professional dimension. Not surprisingly, therefore, those who wrote against atheists often targeted Skeptics as well. Garasse targets Charron in his *Doctrine curieuse des beaux esprits de ce temps* as an abettor of atheists, including him in the diabolical pantheon of morally suspect men known to consort with an exclusive elite of like-minded dissimulators. Though accepting that Charron had had only the best intentions, Marin Mersenne in *L'Impiété des deistes, athées, et libertines de ce temps, combatuë et renversee de point en point par raisons tirees de la Philosophie, & de la Theologie* (1624), rejects fideism as a convenient cover for atheists, while Jean de Silhon, another friend and correspondent of Descartes, seeks to overcome pyrrhonism in *De l'immortalité de l'âme* (1634) by forcing the Skeptic to accept the possibility of infallible knowledge through the admission of his own existence. It is an argument that evidently made an impression on Descartes.[38]

Descartes espoused the anti-skeptical movement of his entourage and even borrowed some of their arguments. His objections to skepticism, nevertheless, differed from those of his contemporaries. The principal aim of Mersenne and Silhon was to arrest the rise of atheism, which they considered a logical consequence of Charron's fideism. For Descartes, in contrast, overcoming skepticism and proving the existence of God were only the means to an end: establishing the orthodoxy of his mechanistic natural philosophy. Alan Boase comments: "It was only by showing official theology that he could do their job for them better than they could themselves that he could hope to get his new mechanistic physics accepted."[39] Descartes's clever gambit was to deploy skeptical arguments to destroy the foundations of scholastic

---

38   Descartes was clearly indebted for his *cogito* not just to Augustine, as Arnauld and Clerselier would later point out, but more immediately to Jean de Silhon's *De l'immortalité de l'âme* (1634): "But in order to satisfy entirely the most difficult minds, and to convince the most opinionated; in order to force those wills most determined to believe nothing at all and to place everything in doubt; and so that there may be no ground for answering in vain, or any for making a bad objection in favor of Pyrrhonism: here is a piece of certain knowledge—in whatever direction you turn it and in whatever light you regard it—of which it is impossible that a man capable of reflection and of discourse could doubt and not be assured. Every man, I say, who has the use of judgment and reason can know *that he is*, that is, that he has being, and this knowledge is so infallible, that, even though all the operations of the external senses might in themselves be deceptive, or even though we cannot distinguish between them and those of an impaired imagination, nor wholly assure ourselves whether we are awake or asleep, or whether what we are seeing is the truth or illusion and pretense, it is impossible that a man who has the power, as some have, to enter into himself, and to make the judgment that he is, should be deceived in this judgment, and *should not be*.... Now this judgment that a man makes, that he is, is not a frivolous piece of knowledge, or an impertinent reflection. He can rise from there to the first and original source of his being, and to the knowledge of God himself." In *Descartes's Meditations: Background Source Materials*, eds Roger Ariew, John Cottingham, Tom Sorell, trans. Roger Ariew and Marjorie Grene (Cambridge: Cambridge U.P., 1998), 199–200.

39   Alan Boase, *The Fortunes of Montaigne: A History of the Essays in France, 1580–1669* (London: Methuen, 1935), xx.

epistemology before in turn discrediting those arguments. The Counter-Reformation had ushered in an Aristotelian revival, which swelled proportionally with the Society of Jesus, not the least at the Collège de la Flèche, Descartes's alma mater. Aristotelian epistemology was based on the senses: "[N]othing is in the intellect that was not first in the senses," went the venerable Thomist refrain. Yet as I showed in Chapter One, the great Renaissance obsession with the Devil's powers of illusion greatly favored the skeptical demolition of Aristotelian epistemology; the psychological study of the human/demon interface revealed the fine—invisible?—line between sense perception and distorted imagination. Pierre le Loyer expanded his *Quatre livres des spectres ou apparitions et visions et esprits, anges et demons se monstrant sensiblement aux hommes* (1586) in 1605 and again in 1608, to refute skeptical arguments on the untrustworthiness of sense perception.[40] Between the composition of the *Regulae* and of the *Discours*, Descartes seems to have realized that the skeptics were his best allies for undermining the authority of the sense-based epistemology of the scholastics. Charles Larmore explains the sequence: "By showing that empiricism cannot withstand the Skeptic's doubt, and by then drawing out a body of truths which those doubts are themselves powerless to impugn, Descartes hoped to convince his reader to move beyond the two warring camps of the day, Aristotelian scholasticism and skepticism, and in the direction of his own philosophy which rested on a non-empiricist theory of knowledge."[41] Doing in the Skeptic would, he hoped, be more than enough to excuse his destruction of scholastic philosophy in the eyes of his orthodox readers. He confides to Mersenne, "I hope that readers will gradually get used to my principles, and recognize their truth, before they notice that they destroy the principles of Aristotle."[42]

Descartes had strong motivation for feigning concern about the dangers of the skeptical arguments he deployed: he knew that the readers he courted most assiduously would be very concerned about them. He himself does not seem to have regarded skepticism as a major threat to the moral state of the reading public, however. This can be inferred from his acknowledgement of the conventional character of the skeptical arguments he deployed against sense experience. One gets a sense of their currency in *La Recherche de la vérité par la lumière naturelle*, an unfinished and unpublished "conversation" between three interlocutors, whose date remains uncertain.[43] Polyander ("everyman") reacts incredulously to Eudoxus's view that it is salutary, even necessary, for people to rid themselves of preconceived notions

---

40 Boase, 43.

41 Charles Larmore, "Descartes and Skepticism," in *The Blackwell Guide to Descartes' Meditations*, ed. Stephen Gaukroger (Malden, Oxford, Victoria: Blackwell Publishing, 2006), 17–29, 19.

42 AT, III, 298.

43 *La Recherche de la Vérité* was one of Descartes's early works, composed before the *Discours*, according to G. Cantecor, "A quelle date Descartes a-t-il écrit La Recherche de la vérité?" *Revue de la Philosophie*, year 2 (July-September 1928), 254–89. Gaukroger places the composition of the work in 1642 (362–3). See as well Geneviève Rodis-Lewis, "Les derniers écrits de Descartes," in *Le développement de la pensée de Descartes* (Paris: Vrin, 1997), 203–23, and Descartes, *La Recherche de la vérité*, eds Ettore Lojacono and Erik Jan Bos (Milan: Franco Angeli, 2002).

once and for all: "Is there anyone who can doubt that sensible things, I mean those that can be seen and touched, are much surer than all the others?" Eudoxus replies: "Have you never seen one of those melancholic individuals who think themselves to be vases or take some part of their body to be enormous; they will swear that what they see and touch is just as they imagine it to be.... Have you never heard this expression of surprise in comedies: 'Am I awake or asleep?' How can you be certain that your life is not a continuous dream, and that everything you think you learn through your senses is not false now, just as when you are asleep?"[44] The recurrent interrogative formula "Have you never ...?" suggests that these kinds of reflections ought to be familiar to Polyander, hence to the *honnête homme* he represents. In that an *honnête homme* "is not required to have read every book or diligently mastered everything taught in the Schools,"[45] some of whom would have been familiar with Honoré d'Urfé's pastoral novel *L'Astrée* (1607–28) in which one reads, "Am I sleeping or waking?"[46] Even the deliberate application of doubt was not Descartes's invention; he took it from *De la sagesse*, which enjoyed almost as many editions in the early seventeenth century as Montaigne's *Essays*.[47] Indeed, there was not much in the supposedly dangerous *Méditations* that a feeble-minded woman could not have encountered elsewhere. Hobbes and Gassendi complained that the skeptical themes of the first meditation were so familiar that they were hardly worth the space allotted to them.[48] Descartes admits that it was not without a certain "distaste" that he dished out doubt: "Nothing is more conducive to attaining a firm knowledge of things than first becoming accustomed to doubt all things especially corporeal ones. So although I had, some time ago, seen several books on the subject, written by Academics and Skeptics, and felt some distaste at heating up that stale dish again, still I had to give it a whole meditation."[49] The malicious demon, to which Gassendi objected as uncharacteristic of skeptical argumentation, was not so foreign, really. "Our own theologians (following the ancients, I imagine) attribute to each person

---

44   AT, X, 511; CSM, II, 407–8.

45   AT, X, 495; CSM, II, 400.

46   Honoré d'Urfé, *L'Astrée*, cited in Geneviève Rodis-Lewis, *Le Développement de la pensée de Descartes* (Paris: Vrin, 1997), 192, n. 4.

47   Michael Williams explains how Descartes's methodological doubt differed from Hellenistic skepticism in "Descartes and the Metaphysics of Doubt," *Essays on Descartes' Meditations*, ed. Amélie Oksenberg Rorty (Berkeley, Los Angeles, London: University of California Press, 1986), 117–39: "[W]hereas skepticism creeps up on the classical skeptic, as the result of his persistent inability to bring disputes to a definite conclusion, skepticism for Descartes is a theoretical problem that he chooses to confront. From the outset, skepticism is under his control: it is not, as it is for the classical skeptic, something with a life of its own, which might affect his motives in unforeseen and, perhaps initially, even unwelcome ways" 120. However, José R. Maia Neto points out that Charron's Sage resolves "to get rid of all received opinions and to this purpose voluntarily considers the reasons of doubt" in "Charron's Epoché and Descartes' Cogito: The Skeptical Base of Descartes's Refutation of Scepticism," in *The Return of Scepticism from Hobbes and Descartes to Bayle*, ed. Gianni Paganini (Dordrecht, Boston: Kluwer Academic Publishers, 2003), 81–113, 97.

48   AT, VII, 171, 257, 258.

49   AT, VII, 130.

from the very beginning of his life two *genii* which they call angels; one is our friend, and procures for us the things that are good, the other is evil, and is intent on bringing about our ruin in every way possible," says Erasmus.[50] Furthermore, thanks to the prevalence of demonology, the Devil's powers of illusion had infiltrated every stage of sense perception, stoking the Skeptics' bonfire of the sense-based epistemology of the school.[51]

In the context of abundantly accessible doubt, Descartes's stated desire to shield feeble-minded women from its dangers cannot be taken as evidence that he was determined to relegate them to the sidelines of the search for truth. Clearly, it was not for the sake of women, but for that of suspicious theologians, that Descartes suppressed radical doubt, the cornerstone of the Latin *Meditationes de prima philosophia*, from the vernacular *Discours*. Descartes's paternalistic gesture to protect women from the potential ravages of skeptical doubt is, at the very least, disingenuous, since he could not have ignored that the Skeptics who emitted so many dangerous arguments were also those from whom he took his inclusive stance in the *Discours*. Descartes incorporated the Skeptics' open attitude towards women— already an antiphilosophical gesture in Montaigne's *Essays*—just as he appropriated skeptical arguments to destroy the sense-based epistemology of the School. And in the same way that his triumph over skeptical irresolution would excuse, he hoped, his initial reliance on skeptical arguments, his supposed reluctance to expose women to skeptical techniques masks his debt to those Skeptics (and fideists) who valorized women as a means of humbling the learned. Stéphanie-Félicité du Crest, comtesse de Genlis, calls Descartes the first person to defend women against "the most barbarous opinions of men" in the preface to her play *Le Club des dames ou le Retour de Descartes* (1784).[52] Genlis credits Descartes for defending women notwithstanding his careful avoidance of polemic and despite his circumspection regarding the social implications of his philosophy. Even more remarkable, in granting him the historical paternity of pro(to)feminist polemics, she ignores much more outspoken predecessors: Christine de Pizan, Agrippa von Nettesheim, Marie de Gournay. Both the idea that Descartes defended women and that he was the first to do so result from his incorporation and transformation of the skeptical tradition. It is often said that Descartes transformed skepticism from an ethical attitude to a

---

50   Erasmus, "Genius malus," Adage I i 72, in *Collected Works of Erasmus*, trans. Margaret Mann Phillips (Toronto: University of Toronto Press, 1982), I, 117.

51   Larmore rightly points out that "Greek skepticism stopped short of putting into doubt the existence of the world, since it aimed to constitute a way of life" (18), but skepticism had undergone the radicalizing influence of demonology during the Renaissance. See Stuart Clark, *Vanities of the Eye: Vision in Early Modern European Culture* (Oxford: Oxford U.P., 2007). Thomas M. Lennon in "Lady Oracle: Changing Conceptions of Authority and Reason in Seventeenth-Century Philosophy," in *Women and Reason*, ed. Elizabeth Harvey and Kathleen Okruhlik (Ann Arbor: University of Michigan Press, 1992), 39–61, makes a suggestive connection between the possession trial at the Ursuline convent of Loudun in 1634 and 1635 and Descartes's radical doubt: "[T]he epistemological project of Cartesianism is an effort at exorcising universal diabolical possession" (47).

52   Cited in Londa Schiebinger, *The Mind Has No Sex? Women in the Origins of Modern Science* (Cambridge: Harvard U.P., 1989), 172.

series of epistemological problems to overcome.[53] In doing so, he profoundly altered one of the Skeptics' favorite topoi. Montaigne had subverted gender hierarchy and suspended judgment regarding sex difference as a means of attaining tranquility. Marie de Gournay seized upon skeptical equipollence to argue for the equality of women and men, blaming sexist customs for their differences. Descartes defined the basis of equality—*bon sens* in the epistemological realm, free will in the moral sphere—in the context of a search for truth in which custom (including law, but also beliefs and other "dogmatic suppositions") could no longer be bracketed from the progress of knowledge. In this sense, Cartesian philosophy was a first for women: though he did not defend women, and certainly would not have been the first to do so if he had defended them, he established the foundations for equality and provided the philosophical justification for the reform of sexist custom. I turn now to Descartes's moral philosophy, where he fleshes out the abstract egalitarianism of his metaphysics.

Problems with the Good Life

Descartes gleaned his overall conception of philosophy as something that unites the quest for scientific and moral truth from the Stoics. His use of the term "the search for truth" reflects the stoic enterprise of bringing to fruition "the seeds of knowledge and virtue," opposing the Aristotelian notion of a blank slate filled by impressions coming in from outside. The subtitle of *La Recherche de la vérité par la lumière naturelle* defines "the search for truth" as a rational enterprise leading to knowledge: one's natural intelligence, on its own "and without borrowing the help of religion or philosophy, determines the opinions that an *honnête homme* should have, with respect to all things that can occupy his thoughts and penetrates the secrets of the most curious sciences."[54] But the expression also denotes the quest to lead a good and happy life. Typical of the Stoics for whom *sapientia* or wisdom is indistinctly a virtue and a science, Descartes viewed the moral and the scientific components of the search for truth as inseparable and mutually reinforcing.[55] True wisdom, he asserts in the preface to the French translation (1647) of the *Principia philosophiae* (1644),

---

53　"The skepticism that develops within a foundational conception of knowledge contrasts sharply with classical skepticism, even in its most purely epistemic form," explains Larmore; "The classical skeptic's undifferentiated *epoche* thus gives way to a form of skepticism organized around specific skeptical problems: the external world, induction, other minds, and so forth. This transformation of skepticism is the legacy of Descartes's *Meditations*" (Larmore 126–7). According to Williams, "[s]ince Descartes' confrontation with skepticism takes place in a context where his fundamental motive, the urge to really know, is unaffected by skeptical reflections, a context where even the teachings of nature are minimally insistent, such reflections serve to intensify the initial uncertainty rather than eliminate it. Skepticism becomes wedded to doubt" (120).

54　AT, X, 495; CSM, II, 400.

55　Edouard Mehl, "Les méditations stoïciennes de Descartes: Hypothèses sur l'influence du stoïcisme dans la constitution de la pensée cartésienne (1619–1637)," in *Le Stoïcisme au 16ᵉ et 17ᵉ siècle: Le retour des philosophies antiques à l'âge classique*, ed. Pierre-François Moreau (Paris: Albin Michel, 1999), 251–80, 253.

consists in "a perfect knowledge of all things that mankind is capable of knowing, both for the conduct of life and for the preservation of health and the discovery of all manner of skills. In order for this kind of knowledge to be perfect it must be deduced from first causes."[56] His quest for epistemological certitude begins with a reform of the self close in spirit to the moral discipline advocated by the Stoics. The epistemological asceticism that leads to the cogito parallels the stoic Sage's paring away of the obstacles to moral perfection.[57] "Because we do not bring a clear mind to Philosophy, but a badly disposed one occupied with upsetting and popular humors [as we would come] to a Physician," writes Du Vair, "we must do as those who treat wounds, who before applying any bandage remove foreign bodies, and begin by ridding our minds of the passions that arise there, blinding the eye of reason with their smoke."[58] The reform of the self leads, ultimately, to the mastery and possession of nature, and thus, as Descartes optimistically speculates in the fifth part of the *Discours*, to scientific knowledge that allows for the betterment and prolongation of human life. "The whole of philosophy is like a tree," Descartes explains in the preface to the *Principes*. "The roots are metaphysics, the trunk is physics, and the branches emerging from the trunk are all the other sciences, which may be reduced to three principal ones, namely medicine, mechanics, and morals. By 'morals' I understand the highest and most perfect moral system, which presupposes a complete knowledge of the other sciences and is the ultimate level of wisdom."[59]

Reflective of the culminating position on the tree of philosophy that Descartes assigned it in 1647, moral philosophy had by then moved from the periphery to the center of his interests. Disillusionment regarding his initial projects (he often complains in his correspondence of the dearth of funds to finance experiments), as well as the desire to be remembered as a philosopher of the ages may have motivated this orientation. Moral philosophy was the science of how to conduct one's life, and offering guidance on this matter is what made one a philosopher in early modern France. Marie de Rabutin-Chantal, Marquise de Sévigné, the mother of the Comtesse de Grignan, an avowed *Cartésienne,* insisted that she was not a philosopher, meaning that she was neither a lover of abstract systems, like her daughter, nor was attracted to "the conceptions of Seneca and Epictetus."[60] Not surprisingly, she preferred Montaigne, who would have sympathized with her stated affection for "weakness": "Ah! What a likeable man! What good company he makes!"[61] Even if Montaigne's skeptical deconstruction of stoic certitudes made him something of

56 AT, IX B, 2; CSM, I, 179.

57 Dana Shelley, "The Stoic Paradigm of Cartesian Skepticism," Descartes I, North American Society for Seventeenth-Century French Literature, Lincoln, Nebraska, 10 May 2007.

58 Guillaume du Vair, *La Philosophie morale des Stoïques,* in *Les Oeuvres de Messire Guillaume du Vair, Evesque et Comte de Lisieux, Garde des seaux de France* (Paris: Sébastien Cramoisy, 1641; Geneva: Slatkin Reprints, 1970), 25.

59 AT, IX B, 14; CSM, I, 186.

60 Marie de Rabutin-Chantal de Sévigné, *Correspondance,* ed. Roger Duchêne (Paris: Gallimard, 1972–78), I, 191. Cited in John Lyons, *Before Imagination: Embodied Thought from Montaigne to Rousseau* (Stanford: Stanford U.P., 2005), 124.

61 Sévigné, *Correspondance,* II, 697.

an anti-philosopher (which Sévigné seems to have realized better than a number of Montaigne's contemporaries, who thought of him as another neo-Stoic), his *Essays* appealed to readers—first among them Gournay—because they could be used as a practical guide; they were, as Sévigné appreciated, good traveling companions in the journey of life.[62] Descartes's autobiographical trajectory in the *Discours de la méthode* was much harder to envision as a guide or even a model; indeed, he actively discouraged people from following it, and he probably would have never approached the topic of the passions had it not been for his friendship with Elizabeth. Descartes had hoped that through the *Meditationes* (and through the replies to the objections that Marin Mersenne solicited on his behalf), he would be able to persuade a group of powerful, suspicious priests of the orthodoxy of his philosophy. When the ecclesiastical approval he had so assiduously courted continued to elude him, Descartes sought moral support and intellectual sustenance elsewhere. Elizabeth proved an ideal interlocutor: her "mental powers [were] so extraordinary that she ... easily [understood] matters which seem[ed] very difficult to our learned doctors."[63] Reminiscent of the anti-scholastic stance of the Skeptics, he clearly savored the point that a woman runs circles around pedants. But he did not need to compare Elizabeth to his less receptive readers to appreciate her qualities; in his letter of dedication in the *Principia* (1644), he describes her mind as "incomparable." The admiration he expresses there is a reworking of one of his letters to her, following his receipt of her solution to a geometrical problem:

> The solution which it pleased your Highness to do me the honor of sending is so accurate that nothing more could be desired in it; and I was not only seized with astonishment at seeing it, but I cannot refrain from adding that I was also overjoyed, and even taken with vanity to see that the calculation used by your Highness is exactly the same as the one I proposed in my *Geometry*. Experience has taught me that most minds that easily understand the reasoning of metaphysics are not able to grasp that of algebra, and conversely that those that easily understand the latter are usually incapable of others; I see only that of your Highness for which all things are equally easy. It is true that I had already had such ample evidence [of your facility], that I should have had no doubt about it; yet I feared only that [you] would lack the patience necessary, in the beginning, to overcome the difficulty of mathematical reasoning. For this quality is extremely rare in excellent minds and in persons of high station.[64]

Of the three kinds of readers discussed in the *Discours*, there could now be no doubt as to which one Elizabeth belonged: her mind was neither weak (he already knew that), nor impatient (here was confirmation), but truly exceptional. How flattering for him that she grasped the originality of his philosophy, which she said, only required her to "extract from my mind knowledge that I had not previously perceived"![65] How

---

62 Boase, 62.
63 AT, XI, 324; CSM, I, 327.
64 Descartes to Elizabeth, November 1643, AT, IV, 45–6.
65 Elizabeth to Descartes, 16 August 1645, AT, IV, 269.

gratifying that she asked hard questions that showed how well she had understood him![66]

Certainly the most important of the questions that Elizabeth asked Descartes was the nature and mode of the mind's union with the body. As of her very first letter of 16 May 1643, she pressed Descartes to explain to her how two substances, the *res cogitans* and the *res extensa*, could be joined.[67] "I will despair of ever finding certainty in anything," she writes in a subsequent letter, "if you do not give me any, you who alone have kept me from embracing the skepticism to which my reason was first leading me."[68] It would not be the fault of her own weak or impatient mind, Elizabeth wryly suggests, if Descartes should make a skeptic of her; it would instead be the fault of a gap in his metaphysics. Over their seven-year correspondence, Descartes never did explain the mode of mind/body union to Elizabeth's satisfaction, but he did at least clarify why he thought that he need not explain it. There was, he claimed, an epistemological duality corresponding to the two realms of our being. We can deduce that the mind is a distinct substance through rational reflection. But we know through experience and by intuition that we are made up of a body and a mind together.[69] Elizabeth's inquiry concerning the way in which mind and body interact open onto what was to be the main subject of their letters: moral philosophy. If the kind of thought that Descartes practices in the *Meditations* should only occupy one for a few hours a year, she wondered, what *is* the best way to conduct oneself the rest of the time?[70] Elizabeth was determined to understand how Descartes's rationalist epistemology and dualist metaphysics could help her to lead a happy life when her

---

66 Descartes had learned not to take such good will for granted; the experience of the *Objections to the Meditations* had been disappointing to him because he felt that some of his objectors, namely Hobbes and Gassendi, had not read his *Meditations* carefully, an opinion shared by Elizabeth. Upon receiving a copy of the French *Méditations métaphysiques* (1647), Elizabeth writes on 5 December 1647: "Mon admiration s'augmente toutes les fois que je relis les objections qu'on vous a faites, comment il est possible que des personnes, qui ont employé tant d'années à la méditation et à l'étude, ne sauraient comprendre des choses si simples et si claires, que la plupart, en disputant du vrai et du faux, semblent ne pas connaître comment il les faut discerner, et que le sieur Gasendus, qui est en la plus grande réputation du pour son savoir, a fait, après l'Anglais, des objections moins raisonnables que tous les autres" (AT, V, 97).

67 On this question see Garber, "Understanding Interaction: What Descartes should have told Elizabeth," in *Descartes Embodied: Reading Cartesian Philosophy through Cartesian Science* (Cambridge: Cambridge U.P., 2001), 168–88; Deborah Tollefsen, "Princess of Elizabeth and the Problem of Mind-Body Interaction," *Hypatia* 14 (1999): 59–77; Andrea Nye, "Polity and Prudence: the Ethics of Elizabeth, Princess Palatine" in *Hypatia's Daughters*, ed. Linda Lopez McAlister (Bloomington: Indiana U.P., 1996) 68–91; Lisa Shapiro, "Princess Elizabeth and Descartes: The Union of Soul and Body and the Practice of Philosophy," in *Feminism and the History of Philosophy*, ed. Genevieve Lloyd (Oxford: Oxford U.P., 2002), 182–203.

68 Elizabeth to Descartes, 1 July 1643, AT, IV, 2–3.

69 Jean Laporte, *Le Rationalisme de Descartes* (Paris: Presses Universitaires de France, 1950), 233; Michael Moriarty, *Early Modern French Thought: The Age of Suspicion* (Oxford: Oxford U.P., 2003), 74.

70 Descartes writes to Elizabeth 28 June 1643: "je n'ai jamais employé que fort peu d'heures, par jour, aux pensées qui occupent l'imagination, et fort peu d'heures, par an, à

body and her familial circumstances caused her to be miserable. She also wanted to know how Descartes's philosophy could help her make the right decision when political developments were such that she did not have time to sequester herself to meditate the outcomes of all possible actions she might take.

It was Descartes's failed attempt to play doctor to Elizabeth's melancholy that led him to take a stand on the moral philosophy of the Stoics. The therapy he initially recommends is stoic, and this is not surprising. He had read Du Vair,[71] Montaigne (whom many thought of as a Stoic), and Charron (who cites Du Vair almost as much as he cites Montaigne); his program of study at the Collège de la Flèche featured a curriculum "imbued with that wholesome and rugged philosophy" of classical Latin literature;[72] and Justus Lipsius' influence remained strong in the humanist circles that welcomed him in the Netherlands. He begins by distinguishing between noble and vulgar souls:

> It seems to me that the difference between the greatest souls and those that are base and vulgar consists principally in that the vulgar souls give themselves over to their passions and are happy or sad only according to whether those things that happen to them are agreeable or pleasant ; whereas great souls are so strong and powerful in their reasoning, even though they too have passions—often even more violent than those of common people— their reason nevertheless prevails, so that even afflictions serve them and contribute to the perfect felicity they enjoy in this life. Considering themselves immortal and capable of attaining great contentment on the one hand, and, on the other hand, considering that they are joined to mortal, fragile bodies that are subject to many infirmities and will inevitably perish in a few years, they do everything in their power to turn Fortune to their favor in this life. They nevertheless attach so little value to Fortune seen in the perspective of Eternity, that they view its vicissitudes somewhat the way we view the events of a play. And just as sad or pitiful stories that we see acted on stage can often provide us with as much diversion as happy ones, even though they bring tears to our eyes, so the noblest souls … feel an inner satisfaction with even the most distressing and unbearable things that befall them.

Descartes nevertheless seems a bit embarrassed to propose such parochial stuff as a remedy for her. He assures the princess that "I am not one of those cruel philosophers, who wishes their Sage to be unfeeling," and he excuses his recourse to stoical platitudes by accentuating their unique appropriateness to her person: "I would fear that this style were ridiculous, if I were using it to write to someone else."[73]

Elizabeth expresses gratitude for Descartes's solicitude; the letters and the friendship they embody provide a salutary, if temporary "antidote to melancholy."[74] She nonetheless makes it clear that his wanting to "cure my body by the soul" is wishful thinking. Elizabeth agrees with Descartes's diagnosis; she even expands on

---

celles qui occupent l'entendement seul, et que j'ai donné tout le reste de mon temps au relâche des sens et au repos de l'esprit" (AT, III, 693).

71 On Descartes's indebtedness to Du Vair, see Anthony Levi, *French Moralists: The Theory of the Passions, 1585–1649* (Oxford: Clarendon Press, 1964), 246–7.

72 Mesnard, 4.

73 Descartes to Elizabeth, 18 May 1645, AT, IV, 201–2.

74 Elizabeth to Descartes, 22 June 1645, AT, IV, 233.

the etiology of hypochondriacal melancholy, the sort of "windy" melancholy that, according to André du Laurens, results from the obstruction of organs in the lower abdomen (the *hypochondria*). "For persons who cannot do much exercise, it does not take sadness's oppression of the heart long to block the spleen and infect the rest of the body with its vapors. I imagine that my slow fever and dry cough, which have not left me yet ... are caused by that."[75] But neither the symptoms nor the cause of her malady are as easy to cure as he imagines. Surrounded by reminders of unpleasant events and having the responsibility of making decisions about them, it is not possible to maintain a rigorous distance that would allow her to anticipate and to master her passionate responses to events, to be the detached spectator, as Descartes advocates, of her misfortune: "If I could make it [the conduct of my life] conform to your recent precepts, there would be no doubt but I would quickly recover from the body's illnesses and the mind's weakness. But I admit that I find it difficult to separate sense and imagination from things that are continually represented in conversation and letters, which I cannot ignore without sinning against my duty." She concedes that such separation could preempt the nefarious effects of the passions. "But I have never been able to put it into practice until after passion has already played its role. There is an element of surprise in calamities, even in those that are expected, which I cannot master until some time goes by, during which my body becomes so disordered, that to recover it takes several months that almost never pass without some new upset."[76]

If Elizabeth's soul is exceptional, as Descartes insists, it is because of her resilience as a survivor of the passions, not because of her mastery of them: "I think that, if my life were fully known to you, you would find the fact that a sensitive soul, like mine, has survived so long, through so many tribulations, in a body so feeble, with no other counsel but my own reason, and no consolation besides that of my conscience, more strange than you find the causes of my present ailment."[77] And whereas Descartes appears to see Elizabeth in terms of resemblance to himself, to the point that he offers his own experience as an example,[78] she reminds him of her

---

75 Elizabeth to Descartes, 24 May, 1645, AT, IV, 208.

76 Ibid., 22 June, 1645, AT, IV, 234.

77 Elizabeth to Descartes, 24 May 1645, AT, IV, 209.

78 Here is Descartes to Elizabeth, May or June 1645: "j'ai expérimenté en moi-même, ... un mal presque semblable, et même plus dangereux ... estant né d'une mère qui mourut, peu de jours après ma naissance, d'un mal de poumon, causé par quelques déplaisirs, j'avois hérité d'elle une toux seiche, & une couleur pasle, que j'ay gardée jusques à l'âge de vingt ans, & qui faisoit que tous les Medecins qui m'ont vû avant ce temps-là, me condamnoient à mourir jeune. Mais je croy que l'inclination que j'ay tousjours euë à regarder les choses qui se présentoient du biais qui me les pouvoit rendre le plus agréables, & à faire que mon principal contentement ne despendist que de moy seul, est cause que cette indisposition, qui m'estoit comme naturelle, s'est peu à peu entièrement passée" (AT, IV, 220–21). His mother died of an illness caused by upsetting passions ("quelques déplaisirs"); his own optimistic outlook—a natural "inclination" or a cultivated habit?—saved him from the fate of his mother, even though he contracted her illness. Interestingly, Descartes says that his mother died only days after his birth, when, in fact, she died when he was fourteen months old. He clearly wanted to establish that he had been raised without a mother. "To choose a means of indicating this

difference: "Know, then, that my body is imbued with many of the weaknesses of my sex, that it easily feels the soul's afflictions and does not have the strength to recover along with it, being of a constitution that is subject to obstructions and located in an environment that contributes greatly to this susceptibility."[79]

At this point Descartes suggests that they read Seneca's *De vita beata* together "so that my letters are not wholly empty and useless" (one senses the doctor's discouragement).[80] The reading of Seneca proves to be a turning point. Expecting to simply "improve upon [*renchérir par-dessus*]" the work of an ancient, Descartes will decide that he needs to subject moral philosophy to a complete overhaul, just as he has done with metaphysics. The immediate source of dissatisfaction stems from the apparent lack of metaphysical foundations—or "roots," to borrow the tree of philosophy metaphor—of the blessed life according to Seneca. Seneca's moral philosophy is based on persuasion, not on science; it is rhetoric, not philosophy. Elizabeth concurs, "I found ... many beautiful phrases and well-imagined *sententia* to inspire pleasant meditation in me, but not to instruct me in the subject he deals with since they lack method and since the author does not even follow the method he had said he would follow"; she suspects that he may have been trying "to acquire admirers, by surprising the imagination, rather than disciples, by informing judgment."[81] Henceforth, clearly, Descartes cannot expect to simply pull a cure for Elizabeth out of his humanist baggage, but that he must, if he wishes to help her, make good on the definition of philosophy that he proposes in the preface to the *Principia* and make moral philosophy result from his metaphysics and his physics, the roots and the trunk of the tree of philosophy. It is therefore to misunderstand Descartes to portray his moral philosophy as simply a stoicized complement to his dualist metaphysics, as Harth does: "Descartes's neostoicism rests on the major epistemological premise that *res cogitans* has a reflexive capacity to disengage itself from the body ... to view it and all that befalls it, and consequently, all accidents that fall *res extensa* with the bemused detachment of a spectator at the theater."[82] The *theatrum mundi* metaphor is certainly stoic, but Descartes and Elizabeth consider passionate response to theater from various angles, symptomatic of bricolage rather than revelatory of a system. Elizabeth will even suggest that the tragic spectacle is pleasurable, because "we like naturally to be moved."[83] Descartes concurs that passions, even distressing ones, are more pleasurable than a-pathos, apathy. That

---

fact is itself surely indicative of some strong feeling on the matter," comments Stephen Gaukroger in *Descartes: An Intellectual Biography* (Oxford: Clarendon Press, 1995), 16–17. It is interesting that Descartes does not mention the much more recent death of his five-year-old daughter Francine, which according to Baillet, left him "with the greatest sorrow that he had ever experienced in his life" (cited in Gaukroger, 353).

79   Elizabeth to Descartes, 24 May 1645, AT, IV, 208.

80   Descartes to Elizabeth, 21 July 1645, AT, IV, 252.

81   Elizabeth to Descartes, 16 August 1645, AT, IV, 268–9; Elizabeth to Descartes, August 1645, AT, IV, 279.

82   Harth, 74. Another scholar who claims that Descartes's moral philosophy "is almost all stoic" is André Bridoux, *Le Stoïcisme et son influence* (Paris: Vrin, 1966), 212.

83   Elizabeth to Descartes, 28 October 1645, AT, IV, 322. On Descartes, Elizabeth, and tragedy, see Carole Talon-Hugon, *Les Passions rêvées par la raison: Essai sur la théorie des*

is why, rather than pity Elizabeth,[84] he pities those who follow the Stoics. Wishing to conquer their passions, they are truly "melancholic, or minds entirely detached from their bodies."[85] For through his correspondence with Elizabeth, which inspires in him "extreme passions," including "happiness," "joy," "vanity," "glory," and "sadness,"[86] he has come to see that the passions, far from harming the soul, are "almost all good, and so useful to this life that our soul would have no reason to wish to remain joined to the body for a moment, if it could not feel them."[87] In this light, learning how the passions function can help us, not to suppress or transcend them, but to "tame" them—that is, to enhance those that are profitable and pleasurable to us and to limit those that harm us. He therefore devotes *Les Passions de l'âme* to explaining the mechanics of the passions, through which we intuit the union of the mind and the body, explaining how it is that a corporeal state can inflect the perceptions of the soul, or how a state of mind can be continued, as it were, in the fabric of the body.

Descartes begins *Les Passions de l'âme* with a familiar gesture: "[T]he teachings of the ancients ... are so meager and for the most part so implausible that I cannot hope to approach the truth except by departing from the paths they have followed."[88] As in his metaphysics, however, this new path is built from the debris of the system he has demolished. The framework and the vocabulary remain stoic, but the content is transformed. Descartes's eclectic redeployment of stoic concepts was typical of the time. The famous predicator, Jean-François Senault anticipates Descartes's reworking of stoicism in *De l'usage des passions* (1641). Senault denies that the passions can be eradicated since they are part of our fallen nature and sometimes even serve as "seeds of virtue." At the same time, he agrees with the Stoics that excessive passion can degenerate into vice and that the Christian bears some responsibility in controlling passion; the techniques he recommends for doing so are recognizably stoic.[89] Like Senault, Descartes acknowledges a distinctly human space of moral activity, but he, too, infuses stoicism with a Christian aura, for the ultimate form of contentment is that which comes from grace: "[O]nly faith can teach us what grace is, by which God elevates us to a supernatural beatitude."[90]

---

passions de Descartes et de quelques-uns de ses contemporains (Paris: Vrin, 2002), 96–7, 103.

84 Descartes to Elizabeth, June 1645: "Je supplie très humblement Votre Altesse de me pardonner, si je ne puis plaindre son indisposition, lorsque j'ai l'honneur de recevoir de ses lettres. Car j'y remarque toujours des pensées si nettes et des raisonnements si fermes, qu'il ne m'est pas possible de me persuader qu'un esprit capable de les concevoir soit logé dans un corps faible et malade" (AT, IV, 326).

85 Descartes to Elizabeth, 18 August 1645, AT, IV, 277.

86 Descartes to Elizabeth, 8 July 1644, AT, IV, 64; November 1643, AT, IV, 46; May 1646, AT, IV, 407; 22 February 1649, AT V, 281. Elizabeth's responses to Descartes are less passionate. See Elizabeth to Descartes, 6 or 16 May 1643, AT, III, 660; 1 August 1644, AT, IV, 131–3.

87 Descartes to Chanut, 1 November 1646, AT, IV, 538.

88 AT, XI, 327–8; CSM, I, 328.

89 On Senault and stoicism, see Talon-Hugon, 48–56.

90 Descartes to Elizabeth, 6 October 1645, AT, IV, 314.

Descartes's moral philosophy is nonetheless unique in its relation to stoicism in that it brings moral considerations into line with epistemological ones, with free will as a moral equivalent to *bon sens*. I have already indicated that Descartes was deeply indebted to the Stoics for the basic components of his epistemology. His notion of innate ideas comes from the stoic "seeds of virtue and knowledge," and he takes the idea of the unity of the sciences from the Stoics as well. That the "seeds of virtue and knowledge" should be found in all people, men and women, is a given not just in Cartesian epistemology, but in ancient stoic epistemology as well, if only because the unity of the sciences rested on the claim that human minds were all endowed with the same basic capacity for discerning between the true and the false.

Now, there can be no doubt that stoic moral philosophy—and the Stoics in early modern France were remembered primarily as moral philosophers rather than as epistemologists or natural philosophers—was the most masculinist moral philosophy that ever strutted the face of the earth. We need only consider Montaigne's first essay, as I did in Chapter Four, to appreciate the extent to which the Sage had been caricaturized not just as non-human (as a rock, because of his apathy), but also as hyper-masculine. The Renaissance ideal was that of moderate masculinity, as Todd Reeser reveals in *Moderating Masculinity in Early Modern Culture*.[91] Moderation in general had been perilously polarized by sectarian strife, and the highly gendered rhetoric of the neo-Stoics was symptomatic of this eclipse of the golden mean. In order to trade the accusation of (an often feminized) Machiavellian manipulation for an image of moral rectitude, the *politiques* ennobled their political pragmatics with a stoic credo. Through the adoption of stoic moral philosophy, they characterized the Catholic League, which had until then occupied the moral high ground (it was, after all, defending the Catholic faith) as pathologically melancholic; to pathologize melancholy—that condition of genial men, according to Bodin—they feminized it. At the same time, they portrayed themselves conquering the seditious passions and acceding to *masle vertu*, sometimes describing this reform of the self (also to be understood as an allegory of the French nation) in terms of a sex change from girl to boy. How striking, in comparison, is Descartes's gender-neutral discussion of the passions! Never does he suggest to Elizabeth that she would become more masculine through the mastery of her melancholy; never does he feminize melancholy, although he certainly presents it as pathology, not just in the letters, but in *La Recherche de la Vérité* and the *Meditationes de prima philosophia* as well. The stoic concepts of virtue and generosity would be virtually meaningless for Du Vair in the absence of the adjective "masle." Indeed, I argued in Chapter Three, that the necessity of performing masculinity resulted from the determining power of the will. How can one rely on a pre-existing masculine essence (humoral or anatomical) when one becomes a man by virtue of the will's dominance over the passions? Descartes views the reliance on rhetoric as a sign of the lack, not of real masculinity, but of true philosophy. Thus, "Seneca did not clearly understand what he meant to say; for the better we conceive of something, the more we are determined to express it in only

---

91   Todd Reeser, *Moderating Masculinity in Early Modern Culture* (Chapel Hill: University of North Carolina Press, 2006). See especially his analysis of Montaigne's "Of Moderation," 11–18.

one way.""[92] In abandoning Seneca, Descartes not only forgoes the gendered rhetoric of stoic and neo-stoic moral philosophy, he seeks to ground moral philosophy in a metaphysical and physical framework. Those metaphysics, based in part on stoic epistemology, were egalitarian by principle. And an important part of Descartes's transformation of the moral philosophy of the Stoics entailed making it egalitarian, which meant, paradoxically, making it more consistent with Stoic epistemology.

The egalitarian tenor of Cartesian moral philosophy results directly from Descartes's exchanges with Elizabeth, but not because she is a woman and he is a man. Rather, Elizabeth causes Descartes to rethink how one measures a person's value, or rather, what one measures in order to determine his or her moral value. Whereas Descartes characterizes intelligence, knowledge, and care for others as static possessions that have intrinsic value, Elizabeth challenges him to assess value in terms of the use made of those possessions, in a way more consistent with his emphasis on the application of *bon sens* in the *Discours de la méthode*. As a result, he defines moral value in a way that incorporates differences between individuals while recognizing their basic equality.[93]

If there is one aspect of Descartes's exhortations that remains consistent throughout his letters to Elizabeth, it is that he cannot understand how she could not find in herself all that she needs to live a life of contentment or "blessedness [*béatitude*]." He remains incredulous that a mind of her "caliber [*trempe*]" could not serve as the basis of happiness.

> Because I consider your Highness as having the noblest and most elevated soul that I know, I think that it must also be the happiest, and that it truly will be happy, on condition that it pleases her to cast her eyes towards what is beneath her, and compare the value of the advantages [*biens*] she possesses, and that can never be taken from her, with those of which fortune has stripped her, and with the disgrace with which fortune persecutes her through people who are close to her; for then she will see what good reason she has to be content with her own possessions [*biens*].[94]

In opposing the "possessions" of Elizabeth's soul and material goods subject to fortune, Descartes suggests that, in finding value in herself, she could also find contentment. The argument is strange. Ostensibly, the difference is that goods in the soul are impervious to fortune, while wealth comes and goes. The soul's possessions are thus a reliable source of contentment, while to put stock in the material goods would mean enslaving one's emotional state to fortune. This would seem to imply that if wealth were, in fact, impervious to fortune, it could be a continuing and, therefore, legitimate source of satisfaction. But this is psychologically implausible,

---

92 Descartes to Elizabeth, 18 August 1645, AT, IV, 272–3. Compare to the *Discours*: "ceux qui ont le raisonnement le plus fort, et qui digèrent le mieux leurs pensées, afin de les rendre claires et intelligibles, peuvent toujours persuader ce qu'ils proposent, encore qu'ils ne parlassent que bas Breton, et qu'ils n'eussent jamais appris de rhétorique"(AT, VI, 7).

93 I was led to think about value by Donald Rung, "Is Knowledge Like Money? Descartes in Amsterdam," Descartes I, North American Society for Seventeenth-Century French Literature, Lincoln, Nebraska, 10 May 2007.

94 Descartes to Elizabeth, 18 May 1645, AT, IV, 203–4.

as is Descartes's expectation that Elizabeth could find relief from her melancholy by taking stock of her soul's possessions and "seeing what good reason she has to be content with her own possessions [biens]." "Happy is he who had all his wealth invested, and keeps only what he needs for his expenses," sighs Molière's miser, Harpagon, recognizing, despite himself, that the value of money is only palpable when it is growing or circulating. [95] To get satisfaction from one's wealth, it is not enough to contemplate it; one must be able to use it.

The "possessions" that Descartes values in Elizabeth include her care for others. [96] Above all, however, it includes her cultivated mind: "Your Highness can draw this general consolation from fortune's calamities: they have perhaps contributed significantly to making her cultivate her mind to the extent she had done; that is a possession that she should value more than an empire." [97] Descartes at first encourages Elizabeth to esteem the value of her intellectual achievements, but soon comes to see that use is more salutary than contemplation as he accepts a more modest role in treating Elizabeth's melancholy. One of the therapies that he initially recommends to her is the epicurean tactic of diversion. He approves of her decision to take the waters at Spa so long as she observes,

> in taking them, what physicians customarily recommend, that is, that one must deliver one's mind completely from all sorts of sad thoughts, and even from all sorts of serious meditations concerning knowledge [*les sciences*], and to busy oneself only with imitating those who, in observing the greenery of woods, the colors of a flower, the flight of a bird, and other such things that require no attention whatsoever, persuade themselves that they are thinking of nothing. [98]

But Descartes abandons these recommendations as soon as he realizes that it is not by prescribing a cure that he can help Elizabeth, but simply by providing her with distraction: "I have the honor of observing [*témoigner*] that my letters may serve as a distraction to you, while physicians advise you to occupy your mind with nothing taxing." [99] Contradicting the doctors, he now recommends serious study as the best distraction:

> I have attempted before to persuade your Highness to cultivate nonchalance, thinking that overly serious occupations weaken the body in tiring the mind: but I would not want for all that to dissuade her from the cares necessary to divert her thoughts from objects which may sadden her; and I do not doubt that the divertissement of study, which would be highly grievous to others, could sometimes offer her respite. [100]

---

95 Molière, *L'Avare*, Act I, scene 4, in *Oeuvres complètes*, vol. II, 248.

96 Descartes to Elizabeth, 18 May 1645: "Je sais …que Votre Altesse n'est point tant touchée de ce qui la regarde en son particulier, que de ce qui regarde les intérêts de sa maison et des personnes qu'elle affectionne; ce que j'estime comme une vertu la plus aimable de toutes" (AT, IV, 202).

97 Descartes to Elizabeth, June 1645, AT, IV, 237.

98 Descartes to Elizabeth, May or June 1645, AT, IV, 220.

99 Descartes to Elizabeth, 21 July 1645, AT, IV, 251.

100 Descartes to Elizabeth, June 1645, AT, IV, 237–8.

De vita beata is their first divertissement, and henceforth (to Descartes's apparent relief) they address the passions as an object of study. The princess still brings the discussion back to her situation when the philosopher gets too abstract, and the philosopher still hopes to edify the princess, but the doctor/patient rapport is much less in evidence.

The other way in which the value of a possession can be felt and appreciated is through comparison. The miser to whom Descartes compares himself upon receiving his first letter from Elizabeth only derives pleasure from his treasures knowing that he hoards what others lack: "I can only say ... that, infinitely valuing your letter to me, I will treat it as misers do their treasures; they more they value them, the more they hide them, and begrudging the rest of the world a view of them, they make it their sovereign contentment to admire them."[101] Despite the fact that Descartes qualifies Elizabeth as "incomparable" in the dedicatory epistle to the *Principia*, it is obvious that he assesses the value of the goods of her soul by comparison. In one instance, hoping to buoy her mood, he even invites her to compare herself to others: "Thus, when your Highness perceives the causes for which she has had more leisure, to cultivate her reason, than many others of her age, if it also pleases her to consider how much more she has profited than these others, I am sure that she will find ample subject for contentment."[102] It is Elizabeth's turn to be surprised: "I am astonished that you would ask me to compare myself to those of my age, regarding something of which I am ignorant rather than something I cannot ignore, even if the former is to my advantage. There is nothing that can tell me if I have profited more, in cultivating my reason, than others have done in the ends they have pursued." Elizabeth calls Descartes back to the opening assertions of the *Discours*. We all have good sense; the most important thing is to use it well. "[T]he greatest souls are capable of the greatest vices, as well as the greatest virtues."[103] How, Elizabeth wonders, could she possibly measure another person's "profit" against her own when he or she may have applied his or her reason, no less legitimately, to other sorts of things? This would be like comparing apples and oranges. It would make much more sense to measure what she has done against what she could have done. "I have no doubt that with the time my body has demanded for respite, there was still more available during which I could have advanced beyond where I am now."[104] It is not that she does not recognize the exceptionality of her achievements, only that she does not see how comparing what her mind has done or is capable of doing to those of others can profit her:

> In measuring the breadth of the human mind by the example of common people, we would find it to be very narrow, for most people's thoughts only go as far as the senses. Even amidst those who apply themselves to study, there are few who employ anything besides memory, or who have truth as the goal of their labor. And if there is something wrong with my not wanting to consider whether or not I have gained more than these people, I do not believe that an excess of humility is as nefarious as presumptuousness, although less ordinary. We are more inclined to fail to recognize our faults than our perfections. And in

---

101 Descartes to Elizabeth, 21 May 1643, AT, III, 668.
102 Descartes to Elizabeth, 6 October 1645, AT, IV, 306.
103 AT, VI, 2; CSM I, 111.
104 Elizabeth to Descartes, 28 October 1645, 321.

fleeing the repentance of faults we have committed, as if it were an enemy of felicity, we might run the risk of losing the impetus to better ourselves.[105]

Elizabeth's point is that the value of a possession can only really be determined by its use, and that measuring her mind against that of the common herd would only give her an excuse not to use it, since they use it mostly for things having to do with the senses. This would do nothing to profit her, since as we have seen, study is her most successful therapy, although here Elizabeth seems to characterize it as a moral duty, whose abandonment would be to commit a "fault."

Descartes insists that for so experienced an appraiser of minds as himself, such a comparison is not difficult at all. He nonetheless grasps her point:

[E]ven if the comparison that your Highness refuses to make to her advantage can be easily verified by experience, it is nevertheless so praiseworthy a virtue to judge so favorably of others, and it accords so well with the generosity that prevents you from measuring the potential of the human mind by the example of common man, that I cannot refrain from valuing the one [her virtue] and the other [her generosity] to the utmost.[106]

This may seem at first like a gratuitous flourish of gallantry, but, in fact, it shows that Descartes has revised how he values Elizabeth as a result of her objections to how she measures value. Significantly, although the princess frequently refers to the philosopher's "excess of generosity" and "perfect generosity,"[107] this is the only place in the correspondence (that I have found) where *he* describes *her* in terms of generosity, which he esteems along with her virtue. Her virtue entails judging others favorably; her generosity consists in refusing to measure the breadth of the human mind through common example. Are these two actions contradictory? To refuse to accept the common herd as an example of the capacity of the human mind would seem to entail a condescending judgment rather than a favorable one. But this is not what Elizabeth is saying, and not what Descartes understands her to be saying. To be sure, very few people (maybe just the two of them!) truly engage in the kind of meditating from which Descartes pretends to protect women by writing his meditations in Latin, the kind of thought that, he tells Elizabeth, should only occupy her time a few hours of any given year (at least before realizing that such thought offered relief from her melancholy). And Elizabeth is not a relativist; she clearly believes that "cultivating her reason" has more value in the absolute than going about one's entire life relying on sense or devoting one's whole career to stuffing one's memory. But distinguishing between noble and vulgar souls only obscures the epistemological premise that each individual, according to Descartes, has within him or her that which he or she needs to distinguish the true from the false. It also detracts from what is more important: how one uses what one has according to the goals one sets for oneself. For after all, the search for truth, as Descartes puts it in the closing pages of the *Discours*, is a collective enterprise "combining the lives and labours of many," and those labors

105 Elizabeth to Descartes, 28 October 1645, AT, IV, 321–2.

106 Descartes to Elizabeth, 3 Novembrer 1645, AT, IV, 330–31.

107 Elizabeth to Descartes, 1 July 1643, AT, IV, 3; 24 May 1645, AT, IV, 207; August 1645, AT, IV 279; 30 June 1648, AT, V, 195.

necessarily entail the widest diversity.[108] In refusing to consider the capacity of the common herd as a standard against which minds such as her own appear superior, Elizabeth is also, implicitly, refusing to impose her (and Descartes's) pursuit as a standard to which these common people would appear inferior. Consequently, her tendency to judge others favorably—her "virtue" according to Descartes—is not a case of ignoring difference, but of recognizing the difficulty of assessing how others have used what they have, given the differences between people. Recognizing that we are ill-equipped to make such judgments, it behooves us to give others the benefit of the doubt. This reasoning is, for Descartes, a lesson in generosity.

Now we are equipped to understand how Descartes transforms the moral philosophy of the Stoics in *Les Passions de l'âme* by fleshing out an egalitarian complement to his rationalist epistemology. There he asserts that the universal basis of moral action and value—the ethical equivalent of *bon sens*—is free will. Just as God creates a mechanistic universe whose laws can be known to humankind, so He equips us with a unique gift that we are entitled to use as we see fit. In a deterministic universe, only humans have the freedom of self-determination, and in this they resemble God. The perpetual wonder we feel at our own freedom is what gives us our sense of value; the gift of free will is the basis of self-esteem: "I see only one thing in us which could give us good reason for esteeming ourselves, namely, the exercise of our free will and the control we have over our volitions. For we can reasonably be praised or blamed only for actions that depend upon this free will. It renders us in a certain way like God by making us masters of ourselves."[109] Descartes never convinces Elizabeth that she can master her passions; the best he can do is to divert her attention from her troubles, and the best she can muster is to pick up the pieces once her passions have already been unleashed. Nevertheless, this concept of free will satisfies Descartes's desire for some common denominator of value, while at the same time satisfying Elizabeth's point that it is not what we have but how we use it that matters. In terms of a "possession of the soul," free will needs no comparison in order for us to grasp its value; it comes from God and makes us like God in our own sphere of action, so that even though everybody has it, this is no way diminishes our appreciation of it. In any case, free will is not something that can be measured or compared, since Descartes holds it to be infinite in each of us. The only possible judgment one can make with respect to free will, and the only distinctions one can legitimately draw between individuals, pertain to its use: "Thus I believe that true generosity, which causes a person's self-esteem to be as great as it may legitimately be ... consists in his knowing that nothing truly belongs to him but this freedom to dispose his volitions, and that he ought to be praised or blamed for no other reason than his *using* this freedom well or badly."[110] Here Descartes clearly disavows his earlier statements about why Elizabeth should feel self-esteem. In the correspondence, he initially encourages her to find satisfaction in the contemplation of her soul's possessions: intelligence, knowledge, care for others. But according to *Les Passions de l'âme*, the only thing that truly belongs to anyone is free will. This

---

108 AT, I, 63; CSM, I, 143.

109 AT, XI, 445; CSM, I, 384.

110 AT XI, 445–6; CSM, III, 384. Emphasis mine.

is not to say that Descartes's appraisal of Elizabeth has changed, that he no longer thinks that she should value her intelligence, learning, or caring. Rather it is the notion of possession that has changed. What truly belongs to us is not a static object of reflection, but the will that we enact in the moment that we enact it. Analogous to the thought, "I think, I am" whose truth manifests itself as a fleeting intuition yet from which we can establish enduring criteria for the truth (clarity and distinction), the enactment of will is a momentary thing in which we nevertheless glimpse the infinite purview of our freedom.

We recognize in Descartes's emphasis on enactment the performative quality of stoic virtue, but whereas the sage enacts will in order to ascertain the presence of his *masle vertu*, Descartes, in linking the use of will to a metaphysics, grants it continuity and substance; the gendered rhetoric that lends meaning and value to the Sage's successful deployment of the will thus becomes superfluous. Equally superfluous are the comparisons through which Descartes had initially assessed the value of Elizabeth's "possessions." The generous person is she who, like Elizabeth, refrains from contempt of others because the "goods" that are easy to compare—intelligence, knowledge—are only the resources on which our will draws, while will, which is truly responsible for our profit, is hard to judge.

> Those who possess this knowledge and this feeling about themselves readily come to believe that any other person can have the same knowledge and feeling about himself, because this involves nothing which depends on someone else. That is why such people never have contempt for anyone. Although they often see that others do wrong in ways that show up their weakness, they are nevertheless more inclined to excuse than to blame them and to regard such wrong-doing as due rather to lack of knowledge than to lack of a virtuous will. Just as they do not consider themselves much inferior to those who have greater wealth of honour, or even to those who have more intelligence, knowledge or beauty, or generally to those who surpass them in some other perfections, equally they do not have much more esteem for themselves than for those whom they surpass.[111]

We recognize in this development Elizabeth's lesson in generosity. Descartes had wanted her to take solace in the possessions of her soul, which he opposed to material goods. She rejected this suggestion, recognizing that static possessions of any sort are not a basis of contentment, except by comparison. Comparison implies judging everyone according to a single standard (mental ability, intellectual achievement), a throwback to the scholastic hierarchy between the learned and the vulgar that contradicted the egalitarian spirit of the *Discours*. In response to Elizabeth's objection, Descartes locates a truly universal possession—free will—and now considers intelligence, knowledge, and beauty no better a foundation for self-esteem than riches. When Elizabeth writes to Descartes on 1 August 1644, that she has received the *Principia*, with the dedication to her, she comments, "Pedants will say that you were obliged to construct a new moral philosophy so that I could be worthy of it."[112] The pedants were right for once. In *Les Passions de l'âme*, written at her behest a few years later, Descartes constructed a new moral philosophy that

---

111 AT, XI, 445–6; CSM, I, 384.
112 Elizabeth to Descartes, 1 August 1644, AT, IV, 131.

would enable her, but also anybody who resolved to use his or her free will well—
"that is, never to lack the will to undertake and carry out whatever he judges to be
best"—to achieve the cardinal virtue of *générosité*. According to André Bridoux,
"the sentiment of generosity is replete with a transformation of human relations. In
revealing the absolute freedom present in man's soul, [Descartes] obligates us to
respect our *semblables*, to recognize them as equals, to act towards them with good
will and gentleness. In so doing, he leads us through trails that we already knew,
because the Stoics blazed them."[113] Perhaps we did know of these trails before,
but it is unlikely that a good number of us actually traveled them, so overgrown
were they with florid, masculinist rhetoric. Thanks to his fertile exchange with
Elizabeth, Descartes succeeds, limpidly, in cross-pollinating the "seeds of virtue
and knowledge" to reveal equality as one of the most precious fruits of the tree of
Cartesian philosophy.

The Question of Custom

Descartes was committed to the basic epistemic and moral equality of all people.
But this equality would not mean much if he had not also provided us with a means
of rectifying institutions that cultivated inequality among people. The feminist
potential of Cartesian philosophy depends heavily on the relation he establishes
between the search for truth and custom, under whose rubric I include the related
concepts of laws, institutions, and common practices or beliefs grounded on
dogmatic suppositions. If Descartes cordons off custom from the search for truth,
then his establishment of equality is an empty, hypocritical gesture. If, on the other
hand, deference to custom is only a palliative measure to remain in place until true
foundations of knowledge have been developed, then the Cartesian search for truth
logically entails the subordination of custom to reason; sexist customs based on
an erroneous prejudice concerning the natural inequality of women with men will
eventually be modified to reflect the true equality of human *semina scientiae*. Here,
too, we can trace the evolution of Descartes's thought by comparing the provisional
morality of the *Discours* to what he says about these matters to Elizabeth.

Descartes introduces the provisional morality in the second part of the *Discours*
as he is on the verge of demolishing everything that he thought he knew. This was
a sensible thing to do in order to continue to operate on a practical level: "[L]est
I should remain indecisive in my actions while reason obliged me to be so in my
judgments, and in order to live as happily as I could during this time, I formed for
myself a provisional moral code."[114] It was also a necessary precaution given the
supercilious readership he anticipated, for even if his readers noticed that he had
destroyed the foundations of Aristotelian natural philosophy that since Thomas of
Aquinas had been the institutionalized partner of Catholic theology, at least they
would see that he did not mean to put the latter in question. The first maxim of the
moral code "was to obey the laws and customs of my country, holding constantly to

---

113 Bridoux, 214.
114 AT, VI, 22; CSM, I, 122.

the religion in which by God's grace I had been instructed from my own childhood, and governing myself in all other matters according to the most moderate and least extreme opinions—the opinions commonly accepted in practice by the most sensible of those with whom I should have to live." Descartes is preempting any possible association between the authority that Luther grants to the individual conscience and the authority that he grants to individual reason. Moreover, he insists that his reform of the self has no common cause with "those meddlesome and restless characters who, called neither by birth nor by fortune to the management of public affairs, are yet forever thinking up some new reform."[115] Descartes probably does not have women such as Marie de Gournay in mind when he scorns people who want to reform general practices. But his comments have ramifications for feminist reform. According to this first maxim, women would have no right to go meddling with long-established traditions, especially not those (like Salic law) that bar them "from the management of public affairs" in the first place. Reread in light of the first maxim, Descartes's (ironic) opening assertion that good sense must be universal (because everyone believes they have as much as they need of it) appears to be little more than a teaser. To the feminist reader, Descartes's first maxim for moral conduct, skeptical in origin, is as disappointing as Montaigne's respect for customs that he shows, through the inversion of the Amazons' crippling of their men, to be not just arbitrary but perpetuated through violence.

Descartes's third maxim, this one of stoic origin, compounds the disappointment. Following Montaigne's ethic of self-reform in "Of Presumption" ("Not being able to rule events, I rule myself"),[116] he resolves "to try always to master myself rather than fortune, and change my desires rather than the order of the world. In general I would become accustomed to believing that nothing lies entirely within our power except our thoughts, so that after doing our best in dealing with matters external to us, whatever we fail to achieve is absolutely impossible so far as we are concerned."[117] To write off a failed attempt to change what is external to us seems a comforting bit of casuistry. However, "making a virtue of necessity"—for example, not desiring "to be healthy when ill or free when imprisoned"—is to recommend conformity to the established order. Here Descartes's apparently inclusive statement that he wanted "even women" to understand the *Discours* suffers a severe limitation. Rather than sharing Gournay's claim that custom must change to reflect the equality of women and men, Descartes's third maxim supports the opinion of Anna Maria von Schurman who, in her *Letters Concerning a Christian Woman* (1640), argues that women should use learning only for their personal edification.[118] We might even suspect that

---

115 AT, VI, 16; CSM, I, 118.

116 DF, II, 351.

117 AT, I, 25; CSM, I, 123.

118 Schurman (1607–78) was the first female student to enroll at the University of Utrecht, where she studied with the Protestant theologian Gisbertus Voetius, before joining Jean de Labadie (1610–74), a former Jesuit, in a mystical, communitarian sect. Descartes's judgment comes to us indirectly through Descartes's first biographer, Adrien Baillet (1649–1706). According to Baillet in *La Vie de Monsieur Des-Cartes* (Geneva: Slatkin Reprints, 1970), "M. Descartes sans être prophète ... avait eu quelque pressentiment de ce qui devait arriver à cette pauvre fille. Il jugeait que cette curiosité démesurée de trop savoir, et de pénétrer dans les

this is why Descartes insists that Elizabeth should find contentment in contemplating her superior learning: there was not much use she could make of it. For let us not think for a moment that Descartes was silent about pro(to)feminist polemics because he was oblivious to them. In his dedicatory epistle to the *Principia*, he recognizes that Elizabeth's intellectual achievements are all the more extraordinary insofar as she attained them despite custom. "That such zeal [for acquiring knowledge of the truth] is abundantly present in Your Highness is clear from the fact that neither the diversions of the Court nor the customary education that so often condemns young ladies to ignorance has been able to prevent you from studying all the worthwhile arts and sciences."[119] The provisional morality of the *Discours* exempts custom from the repudiation of received ideas. With an ethic of this sort, the best one can imagine in terms of self-determination for women is a withdrawal from society for the sake of individual repos, along the lines of the retreat chosen by Madame de Lafayette's heroine at the end of *La Princesse de Clèves*.

The apparent contradiction between the epistemological egalitarianism of the first part of the *Discours* and the social conservatism of the *morale par provision* in the second part raises the old question of exactly how provisional Descartes intended those maxims to be. Some scholars consider the provisional moral code of the second part of the *Discours* a temporary palliative meant as much to mollify theologians as to make his life livable until the fog that enshrouds his judgment is dispersed by the illumination of the cogito. Support for this interpretation can be found in a letter to Mersenne, in which Descartes, accused of encouraging infidels

---

mystères les plus inaccessibles de la théologie pour les personnes de son sexe, pourrait bien l'entraîner trop loin, et dégénérer en une présomption qui lui attirerait le sort des vierges folles et imprudentes de l'Evangile." Pierre Bayle complains in his *Nouvelles de la République des Lettres* of June 1684 that people use the fact that Schurman died schismatic as a pretext to discourage women from studying: "Le monde prend de là occasion & de quelques autres exemples que l'on conserve précieusement dans sa mémoire, d'insulter toutes les femmes qui s'attachent à l'étude, & la moindre chose dont on leur fait peur, c'est de dire qu'elles en perdront l'esprit. La vérité est qu'on ne parle ainsi, que parce qu'on les aime mieux attachées à la bagatelle, & parce qu'on est bien aise de mortifier celles qui se distinguent par cet autre endroit" (I: 388–9). Was this the spirit of Descartes's remark about Schurman: to mortify a woman who had sought to distinguish herself? Descartes had been on friendly terms with Schurman until his dispute with Voetius, who maligned him an "atheist and libertine," associations that Descartes had scrupulously avoided by styling himself either as an average man following a well-trod path (in the *Discours*), or as the traveler of an uncommon path on which he hoped to engage an exclusive, but also exclusively orthodox group of fellow travelers (in the *Meditations*). To the extent that Schurman sided with Voetius and thanked God for "separating her heart from that profane man [Descartes]," Descartes's stated contempt for "persons of her sex" is above all a personal attack. His contention (if Baillet is a reliable source) that theology's "most inaccessible mysteries" were inappropriate for women is utterly gratuitous, since there is nothing sex specific about the "presumption" of seeking to penetrate theological mysteries in any of Descartes's writings; he himself scrupulously bracketed theology. Schurman (in Descartes's characterization of her) pertains to the second kind of reader whom he discouraged from imitating him: those who lose their way as a result of their misplaced confidence.

119 AT, IX B, 22; CSM, I, 192.

to remain in the religion of their parents, insisted that the maxim was, after all, only a provisional one and that he hoped to arrive at the truth by using his God-given faculty of discerning the truth, not being content to accept the opinions of others for a moment.[120] Others argue however that "par provision" does not mean "temporary" but "provisional" in the sense of the "provisions" that one takes along for the journey. Insofar as Descartes is still seeking truth "that is the principal good in my life" in his last letter to Elizabeth four months before his death, they argue that the social conservatism that he professes in the *Discours* concerns the long haul. The latter interpretation, that is, that the *morale par provision* is meant to be an enduring practical complement to purely intellectual activity, seems more plausible given that Descartes alludes to the "three moral rules" of the *Discours* in a letter to Elizabeth. The simple fact that he cites them indicates that he still considers them to be valid. Indeed, he presents them as general moral rules to live by: "[I]t seems to me that anybody can become content with what he has without expecting anything from elsewhere, as long as he observes the three things to which the three rules of moral conduct that I put in my *Discours de la méthode* relate." Curiously, however, he changes those rules considerably in his ensuing summary of them: "The first is, that he always endeavor to use his mind the best he can to know what he must or must not do in all occurrences in life."[121] Religion, laws, and customs have disappeared. Is this omission the influence of Seneca, on whose "blessed life" Descartes begins to comment in this letter? In the next letter, he notes that Seneca "criticizes those who follow custom and example rather than reason.... In regard to which I share his opinion; for, although several people are incapable of finding the right path on their own, there are nevertheless few who do not recognize it when someone else shows it to them."[122] Whereas in the *Discours*, Descartes held custom apart from reason's questioning, here he subjects custom to reason.

The conformity advocated in the third maxim fades, too, in favor of the more pressing consideration of how to be happy. At the same time as he counsels Elizabeth to take heart through the contemplation of the "possessions of her soul," he advises her against desiring what she does not "possess," namely wealth and health:

> Let him consider ... that all the goods that he does not possess are equally beyond his power... and that, in this way, he becomes accustomed to not desiring.... And what makes us not want, for instance, more arms or more tongues than we already have, but wish we could be in better health or have more wealth? It is only because we imagine that the latter could be acquired as a result of our conduct, or that they are due to our nature, which is not the case for the former. We can rid ourselves of this opinion by considering that, since we have always followed the counsel of reason, we have neglected nothing that is in our power, and that illnesses and misfortune are no less natural to man than prosperity and health.[123]

Some things may seem like they are more within our reach than others, but if they are not truly ours, then we must accept that they are outside of our power. But what

---

120 Descartes to Mersenne, 27 April 1637, AT, I, 367.
121 Descartes to Elizabeth, 4 August, 1645, AT, IV, 265.
122 Descartes to Elizabeth, 18 August 1645, AT, IV, 272.
123 Descartes to Elizabeth, 4 August 1645, AT, IV, 265–6.

is truly ours? In the correspondence, Descartes thinks of Elizabeth's intelligence, learning, and care for others as her possessions. According to the *Passions de l'âme*, however, free will alone truly belongs to us. There, Gilles Olivo shows, Descartes modifies the stoic maxim that we should not desire things that are beyond our power to obtain by considering free will in causal terms. The attitude of the Sage is governed by assent to and acceptance of the present; he strives, according to Epictetus, "to learn to want each event as it happens;" he cultivates "patience without hope" (as Leibniz put it), because hope, albeit the opposite of fear, easily changes into fear and robs us of our control over ourselves in the here and now.[124] Descartes, in contrast, allows for hope by distinguishing desires whose realization depends only on us from desires whose realization depends on other causes. If we are able to esteem or scorn other objects capable of doing good or evil, he says, it is because we "consider them as free causes" (Article 55). "Esteem and scorn for oneself as for others is founded on the identification of free will with the exercise of a free cause," Olivo explains. Exercising will freely means exercising a cause freely.[125] In subjecting the stoic distinction between what is and what is not in our power to the imperative of causality, Descartes modifies stoic indifference to the future. "Cartesian virtue is not conquered, like stoic virtue, by obnubilating the will in the present," comments Olivo.

> [T]o the contrary, it is open to the temporality of anticipation, under whose horizon the project of the mastery of the world makes sense ... Equal of the gods, the stoic Sage exercises his virtue in a supreme patience that Christianity will qualify as prideful. In contrast, the Cartesian discovers himself in generosity in the image and the resemblance of God and exercises his virtue through a humble patience, open to the future of his effectivity.[126]

To identify free will as a cause implies that it has effects that go beyond mere assent to the present. Consequently, it is valid to anticipate the future, to hope: as the cause of the things that we will, we have some control over how that future unfolds. Not only does Descartes christianizes stoic moral philosophy, as Olivo suggests; he also adjusts an ethic prescribing mental withdrawal from the world to his own optimistic philosophy in which we strive to improve our lives through science. Thus, in a way, we determine human destiny in the world. This optimism is present in the *Discours*, as Descartes holds out the hope that man will finally become "master and possessor of nature," as well as in the *Passions*, though more subtly, where he says that generosity fortifies the soul in the search for the true good.

In the *Discours*, Descartes juxtaposes a socially conservative *morale par provision* with the blueprint of an unorthodox quest to reform science. Women's participation in

---

124 Epictetus and Leibniz, cited in Gilles Olivo, "Une patience sans espérance?: Descartes et le stoïcisme," in *Le Stoïcisme au 16e et 17e siècle: Le retour des philosophies antiques à l'âge classique*, ed. Pierre-François Moreau (Paris: Albin Michel, 1999), 234–50, 236. Olivo comments: "We might say that the Stoic does not so much exercise a causality so much as he is traversed by the causality of the destiny to which he consents" (243).

125 Olivo, 242.

126 Ibid., 243.

that search for truth is compromised by the exception of custom from the other sorts of received ideas that he repudiates. Women share the same basic epistemic authority as men, yet they must find contentment in "the customary education that so often condemns young ladies to ignorance" caused by their exclusion from institutions devoted to knowledge: the School, the Academies, the Republic of Letters. One can interpret the provisional morality as a temporary modus operandi to tide one over until the foundations of the new science had been laid; in this reading, we are free to attack sexist custom as prejudice as soon as we are armed with the new criteria of truth —clarity and distinction. However, Descartes's subsequent writings do not authorize the compartmentalization of ethics and science into parallel spheres; as he said in the *Principia*, moral philosophy grows out of physics and metaphysics. Consequently, it is not possible to say that after a certain point attained in the scientific search for truth, we can begin to reform the moral code whose authority had been untouchable in the meantime. As moral philosophy moves to the heart of the search for truth in the correspondence with Elizabeth, the provisional quality of the moral maxims of the *Discours* becomes permanent. But this is not to the detriment of the feminist potential of Cartesian philosophy, for Descartes makes the attenuation of custom's authority integral to the moral philosophy that is now permanently relevant to the scientific search for truth. Subordinating custom to reason is just as important to moral conduct as it is to science. Although Descartes only envisions the critique of custom at an individual level, it is obvious that since custom takes its authority from the assent of many, this individual critique, multiplied by many generous souls (which we all have the capacity to be), cannot help but diminish the authority of those customs that are at odds with reason. Similarly, Descartes attenuates the stoic idea (expressed in the third maxim of the *Discours*) according to which we can only change ourselves, not the world around us, by introducing a causal dimension to free will. Free will, he says, is the only thing that truly belongs to us; it is, therefore, the only thing we can legitimately expect to control. Yet far from closing ourselves off from hope for the future by arranging our feelings so that we can always claim to have willed our assent to whatever it is that happens to us in the present, Descartes makes willing synonymous with causing, and thereby introduces an element of anticipation into our deployment of God's esteem-inspiring gift to us. Descartes's mature moral philosophy, construed not as a palliative, but as an integral part of the search for truth, provides, despite its tightly individual frame, philosophical justification for the reform of custom. It legitimates hope—the hope that our will might be the cause of the improvement of our lives. In light of Descartes's profoundly egalitarian presentation of universal epistemic authority in the *Discours* and of moral value as manifested in his definition of *générosité*, it seems only inevitable that a Poullain de la Barre would see in Cartesian philosophy all the ingredients for an apologetics for the immediate reform of "the customary education that so often condemns young ladies to ignorance." If his ideas remained marginal, this was not the fault of Descartes. The reform of custom by reason takes time when it is carried out generous soul by generous soul.

On Closing Narratives

Daniel Garber calls the publication of the *Discours de la méthode* "the revolution that did not happen in 1637."[127] Challenging standard accounts of "the Scientific Revolution," he contends that judging by its reception, few people at the time thought of Descartes's first published work as a foundational moment in modern epistemology. To the Aristotelian devotees whom Descartes tried hard not to alienate, the mechanistic natural philosophy to which he gestures in the fifth part of the *Discours* looked like a rehashing of ancient atomism, along the lines of the physics that Gassendi was then proposing. Some even opined that Descartes's philosophy was not incompatible with that of Aristotle. We have seen, furthermore, that Gassendi and others objected to Descartes's use of skeptical arguments in the *Meditationes* as a waste of paper because they were so familiar. Indeed, in this chapter, I have emphasized Descartes's debt to Montaigne not just for the prolegema leading up to the cogito, but for the inclusive attitude he manifests with regard to women. Montaigne in the "Apologie de Raymond Sebond" describes the handing down of knowledge in terms of softening:

> Having found by experience that where one man had failed, another has succeeded, and that what was unknown to one century the following century has made clear, ... I do not leave off sounding and testing what my powers cannot discover; and by handling again and kneading this new material, stirring it and heating it, I open up to whoever follows me some facility to enjoy it more at his ease, and make it more supple and manageable for him:

> As Hymettian wax grows softer in the sun,
> Takes many shapes when molded by the thumb,
> And thus by usage useful does become.[128]

Heir to Montaigne's skepticism, Descartes aimed to arrest the shapeless ebb and formless flow of zetetic thought. In the second meditation, he subjects wax to a radical regimen, not just softening it, but melting it, and then hardening it once more. He does this to prove his point that the mind, which understands its essence to be thought, is surprisingly easier to know than *res extensa*. Descartes, like many of his generation, was determined to reform the anarchic state of knowledge exacerbated by the Skeptics and to set the search for truth off on solid footing so that truths could indeed be found. The realization of the presence of one's being through thought was the cornerstone of this edifice. In this sense, Descartes's search for truth was teleological: gains were to be made, fruits to be harvested.

Yet Descartes's search for truth, building on the seeds of virtue and knowledge, led by reason but not bound by custom, and open to the future, was just as open-ended as that of Montaigne's *skepsis*. That is why Martial Guéroult terribly misrepresents Descartes's opus when he portrays it as a "profound monument, solid and geometrical,

---

127 Daniel Garber, "Descartes, the Aristotelians, and the Revolution that Did Not Happen in 1637," *Monist: An International Quarterly Journal of General Philosophical Inquiry* 71 (1988): 471–86.

128 DF I: 256; PV, 560.

like a fortress designed by Vauban." It is also why we would be wrong to accept Guéroult's advice: "Historical truth is what it is," he declares categorically. "You should close history books if it is distasteful to you."[129] Postmodern students of the past, we now have internalized many tools for debunking this condescending advice; we know better than to let someone get away with the claim to exclusive omniscience with respect to "historical truth." We know that the best way to defy such claims is to pry open those formidable fortress-like books and show that their meanings are multiple and eminently open to interpretation. And yet, we have been doing just the opposite in the case of Descartes, allowing the image of an impregnable and hostile opus to persist by closing rather than opening his books, as per Guéroult's admonition. Michael Moriarty remarks:

> Much present-day discussions of Descartes, not so much perhaps within the discipline of philosophy as in accounts of the emergence of "modern" culture, is couched in valedictory terms, offered in the spirit of a "closing" narrative. It may well be that the Cartesian model of rendering ourselves "masters and possessors of nature" by the application of scientific knowledge has lost its appeal.... But this does not mean, by a long chalk, that we can put a line under Descartes, as if he could henceforth be nothing more to us than the vehicle of a defunct paradigm, scored with the traces of its own anxieties. The history of philosophy shows that there are philosophers on whom we can never close the book.[130]

The fact that numerous feminists (among others) have been trying to "close" the book on Descartes for some time now suggests that this gesture may be doomed to remain a dramatic one. One of Guéroult's contemporaries, Tristan Tzara, at that point adhering to the French communist party, gave a lecture at the Sorbonne in which he deplored the passivity of his surrealist friends with respect to fascism, a passivity he found out of character with France's tradition of insubordination that he attributes to "Cartesian rationalism." The surrealist André Breton erupted with indignation: "*Chien!* [Dog!] Listen, Mr. Tzara is speaking of Descartes in 1947!"[131] The point that Descartes might claim paternity for the spirit of revolution endemic to the French mind seemed intolerably parochial to the surrealists, who promoted instead a revolt against reason, with Descartes as their main target. Tzara's linking of revolution to Cartesian rationalism stretched Descartes beyond recognition, but Breton's indignation seems equally overblown in retrospect, if only to the extent that we are still speaking of Descartes today. Finally dispensing with Descartes seems as remote a possibility sixty years after this colorful altercation (we are still speaking of his ostensible role in the "Scientific Revolution"), and perhaps, as Tzara suggested, it is ultimately not in our interest to close the book on Descartes once and for all. Indeed, it may be time to set aside what we think we know and to read him afresh. Letting go of the familiar narratives of Descartes as the origin of "later concepts of subjectivity and knowledge," as the "father of modern subjectivity," and so on could allow feminists to claim Descartes in a different way: as a resource rather

---

129 Martial Guéroult, *Descartes selon l'ordre des raisons* (Paris: Aubier, 1968), I, 9.
130 Moriarty, 2.
131 Cited in Azouvi, 9–10.

than a source, and as an interlocutor rather than an obstacle.[132] "There are authors whose end is to tell what has happened," writes Montaigne in "Of the Power of the Imagination;" "Mine if I could attain it, would be to talk about what can happen." In the spirit not of a closing narrative, but rather with an eye to the sense of openness and possibility that inheres equally in Descartes's rationalist search for truth as in Montaigne's zetetic one, I close this book with an invitation to return to the history books we may have written off and to open them anew in the non-presuming spirit of generosity that Elizabeth taught Descartes to appreciate. Who knows what small revolutions might then happen!

---

132 Grosz, 10. Stanley Clarke finds that Descartes's writings on moral philosophy, biology, and psychology provide "resources for a theory of gender that is strikingly contemporary and compatible with feminist critiques" (83). Whereas a "source" denotes an origin, a "resource" is simply something on which one can draw to further one's own researches. The advantage of treating Descartes as a resource is that it posits his writings as an available and unexhausted asset, rather than presuming that they can be distilled into a few key notions (dualism, rationalism, the modern subject, etc.) with which one can then dispense.

Conclusion

In this book I have examined the emergence of Descartes's rationalist epistemology, an event deemed pivotal since the seventeenth century to arguments for the intellectual equality of women and men. I have considered Descartes's legacy from the point of view of the intellectual traditions he inherited, incorporated, and transformed, seeking in particular to understand how he responded to the uses of gender in skeptical and neo-stoic currents in the last decades of the sixteenth century. In the *Meditations*, Descartes rehearsed what were by his day standard, skeptical problems resulting from the confrontation of demonological inquiry (Johann Weyer's *De praestigiis daemonum)* with the humanist revival of Hellenistic skepticism, as detailed in Sextus Empiricus' *Outlines of Pyrrhonism*: How can we be sure that we are awake rather than dreaming? That we are perceiving things outside the mind rather than the illusions of melancholy? That an evil genius has not engulfed us in total illusion? While these skeptical resonances in Descartes's thought are now widely acknowledged thanks to Richard Popkin, Edwin Curley, and more recently, Stuart Clark, Descartes's inclusive stance with respect to women in the *Discours de la méthode* has not so far been recognized as a feature deriving from skeptical thought. This neglect is because little attention has been paid to the persistent link, throughout the Renaissance, between pro(to)feminist discourse and skeptical or fideist attitudes toward knowledge.

I have devoted the first four chapters of this book to demonstrating the connection between skepticism and pro(to)feminism, on the one hand, and between positive conceptions of knowledge and misogynistic attitudes, on the other. I have shown that those intellectuals in the second half of the sixteenth century who construed the search for truth in teleological terms articulated their epistemologies through gender distinctions that excluded women. Johann Weyer, despite his heroic defense of "witches" and his remarkable condemnation of torture, established his authority at the expense of those very women whom he defended, valorizing the physician's common sense over and against their afflicted imaginations. Weyer's emphasis on the Devil's power of illusion nonetheless undermined his empirical epistemology (which I described in Chapter One more precisely as a literalist hermeneutics). Addressing the untrustworthiness of the senses in the face of demonic illusion, Jean Bodin reaffirmed the value of torture for seeking out hidden truth along with the corollary notion of woman as a container of secrets. At the same time, he objected to the natural explanations that Weyer had offered for supernatural effects with a kind of compulsory fideism. Just as social order depended upon the wife's submission to her husband (or so Bodin argued in his *Six livres de la république*), so moral order depended upon nature's submission to God; to put nature over God is, therefore, to be an atheist, no better than a witch. My analyses of *De praestigiis daemonum* and *De la démonomanie des sorciers* suggest that affirmations of sex difference or gender hierarchies often conceal logical weaknesses. Weyer's claim that women were naturally more susceptible to illusions could not guarantee the physician's clear-sightedness; rather, it diverted attention from the question of his own vulnerability to illusion. Bodin similarly masked the arbitrariness of his distinction between the natural and the supernatural by grounding it on a conjugal hierarchy that was supposedly natural and divinely ordained.

It is therefore not surprising that Skeptics chose to deconstruct gender hierarchies as a means of demolishing dogmatism. Agrippa von Nettesheim's declamation on the preeminence of the female sex was consistent with his attack on the vanity of knowledge in that both aimed to humble learned men. In an essay targeting Bodin's *De la démonomanie*, Montaigne drew a parallel between the crippling of boys that ensures the Amazons' dominance and the violence that keeps men on top *par deça* (over here). Whereas for Agrippa and Montaigne inverting hierarchies or suspending sex difference served an ethical outcome (tranquility), for Gournay it worked the other way: the skeptical notion of balance between two things led her to theorize the equality between men and women. Like Agrippa and Montaigne, Gournay blamed women's disgraceful lack of learning on customs elaborated by men in their own interest. Yet she no more than Agrippa or Montaigne proposed measures of reform, since innovation was fundamentally incompatible with skeptical ethics. My analysis of the changes that Descartes made in his correspondence with Elizabeth to the first rule of his provisional morality in the *Discours* show that his philosophy allowed—indeed required—the alteration of institutions and customs that were out of line with truths rationally discovered. Even if Descartes himself seems to have been indifferent to the woman question, his appropriation of the skeptical inclusion of women, on the one hand, combined with his conviction regarding the perfectibility of knowledge and human society, on the other, made his philosophy groundbreaking: He was the first to incorporate women into a nonskeptical search for truth, a search that entailed the pursuit of knowledge as well as the reform of institutions.[1]

Whereas the skeptical origins of Descartes's inclusion of women in the search for truth have thus far escaped scholarly notice, his debt to the Stoics has not. Erica Harth and Jacqueline Broad read the stoic tenor of some of Descartes's letters to Elizabeth as indicative of the implicit masculinism of Cartesian dualism.[2] Yet it is significant that Descartes's neo-stoicism differs from that of his contemporaries precisely in its avoidance of gendered rhetoric. The stoic revival began in the 1580s and 1590s when French *politiques* exhorted loyal subjects to cultivate *masle vertu* rather than participate in the effeminate melancholy of the Catholic League. Neo-stoic virtue, I argued in Chapter Three, would have been virtually meaningless in the absence of the modifier, "masle," to the extent that Guillaume du Vair described his attainment of stoic virtue in terms of a female-to-male sex change. Familiar as he was with both Sextus Empiricus' *Outlines of Pyrrhonism* and Montaigne's *Essays*,

---

1   There is one important question I have not answered in my study: What became of the pro(to)feminist /skeptical correlation after Descartes? Figures such as La Mothe Le Vayer, Blaise Pascal, Pierre Daniel Huet, and Pierre Bayle would benefit from the kind of comprehensive analyses that I have conducted in this book.

2   Jacqueline Broad, *Women Philosophers of the Seventeenth Century* (Cambridge: Cambridge U.P., 2002), 33.

Descartes could not have ignored the Skeptics' lampooning of stoic masculinity, and both he and Elizabeth expressed dissatisfaction with what they viewed as substanceless rhetoric in Seneca's *De vita beata*. Largely as a result of his exchange with Elizabeth, Descartes endowed generosity, a concept derived from the Stoics, with an egalitarian content foreign to neo-stoic moral philosophy but (paradoxically) consistent with ancient stoic epistemology.

At times in my book, I have disagreed with other feminist scholars—primarily historians of philosophy like Genevieve Lloyd who view Descartes's dualism as introducing new and newly surreptitious obstacles to women's intellectual aspirations, and historians of science who characterize Descartes's mechanistic physics as an extension of Bacon's rape or torture of nature metaphors (Carolyn Merchant) or as a repudiation of a worldview somehow evocative of the maternal (Susan Bordo). It is nevertheless obvious, I hope, that I in no way discredit feminist approaches to the history of philosophy or of science. There has been a backlash against feminist scholarship. According to one contributor to a 1998 volume entitled *A House Built on Sand: Exposing Postmodernist Myths about Science*, feminist historians of science occupy a large wing not far from the quarters inhabited by the "French" and the rooms containing "a few assistant professors of literature making fools of themselves."[3] In tones that can only be described as cocky and combative, Michael Ruse and Alan Soble deride "feminist science critics; in particular Sandra Harding, Carolyn Merchant, and Evelyn Fox Keller" as "evangelicals," accusing them of "abusive accusation[s]," "impatience of research," and "personal stubbornness." Ruse asks whether Darwin's sexism is of any significance whatsoever, while Soble "defends" Bacon from the "claim that sexist sexual metaphors played an important role in the rise of modern science."[4] It could be argued that just as Soble "defends" Bacon from feminist bullies, I have "defended" Descartes from longstanding suspicions harbored by feminists. But I have no common cause with Soble. Soble discredits feminist interpretations of Bacon's representations of nature, offering nothing in their place. In contrast, I have attempted to model a methodology in which gender provides the key to unlocking complex and highly individual epistemological and ethical stances. By showing how heavily early modern intellectuals depended on gender notions to articulate their constructions of knowledge, I hope to ensure that feminist perspectives cannot be cordoned off into a separate house.

The past two decades have seen the flourishing of editions and translations of women's long-neglected works, thanks to the University of Chicago Press's Other Voice in Early Modern Europe series and Ashgate's Early Modern Englishwoman collection. Paula Findlen expresses the "hope that the next survey of the Scientific Revolution that appears in print will find it difficult to neglect the fascinating community of seventeenth-century women philosophers that this recent body of

---

3   Alan D. Sokal, "What the Social Text Affair Does and Does Not Prove," *A House Built on Sand: Exposing Postmodernist Myths about Science*, ed. Noretta Koertge (New York and Oxford: Oxford U.P., 1998), 9–22, 12.

4   Michael Ruse, "Is Darwinism Sexist? (And if It Is, So What?)," *A House Built on Sand*, 119–29, 119; Alan Soble, "In Defense of Bacon," *A House Built on Sand*, 195–215, 198, 210, 211 n. 9.

scholarship has rendered accessible in all their humanity."[5] While the accessibility of texts authored by early modern women will certainly facilitate the development of new syllabi, it will not single-handedly reform the way in which we read Descartes, Bacon, and others. There is always the danger that these editions and translations will be relegated to a house to which few scholars will make a detour unless they have a prior stake in it. Consequently, at the same time as we understand the specificity of women's voices (the monographs of Harth and Broad are good examples of this kind of scholarship), it is also incumbent upon feminist scholars to *make the case* for the relevance of women and gender to the canonical narratives of Western history. Feminist studies that reinforce master narratives, while offering differing moral interpretations of them (such as Merchant's interpretation of the Scientific Revolution), become easy targets for unconstructive scholars like Soble who trivialize the scholarly enterprise as a matter of defending or attacking the honor of historical figures. In contrast, feminist research that causes readers to rethink master narratives, such as Katharine Park's *Secrets of Women: Gender, Generation, and the Origins of Human Dissection*, are not so easily dismissed. In *Women, Imagination, and the Search for Truth in Early Modern France*, I have striven to show that to ignore gender is to ignore the logical shortcomings of dogmatic thought, to miss one of the most radical tools of skeptical argumentation, and to overlook one of the most important fruits of Descartes's search for truth.

---

5   Paula Findlen, "Ideas in the Mind: Gender and Knowledge in the Seventeenth Century," *Hypatia* 17(2002): 183–96, 194.

Bibliography

Primary Sources

Agrippa von Nettesheim, Heinrich Cornelius. *Of the Vanitie and Uncertaintie of the Artes and Sciences*. Trans. James Sanford, 1569. Ed. Catherine Dunn. Northridge: California State University, 1974.

———. *Three Books of Occult Philosophy*. Trans. James Freake. Ed. Donald Tyson. St. Paul: Llewellyn Publications, 1993.

———. *Declamation on the Nobility and Preeminence of the Female Sex*. Trans. and ed. Albert Rabil Jr. Chicago and London: University of Chicago Press, 1996.

[Pseudo-] Albertus Magnus. *Women's Secrets: A Translation of Pseudo-Albertus Magnus's De Secretis Mulierum with Commentaries*. Trans. Helen Rodnite LeMay. Albany: State University of New York Press, 1992.

[Pseudo-] Aristotle. *Problems*. Trans. W.S. Hett. Eds. T.E. Page, E. Capps, and W.H.D Rouse. Cambridge: Harvard U.P., 1957–1961.

Aubigné, Agrippa d. *Les Tragiques*. Eds. A. Garnier and J. Plattard. Paris: S.T.F.M., 1990.

Baillet, Adrien. *La Vie de Monsieur Des-Cartes*. Geneva: Slatkin Reprints, 1970.

Bayle, Pierre. *Nouvelles de la République des Lettres*. Amsterdam: H. Desbordes, 1684.

Benserade, Isaac de. *Iphis et Iante*. Ed. Anne Verdier. Vijon: Lampsaque, 2000.

Bérulle, Pierre de. *Traicté des Energumènes, suivi d'un discours sur la possession de Marthe Brossier: Contre les calomnies d'un Medecin de Paris*. Troyes, 1599.

Bodin, Jean. *De la Démonomanie des sorciers*. Paris: Jacques DuPuys, 1580.

———. *Oeuvres philosophiques*. Ed. and trans. Pierre Mesnard. Paris: Presses Universitaires de France, 1951.

_____. *Colloque entre sept scavans qui sont de differens sentimens des secrets cachez des choses relevees*. Trans. anonymous (1923). Ed. François Berriot. Genève: Droz, 1984.

Bourgeois, Louise. *Observations diverses sur la sterilité, perte de fruict, foecondité, accouchements, et maladies des femmes et enfants nouveaux naiz amplement traittées heureusement practiquées*. Paris: A. Saugrain, 1617.

_____. *Observations diverses sur la stérilité, perte de fruit, fécondité, accouchements, et maladies des femmes et enfants nouveaux-nés*. Paris: Côté-femmes, 1992.

Browne, Thomas. *Religio Medici*. Menston: Scholar Press, 1970.

Chapelain, Jean. *La Pucelle ou la France délivrée*. Vol. 1. Paris: Librairie Marpon and Flammarion, 1891.

Charron, Pierre. *De la sagesse*. Paris: Fayard, 1986.

Cicero, Marcus Tullius. *Letters to Friends*. Ed. D.R. Shackleton Bailey. Vol. 3. Cambridge and London: Harvard U.P., 2001.

Crooke, Helkiah. *Mikrocosmographia: A Description of the Body of Man*. [n.p.], 1615.

Demosthenes. *Olynthiacs*. Trans. J.H. Vince, C.A. Vince, A.T. Murray, N.W. DeWitt, N.J. De Witt. 7 vols. Cambridge and London: Harvard U.P., 1984–1992.

Descartes, René. *Oeuvres de Descartes*. Eds. Charles Adam and Paul Tannery. 11 vols. Paris: Vrin, 1964.

------. *The Philosophical Writings of Descartes*. Trans. John Cottingham, Robert Stoothoff, Dugald Murdoch. 3 vols. Cambridge and London: Cambridge U.P., 1984.

------. *La Recherche de la vérité*. Eds. Ettore Lojacono and Erik Jan Bos. Milan: Franco Angeli, 2002.

------. *The Correspondence between Princess Elisabeth of Bohemia and René Descartes*. Trans. Lisa Shapiro. Chicago: The University of Chicago Press, 2007.

Diogenes Laertius. *Lives of Eminent Philosophers*. Trans. R.D. Hicks. London and Cambridge: Harvard U.P., 1931.

Du Laurens, André. *Les Œuvres de Me. André du Laurens, Sieur de la Ferrieres, Conseiller & premier Medecin du Tres-Chrestien Roy de France & de Navarre, Henry le Grand, & son Chancelier en l'Université de Montpelier*. Trans. Théophile Gelée. Paris: Michel Soly, 1646.

Du Vair, Guillaume. *Les Oeuvres de Messire Guillaume du Vair, Evesque et Comte de Lisieux, Garde des seaux de France*. Paris: Sébastien Cramoisy, 1641. Geneva: Slatkin Reprints, 1970.

Duval, Jacques. *Traité des hermaphrodites*. Paris: Lisieux, 1880.

Erasmus, Desiderius. *Erasmi opuscula: A Supplement to the Opera omnia*. Ed. Wallace K. Ferguson. The Hague: M. Nijhoff, 1933.

------. *Adages*. Trans. Margaret Mann Phillips. Ann. R.A.B. Mynors. Collected Works of Erasmus. Vols. 31–35. Toronto; Buffalo: University of Toronto Press, 1982.

Erastus, Thomas. *Deux dialogues de Thomas Erastus, Docteur en medecine à Heidelberg, touchant le pouvoir des Sorcieres: et de la punition qu'elles meritent*. Trans. Simon Goulart de Senlis. Weyer, *Histoires*, 757–875.

Estienne, Charles. *Paradoxes*. Ed. Trevor Peach. Geneva: Droz, 1998.

Ferrand, Jacques. *De la maladie d'amour ou mélancholie érotique*. Paris: Denis Moreau, 1623.

Furetière, Antoine. *Dictionnaire universel*. The Hague and Rotterdam: A. and R. Leers, 1590.

------. *Dictionaire universel*. Paris: S.N.L.-Le Robert, 1978.

Galen, *De l'usage des parties du corps humain*. Trans. Jacques Dalechamps. Lyon: Guillame Roville, 1566.

Garasse, François. *Doctrine curieuse des beaux esprits de ce temps, ou pretendus tels*. Paris: S. Chappelet.

Gentillet, Innocent, and Henri Estienne. *Discours merveilleux de la vie, actions et deportements de Catherine de Médicis, royne-mère*, 1575. Genève: Librairie Droz, 1995.

Gournay, Marie de. "A Michel Seigneur de Montaigne." *Le Proumenoir de Monsieur de Montaigne*. Paris: Abel l'Angelier, 1694.

------. *Oeuvres complètes*. Eds. Jean-Claude Arnould, Evelyne Berriot, Claude Blum, Anna Lia Franchetti, Marie-Claire Thomine, and Valerie Worth-Stylianou. Paris: Champion, 2002.

Grévin, Jacques. *Deux livres des Venins, ausquels il est amplement discouru des bestes venimeuses, thériaques, poisons, et contrepoisons.* Anvers: Christophe Plantin, 1568.

_____. *Théâtre complet et poésies choisies.* Ed. Lucien Pinvert. Paris: Garnier frères, 1922.

Guez de Balzac, Jean-Louis. *Oeuvres diverses.* Ed. Roger Zuber. Paris: Champion, 1995.

Guibelet, Jourdain. *Examen de l'examen des esprits.* Paris: Michel Soly, 1631.

Herodotus. *Histoires.* Trans. Ph-E. Legrand. Paris: Les Belles Lettres, 1951.

Hotman, François. *Francogallia.* Trans. J.H.M. Salmon. Cambridge: Cambridge U.P., 1972.

Huarte, Juan. *Anacrise, ou parfait jugement et examen des esprits propres & naiz aux sciences.* Trans. Gabriel Chappuis. Lyon: François Didier, 1580.

Joubert, Laurent. *La Première et seconde partie des erreurs populaires, touchant la medecine & le régime de santé.* Paris: Claude Micard, 1587.

_____. *Popular Errors.* Trans. Gregory David de Rocher. 2 vols. Tuscaloosa: University of Alabama Press, 1989–1995.

Kramer, Heinrich, and James Sprenger. *The Malleus Maleficarum.* Trans. Montague Summers. New York: Dover Publications, 1971.

Laclos, Choderlos de. *Les Liaisons dangereuses.* Paris: Gallimard, 2003.

La Primaudaye, Pierre de. *Suite de l'Academie Françoise en laquelle il est traicté de l'homme & comme par une histoire naturelle du corps & de l'ame.* Paris: Guillaume Chaudiere, 1580.

Lavater, Ludwig. *Trois livres des apparitions des esprits, fantosmes, prodiges, & accidens merveilleux.* Zurich: Guillaume des Marescz, 1581.

Le Bermen, Louis. *Le Bouclier des Dames.* Rouen: [n.p.], 1621.

Le Caron, Loys Charondas. *De la tranquilité de l'esprit, livre singulier. Plus un discours sur le proces criminel faict à une Sorcière condamnee à mort par Arrest de la Court de Parlement, & executee au bourg de la Neufville le Roy en Picardie, avec ses interrogatoires & confessions. Traictez grandement necessaires pour le temps present : extraicts des discours Philosophiques de L. Charondas le Caron Parisien.* Paris: Jacques DuPuys, 1588.

Lempérière and Magnart. *Response à l'Examen de la possession des Religieuses de Louviers, à monsieur Levilin.* Evreux: Jean de la Vigne, 1643.

L'Estoile, Pierre de. *Registre-Journal du regne de Henri III.* Eds. Madeleine Lazard and Gilbert Schrenck. 5 vols. Geneva: Droz, 2003.

Liébault, Jean. *Trois livres des maladies & infirmitez des femmes.* Ed. Lazare Pe. Rouen: Jean Berthelin, 1649.

Lipsius, Justus. *Six Books of Politics or Political Instruction.* Ed. Jan Waszink. Assen: Royal Van Gorcum, 2004.

Malherbe, François. *Poésies.* Ed. Antoine Adam. Paris: Gallimard, 1982.

Marot, Clément. *Œuvres.* Geneva: Slatkin Reprints, 1969.

Mersenne, Marin. *L'Impiété des deistes, athées, et libertins de ce temps, combatuë, & renversee de point en point par raisons tirees de la Philosophie, & de la Theologie.* Paris: Pierre Bilaine, 1624.

_____. *La Vérité des sciences contre les sceptiques ou pyrrhoniens*. Paris: Toyssaint du Bray, 1625.

Molière, Jean-Baptiste Poquelin de. *Oeuvres complètes*. Ed. Robert Jouanny. 2 vols. Paris: Garnier, 1962.

Monantheuil, Henri de. *Panégyric de Henri IV, Roy de France et de Navarre, treschrestien, tres-invincible, tres-clement*. Paris: Fréderic Morel, 1594.

Montaigne, Michel de. *The Complete Essays of Montaigne*. Trans. Donald Frame. Garden City: Doubleday, 1960.

———. *Essais*. Ed. Pierre Villey. Paris: Presses universitaires de France, 1965.

———. *Journal de voyage en Italie*. Ed. Pierre Michel. Paris: Livre de poche, 1974.

Ovid. *Metamorphoses*. Trans. Frank Justus Miller. Cambridge: Harvard U.P., 1984.

Paré, Ambroise. *Œuvres*. Paris: Veuve Gabriel Buon, 1598.

———. *Des Monstres et prodiges*. Ed. Jean Céard. Paris: Droz, 1971.

Pascal, Blaise. *Oeuvres complètes*. Ed. Louis Lafuma. Paris: Seuil, 1963.

Perrault, Charles. *L'Apologie des femmes*. Paris: Jean-Baptiste Coignard, 1694.

Petit, Pierre. *Traité historique sur les Amazones, où l'on trouve tout ce que les auteurs tant anciens que modernes, ont écrit pour ou contre ces heroines*. Leiden: J.A. Langerak, 1718.

Quintilian, Marcus Fabius. *The Orator's Education*. Ed. Donald Russell. Cambridge and London: Harvard U.P., 2001.

Raemond, Florimond de. *L'Histoire de la naissance, progres, et decadence de l'Heresie de ce siecle*. Paris: [s.n.], 1605.

Ronsard, Pierre de. *Oeuvres complètes*. Eds. Jean Céard, Daniel Ménager, Michel Simonin. 2 vols. Paris: Gallimard, 1993

Ryer, Pierre du. *Les Métamorphoses d'Ovide traduites en François par M. Du-Ryer de l'Académie Françoise, Avec des explications à la fin de chacune fable*. Paris: Veuve Cochart, 1694.

Saint-Amant, Marc-Antoine Girard de. *Oeuvres*. Paris: Nizet, 1971.

Seneca, Lucius Annaeus. *Moral Essays*. Trans. John W. Basore. Cambridge: Harvard U.P., 1928.

Sévigné, Marie de Rabutin-Chantal de. *Correspondance*. Ed. Roger Duchêne. Paris: Gallimard, 1972–1978.

Silhon, Jean de. *De l'immortalité de l'âme* (1634). In *Descartes's Meditations: Background Source Materials*. Trans. Roger Ariew and Marjorie Grene. Eds. Roger Ariew, John Cottingham, Tom Sorell. Cambridge: Cambridge U.P., 1998.

Tacitus, Cornelius. *Dialogue des orateurs*. Trans. Henri Bornecque. Ed. Henri Goelzer. Paris: Les Belles Lettres, 1947.

Tahureau, Jacques. *Les Dialogues non moins profitables que facetieux*. Ed. Max Gauna. Genève: Droz, 1981.

Taillepied, Noël. *Psichologie, ou Traité de l'apparition des esprits sçavoir des âmes séparées, fantosmes, prodiges, et accidents merveilleux qui precedent quelquefois la mort des grands personages ou signifient changemens de la chose publique*. Paris: G. Bichon, 1588.

Thévet, André. *Les Singularitez de la France antarctique, autrement nommée Amérique, & de plusieurs Terres & Isles descouvertes de notre temps*. Anvers: Christophe Plantin, 1558.

Thou, Jacques-Auguste de. *Histoire Universelle de Jacques-Auguste De Thou, depuis 1543 jusqu'en 1607.* London [i.e. Paris]: [s.n.], 1734.

Thucydides. *La Guerre du Péloponnèse.* Trans. Jacqueline de Romilly. Paris: Belles Lettres, 1995.

Tristan L'Hermite, François. *La Mort de Sénèque: Tragédie.* Ed. Jacques Madeleine. Paris: Nizet, 1984.

Tyard, Pontus de. *Solitaire Premier ou discours des Muses et de la fureur poétique.* Ed. Silvio F. Baridon. Geneva: Librairie Droz, 1950.

Varanda, Jean de. *De morbis et affectibus mulierum libri tres.* Lyon: Pierre Myteau, 1619.

Vesalius, Andreas. *On the Fabric of the Human Body.* Trans. William Frank Richardson and John Burd Carman. San Francisco: Norman Publishing, 1998.

Weyer, Johann. *Cinq Livres de l'Imposture et Tromperie des Diables: Des enchantements et sorcelleries... faits François par Jaques Grévin de Clermont en Beauvoisis, médecin à Paris.* Paris: Jacques Dupuys, 1567.

_____. *Histoires, disputes et discours des illusions et impostures des diables, des magiciens infâmes, sorcières et empoisonneurs: des ensorcelés et des démoniaques, et de la guérison d'iceux: item de la punition que méritent les magiciens, les empoisonneurs et les sorcières. Le tout comprins en Six Livres (augmentez de moitié en ceste dernière édition).* Genève: Jacques Chovet, 1579.

_____. *Witches, Devils, and Doctors in the Renaissance: Johann Weyer, De praestigiis daemonum.* Trans. John Shea. Eds. George Mora and Benjamin Kohl. Binghampton: Medieval and Renaissance Texts and Studies, 1991.

Yvelin, Pierre. *Examen de la possession des religieuses de Louviers.* Paris: [n.p.], 1643.

Secondary Sources

Akerman, Susanna. *Queen Christina of Sweden and her Circle.* Leiden: Brill, 1991.

Akkerman, Tjitske, and Siep Stuurman. *Perspectives on Feminist Political Thought in European History.* New York: Routledge, 1998.

Albistur, Maïté, and Daniel Armogathe. *Histoire du féminisme français du moyen âge à nos jours.* Paris: Des Femmes, 1977.

Annas, Julia, and Jonathan Barnes. Introduction. Sextus Empiricus, iv–xv.

Attwood, Philip. *Italian Medals, c. 1530–1600, in British Public Collections.* 2 vols. London: The British Museum Press, 2003.

Austin, J.L. *How to Do Things with Words.* Cambridge: Harvard U.P., 1962.

Azouvi, François. *Descartes et la France: Histoire d'une passion nationale.* Paris: Fayard, 2002.

Balsamo, Jean. "Guillaume du Vair, Malherbe, et les Epistres Amoureuses et morales de François de Rosset." Petey-Girard and Tarrête 231–45.

Balsamo, Jean, and Michel Simonin. *Abel L'Angelier et Françoise de Louvain (1574–1620).* Geneva: Droz, 2002.

Banderier, Gilles. "Du Vair et Du Perron: Deux vies parallèles." Petey-Girard and Tarrête.

Battigelli, Anna. *Margaret Cavendish and the Exiles of the Mind.* Lexington: U.P. of Kentucky, 1998.

Bauschatz, C. "Women as Ideal Readers in Montaigne's Essais." *Journal of Medieval and Renaissance Studies* 19 (1989): 83–101.

Beasley, Faith E. *Salons, History, and the Creation of Seventeenth-Century France: Mastering Memory.* Aldershot and Burlington: Ashgate, 2006.

Berriot, François. "La Fortune du *Colloquium heptaplomere*s." Bodin, *Colloque entre sept scavans*, xv–l.

Berriot-Salvadore, Evelyne. *Un Corps, un destin: La femme dans la médecine de la Renaissance.* Paris: Champion, 1993.

Biow, Douglas. *Doctors, Ambassadors, Secretaries: Humanism and Professions in Renaissance Italy.* Chicago: University of Chicago Press, 2002.

Blair, Ann. *The Theater of Nature: Jean Bodin and Renaissance Science.* Princeton: Princeton U.P., 1997.

Boase, Alan M. *The Fortunes of Montaigne: A History of the Essays in France, 1580-1669.* London: Methuen, 1935.

"Bodin, Jean." *Biographie universelle, ancienne et moderne; ou, Histoire, par ordre alphabétique, de la vie publique et privée de tous les hommes qui se sont fait remarquer par leurs écrits, leurs actions, leurs talents, leurs vertus ou leurs crimes.* Ed. Joseph François Michaud. Paris, 1811–1828.

Bono, James. *The Word of God and the Languages of Man: Interpreting Nature in Early Modern Science and Medicine.* Madison: University of Wisconsin Press, 1995.

Bordo, Susan. *The Flight to Objectivity: Essays on Cartesianism and Culture.* New York: State University of New York Press, 1987.

_____. "Feminist Skepticism and the 'Maleness' of Philosophy." Harvey and Okruhlik 143–62.

———, ed. *Feminist Interpretations of René Descartes.* University Park: Pennsylvania State U.P., 1999.

Boss, Jeffrey. "The Seventeenth-Century Transformation of the Hysteric Affection, and Sydenham's Baconian Medicine." *Psychological Medicine* 9 (1979): 221–34.

Brahami, Frédéric. *Le Scepticisme de Montaigne.* Paris: Presses Universitaires de France, 1997.

Brann, Noel L. "Melancholy and the Divine Frenzies in the French Pléiade: Their Conflicting Roles in the Art of *beaux exercises spirituels*." *Journal of Medieval and Renaissance Studies* 9 (1979): 81–100.

Bridoux, André. *Le Stoïcisme et son influence.* Paris: Vrin, 1966.

Broad, Jacqueline. *Women Philosophers of the Seventeenth Century.* Cambridge: Cambridge U.P., 2002.

Brockliss, Laurence, and Colin Jones. *The Medical World of Early Modern France.* Oxford: Clarendon Press, 1997.

Broedel, Hans Peter. *The Malleus Maleficarum and the Construction of Witchcraft: Theology and Popular Belief.* Manchester and New York: Manchester U.P., 2003.

Busson, Henri. *Le Rationalisme dans la littérature française de la Renaissance (1533–1601).* Paris: Vrin, 1957.

Butler, Judith. *Gender Trouble: Feminism and the Subversion of Identity*. New York and London: Routledge, 1999.

Cantecor, G. "A Quelle date Descartes a-t-il écrit *La Recherche de la vérité?*" *Revue de la Philosophie* 2 (1928): 254–89.

Carlino, Andrea. *Books of the Body: Anatomical Ritual and Renaissance Learning*. Trans. John Tedeschi and Anne C. Tedeschi. Chicago and London: The University of Chicago Press, 1999.

Carr, Thomas M., Jr. *Descartes and the Resilience of Rhetoric: Varieties of Cartesian Rhetorical Theory*. Carbondale and Edwardsville: Southern Illinois U.P., 1990.

Cave, Terence. *Pré-histoires: Textes troublés au seuil de la modernité*. Genève: Droz, 1999.

Céard, Jean. "Médecine et démonologie: Les enjeux d'un débat." *Diable, diables, et diableries au temps de la Renaissance*. Ed. M.T. Jones-Davies, 97–112.

Chomarat, Jacques. *Grammaire et rhétorique chez Erasme*. Paris: Belles lettres, 1981.

Christodoulou, Kyriaki. "Montaigne et la vertu stoïque." Masters and Tetel 175–85.

Clark, Stuart. *Thinking with Demons: The Idea of Witchcraft in Early Modern Europe*. Oxford: Oxford U.P., 1997.

_____. *Vanities of the Eye: Vision in Early Modern European Culture*. Oxford: Oxford U.P., 2007.

Clarke, Stanley. "Descartes's 'Gender'." Bordo, *Feminist Interpretations*, 82–102.

Colie, Rosalie L. *Paradoxia Epidemica: The Renaissance Tradition of Paradox*. Princeton: Princeton U.P., 1966.

Conley, John J. *The Suspicion of Virtue: Women Philosophers in Neoclassical France*. Ithaca and London: Cornell U.P., 2002.

Course, Didier. *D'or et de pierres précieuses: Les paradis artificiels de la Contre-réforme en France, 1580–1685*. Lausanne: Payot, 2005.

Crahay, Roland, and Marie-Thérèse Isaac. "La 'Bibliothèque' de Jean Bodin démonologue: Les bases théoriques." *Bulletin de la classe des lettres et des sciences morales et politiques de l'Académie Royale de Belgique* 73 (1987): 129–71.

Crescenzo, R. "Le traité *De l'éloquence française* de Du Vair (1594): Une réponse à la position de Montaigne sur l'éloquence?" *Montaigne et Henri IV. Actes du Colloque International (Bordeaux-Pau)*. Ed. Cl.-G. Dubois. Biarritz: J and D éditions, 1996.

Crouzet, Denis. "La représentation du temps à l'époque de la Ligue: 'Le clouaque et esgoust des immondices des autres [siècles] passez'." *Revue historique* 270 (1984): 297–388.

_____. "Henri IV, King of Reason?" Trans. Judith K. Proud. *From Valois to Bourbon: Dynasty, State, and Society in Early Modern France*. Ed. Keith Cameron, Exeter: University of Exeter Press, 1989, 74–8.

_____. *Les Guerriers de Dieu: la violence au temps des troubles de religion*. Seyssel: Champ Vallon, 1990.

Cunningham, Andrew. *The Anatomical Renaissance: The Resurrection of the Anatomical Projects of the Ancients*. Aldershot: Scolar Press, 1997.

Cunningham, Andrew, and Ole Peter Grell. *The Four Horsemen of the Apocalypse: Religion, War, Famine and Death in Reformation Europe*. Cambridge: Cambridge U.P., 2000.

Curley, Edwin. *Descartes against the Skeptics*. Cambridge: Harvard U.P., 1978.

Dandrey, Patrick. *Les Tréteaux de Saturne: Scènes de la mélancolie à l'époque baroque*. Paris: Klincksieck, 2003.

Daston, Lorraine, and Katharine Park. *Wonders and the Order of Nature, 1150-1750*. New York: Zone Books, 1998.

Dear, Peter. *Discipline and Experience: The Mathematical Way in the Scientific Revolution*. Chicago: University of Chicago Press, 1995.

———. *Revolutionizing the Sciences: European Knowledge and its Ambitions, 1500-1700*. Princeton: Princeton U.P., 2001.

Debus, Allen G. *The French Paracelsians: The Chemical Challenge to Medical and Scientific Tradition in Early Modern France*. Cambridge: Cambridge U.P., 1991.

Decrusy, Isambert, Jourdan. *Recueil général des anciennes lois françaises*. 29 vols. Paris: Belin-LePrieur, 1821–1833.

DeJean, Joan. *Fictions of Sappho, 1546-1937*. Chicago: The University of Chicago Press, 1989.

Descimon, Robert. *Qui étaient les Seize? Mythes et réalités de la Ligue parisienne (1585-1594)*. Mémoires de la Fédération des Sociétés Historiques et Archéologiques de Paris et de l'Ile de France 34. Paris: Klincksieck, 1983.

Diefendorf, Barbara. *Beneath the Cross: Catholics and Huguenots in Sixteenth-Century Paris*. New York and Oxford: Oxford U.P., 1991.

Dixon, Laurinda. *Perilous Chastity: Women and Illness in Pre-Enlightenment Art and Medicine*. Ithaca: Cornell U.P., 1995.

Donnison, Jean. *Midwives and Medical Men: A History of Inter-Professional Rivalries and Women's Rights*. New York: Schocken Books, 1977.

DuBois, Page. *Centaurs and Amazons: Women and the Pre-History of the Great Chain of Being*. Ann Arbor: The University of Michigan Press, 1982.

_____. *Torture and Truth*. London and New York: Routledge, 1991.

Duden, Barbara. *The Woman Beneath the Skin: A Doctor's Patients in Eighteenth-Century Germany*. Trans. Thomas Dunlap. Cambridge and London: Harvard U.P., 1991.

Dumont, Jean-Paul. *Le Scepticisme et le phénomène: Essai sur la signification et les origines du pyrrhonisme*. Paris: Vrin, 1972.

Eamon, William. *Science and the Secrets of Nature: Books of Secrets in Medieval and Early Modern Culture*. Princeton: Princeton U.P., 1994.

Easlea, Brian. *Witch Hunting, Magic, and the New Philosophy: An Introduction to Debates of the Scientific Revolution 1450-1750*. Sussex: Harvester Press: New Jersey, Humanities Press, 1980.

Ehrenreich, Barbara, and Deirdre English, *For Her Own Good: 150 Years of the Experts' Advice to Women*. Garden City: Doubleday, 1978.

Elliott, Dyan. *Proving Woman: Female Spirituality and Inquisitional Culture in the Later Middle Ages*. Princeton and Oxford: Princeton U.P., 2004.

Enders, Jody. *The Medieval Theater of Cruelty: Rhetoric, Memory, Violence*. Ithaca: Cornell U.P., 1999.

Festugière, Jean. *La Philosophie d'amour de Marsile Ficin et son influence sur la littérature française au XVIe siècle*. Paris: Vrin, 1941.

Ficino, Marsilio. *Three Books on Life*. Ed. and trans. Carol V. Kaske and John R. Clark. Binghamptom: Medieval and Renaissance Texts and Studies, 1989.

Findlen, Paula. "Ideas in the Mind: Gender and Knowledge in the Seventeenth Century." *Hypatia* 17(2002): 183–96.

Floridi, Luciano. *Sextus Empiricus: The Transmission and Recovery of Pyrrhonism.* New York: Oxford U.P., 2002.

Foucault, Michel. *Les Mots et les choses: Une archéologie des sciences humaines.* Paris: Gallimard, 1966.

———. "Médecins, juges, et sorciers au XVIIe siècle." In *Dits et écrits: 1954-1988.* Vol. 1. Paris: Gallimard, 1994. 753–6.

Franklin, Julian. *Jean Bodin and the Sixteenth-Century Revolution in the Methodology of Law and History.* New York and London: Columbia U.P., 1963.

———. *Jean Bodin and the Rise of Absolutist Theory.* Cambridge: Cambridge U.P., 1973.

Friedrich, Hugo. *Montaigne.* Trans. Dawn Eng. Ed. Philippe Desan. Berkeley: University of California Press, 1991.

Frisch, Andrea. *The Invention of the Eyewitness: Witnessing and Testimony in Early Modern France.* Chapel Hill: University of North Carolina Press, 2004.

Fumaroli, Marc. *L'Age de l'éloquence: Rhétorique et 'res literaria' de la Renaissance au seuil de l'époque classique.* Geneva: Droz, 1980.

Garber, Daniel. "Descartes, the Aristotelians, and the Revolution that Did Not Happen in 1637." *Monist* 71 (1988): 471–86.

———. Understanding Interaction: What Descartes Should Have Told Elizabeth." *Descartes Embodied: Reading Cartesian Philosophy through Cartesian Science.* Cambridge: Cambridge U.P., 2001. 168–88.

Gaukroger, Stephen. *Descartes: An Intellectual Biography.* Oxford: Clarendon Press, 1995.

———, ed. *The Blackwell Guide to Descartes' Meditations.* Malden, Oxford, Victoria: Blackwell Publishing, 2006.

Gélis, Jacques. *La Sage-femme ou le médecin: une nouvelle conception de la vie.* Paris: Fayard, 1988.

Gilman, Sander, ed. *Hysteria Beyond Freud.* Berkeley: University of California Press, 1993.

Giocanti, Sylvia. *Penser l'irrésolution: Montaigne, Pascal, La Mothe le Vayer. Trois itinéraires sceptiques.* Paris: Champion, 2001.

Goldberg, Jonathan. *Sodometries: Renaissance Texts, Modern Sexualities.* Stanford: Stanford U.P., 1992.

Green, Monica. "From 'Diseases of Women' to 'Secrets of Women': The Transformation of Gynecological Literature in the Later Middle Ages." *Journal of Medieval and Early Modern Studies* 30 (2000): 5–39.

Greenblatt, Stephen. *Renaissance Self-fashioning from More to Shakespeare.* Chicago and London: The University of Chicago Press, 1980.

Guéroult, Martial. *Descartes selon l'ordre des raisons.* 2 vols. Paris: Aubier, 1968.

Gunnoe, Charles D., Jr. "Erastus and Paracelsianism: Theological Motifs in Thomas Erastus' Rejection of Paracelsian Natural Philosophy." In *Reading the Book of Nature: The Other Side of the Scientific Revolution.* Eds. Allen G. Debus and Michael T. Walton. *Sixteenth Century Essays and Studies* 41 (1998): 45–66.

Gusdorf, Georges. *Introduction aux Sciences Humaines: Essai critique sur leurs origines et leur développement*. Paris: Editions Ophrys, 1974.

Hanley, Sarah. *The* lit de justice *of the Kings of France: Constitutional Ideology in Legend, Ritual, and Discourse*. Princeton: Princeton U.P., 1983.

Harcourt, Glenn. "Andreas Vesalius and the Anatomy of Antique Sculpture." *Representations* 17 (1987): 28–61.

Harrison, Peter. *The Bible, Protestantism, and the Rise of Natural Science*. Cambridge: Cambridge U.P., 1998.

Harth, Erica. *Cartesian Women: Versions and Subversions of Rational Discourse in the Old Regime*. Ithaca and London: Cornell U.P., 1992.

Hartle, Ann. *Michel de Montaigne: Accidental Philosopher*. Cambridge and New York: Cambridge U.P., 2003.

Harvey, Elizabeth, and Kathleen Okruhlik, eds. *Women and Reason*. Ann Arbor: University of Michigan Press, 1992.

Heyd, Michael. *Be Sober and Reasonable: The Critique of Enthusiasm in the Seventeenth and Early Eighteenth Centuries*. Leiden, New York, and Köln: E.J. Brill, 1995.

Horowitz, Maryanne Cline. *Seeds of Virtue and Knowledge*. Princeton: Princeton U.P., 1988.

Houdard, Sophie. *Les Sciences du diable : Quatre discours sur la sorcellerie*. Paris: Editions du Cerf, 1992.

Hsia, R. Po-Chia. "A Time for Monsters: Monstrous Births, Propaganda, and the German Reformation." *Monstrous Bodies/Political Monstrosities in Early Modern Europe*. Eds. Laura Lunger Knoppers and Joan B. Landes. Ithaca and London: Cornell U.P., 2004.

Hunter, Lynette, and Sarah Hutton, eds. *Women, Science, and Medicine, 1500-1700: Mothers and Sisters of the Royal Society*. Thrupp, Stroud, Gloucestershire: Sutton, 1997.

Huppert, George. *The Idea of Perfect History: Historical Erudition and Historical Philosophy in Renaissance France*. Urbana: University of Illinois Press, 1970.

Hutton, Sarah. "The Riddle of the Sphinx: Francis Bacon and the Emblems of Science." In *Women, Science, and Medicine, 1500-1700: Mothers and Sisters of the Royal Society*. Phoenix Mill Thrupp: Sutton, 1999. 7–28.

Isaac, Marie-Thérèse. "De la démonomanie des sorciers: Histoire d'un livre à travers ses editions." *Jean Bodin*, 101–377.

Jacques-Chaquin, Nicole. "*La Démonomanie des sorciers*: une lecture politique de la sorcellerie." *Jean Bodin: Nature, histoire, droit, et politique*. Ed. Yves-Charles Zarka. Paris: Presses Universitaires de France, 43–70.

Janssen, Willem. *Charles Utenhove: Sa vie et son oeuvre (1536–1600)*. Maastricht: Gebrs. van Aelst, 1939.

Jean Bodin: Actes du colloque interdisciplinaire d'Angers, 24 au 27 mai 1984. Angers: Presses de l'Université d'Angers, 1985.

Jed, Stephanie. *The Rape of Lucretia and the Birth of Humanism*. Bloomington: Indiana U.P., 1989.

Jordan, Constance. *Renaissance Feminism: Literary Texts and Political Models*. Ithaca: Cornell U.P., 1990.

Kahn, Victoria. *Machiavellian Rhetoric from the Counter-Reformation to Milton.* Princeton: Princeton U.P., 1994.

Kantorowicz, Ernst H. *The King's Two Bodies: A Study in Mediaeval Political Theology.* Princeton: Princeton U.P., 1997.

Keefer, Michael H. "Agrippa's Dilemma: Hermetic 'Rebirth' and the Ambivalences of *De vanitate* and *De occulta philosophia*." *Renaissance Quarterly* 41 (1988): 614–53.

Keller, Evelyn Fox. *Reflections on Gender and Science.* New Haven and London: Yale U.P., 1985.

Kibre, Pearl. "The Faculty of Medicine at Paris, Charlatanism, and Unlicensed Medical Practices in the Later Middle Ages." *Bulletin of the History of Medicine* 27 (1953): 1–20.

King, Helen. "Once upon a Text: Hysteria from Hippocrates." Gilman, 3–90.

Koertge, Noretta, ed. *A House Built on Sand: Exposing Postmodernist Myths about Science.* New York and Oxford: Oxford U.P., 1998.

Kors, Alan Charles, and Edward Peters. *Witchcraft in Europe, 400-1700: A Documentary History.* Philadelphia: University of Pennsylvania Press, 2001.

Krause, Virginia. *Idle Pursuits: Literature and Oisiveté in the French Renaissance.* Newark: University of Delaware Press, 2003.

———. "Confessional Fictions and Demonology in Renaissance France." *Journal of Medieval and Early Modern Studies* 35 (2005): 327–48.

Kritzman, Lawrence D. "The Neoplatonic Debate." *A New History of French Literature.* Ed. Denis Hollier. Cambridge and London: Harvard U.P., 1989.

Kuhn, Thomas. *The Structure of Scientific Revolutions.* Chicago: University of Chicago Press, 1962.

Ladee, G.A. *Hypochondriacal Syndromes.* Amsterdam, London, and New York: Elsevier Publishing Company, 1966.

Lagrée, Jacqueline. "La vertu stoïcienne de constance." Moreau 94–116.

Langbein, John H. *Prosecuting Crime in the Renaissance.* Cambridge: Harvard U.P., 1974.

———. *Torture and the Law of Proof: Europe and England in the Ancien Régime.* Chicago: University of Chicago Press, 1977.

Lanson, Gustave. *Les Essais de Montaigne: Etude et analyse.* Paris: Librairie Mellottée, 1929.

Laporte, Jean. *Le Rationalisme de Descartes.* Paris: Presses Universitaires de France, 1950.

Laqueur, Thomas. *Making Sex: Body and Gender from the Greeks to Freud.* Cambridge and London: Harvard U.P., 1990.

Larmore, Charles. "Descartes and Skepticism." Gaukroger, *The Blackwell Guide to Descartes' Meditations*, 17–29.

Larner, Christina. "Crimen Exceptum? Witchcraft in Europe." *Crime and the Law: The Social History of Crime in Western Europe since 1500.* Eds. V.A.C. Gatrell, Bruce Lenman, and Geoffrey Parker. London: Europa Publications, 1980.

Lawn, Brian. *The Rise and Decline of the Scholastic "Quaestio Disputata."* Leiden, New York, Köln: Brill, 1993.

Lemay, Helen Rodnite. Introduction. *Women's Secrets.* By [Pseudo-] Albertus Magnus, 1–58.

Lennon, Thomas M. "Lady Oracle: Changing Conceptions of Authority and Reason in Seventeenth-Century Philosophy." Harvey and Okruhlik, 39–61.

Levi, Anthony. *French Moralists: The Theory of the Passions, 1585-1649*. Oxford: Clarendon Press, 1964.

Lloyd, Genevieve. "Reason as Attainment." Bordo, *Feminist Interpretations*, 70–81.

_____. *The Man of Reason: "Male" and "Female" in Western Philosophy*. Minneapolis: University of Minnesota Press, 1984.

Long, A.A. *Hellenistic Philosophy: Stoics, Epicureans, Sceptics*. Berkeley and Los Angeles: University of California Press, 1974, 1986.

Long, Kathleen Perry. "Hermaphrodites Newly Discovered: The Cultural Monsters of Sixteenth-Century France." *Monster Theory: Reading Culture*. Ed. Jeffrey Jerome Cohen. Minneapolis: University of Minnesota Press, 1996.

———. "Jacques Duval on Hermaphrodites." *High Anxiety: Masculinity in Crisis in Early Modern France*. Ed. Kathleen P. Long. Kirksville: Truman State U.P., 2002. 107–36.

———. *Hermaphrodites in Renaissance Europe*. Burlington and Aldershot: Ashgate, 2006.

Lonie, Iain M. "The Paris Hippocratics: Teaching and Research in Paris in the Second Half of the Sixteenth Century." *The Medical Renaissance of the Sixteenth Century*. Eds. A. Wear, R.K. French, I.M. Lonie, Cambridge: Cambridge U.P., 1985. 155–74.

Lyons, John. *Before Imagination: Embodied Thought from Montaigne to Rousseau*. Stanford: Stanford U.P., 2005.

Maclean, Ian. *The Renaissance Notion of Woman: A Study in the Fortunes of Scholasticism and Medical Science in European Intellectual Life*. Cambridge: Cambridge U.P., 1988.

Maia Neto, José R. "Charron's Epochè and Descartes' Cogito: The Sceptical Base of Descartes's Refutation of Scepticism." *The Return of Scepticism from Hobbes and Descartes to Bayle*. Ed. Gianni Paganini. Dordrecht, Boston: Kluwer Academic Publishers, 2003. 81–113.

Martos, Joseph. *Doors to the Sacred: A Historical Introduction to Sacraments in the Catholic Church*. New York: Doubleday, 1981.

Masters, G. Mallary, and Marcel Tetel, eds. *Le Parcours des Essais de Montaigne, 1588-1988*. Paris: Aux Amateurs de livres, 1989.

Mathieu-Castellani, Gisèle. *Agrippa d'Aubigné: Le corps de Jézabel*. Paris: Presses universitaires de France, 1991.

Mathon, Georges. "Antoine de Crussol, comte de Crussol, duc et Pair de France, Premier duc d'Uzès." www.nimausensis.com/personnages/AntoineCrussol.htm.

Mazzoni, Cristina. *Saint Hysteria: Neurosis, Mysticism, and Gender in European Culture*. Ithaca: Cornell U.P., 1996.

McClure, George. "The *Artes* and the *Ars moriendi* in late Renaissance Venice: The Professions in Fabio Glissenti's *Discorsi morali contra il dispiacer del morire, detto Athanatophilia* (1596)." *Renaissance Quarterly* 51 (1998): 92–127.

Mehl, Edouard. "Les méditations stoïciennes de Descartes: Hypothèses sur l'influence du stoïcisme dans la constitution de la pensée cartésienne (1619–1637)." Moreau 251–80.

Meinecke, Friedrich. *Machiavellism: The Doctrine of Raison d'Etat and its Place in Modern Europe*. Trans. Douglas Scott. London: Routledge, 1957.

Melehy, Hasan. *Writing Cogito: Montaigne, Descartes, and the Institution of the Modern Subject*. Albany: State University of New York Press, 1997.

Merchant, Carolyn. *The Death of Nature: Women, Ecology, and the Scientific Revolution*. San Francisco: Harper and Row, 1980.

Mesnard, Pierre. *Essai sur la Morale de Descartes*. Paris: Boivin, 1936.

Midelfort, H.C. Erik. *A History of Madness in Sixteenth-Century Germany*. Stanford: Stanford U.P., 1999.

Millen, Ronald Forsyth, and Robert Erich Wolf. *Heroic Deeds and Mystic Figures: A New Reading of Rubens' Life of Maria de' Medici*. Princeton: Princeton U.P., 1989.

Mora, George. Introduction. Weyer, *Witches, Devils, and Doctors*, xxvii–xcii.

Moreau, Pierre-Francois, ed. *Le Stoïcisme au XVIe et XVIIe siècle: Le retour des philosophies antiques à l'âge classique*. Paris: Albin Michel, 1999.

_____. "Les trois étapes du stoïcisme moderne." Moreau 11–27.

_____. "Calvin: fascination et critique du stoïcisme." Moreau 51–64.

Moriarty, Michael. *Early Modern French Thought: The Age of Suspicion*. Oxford: Oxford U.P., 2003.

Nauert, Charles G., Jr. *Agrippa and the Crisis of Renaissance Thought*. Urbana: University of Illinois Press, 1965.

Newman, William R. "Alchemy, Domination, and Gender." Koertge 216–26.

Nye, Andrea. "Polity and Prudence: The Ethics of Elizabeth, Princess Palatine." In *Hypatia's Daughters*. Ed. Linda Lopez McAlister. Bloomington: Indiana U.P., 1996. 68–91.

Nye, Robert, and Katharine Park. "Destiny is Anatomy." *The New Republic* 24 (1991): 53–7.

Oberman, Heiko A. *Luther: Life between God and the Devil*. Trans. Eileen Walliser-Schwartzbart. New Haven and London: Yale U.P., 1989.

Odorisio, Ginevra Conti. *Famiglia e Stato nella République di Jean Bodin*. Torino: G. Giappichelli, 1993.

Oestreich, Gerhard. *Neostoicism and the Early Modern State*. Ed. Brigitta Oestreich and H.G. Koenigsberger. Trans. David McLintock. Cambridge; New York: Cambridge U.P., 1982.

Olivo, Gilles. "Une patience sans espérance?: Descartes et le stoïcisme." Moreau 234–50.

O'Malley, C.D. "The Inception of Anatomical Studies in the University of Paris." *Bulletin of the History of Medicine* 23 (1959): 436–45.

O'Neill, Eileen. "Women Cartesians, 'Feminine Philosophy,' and Historical Exclusion." Bordo, *Feminist Interpretations*, 232–57.

Osler, Margaret. "The Gender of Nature and the Nature of Gender in Early Modern Natural Philosophy." *Men, Women, and the Birthing of Modern Science*. Ed. Judith P. Zinsser. DeKalb: Northern Illinois U.P., 2005.

Pallier, Denis. "Les Réponses catholiques." *Histoire de l'édition française*. Ed. Henri-Jean Martin, Roger Chartier, Jean-Pierre Vivet. Vol. 1. Paris: Promodis, 1982.

Park, Katharine. "Dissecting the Female Body: From Women's Secrets to the Secrets of Nature." In *Crossing Boundaries: Attending to Early Modern Women*. Ed. Jane Donawerth and Adele Seeff. Newark: University of Delaware Press; London: Associate Presses, 2000. 20–47.

_____. *Secrets of Women: Gender, Generation, and the Origins of Human Dissection*. New York: Zone Books, 2007.

Pearl, Jonathan L. "Le rôle énigmatique de *La Démonomonie* dans la chasse aux sorciers." *Jean Bodin* 403–10.

_____. *The Crime of Crimes: Demonology and Politics in France, 1560-1620*. Waterloo: Wilfrid Laurier U.P., 1999.

Pécout, Thierry. "Féodalisme." *Dictionnaire encyclopédique du Moyen Age*. Ed. André Vauchez and Catherine Vincent. Paris: Editions du Cerf; Cambridge: James Clarke and Co.; Rome: Città Nuova, 1997.

Perkins, Wendy. *Midwifery and Medicine in Early Modern France: Louise Bourgeois*. Exeter: University of Exeter Press, 1996.

Pesic, Peter. "Wrestling with Proteus: Francis Bacon and the 'Torture' of Nature." *Isis* 90 (1999): 81–94.

Peters, Edward. *Torture*. Philadelphia: University of Pennsylvania Press, 1996.

Petey-Girard, Bruno et Alexandre Tarrête, eds. *Guillaume du Vair: Parlementaire et écrivain (1556–1621), Colloque d'Aix-en-Provence 4–6 Octobre 2001*. Genève: Droz, 2005.

Pinvert, Lucien. *Jacques Grévin (1538–1570): Etude biographique et littéraire*. Paris: Albert Fontemoing, 1899.

Pizan, Christine de. *The Book of the City of Ladies*. Trans. Earl Jeffrey Richards. New York: Persea Books, 1982.

Plutarch. *Plutarch's Lives: Theseus and Romulus*. Trans. Bernadotte Perrin. Cambridge: Harvard U.P., 1998.

Polachek, Dora E. "Montaigne and Imagination: The Dynamics of Power and Control." Masters and Tetel 135–45.

Popkin, Richard. *The History of Scepticism from Savonarola to Bayle*. Oxford and New York: Oxford U.P., 2003.

Pot, Olivier. *Inspiration et mélancolie: l'épistémologie poétique dans les Amours de Ronsard*. Genève: Droz, 1990.

Préaud, Maxime. "*La Démonomanie*, fille de *La République*." *Jean Bodin*, 419–29.

Purkiss, Diane. *The Witch in History: Early Modern and Twentieth-Century Representations*. London: Routledge, 1996.

Quint, David. *Montaigne and the Quality of Mercy: Ethical and Political Themes in the Essais*. Princeton: Princeton U.P., 1998.

Rabil, Jr., Albert. "Agrippa and the Feminist Tradition." Agrippa, *Declamation*, 3–37.

_____. "Editor's Introduction to the Series." Agrippa, *Declamation*, ix–xxviii.

Radouant, René. *Guillaume du Vair: L'homme et l'orateur jusqu'à la fin des troubles de la Ligue (1556-1596)*. Paris: Société Française d'imprimerie et de librairie, 1907.

Ramsey, Ann W. *Liturgy, Politics, and Salvation: The Catholic League in Paris and the Nature of Catholic Reform, 1540-1630*. Rochester: University of Rochester Press, 1999.

Ranum, Orest. *The Fronde: A French Revolution, 1648–1652*. New York: W.W. Norton, 1993.

Reeser, Todd. *Moderating Masculinity in Early Modern Culture*. Chapel Hill: University of North Carolina Press, 2006.

———. "Re-reading Platonic Sexuality Sceptically in Montaigne's 'Apologie de Raymond Sebond'." *Masculinities in Sixteenth-Century France*. Ed. Philip Ford and Paul White. Cambridge: Cambridge French Colloquia. 2006. 103–26.

Regosin, Richard. *Montaigne's Unruly Brood: Textual Engendering and the Challenge to Paternal Authority*. Berkeley: University of California Press, 1996.

Reiss, Timothy. *Mirages of the Selfe: Patterns of Personhood in Ancient and Early Modern Europe*. Stanford: Stanford U.P., 2003.

Ricoeur, Paul. *De l'interprétation: Essai sur Freud*. Paris: Seuil, 1965.

Rodis-Lewis, Geneviève. *Le développement de la pensée de Descartes*. Paris: Vrin, 1997.

Roper, Lyndal. *Oedipus and the Devil: Witchcraft, Sexuality, and Religion in Early Modern Europe*. London: Routledge, 1994.

Rose, Paul. *Bodin and the Great God of Nature: The Moral and Religious Universe of a Judaiser*. Geneva: Droz, 1980.

Rousseau, G.S. "A Strange Pathology: Hysteria in the Early Modern World, 1500–1800." Gilman 91–221.

Rung, Donald. "Is Knowledge Like Money? Descartes in Amsterdam." Descartes I, North American Society for Seventeenth-Century French Literature, Lincoln, Nebraska, 10 May 2007.

Ruse, Michael. "Is Darwinism Sexist? (And If It Is, So What?)." Koertge 119–29.

Sallman, Jean-Michel. "Sorcière." *XVIe-XVIIe siècles*. Eds. Natalie Zemon Davis and Arlette Farge. *Histoire des femmes en occident*. Eds. Georges Duby and Michelle Perrot. Vol. 3. Paris: Plon, 1991. 455–67.

Sawday, Jonathan. *The Body Emblazoned: Dissection and the Human Body in Renaissance Culture*. London and New York: Routledge, 1995.

Scarry, Elaine. *The Body in Pain*. Oxford: Oxford U.P., 1985.

Schiebinger, Londa. *The Mind has no Sex? Women in the Origins of Modern Science*. Cambridge: Harvard U.P., 1985.

———. *Nature's Body: Gender in the Making of Modern Science*. Boston: Beacon Press, 1993.

Schiesari, Juliana. *The Gendering of Melancholia: Feminism, Psychoanalysis, and the Symbolics of Loss in Renaissance Literature*. Ithaca and London: Cornell U.P., 1992.

Schiffman, Zachary Sayre. *On the Threshold of Modernity: Relativism in the French Renaissance*. Baltimore and London: The Johns Hopkins U.P., 1991.

Schleiner, Winfried. *Melancholy, Genius, and Utopia in the Renaissance*. Wiesbaden: Otto Harrassowitz, 1991.

———. "Early Modern Controversies about the One-Sex Model." *Renaissance Quarterly* 53 (2000): 180–91.

Scott, Joan. *Only Paradoxes to Offer: French Feminists and the Rights of Man*. Cambridge: Harvard U.P., 1996.

Sealy, Robert J. *The Palace Academy of Henry III*. Geneva: Droz, 1981.

Secret, François. *Les Kabbalistes chrétiens de la Renaissance*. Paris: Dunod, 1984.

Shapin, Steven. *The Scientific Revolution*. Chicago: The University of Chicago Press, 1996.

Shapiro, Lisa. "Princess Elizabeth and Descartes: The Union of Soul and Body and the Practice of Philosophy." *Feminism and the History of Philosophy*. Ed. Genevieve Lloyd. Oxford: Oxford U.P., 2002. 182–203

Shelley, Dana. "The Stoic Paradigm of Cartesian Skepticism," Descartes I, North American Society for Seventeenth-Century French Literature, Lincoln, Nebraska, 10 May 2007.

Siraisi, Nancy G. "History, Antiquarianism, and Medicine: The Case of Girolamo Mercuriale." *Journal of the History of Ideas* 64 (2003): 231–51.

Smith, Pamela. *The Body of the Artisan: Art and Experience in the Scientific Revolution*. Chicago: University of Chicago Press, 2004.

Soble, Alan. "In Defense of Bacon." Koertge 195–215.

Sokal, Alan D. "What the Social Text Affair Does and Does Not Prove." Koertge 9–22.

Soman, Alfred. "The Parlement of Paris and the Great Witch Hunt (1565–1640)." *The Sixteenth Century Journal* 9 (1978): 31–44.

———. *Sorcellerie et justice criminelle: Le Parlement de Paris (16ᵉ–18e siècles)*. Hampshire and Brookfield, Vermont: Variorum/Ashgate, 1992.

Stanton, Domna. "Woman as Object and Subject of Exchange: Marie de Gournay's Le Proumenoir (1594)." *Esprit Créateur* 23 (1983): 9–25.

Steinberg, Sylvie. "Le Mythe des Amazones et son utilisation politique de la Renaissance à la Fronde." *Royaume de Fémynie: Pouvoirs, contraintes, espaces de liberté des femmes de la Renaissance à la Fronde*. Ed. Kathleen Wilson-Chevalier and Eliane Viennot. Paris: Champion, 1999. 261–73.

Stephens, Walter. *Demon Lovers: Witchcraft, Sex, and the Crisis of Belief*. Chicago and London: University of Chicago Press, 2002.

Stolberg, Michael. "A Woman Down to Her Bones: The Anatomy of Sexual Difference in the Sixteenth and Early Seventeenth Centuries." *Isis* 94 (2003): 274–99.

Stuurman, Siep. *François Poulain de la Barre and the Invention of Modern Equality*. Cambridge: Harvard U.P., 2004.

Talon-Hugon, Carole. *Les Passions rêvées par la raison: Essai sur la théorie des passions de Descartes et de quelques-uns de ses contemporains*. Paris: Vrin, 2002.

Tarrête, Alexandre. "La Querelle qui opposa Du Vair au duc d'Epernon (1618) et le pamphlet de Guez de Balzac." Petey-Girard and Tarrête 123–40.

Thiher, Allen. *Revels in Madness: Insanity in Medicine and Literature*. Ann Arbor: The University of Michigan Press, 1999.

Timmermans, Linda. *L'Accès des femmes à la culture (1598-1715): Un débat d'idées de Saint François de Sales à la Marquise de Lambert*. Paris: Champion, 1993.

Tin, Louis-Georges. "Ambiguïtés de la vie civile au XVIe siècle." Petey-Girard and Tarrête 263–74.

Tollefsen, Deborah. "Princess of Elizabeth and the Problem of Mind-Body Interaction." *Hypatia* 14 (1999): 59–77.

Trillat, Etienne. *Histoire de l'Hystérie*. Paris: Seghers, 1986.

Tuana, Nancy. *Women and the History of Philosophy*. New York: Paragon, 1992.

Turchetti, Mario. "Religious Concord and Political Tolerance in Sixteenth- and Seventeenth-Century France." *Sixteenth Century Journal* 22 (1991): 15–25.

Tyson, Donald. "The Life of Agrippa." Agrippa von Nettesheim, *Three Books of Occult Philosophy*. Trans. James Freake. Saint Paul: Llewellyn Publications, 1993.

Vaillancourt, Pierre-Louis. "Bodin et le pouvoir politique des femmes." 63–74.

Van Damme, Stéphane. *Descartes: Essai d'histoire culturelle d'une grandeur philosophique*. Paris: Presses de Sciences Politiques, 2002.

Veith, Ilza. *Hysteria: The History of a Disease*. Chicago: University of Chicago Press, 1965.

Waele, Michel de. *Les Relations entre le Parlement de Paris et Henri IV*. Paris: Publisud, 2000.

Walker, D.P. *Unclean Spirits: Possession and Exorcism in France and England in the Late Sixteenth and Early Seventeenth Centuries*. Philadelphia: University of Pennsylvania Press, 1981.

Weeks, Andrew. *Paracelsus: Speculative Theory and the Crisis of the Early Reformation*. Albany: State University of New York Press, 1997.

Williams, Gerhild Scholz. *Defining Dominion: The Discourses of Magic and Witchcraft in Early Modern France and Germany*. Ann Arbor: The University of Michigan Press, 1997.

Williams, Michael. "Descartes and the Metaphysics of Doubt." *Essays on Descartes' Meditations*. Ed. Amélie Oksenberg Rorty. Berkeley, Los Angeles, London: University of California Press, 1986. 117–39.

Wirth, Jean. "La Naissance du concept de croyance (12e–17e siècles)." *Bulletin d'Humanisme et de la Renaissance* 45 (1983): 7–58.

Wolfe, Michael. *The Conversion of Henri IV: Politics, Power, and Religious Belief in Early Modern France*. Cambridge: Harvard U.P., 1993.

Woodbridge, Linda. *Women and the English Renaissance: Literature and the Nature of Womankind, 1540-1620*. Urbana: University of Illinois Press, 1984.

Yates, Frances A. *The French Academies of the Sixteenth Century*. London: Jarrold and Sons, 1947.

Zilboorg, Gregory. *The Medical Man and the Witch during the Renaissance*. Baltimore: Johns Hopkins Press, 1935.

Index